Reducing Youth Gang Violence

D1563452

VIOLENCE PREVENTION AND POLICY SERIES

This AltaMira series publishes new books in the multidisciplinary study of violence. Books are designed to support scientifically based violence prevention programs and widely applicable violence prevention policy. Key topics are juvenile and/or adult community reentry programs, community-based addiction and violence programs, prison violence reduction programs with application in community settings, and school culture and climate studies with recommendations for organizational approaches to school violence reduction. Studies may combine quantitative and qualitative methods, may be multidisciplinary, or may feature European research if it has a multinational application. The series publishes highly accessible books that offer violence prevention policy as the outcome of scientifically based research, designed for college undergraduates and graduates, community agency leaders, school and community decision makers, and senior government policymakers.

SERIES EDITOR

Mark S. Fleisher, Director, The Dr. Semi J. and Ruth W. Begun Center for Violence Research Prevention and Education, Case Western Reserve University, 10900 Euclid Avenue, Cleveland, OH 44106-7164, USA, 216-368-2329 or msf10@po.cwru.edu

EDITORIAL BOARD MEMBERS

BOOKS IN THE SERIES

Reducing Youth Gang Violence

The Little Village Gang Project in Chicago

IRVING A. SPERGEL

ALTAMIRA
PRESS

A Division of
ROWMAN & LITTLEFIELD PUBLISHERS, INC.
Lanham • New York • Toronto • Plymouth, UK

AltaMira Press
A division of Rowman & Littlefield Publishers, Inc.
A wholly owned subsidiary of The Rowman & Littlefield Publishing Group, Inc.
4501 Forbes Boulevard, Suite 200
Lanham, MD 20706
www.altamirapress.com

Estover Road, Plymouth PL6 7PY, United Kingdom

British Library Cataloguing in Publication Information Available

Library of Congress Cataloging-in-Publication Data

Spergel, Irving A.
   Reducing youth gang violence : the Little Village Gang Project in Chicago / Irving A. Spergel.
      p.   cm. – (Violence prevention and policy series)
   Includes bibliographical references and index.
   ISBN-13: 978-0-7591-0998-8 (cloth : alk. paper)
   ISBN-10: 0-7591-0998-2 (cloth : alk. paper)
   ISBN-13: 978-0-7591-0999-5 (pbk. : alk. paper)
   ISBN-10: 0-7591-0999-0 (pbk. : alk. paper)
      1. Little Village Gang Violence Reduction Project (Chicago, Ill.).   2. Gang prevention—Illinois—Chicago.   3. Gang prevention—Illinois—Chicago—Citizen participation.   4. Gang members—Rehabilitation—Illinois—Chicago.   5. Juvenile delinquents—Services for—Illinois—Chicago.   I. Title.
   HV6439.U7C384 2007
   364.4–dc22
                                                                                2006022508

Printed in the United States of America

For Annie

Contents

Illustrations

Preface

The youth gang problem exists in an increasing number of urban, suburban, and rural areas in the United States and other countries. Gangs and their members—mainly adolescents and young adult males—are usually concentrated in minority, low-income, and socially, if not physically, isolated sectors of communities. The problem is characterized not simply by the violence, increasing drug activity, and chronic delinquency of the gang members themselves but also by the lack of interactive, collaborative, and balanced strategies by organizations such as law enforcement, youth agencies, churches, businesses, grassroots groups, and government leaders.

Gang homicides and gang drug activity have become chronic in certain relatively new and rapidly changing communities, as well as in the older metropolitan areas of the United States. Suppression-focused efforts to deal with the problem have been generally unsuccessful.

A veteran gang scholar and researcher, Malcolm Klein, states, "My best guess is that the majority of legislation and suppression programs are counter productive. . . . They have the effect of increasing the bonds between gangs and a common enemy" (Browne 2004, 3).

An editorial in a Los Angeles newspaper states as follows: "Los Angeles' response to street gangs has been a failure for decades. The threadbare patchwork of prevention and intervention programs has allowed gangs to flourish and become more violent. It is time for a new approach, time to consider new ideas" (*Los Angeles Daily News* 2004).

A Chicago newspaper, generally supporting police suppression strategies, reported that the city had the highest homicide rate (particularly gang homicide) of any large city in the country in 2003. It suggested in an editorial that the Chicago Police Department, which traditionally operated on its own, may now have been willing to cooperate with other law-enforcement agencies to suppress gangs. "More than 100 street gangs prey on Chicago and its suburbs. ... Most of the gangs have flourished for decades, secure in the knowledge that law enforcement officials here were too disorganized, too busy jealously guarding their respective fiefdoms to be much threat ... that's changing" (*Chicago Tribune* 2004).

Despite cycles of gang crime, especially violence, there is no hard evidence to support claims that law enforcement, citizen involvement, or social agencies— independent of each other—have prevented, controlled, or reduced street-gang crime, particularly serious gang violence or drug-related activity. Criminal justice, community organization, and youth social development require a "science of policy" (Marburger 2005) that offers compelling research guidance for interrelated program and practice decisions. Evidence of success must be provided at least through detailed observations of policy and program development, and the findings of quasiexperimental evaluation research. The key question that underlies the Little Village Gang Violence Reduction Project is whether, and why, its model of structure and practice was more effective than existing approaches that emphasize either police suppression or outreach youth-work intervention alone.

Policy development and program evaluation of comprehensive youth gang programs require a framework that encompasses a range of integrated perspectives about the nature of the gang problem, and interdependent and balanced program strategies closely related to research evaluation. Program strategies and worker practices have to be integrated with well-designed data collection and analyses, if program effectiveness is to be adequately determined. The Little Village Gang Violence Reduction Project illustrates key issues and obstacles in the implementation of a complex, comprehensive gang program design and its interrelated evaluation. But more, it provides lessons for policy makers, program administrators, and street-level practitioners about what it takes to design effective community-based gang programs, and how best to design quasiexperimental evaluations.

The book is divided into two interrelated major segments: part I, Project Background and Program Strategies, and part II, Evaluation: Program Analysis and Project Outcome. The policy maker, program manager, and practitioners as well as the research evaluator must be both dependent on and independent of the others' ideas and resources. The policy maker and program personnel cannot know how the program develops unless the research evaluator systematically feeds back information about what is happening. The evaluator must know what the program operations are and will be, and arrange for comparison groups, with good research design and adequate data collection. As the policy maker and program personnel facilitate access to data for the evaluator, so the evaluator assists the program manager with preliminary process findings.

Part I describes early and contemporary community-based street-gang programs, elements and approaches of which were integrated into the Little Village Project's comprehensive model, including community mobilization, social intervention, provision of social opportunities, suppression, and organizational change and development. The circumstances under which the project was conceived and implemented are recounted. Details of the project's early days—including contacts with hard-core gang youth on the streets, how the component strategies of the model were carried out, and obstacles encountered and resolved—are provided. While attention is directed to the Chicago Police Department's relationship with the project, focus is on project street-team efforts of police, probation, outreach youth workers, and the neighborhood organization worker.

Part II enumerates the specific contacts and services provided by project workers to program youth. It describes the characteristics of individual program and comparison youth in two major street gangs, the Latin Kings and Two Six. The researchers gathered police arrest data for the total sample of youth (program and comparison), but interview and self-report data only for the program youth. Approximately five hundred youth in the two gangs (some of whom received intensive or less-intensive project services, and others no services) were matched and tracked over a five-year preprogram period and a five-year program period. Specific patterns of project-worker contacts and services and their effects, separately and together, predicted changes in the program youth's arrests and self-reported offenses. The program was most effective with certain types of hard-core gang youth. In addition, the project accounted for gang and community-level changes and reductions in the gang problem—particularly violence—based on a comparison of police incident, arrest, and offender data on Little Village gangs, and from six similar high-gang-crime communities in Chicago. And the project accounted for change in the perceptions of levels of gang crime by residents and local agency and organization administrators in Little Village compared to an almost identical, high-gang-crime community nearby. The book ends with a summary of key findings from the chapters in part I and part II.

Acknowledgments

The Little Village Gang Violence Reduction Project could not have been carried out without the wisdom, dedication, and hard work of many people. Those especially helpful during the course of the project were as follows: Dr. Candice Kane, director of the Illinois Criminal Justice Information Authority; Keith Madderom, associate dean, School of Social Service Administration, University of Chicago; Barbara McDonald, deputy superintendent, Chicago Police Department; Nancy Martin, chief probation officer, Cook County Department of Adult Probation; William Hibbler, presiding judge, Juvenile Justice Division, Cook County Circuit Court; Commander Robert Dart, Lieutenant Philip Chomiak, and Detectives Ray Caballero and Gene Schleder, Chicago Police Department; Tim Flanagan, supervisor, and Tom Fashing, probation officer, Little Village Probation Unit, Cook County Department of Adult Probation; Alderman Ricardo Muñoz, Chicago City Council; Father Jim Miller, Our Lady of Tepeyac Church; Father Kevin Hays, Epiphany Catholic Church; Reverend Noel Castellanos, La Villita Community Church; Mary Lou Gonzales, Neighbors against Gang Violence; project outreach youth workers Bobby Garcia, Benny Estrada, Angelo Torres, Roy Martinez, and Jorge Roque; and field supervisors Javier Avila, Frank Perez, and Richard Scott.

The program and the evaluation evolved together, based on the comprehensive community-wide model of gang intervention involving critical agencies and parts of the community. Dr. Carolyn R. Block and Tracy Hahn of the Illinois Criminal Justice Information Authority were invaluable in their support of the prospective evaluation. Dr. Susan F. Grossman, Dr. Joshua Levy, Ayad

Jacob, Sungeun Choi, Rolando V. Sosa, Lisa DeVivo, and Louis Arata developed and implemented important components of the research design. Kwai Ming Wa was largely responsible for design and implementation of the statistical analyses. Elisa Barrios and Annot Spergel were invaluable in completing various phases of data collection, data organization, writing reports, editing, and producing the manuscript in its various forms. The program, the evaluation, and the book are the product of the collaboration of hearts and minds of many people, including the project's program youth—the gang members.

   The Little Village Project and its evaluation were supported by grants from the Illinois Criminal Justice Information Authority, the U.S. Department of Justice, Office of Justice Programs, and assistance provided by the School of Social Service Administration, University of Chicago. The views and conclusions expressed in this book are those of the author and do not represent the views of these agencies, the Chicago Police Department, the Cook County Department of Adult Probation, or the University of Chicago. Finally, I deeply appreciate the suggestions for changes and support of the manuscript provided by Buddy Howell, David Curry, and Jim Short.

                                                                    —Irving Spergel

I

Project Background and Program Strategies

1

Gang Programs

This book is about the Little Village Gang Violence Reduction Project, which was based on the idea that the youth gang problem is defined not only by the delinquent or criminal behaviors of gangs and gang members but also by what the community's institutions do or do not do to address (prevent, treat, and control) the problem.[1] Certain youth and the local community—including its component parts, particularly police, schools, youth agencies, probation, churches, businesses, and neighborhood organizations, and also families, gangs, former gang youth, and local government leaders—as well as larger social, economic, and cultural factors together are responsible for the creation and development of the problem.

The project model proposes that single-type strategies—whether suppression, social intervention, provision of special education, and job opportunities—and neighborhood-citizen participation or agency and community-leadership mobilization are not sufficient to prevent or reduce the youth gang problem. An interrelated, balanced, interorganizational, and community-based set of these strategies is required. Furthermore, a cross-organizational structure of key agencies and community groups must be developed to guide and implement these strategies, targeting youth in their gang context in gang-problem communities.

The Little Village Gang Violence Reduction Project was born at a time of gang-problem crisis (neighborhood turf-based gang violence) in certain Chicago neighborhoods in the early 1990s. A new city administration and several leaders of criminal justice agencies considered that a single-type approach, that is, police suppression and incarceration, was not adequate to address the problem of gang violence, and thought perhaps a more comprehensive or coordinated institutional and community-based approach, particularly under the aegis of the Chicago Police Department, might be worth trying. The pilot gang program that evolved modified and integrated traditional gang-program approaches. It emphasized the interrelationship of outreach youth services, social opportunities, and suppression in a gang-problem community.

BACKGROUND

American society and its urban centers did not invent gangs. African American and Latino youth—currently the most identifiable as gang members—did not originate delinquent or criminal gang behavior in the United States. Youth gangs, gang-involved youth, and gang problems have been present in almost all societies, particularly in the poor, segregated, and newcomer minority neighborhoods of large urban centers during times of rapid social and economic change. Youth gangs and their behaviors are historical and cross-national social and cultural phenomena. The gang problem is often associated with adult criminal structures and the development of political, sometimes radical or revolutionary, movements (Asbury 1971; Covey 2003; Hobsbawm 1963).

Gangs of various types have currently been identified in the following countries: the United States, Japan, China, Taiwan, Thailand, Korea, Cambodia, Vietnam, the Philippines, Laos, Russia, Israel, Palestine, Syria, Turkey, Lebanon, Iraq, the United Arab Emirates, Iran, Pakistan, India, Myanmar (formerly Burma), Albania, Serbia, Poland, Bulgaria, Slovakia, Hungary, Russia, France, Germany, the United Kingdom, Switzerland, Italy, Belgium, the Netherlands, Poland, Australia, New Zealand, Papua New Guinea, Mexico, El Salvador, Honduras, Colombia, Brazil, and so forth (Grennan et al. 2000; Klein 1995).

In recent decades gang problems have generally increased and spread across local communities in the United States (Egley, Howell, and Major 2004), and in varied form in many developed and developing countries. Certain youth gangs are now larger, better organized, and more specialized than they have been traditionally. They are becoming significant institutions in their own right. Gang youth may engage in serious criminal activities, violence, and drug dealing, as well as a range of other serious and less-serious crimes and age-related status offenses. Gang members may not all be offenders or have arrest records. The great majority of gang youth, particularly in the United States, seem to mature and age out of active gang status and serious violent crime in their late teens or twenties.

The youth gang problem in this country is largely an adolescent and young-adult social problem, mainly of males twelve to twenty-four years old, resulting from an accumulation and interaction of failures of family support, pressures of neighborhood gangs, defective school socialization, insufficient job-market opportunities, a neighborhood gang-crime tradition, and inadequate public policy to facilitate the transition of certain vulnerable youth to conventional adult roles as defined by the local community and the larger society. Youth gangs, and the subcultures that develop, are a means for particular youth to achieve a personal identity and social status, resolve personal problems, secure peer support, acquire economic resources, and find personal challenge and excitement over a limited period of time, but gangs may not be a means to achieve successful, legitimate adult or even criminal careers.

AMERICAN YOUTH GANG OUTREACH PROGRAMS

Youth gangs have existed in the slums and ports-of-entry areas in urban centers of the United States at least since the beginning of the nineteenth century (if not earlier) (Hyman 1984). The roots of contemporary outreach efforts to socialize street youth are found in charitable and religious organizations that attempted to contact "young roughs" and "vagabond" youth on the street through "Boys' Meetings." Mission workers in the late nineteenth century hoped to persuade groups of such youth to change their ways. These early "efforts to combat delinquency through moral suasion took place outside the physical structure of a agency" (Spergel 1966, xiv; Brace 1973).

Boys Club and YMCA workers in urban centers in the early part of the twentieth century occasionally recruited street youth to their organized agency programs, but it was not until the Chicago Area Project of the 1930s and 1940s that "curbstone" counseling as part of a systematic neighborhood-development approach was used to address the street-based youth group or gang-delinquency problem. The Chicago Area Project, located in low-income communities (often of newcomers), stressed the autonomy of local residents in planning and operating programs focused on neighborhood improvement, along with delinquency control and youth socialization. Programming for youth was regarded as a device to enlist the participation of local residents, to cohere and empower them through local community participatory efforts. The important feature that distinguished the Chicago Area Project from established social-agency approaches to the delinquency problem was its emphasis on street outreach, and high levels of commitment and activity from indigenous residents and local groups in dealing with delinquent youth, rather than on professional social-agency workers.

Local adults, including ex-convicts from the neighborhood (many of whom may earlier have been members of the same delinquent groups), went out to the streets to counsel youth. "Curbstone counselors," now law-abiding citizens, could effectively advise the boys in local language and manner to engage in legitimate behaviors. The "curbstone counselors" mediated and advocated for youth with school officials if they were truant or had conduct problems, and with police, court officials, and probation officers if they were arrested or violated probation. They were vigorous in their efforts to get representatives of bureaucratic, established institutions to better understand neighborhood youth and respond to their special interests and problems (Schlossman and Sedlak 1983).

Clifford Shaw, who founded the Chicago Area Project approach, emphasized local neighborhood responsibility and effort in addressing the delinquency problem, but he did not address larger governmental, commercial, and other factors that were significantly accountable for local problems. The Chicago Area Project was designed for gradual civic improvement through local citizen-group action. It was not designed to create organized pressures on government leaders and external agencies to modify their rules and policies or provide greater social and economic opportunities for such youth (Snodgrass 1976). Saul Alinsky, one of the early Chicago Area Project workers, would later redefine and refocus Shaw's approach by building broader local community coalitions, organizing local citizens, and empowering them to attack and negotiate with institutions responsible for a variety of local neighborhood social and economic problems. He also moved away from a focus on delinquency and the developing youth gang problem (Alinsky 1946).

POST–WORLD WAR II YOUTH GANG WORK

Waves of populations from the southern United States, Mexico, and Puerto Rico came to the factories of the North to help sustain America's World War II effort. In the late 1940s and early 1950s attention was directed to many of the sons and daughters of these newcomer populations. Low-income families, schools, and social agencies could not adequately meet the socialization needs of youth, particularly males. Some African American and Latino youth who were not acceptable to, or did not accept, established youth programs or traditional schooling approaches formed troublesome street groups, later identified as youth gangs. Youth gang delinquency was chiefly characterized by disorderly conduct and nonlethal intergang fighting. Fighting gangs were perceived as a threat to civil order and property in the local neighborhood and were of concern to citywide leadership.

In New York, Los Angeles, and other cities, a series of youth-outreach programs was established by city welfare councils, state and citywide youth boards, and county probation departments to identify and contact suspected neighborhood antisocial or warring youth gangs. Detached workers from established youth agencies or special gang projects (also known as street-gang workers, street workers, or outreach workers) were expected to counsel youth gangs and convert them to social groups. The detached, mainly male, workers operated alone on the streets in relative isolation from regular, structured youth-agency programs. A few female workers also were assigned to female (or "deb") groups, usually affiliated with male gangs. The workers were recruited from colleges and universities; a few were former gang members, but most were not indigenous to the particular gang communities in which they worked (Klein 1965, 1968, 1971; New York City Youth Board 1960; Welfare Council of Metropolitan Chicago 1960).

The youth-outreach workers were described as independent, self-assured, charismatic, caring, and socially committed. They themselves may have rebelled against middle-class norms and identified with the personal problems and struggles of gang youth. They had "little patience with the society and the community institutions which seemed to neglect" gang youth (Bernstein 1964, 114). At first, the various agencies sponsoring youth-outreach workers sought to "preserve the independence of the street workers" (Kobrin 1982). They were not to be routinized.

> The street worker is an agency worker on the streets who is striving to help the delinquent gang to change its pattern of behavior. He is on the streets of the neighborhood at odd hours of the day or night. He may have little immediate structure or support, such as an office, regular hours, guidance from colleagues or supervisors. He belongs to two worlds. He is of the delinquent group and its subculture, but also of the world of respectable and conforming people.... He tries on the one hand, to change the delinquent, and on the other, the people and institutions which have, in large measure, produced him. (Spergel 1966, xiii)

> A detached worker (gang worker, social worker, street-club worker) is an individual, usually with a streetwise orientation, who is assigned to one or more urban

street gangs. His modus operandi differs from that of the usual agency worker in that his primary task is to attach himself to the delinquent gang where and as it exists—on a street corner, on the playground, in a garage, at a hamburger stand, or in any other spot, where boys seem to congregate. (Klein 1965, 183)

In the late 1940s and 1950s the Group Guidance Project of the Los Angeles County Probation Department saw the newcomer Mexican American youth "zoot suit" problem as a gang problem and attempted through use of detached workers to reduce "gang acts" by (1) identifying street groups and their members who were oriented to delinquent gang activity; (2) developing a group-counseling relationship with them and their parents to aid in adjusting them to community standards; (3) reducing the isolation of these youth and their parents from established mainstream institutions; and (4) promoting better understanding and cooperation among citizens and established agencies in the community in addressing the problem (Los Angeles County Probation Department 1982).

The New York City Youth Board created the Council of Social and Athletic Clubs in 1950, comprising youth board gang workers who were expected to establish a special relationship with warring gangs. The workers were to help modify the gangs' antisocial attitudes and behaviors, persuade them to have friendlier relations with other street gangs, increase democratic participation within the gang, improve the social adjustment of individual gang members, and induce better relations with neighborhood residents. Street-gang work developed into a specialized program of work with street groups, largely unrelated to other community or agency programs treating or controlling individual delinquent youth, or to other general delinquency issues (New York City Youth Board 1960).

The New York City Youth Board street worker viewed the gang as a "natural neighborhood group," whose activities were not entirely negative or criminal. This natural street group was assumed to provide adolescents with opportunities for "positive youth development," even in socially disadvantaged neighborhoods. The street gang could be "reached," and it was expected to respond to "sympathy, acceptance, affection, and understanding" (when provided by a street worker with the right abilities). Their members would grow up to be conventional, socialized youth (New York City Youth Board 1960, 56–57; see also Shireman 1958; Roth 1961).

Social-work ideology guided the development of the specialized youth gang projects of the 1950s and 1960s. However, the "curbstone" worker idea, as one element of a grassroots community approach pioneered by the Chicago Area Project, was not essentially adopted. The gang worker (or street worker) of this period did not operate within a framework of accountability to local citizen groups or a consortium of local agencies. Also, the focus of the gang worker was more on group or recreational work than on individual-youth counseling, relations with family, or modifying established youth-agency or school approaches to delinquent youth. A social worker and director of the Mid-City Project in Boston described street work as a

> professional service to groups.... Even though the worker may have a number of individual contacts with the families, essentially he is involved in and working with the interaction and forces within the group.... The type of behavior that responds most readily ... is *public group behavior*—the behavior of the football team, participation in gang fights and group vandalism." (Austin 1957, 50)

Alex Norman, a senior staff member of Special Service for Groups in Los Angeles, also focused on the group method. He expected gangs to break up naturally.

> Because the gang acts as a source of delinquency for its members, Special Service for Groups attempts to use the group process to modify behavior to effect change, and enable the discontinuance of the antisocial group associates.... At the initial stage of the investigation, the worker's goal is to establish a trust relationship with these youth who are suspicious, mistrustful, and hostile toward adults and other "outsiders." ...After the group accepts service, weekly meetings are set up utilizing facilities which are available.... Groups tend to disintegrate ...the break-up must be a natural process.... As a supplement to the work being done with the groups, there are contacts with individual members around specific problems. (Norman 1963, 6)

By the early 1960s it was apparent that youth gangs and their members were more prevalent, probably more seriously delinquent, and better organized—more than simply deviant or isolated groups. They had become integral features of changing urban environments. They were more difficult to deal with than had been previously estimated. A changing economy made it difficult for older

youth who had limited education to leave the gang, find jobs, and become socially acceptable adults. Fewer factory and unskilled jobs were available. Gangs
were larger, more enduring, and more complexly organized, at least in major
urban gang centers. Agencies formerly interested in outreach youth gang work
turned their attention to other types of troubled youth and their families in
a greater range of often middle-class communities, including status offenders (particularly runaways) who were generally less overtly hostile and violent.
Nevertheless, some urban Boys Clubs, YMCAs, youth agencies, and Settlement
Houses continued outreach efforts with youth not in their programs (Carney,
Mattick, and Calloway 1965). They emphasized work with youth, some of
whom were on the streets and may not have been gang members. Outposts
and decentralized agency programs were established in isolated, low-income
housing projects. Some street workers were called "extension workers," functioning to bring more street youth into existing or developing youth-agency
social and recreational programs (Mattick and Caplan 1962; Doty and Mattick
1965).

The extension worker still based his approach on the development of personal influence relationships with significant numbers of the youth population.
"Now...detached workers can be described as offering service to unaffiliated
inner-city youth populations" (Cooper 1967, 185). The extension worker's efforts were expected to result in a measurable reduction of area delinquency
rates and "make a positive difference in the behavior of the youngsters residing
in the action areas" (Doty and Mattick 1965, 34; see also Caplan et al. 1967; *New
York Times* 1994). Extension workers also began to utilize leaders of the gangs
or street groups as part-time workers to influence other youth in the groups
toward more conforming behavior. The street-gang or street-group leaders
became assistants to the full-time extension workers. The outreach approach
continued to develop.

Researchers conducted evaluations of several traditional street-gang and
extension-work programs in Los Angeles, Boston, and Chicago in the late
1950s and early 1960s. They concluded that the programs were ineffective. The
programs still emphasized group work and recreational activities. Malcolm
Klein claimed that such programs cohered antisocial youth groups and contributed to an increase in delinquency. He recommended that such programs
be abandoned; he claimed that the programs directly increased gang cohesion
and paid limited attention to individual counseling, job placement, mediation,

or other youth-worker interventions, which were also occurring in the programs. Based on his evaluation of the Group Guidance Project (Klein 1968) and the Ladino Hills Project (Klein 1971), he concluded that detached youth work focusing on the gang-as-a-group structure was ineffective.

Klein concluded that "group programming for gang boys serves to increase gang size and cohesiveness. . . . There was good reason to doubt the desirability of continuing such programs or starting new ones" (Klein 1969, 164). Joan Moore, another major gang researcher and observer of gang programs in Los Angeles during the same period, challenged this conclusion, or at least lamented its consequences. She claimed that Klein's recommendation "was taken as an injunction by Los Angeles policy makers to end gang programs altogether. It was espoused with special enthusiasm by police and sheriffs, who were increasingly successful in persuading policy makers to substitute beefed-up police gang squads" to break up and suppress clusters of so-called gang youth (Moore 1991, 37–38).

THE COMMUNITY APPROACH
Youth-agency outreach programs to delinquent groups or gangs were largely abandoned by the middle 1960s. There had been a shift in ideology regarding the causes of urban problems (including delinquency). The Civil Rights Movement, urban riots, and subcultural gang theory (Cloward and Ohlin 1960) inspired federal legislation to address poverty through community-action programs and contributed to an institutional or structural (rather than an individual-youth or small-group) approach to addressing the delinquent gang problem. Street (or detached) workers were still available. They were now expected to be elements of local community institutional-change efforts, referring low-income, minority-group youth (including gang youth) to the "world of education" (street academies), the "world of work" (manpower training and job corps), and a broader range of community-based services to help them "make it" in the wider, legitimate world (Bibb 1967). Detached workers were now to be integrated into a community-service system. They were to connect youth to organizations such as the Youth Jobs Center, the Youth Services Corps, schools, and juvenile courts. Mobilization for Youth in New York City developed a network of agencies, schools, employment, and citizen (action) groups, and also included a unit of street-gang workers (Mobilization for Youth 1961). Greater access to legitimate opportunities was to be provided. The expectation was that

gang youth would not have to use conflict behavior or illegal opportunities to achieve social and economic status (Cloward and Ohlin 1960; Coleman 1974). But significant changes did not occur. Street workers continued their traditional practice of outreach group work, recreation, and brief individual-youth counseling. Other agencies, particularly youth and criminal justice agencies, did not significantly change their established approaches.

The Mid-City Project in Boston—a not-well-designed major community-wide approach—still used detached workers to emphasize the involvement of gang youth in formal club meetings, athletic contests, dances, and fundraising activities, rather than focusing on better access to social and economic opportunities. The Mid-City Project's "total community" approach did not facilitate community institutional change, strengthen local citizen groups, or encourage cooperation among different types of organizations. Criminal justice elements, especially the police, were not significantly involved in collaboration with street workers. Miller stated in his extensive evaluation that the project was not successful. It did not reduce delinquent-behavior arrests or court appearances of program youth.

But there were serious flaws in the conceptualization of these community-based gang programs. There were serious gaps in the Miller and Klein evaluations. They did not address the effects of different services or worker-activity patterns on program youth and what results were produced. They also did not account for gang, agency-organization, or community characteristics that could have contributed to program results (Miller 1962).

One of the most egregious failures of the still-not-clearly-defined "total community" approach was the Youth Manpower Project of the Woodlawn Organization (TWO) in Chicago in the mid-1960s (Spergel 1972). A grassroots organization with a reputation for effective, militant, Alinsky-style community organizing, TWO was selected by the U.S. Office of Economic Opportunity to address a burgeoning gang-violence problem in the area. Woodlawn was a neighborhood in transition from a mainly white to an all-black, lower class population. The project's objectives were to provide training, jobs, educational opportunities, and conflict mediation to two major warring Chicago Southside gangs. Collaborating with or advising TWO staff members were the Chicago Urban League, the Xerox Corporation, the First Presbyterian Church, and selected faculty of the University of Chicago. The goal of the project was to reduce gang conflict of alienated youth, mainly gang members, as well as area crime rates, and also minimize the potential for urban riots. (The assumption was that gangs and gang members contributed to urban riots in the mid-1960s.) Job-training centers were established in each of the territories of the two gang constellations—the Blackstone Rangers (also known as the Black P. Stone Nation and the El Rukns) and the Devils' Disciples (also known as the Black Disciples and the Black Gangster Disciples).

The Youth Manpower Project had other objectives, which undercut its gang-control goals and objectives and contributed to its failure. TWO, representing the interests of the residents and local organizations of Woodlawn, was opposed to policies of certain Chicago city agencies, mainly the Board of Education and Chicago's planning department. TWO also wanted to integrate the gangs as organizational equals into its own comprehensive, local, community-action and community-development efforts. Further, the minister of the First Presbyterian Church in Woodlawn, interested in addressing the gang problem (separately from the efforts of TWO), emphasized training Blackstone Ranger gang leaders to become local community leaders. A multiplicity of conflicting organizational goals and objectives was further confounded by the Chicago Police Department's newly organized gang unit's emphasis on suppression of targeted gangs in the Woodlawn area, generally opposed to the efforts of TWO and the First Presbyterian Church. Gang leaders were the principal staff of the three job-training centers, two controlled by the Blackstone Rangers and one by the Devils' Disciples. The TWO professional staff of three workers was too small to adequately supervise project operations, which targeted six hundred youth, sixteen to twenty-one years of age, in the two gangs. Gang members and their leaders did not accept the purpose of the project or substantially participate in the job-preparation program at the training centers. Attendance at the centers was used to plan and develop ongoing gang organizational and criminal activities. Gang leaders of the Blackstone Rangers collected weekly "stipends" from youth who attended (or did not attend) the training sessions. TWO project staff did not know how to control the illegitimate activities of the gang-leader program staff at the training centers. The project was attacked by the Chicago Police Department and several local citizens. A great deal of political controversy at local and national levels resulted. Leadership of the Office of Economic Opportunity (OEO) was questioned. The U.S. Senate conducted a well-publicized investigation of the project. The project was not funded for a second year of operations.

Area crime rates did not change. Few youth in the program were trained for or obtained legitimate jobs. The failure of the local community, and city and federal government institutions, to address the gang problem in some well-reasoned, coordinated sense may have contributed to the subsequent enhanced development of the two gang organizations. Leaders of the El Rukns and Gangster Disciples were later prosecuted and convicted of a series of felony crimes, including major drug operations and killings. Key gang leaders were imprisoned for long terms or killed in internal gang or intergang rivalries. Yet the two gangs continued to grow in size and varied criminal activity, and their influence spread to other cities (Spergel 1969, 1972, 1995). The first project to begin to fashion a comprehensive program design focusing on the youth gang problem with substantial attention to youth-agency, community-group, and justice-system characteristics was Crisis Intervention Network (CIN), formed in Philadelphia in 1975. The goals and objectives of the team of CIN street workers and community organizers were "to lower the incidents of youth disputes [gang fighting] in the city through dispute-resolution, follow-up, counseling with individual youth and their families, and by strengthening community organizations, formal and informal" (Darden, Peinsley, and Digre 1985, 54; see also Swans 1981). The CIN program also utilized a network of personnel from various organizations to achieve its objectives, including city probation and local neighborhood associations.

The key members of the CIN crisis team comprised youth gang or street workers who were mainly former gang members from the gang-problem community areas where they were assigned to work. The street workers patrolled the crisis areas and were available to address problems on a twenty-four-hour basis. An important component of the program was parent councils, which were "established as both a forum for information-sharing and a mobilizer of parents to reduce gang-related incidents" (Swans 1985, 2). A city of Philadelphia adult probation unit closely associated with CIN targeted and supervised young-adult gang leaders. Less closely linked to the program were the city schools and the Philadelphia Police Department. Other local community groups and agencies also developed programs to reduce gang violence and were partially associated with CIN, for example, the House of Umoja (Fattah 1987).

Gang homicides decreased sharply by the late 1970s, although the drug problem seemed to increase at the same time. Various agencies, including CIN, claimed credit for the reduction of gang homicides. But exactly who or what specifically was responsible for the reduction in gang violence was not clear. A formal evaluation of the structure, activities, outcome, and impact of CIN was not conducted (Crisis Intervention Network 1981). One prominent gang researcher observed that a change in Philadelphia Police statistical recording procedures may have accounted for some of the violence reduction that had taken place (Miller 1982).

SPECIALIZED GANG-SUPPRESSION APPROACHES

James Short (1985) observed two decades ago that "the behaviors of law en-forcement officers and court officials and actors in other institutions and the relationships among these actors and systems are critical to the understanding of both etiology and controls of crime and delinquency" (66, 67). An extraordi-nary focus on suppression as the key means to address the youth gang problem was developed by the criminal justice system and city and federal government. It is best represented by the activities of gang unit police (Klein 2004).

Specialized gang units originated in large urban areas (particularly Los An-geles and Chicago) in the 1960s in response to an increase in gang violence. Traditional youth-division police, juvenile court, and juvenile probation offi-cers seemed unable at the time to handle the problem effectively. The police became the first criminal justice agency to deal with the gang problem through units of officers trained in special procedures to target and suppress youth gangs. They provided models of approaches to gangs and gang members that later were adopted by prosecution, probation, corrections, and special school officers, and further enabled and legitimized by city ordinances, state laws, and public opinion. Urban disorders in the 1960s impelled police departments to focus somewhat indiscriminately on control of gangs along with other illegit-imate or radical groups that threatened local order and political and business interests. The Gang Crime Unit of the Chicago Police Department was orig-inally formed through the reassignment of some youth-division officers to suppress the behavior of gangs on the south side of Chicago, particularly those involved in TWO's Youth Manpower Project.

Gang units then, and still today, attract tough, moralistic, proactive officers operating in plainclothes and unmarked cars. Gang youth may be considered evil, remorseless in their criminal activities, and not worthy of civil treatment. They are identified, photographed, and recorded in gang books. Arrests of these youth are now based on a range of special gang-motivated or gang-related charges. Minority youth (particularly African American and Hispanic) located in ghetto communities are especially vulnerable to being labeled as gang youth, targeted, subjected to increased surveillance, and charged with gang offenses. Names of youth on police gang lists are not readily expunged. (In some cities, gang problems are assessed as involving mainly young adults in part because their names as juveniles are not removed after a period of years, although they may have committed no crimes.)

Klein (1995, 2004) has described the typical "hard" suppression activities of specialized gang police, probation, prosecution, corrections, and school officers. He maintains that the essence of gang-youth suppression is the punishment, control, and separation of gang youth, which goes beyond normal criminal justice procedures and institutional arrangements for dealing with youth who do not seriously transgress civic norms and criminal laws. Police gang units, vertical gang prosecution, probation gang units, and special school-resource officers have developed various surveillance and information systems and other procedures to control gang behaviors, particularly violence and a range of nuisance behaviors.

Low priority is given to understanding or addressing the complex community and institutional conditions that induce youth to join gangs and participate in criminal behavior. Gang-unit officers focus single-mindedly on gang activities such as street loitering, graffiti, disorderly conduct, mob action, fighting, and drug possession and sales. They aggressively stop and search gang youth (and sometimes non–gang youth) on street corners, in cars, in school yards, in parks, and on beaches, and may sweep them (often randomly) into paddy wagons and detention facilities, charging them with a range of offenses that are often dismissed at court arraignment. Gang police have been known to stimulate the gang problem by deliberately dropping off youth from one gang in opposing gang territories (and then watching for the fights that ensue and arresting the youth); marking out gang graffiti and replacing it with other gang markings; and (infrequently) engaging in a variety of illegal practices, sometimes in collaboration with other gang youth, for example, engaging or providing protection for drug deals.

These activities result inadvertently or deliberately in increased hostility to the police and stronger commitment by youth to the gang, with little effect on law-violating behavior. Sweeps of opposing gang members into the same paddy wagons also create enhanced animosity and further rationale for attacking members of opposing gangs. Gang youth may develop reputations for "beating the rap" and advance in the gang structure. Webb and Katz (2005) conclude that "the growth of gangs during the last two decades has been accompanied by the development and growth of specialized law enforcement responses to gangs." Suppression activities are "of central value in the gang unit's work ... even though the amount of time actually spent on such activities can vary immensely from one gang unit to the next." They also note that prevention activities by police gang units "have received much less priority than intelligence, suppression, or investigations ... prevention is probably at best a residual category"(380, 387, 398).

By contrast, Decker (2004) observes that "the responses to gangs in Europe are decidedly different than those in the United States.... Though suppression is a part of the response to gangs in European societies, it is decidedly the second or third alternative. And even when the police are involved ... social opportunities receive first priority ... police work closely with school officials and social authorities to find jobs, mentor youth, and work with families" (16).

City ordinances and state laws have increasingly widened the range of punishments for gang youth in respect to certain offenses. Courts now tend to deny diversion and rehabilitation services to gang youth, or deny juvenile-court processing, generally referring them to adult court. More than one state bylaw classifies gangs as terrorist organizations (Klein 1995; Spergel 1995). Under a recent gang bill debated in the U.S. Congress, a sentence of at least ten years would be required for an act of violence, at least twenty years for assaults resulting in serious injuries, and at least thirty years for kidnapping, aggravated sexual abuse, or maiming. The bill would demand life imprisonment or the death penalty for any crime resulting in death (Kirkpatrick 2005).

MORE COMPLEX CROSS-INSTITUTIONAL APPROACHES
The increase in gangs and gang members outside of urban centers in the 1980s, 1990s, and 2000s was associated with new waves of immigration, population movements, and growing segregation of low-income Latinos and African Americans in certain areas. Youth gangs developed in the suburbs, in medium and smaller-sized cities, on Indian reservations, and in rural areas. Gang violence grew more lethal, and gang youth increasingly were selling drugs. The gang drug problem escalated more rapidly than intergang violence in most

communities. Still, communities grew more wary, more fearful, and less toler-
ant of gangs and gang youth.

Government leaders continued to declare periodic wars on gangs, particularly on gangs in low-income minority areas. The police, schools, and
community groups—while primarily committed to suppression—also became
somewhat more involved in gang prevention and community mobilization
to counter gang activities. Traditional detached-worker or street-worker programs continued to exist but still in ambiguous relationship with other programs and agencies concerned with the gang problem. Specialized gang units,
as well as community policing unrelated to the gang units, grew rapidly in most
urban centers (Webb and Katz 2005).

Boston made new, extensive, cross-agency comprehensive efforts to deal
with the juvenile violence problem, including juvenile gang violence, in the
early and mid-1990s. Emphasis was on the gun violence problem. Social service agencies concerned with youth violence used street workers to perform
traditional outreach group-oriented tasks, contacting "kids who hung with
crews [i.e., gangs], dealt drugs, suffered from and perpetrated violence." Street
workers also assisted youth with employment, social services, dispute resolution, and youth participation in a "Peace League" of "gang-on-gang" basketball
games held in neutral sites. Probation officers were on the streets in partnership
with a special group of Youth Violence Cease Fire (police) Officers in Operation
Night Light (Piehl, Kennedy, and Braga 2000).

The various personnel in the Boston Cease Fire programs seemed to cooperate well with each other. Street workers, probation officers, and police
were in periodic face-to-face street contact with ministers of the Ten Point
Coalition—an activist African American clergy walking the streets late into the
night. Teachers and mental-health workers taught violence prevention in the
schools. "What emerged in Boston in the early 1990s was an extensive network
of front-line practitioners with a mix of capacities who were well-informed
about what was happening in the streets" (Piehl, Kennedy, and Braga 2000,
72–73).

The various Boston Cease Fire programs were not based on an "anti-gang
strategy." Youth homicides sharply declined, but the decline "cannot be at-
tributed to a cessation of gangs or gang activities." Evaluators of the Boston
effort also could not attribute the decline in youth homicides to any particular program component. The success of the Boston "Gun Project," according

to evaluators, was that it "involved multiple agencies and the community and substantial investments in analysis, coordination and implementation." Gun-control efforts apparently did nothing to reduce "the existing stockpile ... of guns held by gang members in Boston which was still held when violence reached its new low equilibrium." Youth and adults were apparently not using the guns they had. The principal impact, therefore, was certainly a "demand-side deterrence-based effect rather than a supply-side effect." The Boston program evaluations clearly emphasized deterrence of violence but not necessarily youth-development or institutional-change factors that might have contributed to a reduction of the causes of the violence or the gang problem (Piehl, Kennedy, and Braga 2000, 102). We do not know what particular workers did with gangs and violent youth and with what specific short- and long-term effects.

The Chicago Project for Violence Prevention/Cease Fire initially aimed to reduce gun shootings in various neighborhoods in Chicago, as well as in other Illinois cities. Its efforts between 1995 and 1999 in Chicago were focused on "strategy, development, and infrastructure building." It claimed to borrow from and adapt other models, such as the Boston "Gun Project" and later the "Spergel" Comprehensive Community-Wide Gang Program Model, within a public-health framework. Its recently stated eight-point plan involved

(1) developing and maintaining strong community coalitions; (2) sending a unified message about gun violence (no shooting); (3) mediating and intervening in all conflicts; (4) rapidly responding to all shootings; (5) providing alternatives and linkages for most at-risk persons; (6) providing safe havens and programs for youths; (7) enforcing penalties for gun use and gun trafficking; and (8) ensuring prosecution of offenders. (National Institute of Justice 2004, 4)

The last two strategies were not the direct responsibilities of the project, however.

The project continues to operate under the direction of a psychiatrist at the School of Public Health, University of Illinois, Chicago. A process-and-outcome evaluation of its multicomponent program may be in progress. Recently, it has more sharply centered attention on gang-related violent incidents and threats of gang violence, particularly through its outreach workers, many of whom have former gang and prison backgrounds. It appears to have achieved local community and public-official support in some communities but not in others.

Its efforts remain largely separate from those of the Chicago Police Department or other justice-system agencies, in regard to the specific youth or young adults contacted. Chicago government leadership continues to be resistant to close criminal justice and social-agency collaboration, particularly in relation to interactive programming and controls for gang youth. Chicago law-enforcement approaches, despite the presence of a community-policing component, remain dominantly suppression oriented. Also, community-based efforts and a few traditional agency-based street-work programs continue to operate generally unrelated to each other throughout the city.

The efforts and problems of one grassroots program in the Robert Taylor Homes housing project in Chicago in the early 1990s were reminiscent of the flawed TWO Youth Manpower Project of the 1960s. The director of a community center in the homes began to meet privately with gang leaders to reduce gang conflict. While there was some reduction of intergang conflict over a short period of time, the problems of drug trafficking were not addressed. (Tenants in the housing project were on public aid and vulnerable to "check day" blandishments—or intimidation—of gang drug dealers to purchase drugs.) The community center sponsored meetings between tenants and gang leaders to encourage gang members to assist with trash pickup, hallway cleaning, curbing of public drinking, and so forth (Venkatesh 2000, 218).

The community-center director and local tenant group failed to curb the development and expansion of the gang's other criminal-gain activities, especially drug trafficking, which were regarded by some as more destructive and corrupting than gang violence—although the two problems were not entirely separate. Venkatesh's conclusion was that with the expansion of the local gang's major influence across public housing projects in Chicago, and even across other cities and states, the gang was "locally . . . a social and economic enterprise . . . [but] regionally, it was an organized crime enterprise . . . whose leaders paid little attention to non-economic and non-criminal activities" (218).

A recent interagency collaborative arrangement in Los Angeles—the BRIDGES program—involved twenty-six of the city's middle schools in areas where gang activity was highest, and relied heavily on the use of street workers. A detached worker was assigned to each of the schools, with a caseload of thirty clients (gang-involved or gang-crime youth in school, and living within a 2.5-mile radius of the school). The indigenous workers performed a mix of counseling and negotiating truces as well as gathering information about gang problems. An association of Community-Based Gang Intervention Workers was also formed in Los Angeles County. Of its 198 members, representing 56 agencies in the Los Angeles area, "approximately 70% . . . are ex-gang members and a majority of these may have criminal records" (Meyers 2000, 42). Under the regime of a newly elected mayor in Los Angeles, a more comprehensive approach to a burgeoning gang problem was again contemplated involving schools, youth agencies, police, and churches in various parts of the city.

In some cities, academics, former gang leaders, local political aspirants, and minority-group leaders have occasionally engaged in efforts to reform gangs and include them as viable social organizations concerned with and part of a wider civic movement, advocating improved services and institutional reforms on behalf of low-income minority populations in ghetto areas. A result has been the recent evolution of informal support groups to meet the myriad and often critical personal, social, and economic needs of gang youth and older, former gang-affiliated adults. Some of the groups, engaging in activities of a political nature, are closely observed with suspicion by key police gang units (Kontos, Brotherton, and Barrios 2003).

APPROACHES OF THE U.S. DEPARTMENT OF JUSTICE

In the 1990s, the U.S. Department of Justice initiated two different, so-called comprehensive approaches to the crime problem, both with considerable focus on youth gangs but that became increasingly difficult to reconcile. The Office of Juvenile Justice and Delinquency Prevention (OJJDP) sponsored a Comprehensive Community-Wide Approach to Gang Prevention, Intervention, and Suppression Program (1994), based in some measure on the ideas of the Little Village Gang Violence Reduction Project—a comprehensive, community-wide, integrated suppression and intervention program. However, the OJJDP approach became increasingly service oriented over time. At the same time, the Office of Community Oriented Policing Services (COPS) of the U.S. Department of Justice sponsored an Anti-Gun Initiative (AGI) (1995) that adopted the Boston Cease Fire or "Gun Project" model, which became increasingly suppression oriented.

The initial OJJDP Comprehensive Community-Wide Gang Program was demonstrated in five cities (Bloomington, Illinois; Mesa and Tucson, Arizona;

San Antonio, Texas; and Riverside, California). OJJDP supported the program at each site for a four- or five-year period. A consortium of justice-system, social service, educational, and community-based agencies was expected to develop an integrated approach to the youth gang problem in high–gang-crime neighborhoods. In three of the cities, the lead agency was a police department; in two cities it was a social service agency. An effective youth-outreach-worker approach, however, was not established in any of the cities. Police and youth agencies continued in varying degrees to operate in their respective suppression or social-intervention ways. At two of the program sites, where police departments were the lead agencies, a somewhat integrated team approach was substantially achieved, with a resulting decrease in violence arrests for program youth, and also a reduction of gang violence on a community-area basis, at least during the program period (Spergel, Wa, and Sosa 2002, 2003, 2005).

The OJJDP Comprehensive Gang Program was followed by broad, social service–oriented Safe Futures Projects to reduce delinquency and youth violence. Six local government grantees were funded: Boston, Massachusetts; Contra Costa County, California; Fort Belknap Indian Community, Montana; Imperial Valley, California; Seattle, Washington; and St. Louis, Missouri. Safe Futures Projects sought to "prevent and control youth crime and victimization through the creation of a continuum of care in communities.... This continuum of care enables communities to respond to the needs of youth ... with appropriate prevention, intervention, and treatment services and comprising graduated sanctions" (Morley et al. 2000, ix). The nine components of the program (after-school activities, juvenile mentoring, family-support services, mental-health services, gang-free schools, delinquency prevention, drug treatment, continuance of services for at-risk and delinquent girls, and serious violent juvenile offenders) emphasized social development for at-risk youth and violent or gang youth. The evaluators noted in their interim report that the programs at the six sites varied considerably in their "configurations, partnerships, and other aspects" (Morley et al. 2000, x). However, the projects appeared to pay limited attention to the interrelationship of the various service-agency programs.

The COPS anticrime initiative, established in fifteen cities, was an attempt to adapt the Boston Cease Fire efforts. It called for "zero tolerance enforcement against gang members" but also "a carrot and stick approach." One of the programs—in the Hollenbeck area (Boyle Heights) of Los Angeles—developed a strategy to hold gangs collectively responsible for the gun violence of individual gang members. The assumption was that most gang shooters would be known to probation or parole officers and would most likely be responsible for the youth violence in the area. But the results were disappointing. Of the identified shot callers or shooters, only half were known to the justice system. The "carrot" side of the Cease Fire program, that is, prevention and social intervention for target youth, was hardly utilized (Tita, Riley, and Greenwood 2003).

The most interesting divergence from an integrative justice- and social service–system approach to address the youth gang problem occurred in St. Louis, where Safe Futures and COPS programs operated separately in different neighborhoods over the same period. The Safe Futures program, designed to integrate suppression, social intervention, and opportunities provision, was deficient and fragmented in its program efforts. Many of the agencies associated with the program were "incapable of either reaching or serving the at-risk population." Juvenile court did not make referrals to particular agencies, and the police declined to become full participants in the program, since some of the agencies included former gang members as outreach youth workers. Some social agencies were even unwilling to make referrals to other social agencies, or to serve the same youth in a coordinated way. The conclusion was that the program's failure to demonstrate change in crime rates was due to the lack of "integration of suppression and the provision of social opportunities" (Decker and Curry 2003, 211–212).

The continuing dominance of suppression approaches, now somewhat better coordinated among law enforcement and other justice-system agendas, remained basically unrelated to social service, social-opportunity-providing agencies and local community groups. The elements of the Boston approach now emphasized are as follows: "recognizing that violence problems are concentrated among groups of chronic offenders who are often but not always gang-involved"; belief that such groups "are locked into a self-sustaining dynamic of violence, often driven by fear, respect issues, and vendettas"; use of a targeted justice-system "pulling-levers" strategy that would make these groups "believe that consequences would follow violence and gun use"; "combining official data sources with street-level qualitative information"; "convening an interagency [criminal justice system representatives] working group with a locus of responsibility"; and "research involvement in an action-oriented enterprise." The popular, mainly suppression-oriented approaches are estimated to produce "promising results," but none of the projects thus far "have been fully evaluated" and none "have used desirable controlled experimental designs" (Braga, Kennedy, and Tita 2005, 376–78).

FRAGMENTED APPROACHES TO THE GANG PROBLEM

A variety of initiatives have occasionally explored the possibilities of integrating social-intervention and suppression and, less frequently, opportunities-provision and community-mobilization approaches in order to prevent and control youth gang activities, especially violence. To date, the effective integration of the various approaches has not been adequately articulated, planned, or achieved.

Gang programs run by social agencies have continued to use social services, and occasionally outreach youth-worker approaches, with focus on addressing the social and psychological problems of youth and their families. They have attempted to reduce violent gang activity, mediate conflicts between gangs, and provide mentoring, school tutorials, and job referrals. There has been little, if any, individual-youth or gang-level collaboration with criminal justice agencies, particularly law enforcement.

Educational organizations and neighborhood groups emphasize gang-prevention, cultural, and race/ethnic integration issues, and prefer generally to bring in law enforcement to avoid or control crises involving gang youth. The priorities of schools remain, that is, providing education and training of most students but with "zero tolerance" of gang behavior, if not the elimination of the presence of gang-youth altogether. Neighborhood groups, including homeowners, business proprietors, and local citizens with young children, seek protection and quickly call for the arrest and removal of gang youth from the community, especially those engaged in gang fighting and drug dealing. They look to law enforcement and suppression as the principal means of addressing the problem. Law enforcement has become the major institutional approach to addressing the youth gang problem, through single-minded suppression measures.

On the other hand, some gang experts and gang researchers believe that former gang members—even active gang members—are essential to successful gang-control and gang-prevention programs. Hagedorn (1988) insists "public policy must utilize older gang members as consultants in developing new programs" (167). Bursik and Grasmick (1993) recommend "the recruitment of gang members as core members of locally based gang prevention programs" (177). Bartollas is more specific; he suggests that "gang-member volunteers serve as disciplinary monitors within community schools" (Curry 1995, 159). However, other gang researchers such as Klein (1971), Miller (1962), Spergel (1995), and Venkatesh (2000) question primary reliance on former or active gang members to control gang-member delinquency and crime. They emphasize that gang or former gang members have little legitimate authority and are at risk of overidentifying with the gang youth's criminal interests, norms, and values. Neither a single-minded suppression nor a single-minded social-intervention approach has demonstrated success in reducing gang crime, especially gang violence. These authors and others support the need for modified suppression strategies, juxtaposed and integrated with social-opportunity strategies. But none of these views or approaches have been articulated in a model and adequately tested through empirical research. It was not until the Little Village Gang Violence Reduction Project that a model was formulated and a program of integrated suppression and social intervention—through a team arrangement and with community involvement, along with provision of opportunities, community mobilization, and agency change to address the gang-violence problem—was established and systematically tested. A functional, integrated, interinstitutional, community approach had to evolve, the purpose of which was to reduce violence between two major gang constellations. The Little Village Project required a shift in the outreach youth worker's role—to collaborate in a suppression approach—and also a shift (albeit limited) in law enforcement's role—to collaborate in some form of social intervention and even opportunity provision to address the gang problem. An interagency sponsorship and grassroots coalition would have to be formed.

The Little Village Project was a test of a program approach based on the integration of a set of specialized strategies, traditionally implemented in mutually exclusive fashion. It would be a test of the capacity and willingness of city political and criminal justice organizations, youth agencies, and community leaders to slightly modify policies and alter administrative arrangements to develop a comprehensive approach to the gang problem. The approach did not seek to eliminate gangs but to significantly reduce gang violence. The project was only indirectly and partially expected to modify the causal aspects of the problem of community disorganization, which was a product of larger societal and community forces including population movement, poverty, racism, segregation, and family disorganization. The project was also an attempt to determine, prospectively through a quasiexperimental research evaluation, whether an interinstitutional and interdisciplinary community-based approach could be achieved and contribute to the reduction of gang violence.

The essence of the project would be not simply to implement a comprehensive community-wide gang program model but also to simultaneously and interactively develop a comprehensive evaluation of its program process, outcome, and impact in a chronic gang-violent community and politicized urban context—a tall order!

NOTE

1. Irving A. Spergel, *The Youth Gang Problem: A Community Approach* (New York: Oxford University Press, 1995). See also Irving A. Spergel, Susan F. Grossman, and Kwai Ming Wa, "Reducing Youth Gang Violence in Urban Areas: One Community's Effort," *On Good Authority* 2 (5) (March 1999): 1–4; Irving A. Spergel and Kwai Ming Wa, "Combating Gang Violence in Chicago's Little Village Neighborhood," *On Good Authority* 4 (2) (August 2000): 1–4; Irving A. Spergel and Kwai Ming Wa, "Outcomes of the Little Village Gang Violence Reduction Project," *On Good Authority* 3 (3) (August 2000): 1–4; Irving A. Spergel et al., "Evaluation of the Gang Violence Reduction Project in Little Village" (Chicago: School of Social Service Administration, University of Chicago, September 2000).

2

Project Formation

The idea for the Little Village Gang Violence Reduction Project (GVRP) evolved from my field experience in earlier gang programs, as well as my research and that of others indicating that past, single-type strategic approaches were apparently not successful. It was an empirically and also theoretically informed demonstration to address the youth gang problem in comprehensive and community-based terms. The basis for the model was a series of perspectives about societal, family, community, interorganizational, subcultural, and personality factors explaining the development of youth gangs and their behaviors. Emphasis was on social disorganization theory, especially at community and interorganizational levels, but also at family-relationship and adolescent developmental and personality levels, to explain violent behavior of youth gangs. Theories of poverty, lack of social opportunities, and racism often interacted with social (and personal) disorganization to explain the involvement of youth gangs and their members in illegal gain-oriented behavior (figure 2.1).

The program model was developed in the course of the implementation of the Juvenile Gang Suppression and Intervention Research and Development Program, sponsored by the Office of Juvenile Justice and Delinquency Prevention (OJJDP), U.S. Department of Justice (1987–1991). The model was based on a set of five interrelated strategies directed to the youth gang problem: community mobilization, social intervention, provision of social opportunities, suppression or socialized control, and organizational change and development (figure 2.2; Spergel 1995).

These strategies were specified in twelve technical assistance manuals, each providing rationales and recommending policies and practices for different organizations or institutions, for example, governmental planning agencies, police, probation, youth-serving agencies, schools and businesses addressing (or that could address) the gang problem (Spergel and Chance 1992). The GVRP was an opportunity to further develop and test the model in the real

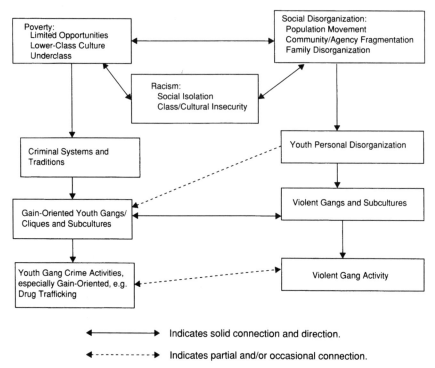

FIGURE 2.1
Youth gang crime: a theoretical framework.

world of community gang-violence problems, fragmented interorganizational relationships, and city politics. Not all of the model's elements, strategies, and policies/practices were implemented.

What distinguished the Little Village Gang Violence Reduction Project was its sponsorship by the Chicago Police Department (CPD). The project model envisioned the collaboration of components of the criminal justice system, youth-service agencies, grassroots groups, and former gang members. Outreach youth workers (mainly former leaders of gangs in the project area) and residents of Little Village were to be key elements in this local, community-based program. Evaluation research was also to be highly integrated into project operations. Extensive data systems describing arrest backgrounds of program and comparison youth, and mapping and analyses of gang crime on a Chicago neighborhood basis, were to be made accessible to the project from the CPD and

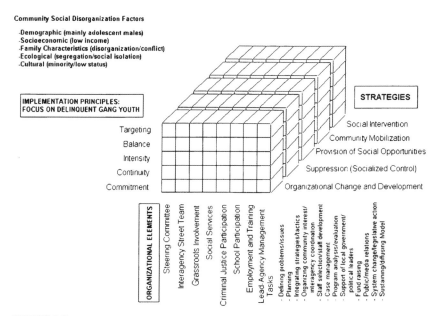

Community Social Disorganization Factors

-Demographic (mainly adolescent males)
-Socioeconomic (low income)
-Family Characteristics (disorganization/conflict)
-Ecological (segregation/social isolation)
-Cultural (minority/low status)

IMPLEMENTATION PRINCIPLES:
FOCUS ON DELINQUENT GANG YOUTH

Targeting
Balance
Intensity
Continuity
Commitment

STRATEGIES

Social Intervention
Community Mobilization
Provision of Social Opportunities
Suppression (Socialized Control)
Organizational Change and Development

ORGANIZATIONAL ELEMENTS

Steering Committee
Interagency Street Team
Grassroots Involvement
Social Services
Criminal Justice Participation
School Participation
Employment and Training
Lead-Agency Management
Tasks
- Defining problems/issues
- Planning
- Integrating strategies/tactics
- Organizing community interest/
  interagency coordination
- Staff selection/staff development
- Case management
- Program analysis/evaluation
- Support of local government/
  political leaders
- Fund raising
- Public/media relations
- System change/legislative action
- Sustaining/diffusing Model

FIGURE 2.2
Comprehensive gang program model.
Goal 1: improve local community and interorganizational capacity to address youth gang crime.
Goal 2: reduce gang crime, especially gang violence.

the Illinois Criminal Justice Information Authority (ICJIA), both for program-development and research purposes. The ICJIA, the state's criminal justice planning agency, strongly encouraged and supported the project, with the aid of U.S. Department of Justice funds.

GENESIS OF THE LITTLE VILLAGE PROJECT

In the spring of 1992, a series of changes occurred in Chicago government and among criminal justice agencies in Chicago and Cook County that made possible the development of the Little Village Gang Violence Reduction Project. A new mayor had been elected, and he appointed a new police superintendent. The structure and direction of the CPD began to change as new senior staff came on board. The then director of the ICJIA resigned her position and was appointed director of the research and development (R&D) unit of the CPD under the newly appointed deputy superintendent, both of whom were given major responsibility for creation of the city's community policing program, the Community Alternative Policing Strategy (CAPS). A former assistant state's attorney in Illinois became the director of the Cook County Department of Adult Probation (CCDAP), with interest in the gang problem.

In 1992 the ICJIA received a four-year grant from the U.S. Justice Department's Violence in Urban Areas Program, of which one million dollars per year was to be allocated to the development of pilot projects in the Chicago Police Department, half to be used to address the problem of domestic violence in an African American community, and half to be used to address the gang-violence problem in a Latino community. The new director of the ICJIA was responsible for the grant application to the federal government and for the distribution of the funds. She had been involved earlier in the development of the OJJDP's Juvenile Gang Suppression and Intervention Program, and later—after the Little Village Project—the implementation of OJJDP's Comprehensive Community-Wide Approach to Gang Prevention, Intervention, and Suppression Program. In the spring of 1992, she contacted me at the School of Social Service Administration, University of Chicago, to request a concept paper to address the gang-violence portion of the federal grant in Chicago. The commander of the CPD's gang-crime unit, who was also involved earlier in the development of the model of the OJJDP Juvenile Gang Suppression and Intervention Program, expressed interest in its adaptation in Chicago. Gang homicides had reached an all-time peak in certain Chicago inner-city communities. The commander provided statistics of gang crime and aided in the selection of possible local sites for the project. At the same time, the effectiveness of the gang-crime unit was being challenged, based on a report of a consulting firm hired by the CPD. In its report to the superintendent of the CPD, the firm recommended the downsizing and decentralization of the gang unit's enforcement operations. The city Department of Human Services (DHS) also expressed interest in its outreach youth workers participating in the project, as it was terminating its Gang Crisis Intervention Network program in the open community.

My concept paper was submitted to the ICJIA and the CPD and was well received. The R&D unit of the CPD agreed to administer the project. The gang-crime unit, the Chicago Department of Human Services, and the Cook County Department of Adult Probation were expected to be key operational components in a coordinated interagency approach. A local community advisory group was also to be established. The grant required that the project target

youth and young adults, seventeen to twenty-four years of age, in a community where serious gang violence was prevalent. Data on gang crime was to be
supplied by the CPD and by a senior researcher at ICJIA who had developed
the early warning system for the collection and refinement of CPD gang-crime
data on a community, gang, gang-offense, gang-offender, and gang-victim basis. Originally, I was to assist the R&D unit and the gang unit in the development
of the project but not to play a program-operational role. I was to receive a separate contract from the ICJIA to evaluate the project. The goal of the project was
to reduce gang violence (especially gang homicide and felony gang-motivated
battery and assault) in the target area, compared to similar areas in the city. A
significant decrease (or a lower rate of increase) in the gang-violence problem
was to occur at the end of the first year's twelve-month test period, compared to
changes in the gang problem in similar areas. At least one hundred hard-core,
violent, or potentially violent gang youth were to be targeted. The strategy to
achieve project goals and objectives required collaboration and the integration
of the efforts of law enforcement and other criminal justice agencies with those
of community-based human service agencies and grassroots organizations.
The entire project originally was to be developed in close cooperation with the
gang-crime unit of the Chicago Police Department.

A high gang-violence Latino community was to be selected as the test community but not necessarily one with high rates of drug-related gang crime.
The police districts in Chicago containing the Latino communities with the
highest rates of gang violence were Humboldt Park on the north side, and Little
Village on the south side. The gangs in Little Village, however, were somewhat
less involved in drug-related gang crime than the gangs in Humboldt Park or
in Pilsen (the community next to Little Village—an almost socioeconomically
identical Mexican American area), which was to become a key comparison
community. It was assumed that a serious drug problem, when closely joined
to the gang-violence problem, would be more complex and resistive to a program model integrating suppression, community mobilization, services, and
job opportunities. The project was expected to have a better chance of success by focusing on the reduction of gang violence, rather than also on the
reduction of drug-related gang crime. Little Village was chosen as the project
site. The Little Village community comprised six police beats in the southern
half of the Tenth District. It was five miles southwest of Chicago's "Loop," the
city's major business center. Formerly a community populated by first- and

second-generation Middle-European residents, it was (since the 1970s) settled by an increasingly Mexican and Mexican American population. The northern sector of the Tenth District was African American and was part of a swath of low-income, high-rise, segregated African American communities extending from the Loop to the western limits of the city.

Little Village was a community of working-class families with two-story homes on its west side, and low-income residents in three- and four-story tenements on its east side. It had well-established Catholic churches, a thriving business strip, and major hospital and university complexes nearby. The resident families were large, with many children and adolescents. The community was also in transition. Latino families were moving in and out of the area from and to other parts of the city and suburbs, downstate Illinois, the southern states (especially Texas), and Mexico. In 1990, the United States Census reported a population of only 60,829, but in 1992, 30 percent of its estimated total one hundred thousand population was believed to be undocumented.

The GVRP model called for an interagency team approach, with community support and involvement, that employed a set of interrelated strategies—community mobilization at local and citywide levels, social intervention or youth outreach, provision of social opportunities (particularly jobs, training, and access to school programs), suppression, and organizational policy-and-practice changes to accommodate the strategies. The team approach was to involve close collaboration among police, probation, outreach youth workers, and a local neighborhood organization that would target violent gang youth. Other criminal justice, social, employment, and educational agencies and organizations would be added as soon as possible. From the start, expectations were that the GVRP, if successful, could be adapted citywide, as part of the CPD's community-policing initiative being planned almost at the same time. Community policing in the Tenth District (one of the five planned pilot sites) did not get off the ground until approximately six months after the start of the Gang Violence Reduction Project. The development of community policing became a major undertaking, more difficult and complex than the CPD anticipated, and consequently took up the bulk of the R&D unit's attention and energies. The CPD's interest in the development of the Little Village Project was tentative and limited. The objectives of the program were not well understood. Community policing went citywide about a year after the Little Village Project was initiated.

MODIFYING THE PLAN

The Little Village Gang Violence Reduction Project was reorganized almost before it began. The commander of the CPD's gang-crime unit resigned. The unit was eliminated, and its intelligence functions transferred to the organized-crime unit. Its enforcement duties were diffused and taken over by the patrol division's tactical arm, which was given operational responsibility for implementing the project. Two full-time officers from the Tenth District tactical unit and two part-time neighborhood-relations officers (including a sergeant of the Tenth District) were assigned to the project, replacing the commander and two operational officers of the gang-crime unit, which no longer existed. The director of the Cook County Department of Adult Probation followed through on its agreement to provide a unit of three full-time probation officers and a supervisor. The Chicago Department of Human Services, which initially planned to provide a unit of three outreach intervention youth workers, did not do so. It shifted its focus to delinquency prevention and assigned its workers to elementary and junior high schools. The agency was no longer interested in a street-worker approach to gangs, or in participating in the Little Village Project.

With rapid changes and shifts of responsibility of administrative personnel, the CPD was unsure about how and who was to manage the project. Perhaps most importantly for purposes of overall project development, it was not clear who the police project coordinator or operational manager of the project would be, that is, who would take day-to-day responsibility for leading and running the program. I was not expected to fill this role, but in the fog of CPD structural changes I initially took a certain amount of operational responsibility for getting the program off the ground operationally. Having designed the model, I believed that a critical program component had to be the use of outreach youth workers to make early contact and provide services to targeted gang members on the street. According to the project plan, progress in creating the program and reducing violence had to be demonstrated within a twelve-month contract period. The youth-work component was now expected to collaborate closely with the CPD's tactical or gang-unit officers for purposes of suppressing gang violence. The project plan also called for the development of the worker team, including tactical officers, probation officers, and a neighborhood organizer. The team would not only employ interrelated strategies of suppression and social intervention but also would begin to mobilize community interest and

develop resources to provide social opportunities for target youth. A huge set
of operational responsibilities confronted me.

The immediate problem in implementing the design was to select an agency
to replace the Department of Human Services, which could provide outreach
youth-work services. A variety of youth-serving organizations were present
in the Little Village area: three Boys and Girls Clubs, Latino Youth (a comprehensive youth-service agency), the Chicago Park Department's Piotrowski
Recreation Center, and several churches with youth programs and gyms. However, none of the organizations had outreach youth workers, and their programs were not directed to hard-core or older gang youth. None worked in
alliance with the Tenth District police around the gang problem. Several citywide youth agencies—BUILD, Chicago Commons, Settlement House, and the
YMCA—had experience with recreation-oriented outreach youth gang programs focused on younger youth but were reluctant to collaborate with the
Chicago Police Department.

Unwilling to modify a basic element of the model, I suggested that the School
of Social Service Administration (SSA), University of Chicago (UC)—already
under contract to evaluate the project—also carry out a service function, replacing the youth-work component the Department of Human Services was
to supply. I had a history of experience at various levels of youth-worker intervention and community organization with gang projects. I proposed that I
would create an outreach youth-worker component to be operated temporarily
through SSA. This idea was acceptable to the CPD, the ICJIA, and the University of Chicago. The possibility existed of involving the DHS at a later time or
persuading one of the local youth agencies to adapt the model and take over
the outreach youth-worker component.

It was important to get the project underway as soon as possible. The interests of the CPD and the CCDAP in interorganizational collaboration, and the
political feasibility of this collaboration, were not solid. The CPD and CCDAP
were not meeting with each other to plan the nature of their collaboration in
the project. I believed the model had to be initiated, developed, and tested with
whatever critical components were available while an opportunity existed to
do so.

The R&D unit of the CPD continued to be deeply involved in departmental
reorganization almost exclusively related to the community-policing initiative,
which would focus on general crime prevention and law enforcement as well

as more efficient contacts for provision of city services to local citizens, but not on gang control. The Tenth District commander was assigned for 5 percent of his time to nominally oversee the Little Village Project, but he retired almost as soon as the project got underway. The replacement commander stayed in the position for only a few weeks. The chief of the patrol division continued to express support for the project. He would appoint a second and then a third Tenth District commander, but direct responsibility for project operations was still not clear.

It appeared that only a lieutenant assigned to the project from the R&D unit and I were committed to the project model and prepared to invest significant effort in its development. Police and probation administrators were interested in the project but not clear about the nature and structure of the program and what their specific responsibilities to the project would be, that is, who should be doing what with whom. By default, I soon became (unofficially) responsible for getting the project off the ground, determining its direction, and coordinating its worker components.

The CPD liaison lieutenant was almost the only one in the department who had a solid grasp of the project concept and the importance of the interrelationship of its components. He was clearly aware of the necessity of acceptance of the project within different levels and units of the CPD, and between the CPD and its subcontractees—the CCDAP and the UC. He took responsibility for communicating the purpose and nature of the project to officials across the various agencies whose staffs were to participate in the project. He was committed to research. He provided his research staff and me with access to detailed police data in order to assess the gang problem in the program and comparison areas. The lieutenant was also interested in whether changes in the views of local citizens regarding the gang problem developed and could be related to the program. He recommended conducting community surveys to determine this. However, before the end of the first year of project operations, the lieutenant transferred out of R&D back to the field and patrol duty. He insisted the project required the active and collective involvement of the police, adult probation, the community, and outreach youth workers in the control and prevention of street crime, particularly gang violence. He said that the project could be an example of community policing in the truest sense of the term. His views were apparently not shared by leaders of R&D, and so he transferred out of the unit.

The failure of the CPD to assign a senior officer to take responsibility for the development of the project may have been due not only to new ideas and procedures confronting administrators in the implementation of community policing but also to its history of skepticism (if not distrust) about the value of outreach youth workers addressing the gang problem. Their prevailing view was that outreach youth workers were essentially still gang members. To further complicate the issue, there was little history of collaboration between police and adult probation in regard to the gang problem. The CPD seemed to take only a muted interest in setting up an interagency administrative structure for such collaboration. To what extent the mayor's office supported the project's objectives of interagency collaboration along with suppression, integrated with youth development, was a question. Fighting the gang problem through increased police suppression was a prime device used by the mayor to coalesce political support for a variety of other policies from segregated, economically fractured, and mutually distrustful or antagonistic African American, Latino, and fearful white communities in Chicago.

MIXED SUPPORT FOR A NEW APPROACH

The project did not begin in an orderly or carefully considered fashion. The lack of clarity about the purpose and structure of the project later presented obstacles to its full development and institutionalization. Although a reasonably well-articulated program model and some leadership were in place to initiate the program, basic operational agency policy and administrative leadership for the project were missing. Officials from the CPD, CCDAP, UC, and ICJIA—and leaders of other local and citywide public and nonprofit agencies interested in the gang problem—did not meet to discuss community concerns and interagency policy and administrative arrangements for the project. Support for a specific program structure and coordinated plan of action was not created. The project was somehow expected to jump quickly from an idea into action, with limited specification of goals, objectives, problem assessment, and formulation of tasks to be accomplished.

Administrative and street-level personnel were selected for the project but were not initially prepared or trained about how to collaborate with each other. I became the default project coordinator. I would also have to recruit an outreach youth-work staff to contact gang youth, establish working contacts with police and probation, and create a steering-committee or advisory-group structure, as well as begin a research evaluation process—all within a one-year period.

Multiple circumstances interacted to support the idea behind the Little Village Project: the presence of an escalating gang-violence crisis, a change of mayor and CPD superintendent, the influence of academic and professional leaders committed to new ideas to address the gang crisis, and the availability of federal funds to control urban violence. The idea of the Little Village Project made sense in light of these interacting circumstances. But how this idea would be developed into a program supported by community leaders, and useful to the mission and purposes of the organizations involved, was not fully discussed or agreed upon by community and city leaders or those within or across the key organizations.

3

Entering the Field

By late June 1992, it was clear that the Gang Violence Reduction Project would be undertaken, although arrangements for funding the project were not consummated until March 1993. While the contract in draft form with the University of Chicago stated that the beginning date of the project was July, my preparation began earlier. As de facto project coordinator, I knew that I had to engage in various interrelated tasks immediately: getting a senior staff person on board; hiring and orienting outreach youth-work staff; assessing the gang problem; making preliminary contacts with gang influentials and street-gang members; establishing working relationships with key police and probation administrators and their street-level personnel assigned to the project; contacting local community organizations and youth agencies; and drafting community and individual gang-member research surveys. My research staff and I, as evaluator, had to begin gathering background program data as soon as possible, including baseline interviews of gang youth. The first order of business was to get into the field, assess the gang-conflict situation, and with the aid of the outreach youth workers, make direct contact with target gang youth, even before the police, probation, and neighborhood organizer came on board.

STAFF HIRING

I had been in touch with Reynaldo, who was to become the project's assistant director with responsibility for the development of the youth-work and community-organization components.[1] In his forties, Reynaldo had been helpful to me in the implementation of an earlier program—Crisis Intervention Services Project (CRISP)—on Chicago's north side in 1983 and 1984. He had been a peripheral member of a gang in his youth and still had connections with leaders of various street gangs, some of whom were still in jail. He had also obtained a college degree, headed an American Friends Service Committee project in Humboldt Park in the early 1980s, was a consultant to alternative education programs, and in 1992 was completing a stint as housing assistant to the local alderman, who was soon to be elected to the U.S. House of Representatives from his mainly Hispanic congressional district, which included Little Village.

Reynaldo was interested in the project concept and seemed well qualified for a job requiring diverse talents. He said he could be helpful, especially in assessing the gang situation, contacting gang influentials in the area, and organizing the community to support the project. He joined the project staff, first as a volunteer, and then as a full-time staff member when the project's contract became effective. At the alderman's office to meet Reynaldo, I also happened to meet the chief of patrol and a departing Tenth District (Little Village) commander, who was being transferred to take responsibility for the Police Training Academy. These two high-ranking Chicago Police Department (CPD) officers were in the alderman's office probably for political purposes related to the forthcoming November elections, in which the alderman was running for the U.S. Congress. The officers—both Latino—were friendly; they knew about and seemed to accept the idea of the project. They knew that the project was to focus on the two major gang constellations, the Latin Kings and the Two Six, who were responsible for 75 percent of the heavy violence (gang homicide, aggravated batteries, and aggravated assaults) in Little Village. Reynaldo and I believed we had to assess the gang situation not only from police and other agency and community-leader sources but also directly from gang members on the street. It was therefore important to recruit staff members who could make contact with street gangs in the area. Reynaldo and I renewed contact with two young men, former gang leaders, who had been helpful and influential in the earlier project on the north side. Julio, in his late twenties, had been one of the original organizers of the Spanish Cobras, a major Northside gang, but was now a building contractor and no longer involved in street-gang activities. Although there were no Spanish Cobras in Little Village, the Two Six were members of the same coalition of gangs—the Folks. I was introduced by Reynaldo to Isaac, a young man in his mid thirties, formerly a general and key enforcer in the Latin Kings' Humboldt Park section, who was currently employed in Chicago's Traffic Department. Although Isaac was not immediately connected with the Little Village Latin Kings, he knew some of the leaders from his earlier contacts with them in prison. Both Julio and Isaac were interested in the project idea and in volunteering to help out for a few months until regular staff were hired. Both agreed to work twenty hours per week as part-time outreach youth workers.

Formerly from opposing gangs and gang coalitions, Julio and Isaac knew and were friendly to each other. Both also knew several of the original gang-crime-unit street officers who were still operating in the area and believed they would have no problem getting along with them. Reynaldo, Julio, and Isaac took major responsibility for making initial contacts with gang youth, mainly through direct "walk-ups" to clusters of gang youth on the various streets. My own tours of the neighborhood and contacts with gang youth or gang leadership came a little later, usually in the company of Reynaldo.

I was able to recruit a full-time Two Six worker in October of 1992 and a full-time Latin King worker in November. Recruitment of the Two Six worker, Al, was fortuitous. Reynaldo and I were visiting the director of Latino Youth, the major youth-serving agency in the area, to acquaint him with the purpose and nature of the GVRP and solicit his support. In the course of a casual conversation with the agency's job-placement counselor in the lobby, she mentioned that her nephew, recently home and honorably discharged after serving in the Army during the first Gulf War, was looking for a job. I arranged to meet him. Al was a tall, heavy-set, voluble young man. He had been looking for, but having trouble finding, a job as a bricklayer. He claimed that he had held a high position— lieutenant governor—in the Two Six before moving out of the area and joining the Army. He said he still knew many of the senior members of the Two Six and could readily contact the younger ones. He was very interested in the idea of the project and said he could be helpful. He had been a sergeant in the military police and was ultimately interested in getting a job with a security firm.

Isaac recruited Ernesto, a young man in his thirties with facial gang tattoos, who claimed to still be influential in the Latin Kings. He had grown up in Little Village, knew most of the gang sections, and had already been helpful to Isaac in getting various Latin King factions to accept the idea of the project. He said he had served two long sentences for gang-aggravated battery and had recently completed two years of community college; he had some prior factory work experience but was interested in clerical work. Reynaldo and I were aware of the risks in hiring Ernesto, since it was apparent that he had been a senior member of the Latin Kings and was still identified with gang values, although he said he was no longer an active gang member. He claimed he had access to many of the leaders of the Latin Kings, who were still suspicious of the project and hostile to outsiders.

About a half dozen other applicants were interviewed for the outreach youth-worker positions, including two former outreach youth workers of the Department of Human Services who expressed interest, particularly in conducting recreational activities. However, they did not know gangs in Little Village and were reluctant to collaborate with police officers. Some of the applicants had either little relevant youth gang experience or refused the jobs once they understood they would be operating (often on their own) on the streets with violent gang youth. Additional workers, part time and full time, were not hired until six months after Al and Ernesto were on board.

Implementation of the project design required collaboration among staff of various backgrounds and agency affiliations. I first wanted to develop a pattern of quick and easy communication among the youth workers assigned to, and still possibly identified with, each of the opposing gangs. This had to be done before collaboration developed with project police and probation officers (who were yet to be assigned to the project). Field operations required the development of a consensus understanding among the outreach youth workers of what the current gang situation in the community was: which sections of one gang were fighting which sections of the other gang; whether sections of the same gang were at odds with each other; and who the key shooters and shot callers were. We had to agree on the best way to contact youth of the different gang sections and orient them to the purpose of the project and its special staffing arrangements.

INITIAL CONTACTS WITH GANG MEMBERS
The objective of the initial field contacts by outreach youth workers was to establish the legitimacy of the project and identify who were the influentials or who "called the shots," as well who participated in key violent gang activities. It was especially important to persuade those influential youth on the street who could get others to accept the project. The outreach youth-work staff would reenter the life space of these youth, learn their concerns and needs, and establish a positive working relationship to best influence their attitudes and behaviors. We needed to find out where the various violent sections of the gangs were located—the sections that contained the youth who were heavily involved in violent gang activity. They would be the groups to be focused on.

The Latin Kings and Two Six were well established in Little Village; they were complex and fluid in structure, with different street sections and cliques of varying interest and status. Our focus was not on modifying gang structures, either in the near or possibly the long term. We planned to target, control, and redirect the violence-prone youth in the cliques to more productive activity. We were essentially interested in the "shooters," not the drug dealers, or those involved in other types of criminal activity. Our focus would be primarily on individual violent gang youth and secondarily on the network of relationships they developed with other violence-prone gang youth. It was important for the outreach youth workers to understand that in order to curtail intragang and intergang violence, their main role would be to help the "guys" with jobs, schooling, and personal or family problems. The outreach youth worker had to indicate that he was part of a team that included other outreach youth workers, police, and probation officers. While the youth worker early on would emphasize his helping role in the development of the relationship, he would fairly quickly explain the project team's inclusion of police and probation officers. The positive, informed contacts by the youth workers with the gang members would set a foundation to facilitate later, useful contacts with police, probation, community residents, and workers of other agencies.

The youth workers had no trouble contacting members of the two gangs. Gang youth were omnipresent on the streets at night in different sections of the community, in varying clique sizes and age groupings, often involved in various types and degrees of disorderly and delinquent or criminal behavior. In the Latin King territory, active gang members were generally older, more aggressive, and identified with cohesive cliques and gang sections. In the Two Six territory, gang members were younger, more nuisance- and property-crime oriented in smaller, more diffuse groupings.

At first, the Latin Kings were quiet, antagonistic, and suspicious of the project. The Two Six were more articulate and friendly but also more elusive and indecisive. The Latin Kings had an "us against the rest of the world" attitude: they were pessimistic about any changes that could affect them for the better. Who their leaders were was reasonably clear. The Two Six expressed a need and willingness to reduce gang violence but were more volatile and unpredictable in their activities. Who their leaders were was less clear.

The youth workers were on the streets mainly in the late afternoon, night, and early morning hours, six or seven days a week. Based on their notes of field contacts with gang members on the streets in the first five weeks of project operations, they encountered 202 Latin Kings in thirty groups, an average of 7 youth per group, and 110 Two Six in twenty-five groups, an average of a little more than 4 youth per group. The Latin Kings were located in at least ten different street locations, the Two Six in fifteen street locations.

Reynaldo and I accompanied the youth workers frequently and explained the purpose, structure, and process of the project to the youth, emphasizing the objectives of helping to reduce gang violence, getting youth back to school, referring them for job training, and placing them in jobs. Reynaldo, the youth workers, and I did not emphasize the suppression role of the police and probation staff who would be in the project or how exactly the youth workers would collaborate with them. This would develop over time, as gang youth observed youth workers contacting project police, probation, and later, the neighborhood organizer at various places and times in the community. We expected there would be a lot of gang youth communicating with each other about such observations.

The following are extracts of initial activity from records of youth workers with gangs during the first six months of the project.

TWO SIX

August 26—met with Danny, leader of one of the Two Six street sections, to explain the program. Danny was receptive but kept his distance. He mentioned that his brother had been shot recently.

August 29—met with the Augusto brothers. They were "cool and distant" but promised to talk to other gang members just out of jail to get their opinions.

September 4—met with six members of Thirty-first and K Street. They complained they were locked out of Piotrowski Park recreation center [in the heart of Two Six territory] because they were gang members.

September 10—met with fourteen members, twenty to twenty-six years of age [the oldest grouping of the Two Six that we encountered]. They were part of the "Dark Side" section. The key leader, Manny, was "negative" about the project idea. [This group or faction would prove to be the most violent, criminal, and resistive of the Two Six to the project. They were heavily engaged in drug dealing and extremely violent in protecting their drug activities.]

November 7—talking to some guys and girls and found that the girls do a lot of fist fighting. One of the girls had a black eye. She had been fighting with one of the Two Six guys from Thirty-eighth Street.

November 10—started the day at 4:00 p.m. and met with two guys who run the block. They told me that the Kings from L Street are in the neighborhood a lot. . . . As we talked two cars with Kings passed by. I went with the guys to one of their houses to get some money to buy guns. I tried to direct them to other activities and suggested we play some basketball, which we did. Then we talked about the different invasions by the Kings.

[I] met two guys, one fifteen and the other eighteen years old. They said they had just shot at one King and two Vice Lords in a car cruising in the area, and the car crashed. They ran to the car and had a fistfight. They said one of the Kings ran down Twenty-sixth Street [Two Six territory]. He had blood on his face and hands. A few minutes later when we were alone, I beeped Rob [one of the project police now on board] and mentioned the incident to him.

November 12—the sixteen-year-old Two Sixer told me that his girlfriend was pregnant. I called some people at the Boys and Girls Club. They gave me some phone numbers, which I gave to the kid. We went to his girlfriend's house and then to a doctor. I showed them where the WIC [Women, Infants, and Children] food-aid program was.

November 13—drove up to Pontiac Corrections Center to see David. I had a pass to see him. He was the overall leader of the Two Six. He was in prison with two life sentences. We talked about the program and what it could do for the guys—also what he could do to help the project. He said that he liked the program idea, especially since it uses ex–gang members as staff. He asked what we can do for the girls. I told him we were still trying to figure out whether we had the money to hire a worker for the girls.

December 21—Hector, a new gang member, beeped me. He wanted me to go to his house and talk to his dad. I told the dad about the program and what I was doing to help his son.

December 23—John from L Street beeped me. He told me about the guy who shot Tony [Latin King]. I called Gary and Rob [project police] and relayed the information. Rob in turn told me about a kid who needed a job and who wanted to talk to a youth worker. I knew where the kid was located and went to talk to him until about 11:00 p.m., then I went home.

LATIN KINGS

August 27—met with "Big Mama." She was about thirty-five years of age. She had a long history as a key lady with the Latin Queens. Her two sons, aged eighteen and twenty years, were also Latin Kings. She wanted them to return to school and get their GEDs.

September 3—met with Little Stevie, aka "Turtle." He was reported to be a chief with three of the groups. He agreed that there was too much violence in the neighborhood and would like to get guys off the streets, maybe into some job training. He said he had a court case pending.

September 11—met with Ernesto again [who would become one of our outreach youth workers]. He volunteered to talk to other Latin Kings to get their support for the project. There were about twenty members on the street with him, ranging in age from about sixteen years to nineteen years; they were positive to the idea of the project working with them, but one of them asked, "How do we know you're 'for real'?"

November 4—had a general conversation with five youth, ages fourteen to sixteen, at T Street and Twenty-fifth. None are in school or working. They deal small amounts of grass to make some money.

November 5—met with two Kings at Twenty-sixth and M Street. We discussed racial tensions at Farragut High School. They discussed the probability of the Kings calling an amnesty with the Black Gangster Disciples who were also at Farragut, but they could not make a decision until they talked with the King higher-ups.

November 6—observed eight Kings, fifteen to nineteen years old, throwing bottles and bricks at a vehicle known to be owned by a Two Sixer from K Street. When we approached, they were upset about the Two Sixer and tried to avoid us. We talked two of the Kings, potential shooters, out of "going down" to K Street and retaliating.

November 21—talked with more Latin Kings, fifteen to seventeen years of age. No police were nearby. The Kings were bored. They were hanging out consuming alcohol, leaning over the hoods of cars, waiting for Two Sixers to come cruising along.

November 25—fifteen Latin Kings, ages fifteen to twenty-three, were hanging out at the gas station intimidating local citizens. We asked them to leave before the police arrived.

December 12—heard shots at Twenty-fifth and T Street. I went over and found fourteen youth, seventeen to twenty-seven years, around a gray-colored vehicle with one headlight. It was parked in the middle of the street. The driver and the passenger seemed drunk. The Latin Kings approached the car and recognized the passenger as a Two Six and shouted "Flakes." The Two Sixers fired seven times with a .380 handgun. They drove off. No one was hurt.

December 22—observed twelve youths eighteen to twenty-one fighting among themselves. One youth accused another of being a "wicky head." I broke up the fight and suggested that they cruise because the police were coming. They left.

December 24—drove to Twenty-first and C Avenue. Paid my respects to the mother of the Latin King who was killed the previous Saturday night. Later I called Rob and Gary to ask for outside assistance so that Kings at the youth's wake the following night would not be harassed by Two Sixers.

December 26—Anthony and Larry [Latin Kings] approached me asking for help to get back to school and jobs.

By the end of the first six months there was a preliminary acceptance of the purpose of the project and the role of youth workers, particularly in respect to their helping with school and job opportunities. Contacts between youth workers and gang youth were more relaxed. Gang youth more freely provided information about gang situations. Also, communication by youth workers with other members of the project team, particularly police, began to occur. In the period through the end of October, more youth requested help with returning to school (mainly Farragut High School), and the same number asked for help with jobs. About half of the requests came from hard-core gangbangers.

In addition to the tension between the Latin Kings and Two Six (both Latino gangs), there was a high level of interracial hostility between the African American and Latino gang youth (mainly Latin Kings) who were attending Farragut. The reason given was that the African American youth were "harassing their girls." The African American youth were largely represented by Black Gangster Disciples, who lived in the area just north of Little Village. The gangs did not want to fight each other. The Latin King youth worker advised both the Latin Kings and the Gangster Disciples to cool it before they were expelled. Parent meetings were taking place, and a new principal was being installed. Peace was restored. There was little interracial hostility involving the Latin Kings and African American gangs in the course of the project period. There was more hostility and fighting between the Two Six and the African American gang kids, who attended Curie High School just south of the Two Six area. A year later, a Two Six would shoot and kill a Vice Lord returning home from school, as he transferred onto a bus while still in the Two Six territory.

In other field situations, one Two Six worker was able to mediate a dispute between nine Two Six youth and an Ambrose youth who lived in Pilsen, just east of Little Village. (The Ambrose youth was visiting his girlfriend, and a minor confrontation might have broken out between the two gangs, although the two gangs were brother clubs.) In another situations, a second Two Six worker, recently hired, was able to assist a gang youth find lodging at an emergency shelter. He also helped the girlfriend of a target gang youth find day care for one of her children. According to the same worker, neighbors and even the gang youth in the Two Six territory were complaining about the unsightliness of the streets; the worker planned a graffiti-removal project with one of the Two Six sections.

DEVELOPING YOUTH-WORKER RESPONSIBILITIES

The roles of the outreach youth workers, the responsibilities they had to take, and the decisions they would have to make had to be articulated again and again over the first months.

Targeting

Again, the types of gang youth the workers were to target and try to help or control were to be shooters, hard-core or influential in regard to provoking violence. We were not primarily concerned with peripheral youth, nonviolent gang youth, or even family members except as they were integrally involved with our target youth and contributed directly or indirectly to their violent behavior, or control of such behavior. Initially, we were not primarily interested in certain types of nonviolent delinquent behavior by gang youth—for example, truancy. As time went on, we took a more comprehensive view of activities that might lead to gang violence. Gang youth, thirteen or fourteen years of age, hanging out in groups on the streets during school hours, could engage in drug use, making gang signs, or lying in wait for enemy-gang youth to invade their turf. Graffiti-related activity was a major contributor to the onset of gang violence, as it was often a means of advertising the gang member's own section, his own persona, as well as challenging opposing gangs. Members of both gangs repeatedly penetrated each other's territory to put up their own gang icons and cross out opposing gang signs.

Target youth did not register for the program, nor were they referred through existing agencies. The youth workers (with assistance from project police, probation officers, and neighborhood workers at team meetings) determined or confirmed which youth were to be in the program and which were to receive special services or controls. The question of who the target program youth were to be had to be resolved early. This was no easy matter for the youth workers, who tended mainly to meet gang members in groups on the street. Many of the gang youth did not have reputations as shooters. Some were interested primarily in drug selling, partying, or simply hanging around. At first, youth workers did not readily make these discriminations, arguing that all gang youth had the potential for violence by virtue of the neighborhood tradition of gang violence, and the general readiness of gang members to respond to incursions of opposing gang members into their turf. However, in due course, the youth workers became fairly adept at identifying those youth who were particularly proactive, ready to go on drive-bys or habitually cruising opposing gang-member turf looking for trouble and excitement.

Initially, we focused on contacting individual gang youth. We wanted to emphasize participation in nongang contexts and mainstream activities. We gradually modified this approach, in recognition of the strength of the gang culture in Little Village and the high degree of gang-member interaction, organization, and gang cohesion. The influence of gang structure and context could not be avoided. Nevertheless, youth workers were instructed to engage only in a minimum amount of group activities, particularly athletic events, so as not to further cohere and possibly reinforce violence norms of particular cliques.

Decisions about which specific program youth would be targeted were made in weekly staff discussions, based on observations of youth workers about the aggressive activities of particular gang youth. Information from other project staff who knew the youth or had second-hand information (often from other youth in the same clique) was also useful. Much of the targeting depended not only on the observations of youth workers but also on arrest reports provided by police. The project police reviewed arrest reports of all Tenth District officers each day. The target youth, once agreed upon, were to receive special, individualized attention—counseling, job or school placement, and also frequent surveillance by various members of the project team, including the police, and probation officers if the youth was on probation. When we planned certain group activities—particularly group discussions or athletic activities, often with opposing gang members involved—all project team members had to be present.

The program was a two-way process of contact and communication. Gang youth often contacted workers, as well as vice versa. Jobs were a continuing reason for youth to initiate and sustain contact with youth workers, even though the youth often did not follow through on job referrals or stay on jobs very long. An early and continuing concern of the youth workers was their inability to adequately respond to gang members who wanted jobs or to refer the youth to agencies for jobs. The workers were not yet knowledgeable about resources or agencies that could be helpful. Reynaldo promised that he could provide jobs for several of the youth, but this did not materialize and was an embarrassment to him as well as to the other workers. More and better job preparation and placement would be needed. At one point, the leaders of one Latin King section again said that they were putting the youth workers and the project on "probation," waiting to see evidence of real job assistance.

Collaboration

A key responsibility of the youth workers was communication and contact with members of the project team—other youth workers, and especially police and probation. These were basic requirements of their job. Information was to be continually shared about gang events that were likely to result in violence, as well as identifying target youth for special attention in regard to both social development and controls. Youth workers were to be responsive to police requests for information about program youth, where they hung out, and the nature of activities of their gang sections, as much before as after violent acts occurred. Youth-worker sharing of information, however, did not necessarily extend to providing information to project police and probation about all forms of crime (usually less serious) in which target youth participated.

Information about violence had to be shared and transmitted to appropriate project workers at team staff meetings, individually (formally and informally), before or after staff meetings or by telephone at almost any time of the day or night. Information about other kinds of crime (such as burglary, robberies, or drug selling) in which gang youth were involved might also be communicated by youth workers to project members. But this kind of communication depended on the degree of comfort and trust youth workers developed with other members of the team, especially the project police. Nevertheless, the youth workers were required to understand clearly that their role was, first and foremost, that of a social service worker, and not that of an undercover policeman. The youth worker was not to operate proactively as an aide to project police in arresting (or to probation officers in violating) a gang youth, except as it contributed to violence prevention or control—of benefit both to the youth and the community, whether in the short or long term. Youth workers were to assist other members of the team in doing their respective project-related jobs.

Project police and probation officers were also expected to aid youth workers in the fulfillment of their social service role; they would have to be respectful of the youth worker and acknowledge the critical importance of the street-level information they provided. Project police were to provide a certain degree of social assistance and advice to program youth, as well as refer them to project youth workers for help with school problems and job placement. Some of these tasks were handled directly between team members, as well as indirectly through me or the assistant director, project police sergeant, or probation supervisor.

Accountability and Risk

The outreach youth workers were largely on their own in the field. Weekly planning schedules were required for accountability purposes and continued throughout the project years. Accountability was also achieved through other procedures, such as face-to-face field contacts with the assistant director (usually at least once per day), youth-worker quick response to beeper calls from me or the assistant director, and attendance both at weekly youth-worker meetings and at alternate-weekly project team meetings.

Originally, youth workers were expected to prepare weekly work plans, keep daily logs of their activities, and complete crisis reports as well as monthly summaries of the progress of individual youth. The completion of all these forms, however, proved to be onerous. The youth workers generally had completed only high school (or had GEDs) and were not diligent in their record keeping. As time went by, weekly debriefings of youth workers by a project administrative assistant proved to be more useful. In addition, youth workers as well as project police, probation officers, and the neighborhood organizer were interviewed by field researchers over a series of days, on an annual basis, to summarize their efforts and results with each target youth. Annual interviews of target youth also provided evidence of youth-worker efforts and accountability, as well as further information about the youth's response to program services.

Project administrators and other team workers also had to be accountable to the youth workers. The youth workers, who often operated alone in the community, had to be protected. They were provided with letters of project identity describing their functions, since they were required to be in the company of gang youth on the street and were prone to being questioned or harassed by police. At the end of the first year, photo IDs were provided. My efforts to introduce and legitimize the role of youth workers to district police officers at roll calls were only partially successful, since some of the youth workers had been known to them as suspects and arrestees prior to the project. However, many of the problems of youth-worker harassment by patrol officers in the district were overcome with the support of project police and special meetings between youth workers and the district tactical gang-unit officers. I reported patrol officers who continued to give youth workers a hard time or even to arrest them without legitimate reason, to the district commander. Some of the abusive patrol officers were transferred to other districts.

Also, because of the many indiscriminate shootings occurring between members of the two gangs throughout Little Village, protective vests were provided to youth workers. The vests were not worn regularly, usually not in the warm weather, or during the latter years of the project as violence abated. While several workers claimed near misses, no worker was ever hit by a bullet. The youth workers used their own cars in their work, and there were half a dozen instances of damage to workers' cars in the cross fire of bottle or brick throwing by opposing gang members. In two instances car windows were shattered by bullets gone astray, but the workers were not injured.

All youth workers were supplied with beepers. The assistant director and later the youth-worker supervisor were supplied with cell phones. Beepers were occasionally lost or damaged, and the use of cell phones had to be carefully monitored so that only business or emergency calls were made. Youth workers were required to be on the street at night, on weekends, and during times of gang crises. They had no official office space, except for meetings at the local probation office in Little Village, or at the University of Chicago (located about six miles southeast of Little Village). Youth workers were expected to be on the streets or to use local community facilities such as churches, park department recreation centers, or youth agencies for individual contacts or group meetings with youth for recreational purposes.

INVOLVEMENT OF LAW ENFORCEMENT AND PROBATION
Police

Police-department involvement and support of the project developed in complicated ways. The CPD was fiscally and administratively responsible for the project. Primary contact with the Tenth District police in Little Village was facilitated by the liaison lieutenant of the R&D unit, who initially introduced the assistant director and me to the Tenth District commander. A district neighborhood-relations sergeant was assigned half-time to the project, but his major responsibility was developing community policing in the district. A quarter-time police clerical assistant, and two new, young Tenth District gang-tactical-unit officers were assigned full time to the project, to replace two veteran tactical officers who had been offered the assignment but refused to be "kiddy cops." Meanwhile, the two original officers of the dissolved gang-crime unit transferred to the organized-crime unit and were still interested in the project. There was a temporary lack of police coordination during major shifts of their personnel.

The two Tenth District tactical officers, the clerical officer, and the part-time sergeant began to meet with youth workers, the assistant director, and me at the School of Social Service Administration. The sergeant, however, was not sure what his role was. He was not sure that he would also be supervising the two tactical officers, who were still attending Tenth District tactical unit meetings and relating closely to the Tenth District tactical unit lieutenant. In due course, an arrangement was made whereby the two tactical officers would also report regularly to the sergeant and provide him with weekly reports of project operations. Certain particulars about the scope of project activity in the district—that is, which beats in the Tenth District would be targeted, the nature of specific tasks of the assigned project police, and especially the scope of information to be exchanged with project youth workers—were not specified. The sergeant was reluctant to be responsible for youth-worker activities. To what extent he would be responsible for the coordination of the project team was never made clear. Probation officers were not yet on board, and the sergeant deferred to me in conducting the early project meetings. The R&D office, downtown, had not prepared the Tenth District administrators and officers for what they were to do.

Nevertheless, relations between the two project tactical officers and the youth workers were remarkably positive from the start. Part of this could have been because the officers operated in plainclothes, were young, with limited experience in the department, and were new to the district. They had volunteered for the project and quickly subscribed to its purpose. They were pleased to be detached from the tactical unit, free to move around the area in their unmarked car and not have to make a certain quota of arrests each day. They worked together in their vehicle, with no superior officer directly supervising them. They requested help almost immediately from the youth workers to identify gangs, gang locations, and particular gang members who should be targeted. They were not comfortable—probably for status reasons—acquiring such information from the district or central gang-crime-unit officers still present, who knew gangs in the area.

The project police officers established direct lines of communication with each of the youth workers. At the invitation of the youth workers, they met on the street with seven or eight members from one section of the Two Six, then with an equal number of members from a section of the Latin Kings. Unexpectedly, positive relationships among the two officers and gang members were quickly established. The assistant director noted that "the gang members developed good respect" for the two officers because they were "not disrespecting" the gang members. The officers, however, soon began to "feel that the gang members [were] getting too friendly and making [them] look bad to the other officers."

However, project police overidentifying with youth workers or with gang members did not develop. Gang and law-enforcement cultures were highly antagonistic to each other in Little Village. At the time the project began operations, the district police were upset because a Latin King, an older drug dealer, had "put a gun to the head of an off-duty police officer." The Tenth District police were opposed to any "soft" approach to gang youth. Nevertheless, positive and useful relations between the project tactical officers and the youth workers continued to develop. Youth workers informed project officers that a retaliation by one unit of the Two Six against another unit of the Latin Kings would take place at a particular location. In turn, the project police informed the youth workers about a pattern of stickups of innocent citizens by Latin Kings that was occurring on Sunday mornings and asked them if they could prevent such incidents. "The King offenders had blocked off a street, pulling people right out of their cars." The project officers asked the youth workers to notify them if any of these types of incidents occurred and which Kings might be involved. Early in the project, the tactical officers suggested that Latin King workers "concentrate on one section of the hard-core Kings at Twenty-seventh and T Street." Youth in this section were fifteen to eighteen years old. "They're crazy and no one has been able to do much with them." Also, in a discussion with youth workers about lack of job resources for gang members, they mentioned a particular administrator at a local trades high school they knew who might be helpful getting program youth into training programs.

Despite such early promise, the project-team concept did not develop smoothly. After the first flush of collaboration, project police complained they were not getting as much information as they wanted from the youth workers about what was happening on the street. The youth workers were also still ambivalent about working with the police, preferring not to have extra meetings with them. They said that biweekly staff meetings were sufficient to exchange field information. Also, tensions continued to develop between the tactical officers and the old gang-crime-unit officers originally assigned to the project who were still in the area.

Probation

The Cook County Department of Adult Probation (CCDAP) was primarily interested in developing a closer, general working relationship with the CPD, and their participation in the project was a way of doing this. Administrators of the CCDAP said they wanted a formal relationship with the CPD around the gang problem. It was not clear at the start what the role of adult probation would be in the project, and what probation officers assigned to be part of the team would be doing. The project neighborhood-relations sergeant claimed that he hadn't had contact with the CCDAP in his eighteen years on the police force. The tactical officers assigned to the project indicated that they had no experience working with adult probation. My initial contacts were mainly with the deputy chief and assistant deputy chief of adult probation. The CCDAP decided to contribute three or possibly four full-time officers to the project and have them establish a decentralized gang probation office in the area. They planned to make the local office available for the two project police officers, if they wanted. Meanwhile, probation administrators volunteered the use of one of their office meeting rooms at the main office of the CCDAP until a Little Village office was set up.

At a team meeting six months after the start of the project, the deputy chief of CCDAP announced that a unit of three probation officers and a supervisor would be assigned to the project. The probation officers would first be undergoing weapons training and would have to be fully and properly equipped. A key responsibility of probation would be to get the criminal-court judges to place "special conditions" on probation youth who were identified as gang members by project personnel. However, most targeted youth—although they had extensive prior arrests and confinement histories—were not currently on probation. The probation officers would struggle in the course of the project to develop a large enough caseload of program youth. The deputy chief of CCDAP, who was especially supportive of the project, suddenly resigned to take an administrative position in another county, before the scope of probation's involvement and the role of probation officers in relation to other team members could be sufficiently developed.

A probation operations problem immediately arose. The first probation supervisor assigned to the project emphasized suppression. He ordered the probation officers to be on the street at least two nights per week and focus on "passive interdiction," that is, checking names and supervising probation youth. The probation officers would call on the project police, when necessary, to make arrests. Project gang probationers would automatically be placed on home confinement, intensive probation, and under special court conditions. Information would be exchanged on a needs basis with police, but probation officers were not to provide information to the youth workers about program youth on probation. I questioned this limited and restrictive involvement of the probation officers.

COMMUNITY CONTACTS AND COMMUNITY ORGANIZATION

A critical component of the project was community mobilization, that is, the involvement, support, and guidance of key organizations, neighborhood groups, and residents in the development of the project. Community mobilization suggested some responsibility by the CPD (the lead agency) and project personnel in building local community capacity to address the gang problem. Basic assumptions were that the gang problem was present or grew worse when local organizations and citizens did not satisfactorily address the gang problem, were fearful or tolerated gangs, or especially, when organizations used the problem primarily to meet their own organizational interests rather than developing a comprehensive approach to the problem. Patterns of organizational and community relationships about the problem would probably have to change if the project was to be successful.

Important project objectives were not only to contact key organizations, citizen groups, and local residents concerned with the gang problem but also to engage their interest and solicit their advice and, in due course, help the community develop a collective ownership in the project. More specifically, an advisory group first needed to be created to support and guide the project over the short term. An advisory group would build a network of local organizations that would develop resources and provide a range of services and controls for hard-core gang youth in the community. Building a modest neighborhood advisory group to support the project (but not necessarily a comprehensive, neighborhood or citywide association of citizens and agencies) was one of the CPD's original objectives.

The first order of business for the assistant director and me was to contact a variety of local organizations, obtain their views about and experiences with the gang problem, and explore possible areas of collaboration. Primary interest was in the development of access to local service resources for program youth, rather than immediately building a coalition of organizations to guide the project in addressing the gang problem. The first of these interests was regarded as more feasible. There were two Boys and Girls Clubs within the program area, and one immediately outside of it. Each of the clubs served gang youth (mainly young teens or preadolescents), although none of their programs had an outreach component specifically interested in hard-core gang youth. Most gang problems (presumably) occurred outside the clubs. One of the clubs was willing to provide services to the targeted program gang youth but would require extra resources to hire and pay its staff for this special and difficult task. Each of the clubs supported the project concept but because of limited resources and insufficiently qualified staff could not be of much service assistance to program youth. However, the idea of an advisory, coordinating committee or council that would somehow address the problem also appealed to the directors of the Boys and Girls Clubs in the area.

Project staff made contacts with the director of the park department's recreation center in Piotrowski Park, located in the Two Six area of the community, to request access to their services. Two Six youth pressured project staff to assist them to gain entry to the recreational center's gym for basketball games. The center had excellent athletic facilities, and the director was interested in service to the broader community—including gang youth, so long as they behaved themselves in the building and on its baseball grounds. Many of the Two Six had already been "kicked out" of the center. The possibility of making the gym available to the project on certain nights was explored. This would require some payment to center staff for maintenance and general supervision, as well as making the project staff available (including the project police) to maintain order. The arrangement and all conditions were agreed to.

Contacts were made with local churches, priests, and ministers. Some of the parish priests were friendly but not particularly interested in the project (including one priest who would shortly become the bishop for the Catholic Latino community in Chicago). Two other priests of large Catholic churches—one in Latin King and the other in Two Six territory—were very interested and promised access to facilities and cooperation with the project. (I renewed a positive relationship with one of the Little Village priests who was involved with me in a gang project on the north side of the city several years before.) Both priests were deeply concerned with gang violence, the tragedy and disruption it caused to families, and especially having to bury so many young people. The two priests quickly volunteered their gyms and meeting facilities. They later proved to be a mainstay in the project's effort to develop a neighborhood advisory group. One protestant minister of an evangelical community church was also very interested and quickly offered to make space available in his church for a planned GED class for the Latin Kings. He would later become one of two key organizers and cochairpersons of the project's local advisory group, Neighbors against Gang Violence (NAGV). He and another evangelical minister from outside of the city would be helpful in locating additional gym facilities for program youth in the years ahead.

Contacts were also made with administrators of the only high school in the community—in Latin King territory (Farragut High School). The principal asked for the assistance of project youth workers to inform teachers about the nature and scope of the gang problem in the area and how to be effective in dealing with gang youth within the school. The youth workers were called on to assist school security personnel to control violence occurring between the gangs just outside the school, especially between Latino and African American gang youth. Of special concern was that the school administrators were not able to assure the safety of the few Two Six youth who were attending the school. Most Two Six had by then decided to attend a high school just south of Little Village.

In addition, contacts were made with heads of a variety of local organizations: hospitals, aldermen, a major nonprofit youth and family agency, the local office of the Department of Human Services, the Chamber of Commerce, the area mental-health center, and other local and citywide organizations with interest in the community's gang problem. Several job-training and placement agencies expressed a willingness to accept referrals of program youth. Suburban JobLink Corporation, a job-placement agency with an office in the area, was interested in recruiting young workers for low-level factory jobs in the suburbs. Its administrator would later become a regular member of NAGV.

One of three aldermen whose districts cut through Little Village expressed strong interest in the project. He was a young man in his thirties, a college graduate, who had been a fringe member of the Latin Kings in his youth. He was concerned with social reform and improvement of living conditions in Little Village. His aldermanic district was located in the Two Six area of the community. He knew many of the Two Six families and was deeply troubled about the gang problem. He offered the use of his network of block clubs to stimulate residents to become active and support the project. Later, he would also become a member of NAGV.

We solicited the interest and assistance of the United Neighborhood Organization (UNO), a citywide Latino community organization, and its branch, the Alliance for Community Excellence (ACE), located in Little Village. A meeting with UNO's director at his downtown office did not prove productive. He and the ACE organization were mainly interested in issues of housing, schools, and jobs. The solution he offered for the general crime problem was simply stronger law enforcement, particularly through the use of a series of mobile police substations in Little Village. (The mayor would ultimately appoint him alderman for the eastern political district of Little Village.) The three Little Village aldermen had little shared interest in various local problems. Two of the aldermen were strictly beholden to the mayor and the Chicago Democratic Party machine and had no interest in the Little Village Project.

The local Little Village/Pilsen UNO organizer (the director of ACE) attended several of the early NAGV organizing meetings to find out what was going on with the project. He made no offers of assistance or cooperation. He had strong political interests and would later run for alderman in the following democratic primary, competing with the then current, young, social-reform alderman, who was helpful to the project.

Reynaldo was able to arrange for project staff to attend the monthly meetings of ACE downtown. The local UNO organization included eighteen Little Village and Pilsen organizations—churches, businesses, social agencies, and representatives of schools, banks, and the Tenth District neighborhood-relations unit. Again, the group's primary interest was in housing, schools, and business improvement, not in the gang problem. The focus of the meetings in the months ahead was on school construction and improving the image of Little Village, which was becoming an increasingly active working and lower-middle-class Latino community.

At the end of one of the ACE meetings, Reynaldo spoke to Gloria Lopez, a community activist, about the GVRP. Gloria was closely associated with several of the local catholic churches. She was a paid youth consultant to one of the national youth agencies concerned with alternative education and job train-ing and was interested in the construction of additional elementary and high schools in the area. Both she and Reynaldo were active in citywide alternative-school issues. She was especially interested in the gang problem. She had been a member of a gang in her youth and knew many of the families with gang youth in the Two Six area. She would become the central figure in the development of NAGV and later a part-time neighborhood organizer on the project. At my invitation, both she and Reverend Mike (from the local protestant community church) attended one of the early project staff meetings and offered their sup-port. Project probation, police, and youth workers were preoccupied with their own developing relationships with each other and did not seem interested in the presence of these two at the meeting.

The Evaluation Component

Many aspects of the project were taking place at the same time: the outreach-youth-work component, staff team building, community resource access for program youth, and creation of an advisory committee, as well as attempting to improve the police and probation administrative context for project operations. Added to this, the Chicago Police Department required a community survey, and the Illinois Criminal Justice Information Authority required a program-process and outcome evaluation of the project.

Community Survey

The CPD liaison lieutenant was especially interested in the effects of the program on community perceptions of the gang problem and requested a baseline community survey. The request was possibly related to the CPD's planning a pilot community-policing program in Little Village. The project's research staff developed a community survey to measure whether there were changing perceptions of the gang problem among residents and organizations in Little Village and whether they were different from those in the comparison community of Pilsen (which was not exposed to the project). Pilsen, in the adjoining Twelfth Police District, had an almost identical population to Little Village, with a similar serious gang problem. There were several major gangs in Pilsen with no connection to Little Village gangs, except for several smaller gangs operating across the border with Little Village.

The project research staff planned to carry out a baseline community survey and repeat it two years later to measure changes in perceptions of the gang problem that might possibly be related to the impact of the project. Focus was on those residents in the streets most affected by the gang problem and on organizations that served the community. The gang-crime-unit officers at central police headquarters—who were still functioning and knew the gang problem in both Little Village and Pilsen—provided maps of locations of gangs and gang incidents. Such information for the preprogram and program periods in Little Village and the comparison community was further elaborated by crime-incident data from the Early Warning System of the Illinois Criminal Justice Information Authority and from the crime analysis section of the CPD.

The project research assistants visited agencies, businesses, and particular streets to verify and obtain further information on gang hangouts, graffiti concentrations, and gang problems. A local Pilsen neighborhood organization offered lists of various organizations and their key, relevant personnel to contact for the survey. The neighborhood-relations sergeants in the Little Village and Pilsen police districts, along with various youth agencies in both communities, pinpointed high gang-violence-incident streets and buildings where citizens should be interviewed. The survey instrument and sampling design were developed in the first months of the project, but it took six months—well into 1993—to collect time I survey data. All project administrative and street-level staff, as well as representatives of key organizations and community residents of Little Village (who would later comprise NAGV) and the director of a major Pilsen community organization, assisted in the development and review of the survey questions.

Individual-Youth-Outcome and Program-Process Data

The major evaluation component was the collection of program-youth interviews, program-process data, and outcome data based on complete police arrest histories for program and comparison youth over time. The analysis of these data, especially any arrest changes, were the primary bases for determining the project's effectiveness in reducing violence and other criminal activities.

Planning for the individual gang member survey occurred in the late fall and early winter of 1992–1993 (see chapters 9 and 10). The survey interviews were directed to all targeted youth when they entered the program and repeated at two annual periods for each youth during the course of the five-year project. The initial interviews served both program-development and evaluation purposes. They were a way of emphasizing again the purpose of the program to targeted youth and also a means of eliciting information about the gang problem in the community, the youth's self-reported gang-delinquent behavior, his relations to family, gang, school, work, and so forth, and determining reasons for his deviant behavior. The interviews were conducted by field interviewers, many hired from the local community and local colleges. Program youth were paid twenty dollars for each one-hour interview, and informed consents were obtained from each youth and also from the parent(s) if the youth was a juvenile. Obtaining interviews required the interviewers and their field supervisor to work closely with the youth workers, who had already established positive relationships with the targeted youth. Only Little Village program youth were interviewed, since funds were not available to select a comparison group from Pilsen or Little Village.[2] (Also, the issue of contamination would arise if comparison youth in the community from the same target gangs and cliques as the program youth were interviewed.) In later chapters, I describe the research methods used in collecting and analyzing program-youth interviews, police arrest histories of program and comparison youth, and the nature of the program-process records completed by the project team workers.

Aggregate Area and Gang Data

A further project research task, essential for measuring program impact on a gang-as-a-unit and community basis, was the collection of aggregate-level gang and nongang crime data in Little Village as well as in comparable Latino gang–violence areas in the city over time. Data on a series of twenty-one gang and nongang-violent, property, and drug incidents were already being collected by the Chicago Police Department's crime-analysis section. With assistance from the liaison lieutenant, six police districts comparable to Little Village, and a total of fifty high-gang-crime beats in these districts, were selected for the project's evaluation. Current gang and nongang data were provided on a monthly basis, as well as crime data back to 1987, to cover the preprogram and program periods.

These data were useful to project staff for ongoing problem assessment and teamwork planning, and particularly to project researchers analyzing whether and how gang and nongang crime patterns changed over time in Little Village compared to other areas. The need for and use of gang and community-area data for program-development and evaluation purposes was a constant from the start (and even earlier) to the conclusion of the project.

OPERATIONALIZING THE PROGRAM MODEL—COMPLEX BEGINNINGS

The comprehensive community-wide gang program model had to be operationalized to accommodate and address the complex reality of the varied interests of key agencies and community groups (as well as the gangs themselves) related to the gang problem in Little Village. The model was a framework, a set of ideas, with no clear steps or priorities that could be readily adapted. Perhaps a first logical and critical step should have been the development of a steering committee of major citywide and local community leaders to support the project idea. But interest was not present and would have been difficult to develop within the framework of resources and time constraints of the project grant. The project was viewed by the sponsoring agencies (including the Illinois Criminal Justice Information Authority and the CPD) as a small demonstration of an integrated, cross-disciplinary approach to be supported by a neighborhood community group of agencies and citizens. An evaluation of the project was also requested.

Based on the CPD's problems of transition and very limited interest in the project, it seemed important and feasible for me to get the show on the road as quickly as possible. The first order of business was to know what the gang problem was, using available data from police sources and especially information gathered by outreach youth workers who had connections to the target gangs. Also important was the development of a team of workers from the CPD and the CCDAP, along with project outreach youth workers, and the support of a neighborhood organization to address the gang problem in terms of a balanced set of interacting strategies. Despite many uncertainties, the start-up of the project at the program-youth, gang, community-group, and local agency levels and the start-up of the project evaluation were reasonably well accomplished.

NOTES

1. Real names of persons associated with the project are not used in this and other chapters.

2. A nonprogram comparison group from Little Village was later created based on police and court information about gang youth from the same gangs who were arrested with the program youth at about the time of their entry into the program.

4

Team Development

After preliminary contacts with gang youth on the streets (mainly by outreach youth workers and police) and orienting local agencies and community groups to the nature of the project and soliciting their interest and assistance, the next order of business was developing a team of workers of different backgrounds or persuasions to work together. The policy context for the development of the project team was nebulous and never satisfactorily clarified. An administrative structure did evolve, which was sufficient only to support project staff at a limited, pilot-demonstration level. My assumption and that of the director of the Illinois Criminal Justice Information Authority—as well as of the Chicago Police Department's (CPD) liaison lieutenant—was that the project, if successful, could contribute to a broader interagency and possibly a team approach to solving the gang problem.

We examine issues of teamwork at the interprogram worker level, especially the development of effective information exchange, service and territorial boundaries, team collaboration, and institutional-relationship patterns. Focus is on coordination at the level of worker activities, rather than on the interrelationship of policy and administrative issues across agency leadership, community groups, and government leaders. (We address these last issues in chapter 7 and chapter 16.)

COORDINATION

A major purpose of the project was to shape and interrelate a variety of selected service-agency strategies. Gang-program strategies traditionally had operated separately and sometimes in opposition to each other in low-income, marginal areas of many cities (including Chicago's Little Village). The project sought to address the gang problem primarily at the individual-youth level within a gang context, by coordinating the functions of street-level staff from criminal justice and youth-serving organizations—particularly police, youth agencies, and probation—and also, to a lesser extent, from churches and neighborhood groups. A key objective was to build a close team relationship among staff assigned to the project. Staff members were expected to modify their traditional agency-worker roles and ideologies as they worked together interdependently. Workers would learn to better understand, accept, and complement the roles of other staff members through a common purpose—gang-violence reduction.

Building the Team Structure

After meeting with those workers who were assigned to the project team and accompanying them on their initial but separate tours of duty in the area, I felt it was important that the police, probation, and youth workers meet together on a regular basis. The model of work was not to be each set of workers doing his or her own traditional agency work or "thing" in isolation from (or even parallel with) that of other members of the team. Communication, for example, was not to occur in ways dictated simply by traditional, separate bureaucratic arrangements: from particular agency worker to agency supervisor, then across to other agency supervisors, and down to the worker. Direct reciprocal communication and working relationships among team members had to develop in order to meet immediate crises or ongoing gang-problem situations in the field, while still acting within the parameters of the respective agencies' purposes and regulations.

The location of a project office and a common meeting place was expected to be an important way to facilitate team interactions and develop a common project identity. The two project police tactical officers were interested in more room to keep notes and records and access to a computer (which they did not currently have in their district station). Probation officers also wanted, and expected to have, a decentralized probation office somewhere in Little Village (preferably in neutral gang territory) that would be accessible to probationers from the area, including program youth from both gangs. There was little interest in meeting at the Tenth District police station, which was first suggested. It was an old and forbidding structure with insufficient space even for district police staff and operations. The outreach youth workers were especially resistive to meeting at the Tenth District station; most of them had been arrested or detained there in earlier times. They preferred to establish a separate place of their own to carry out traditional youth-work counseling or recreational activities. I was reluctant to pursue this possibility, as I wanted to avoid any temptation for gang youth to "hang out," or a particular gang to take over such a facility.

Early meetings of project staff took place at adult probation headquarters just outside of Little Village, where a temporary meeting room was made available. The meetings were frequently attended by administrators of various agencies, project-operations staff, and some community representatives. Initial agenda items included reviewing the purpose and nature of the project, and how different staff would relate to each other. Attendees included a Tenth District police lieutenant; the project police sergeant and clerk; the two project tactical officers; the two originally assigned gang-crime-unit officers; two central-office adult probation administrators; the three project probation officers and their supervisor; and me as the project coordinator, my assistant, and three outreach youth workers. On occasion, an assistant Cook County state's attorney and two Little Village representatives—Gloria (the community activist) and Reverend Mike (the protestant evangelical community church minister)—attended.

A project-related adult probation office was established in Little Village nine months after project operations began. It was the only appropriate office space available, but it was located deep in Latin King territory, on a major business street. Only Latin Kings would come to the office, mainly for required contacts with project probation officers; Two Six gang youth who were on probation usually contacted their project probation officers at adult probation headquarters in the main criminal-court building just outside of Little Village. At first, the Two Six outreach youth workers were hesitant to meet at the decentralized probation office, but no serious confrontations with Latin King youth ever occurred during the course of the project. Eventually, both Two Six and Latin King youth workers began to regularly attend meetings at the local Little Village probation office.

Information Exchange

The key element in the development of the team structure was the exchange of information about the gang problem and who the youth being targeted by the team members in Little Village were. Such information was of special interest to gang-crime-unit officers in the very early meetings at the main adult probation office. They wanted to be current on the gang situation. While they had some knowledge of gangs and key gang influentials or hard-core members in the area, the two new tactical officers assigned to the project had almost none and were eager to learn as much as possible about gangs in Little Village. The tactical officers had no specialized training or experience with gang youth. The probation officers were also new to the area and had only a general familiarity with gangs in the suburbs (with the exception of one officer who had grown up in Little Village). The youth workers were critically important at these first meetings because of their current knowledge of local gangs, the gang youth to be targeted, and current gang incidents, but they were suspicious and distrustful of police and, to a lesser extent, of probation. They sat at the rear of the large conference room, listening and observing. When asked specific questions by the gang-crime-unit officers, they tended to give evasive answers and preferred not to name specific gang youth. Participants at these early meetings seemed to be talking past each other.

As gang-crime-unit officers and youth workers began to exchange "war stories"—special events in local gang history, particularly prominent gang shootings—a certain communication barrier was broken. One of the youth workers mentioned that the annual three-day regional Christmas meeting of the Latin Kings had recently been held in Little Village. It was considered a holy-week meeting in which members and leaders of the Latin Kings from throughout Chicago and from cities and states nearby took part. The youth worker said the meetings involved partying and planning of future activities. This information was an eye-opener for the gang-crime-unit officers. Whether the information was accurate or verifiable was unclear.

A problem of communication arose when the project tactical officers requested help in associating real names with the nicknames of street-gang members. They had obtained names of gang members from the Tenth District arrest reports but could not associate them with the street names or nicknames used in the discussions between the gang-crime-unit officers and youth workers. The youth workers were hesitant or unable to reveal the connection between street and real names; they often did not know the family names of particular gang youth. The gang-crime-unit officers knew both but refused to reveal the information they possessed. This refusal immediately became a source of tension between the project tactical officers and the gang-crime-unit officers. The tactical officers and the neighborhood-relations officer assigned to the project stood up and shouted that such information had to be shared. The gang-crime-unit officers still refused. The sergeant may have pulled rank and communicated with his superiors. The gang-crime officers did not show up at succeeding meetings. Nevertheless, all of the remaining participants agreed to make lists of the real or street names of gang members they knew and viewed as potential target youth, which they would share at the next meeting.

In mid-January 1993 the youth-work staff provided a list of approximately forty-five street names of gang members they were working with. The project police officers reported the real names of ten youth derived from recent arrest reports, youth whom they were attempting to target. The gang-crime-unit officers said they were still working on their list. The project police and the youth workers were partially successful in relating street names and real names. Suddenly, the probation supervisor announced he could *not* provide names of youth on probation from Little Village who might be gang members. This information, he said, was strictly confidential.

The statement puzzled the rest of the project team. The project police officers were particularly uncomfortable with this decision. I raised the question of how it would be difficult to work together as a team if all the team members did not know whom each team member was working with. It was essential to share this information about particular youth if the basic project objective of information sharing and collaboration was to be achieved. He suggested that this information would be useful to probation officers in their decision making about needed services or violations of probation for youth. The probation supervisor was adamant in his refusal. After the meeting, I spoke to the CPD liaison lieutenant and then to the deputy director of the Cook County Department of Adult Probation (CCDAP). I proposed a preliminary way around the impasse: (1) the youth workers would continue to submit updated lists of gang members and in return would expect to receive verification that particular youth were currently probationers, and (2) the youth workers would regard such verification information as confidential, to be used strictly as an aid in their social-intervention, control, and opportunity-provision efforts. The information received would not be used or exchanged with any youth or agency personnel outside of the project team.

The deputy director could not make a final decision. However, at a later meeting with the director of CCDAP, the new executive director of Illinois Criminal Justice Information Authority (ICJIA), the CPD liaison lieutenant, and me, the probation department director said she would not adhere rigidly to the general policy that information about probationers could not be shared without a court order. While the department had a "statutory" obligation to maintain a degree of confidentiality regarding "particular types of information," she had no objection to such information being provided to me and then shared at my discretion with the outreach youth workers. Probation information could be fully and directly shared as necessary with the project police.

Over the next months, the issue was progressively resolved. Information about target youth was readily shared with the project police and me, carefully and selectively sharing the information with youth workers. The information included probation status, recent offense charge, and present criminal-court status of target youth. Later, as confidence and trust among the various project team members grew, a great deal of probation and criminal-history, youth-behavioral, and family-background information was shared by probation officers directly with youth workers. The initial fear that such information would find its way to gang members was not realized.

The continual sharing of information was important. Youth workers increasingly provided knowledge about gangs and shooters, the location of "hot spots," expected places and times of confrontations between gangs, and about drug sales in the community. They assisted project police in solving several homicides by revealing who the actual shooters and noninvolved gang members were. They also helped gang members show up for probation appointments but in turn requested special kinds of help that probation officers could provide to particular target youth. On one occasion, the probation supervisor asked youth workers how a specific program youth could get out of a particular gang without punishment. The youth worker contacted several senior members of the gang who granted such permission. Youth workers alerted probation officers that certain gang youth not on probation in Cook County were on probation in other nearby counties. These youth were then transferred to Little Village's special gang-probation caseloads. Project probation and police officers began to tell youth workers about Latin King and Two Six gang youth not known to them who had been arrested or placed on probation, and who should be targeted for project services. Problems in the exchange of information that occurred early in the development of the project were substantially resolved by the end of the first year of program operations.

Youth-Worker Information Sharing

One major obstacle to communication was internal to the youth-worker component. Youth workers would not at first share information with other

youth-worker staff assigned to the opposing gang, or even other youth workers working with different sections of the same gang. The youth workers were
not professionally trained and had little or no prior youth-agency experience.
They were highly individualistic, self-contained, and some still partially identified with past gang experience and gang norms. In the beginning, youth
workers were in competition with each other for project status. There was insufficient communication about field events and collaboration. For example,
when Latin Kings attacked Two Six gang members, or vice versa, the assigned
workers attempted to deal with the conflict alone, rather than on a team basis.
Information about intergang problems was first provided to the field youth-
work supervisor, rather than directly with the youth workers assigned to the
opposing gang section. Gradually, the information was shared at weekly youth-
worker staff meetings and selectively with individual police and probation team
members.

Two of the youth workers continued to be overly identified with gang youth
and remained for many months opposed to the idea of working closely with
the project police. They were concerned about contributing to the arrest of
gang members; they also did not want to be accused of being "tricks." They
provided only limited information about gang youth engaged in certain crimes,
particularly drug dealing. Over time, a variety of ways were established whereby
information to police and probation could be revealed, with less likelihood of its
being traced back to particular youth workers. They increasingly used beepers
and phones to communicate with other team members, particularly about
crisis situations. Face-to-face meetings of youth workers with project police
were sometimes held outside of the Little Village area. Often, information about
particular youth and field situations was communicated sotto voce, before and
after as well as during team meetings.

In one case, when open communication and cooperation between one youth
worker and the project police was not successful, the youth worker had to be
terminated. In another case, a youth worker was communicating too much
information (or not carefully enough) to project police. He wanted to become
a police officer and flaunted his connection with project police by riding in
their unmarked car in opposing gang territory. He contributed to a significant
number of arrests of gang youth, particularly around drug-dealing situations.
His role in the arrests was discovered by the Two Six leaders, and he was
threatened, that is, a "contract was put on him" by key members of the highly

criminal section of the Two Six. He had become identified with the role of police officer and insufficiently with the role of providing outreach youth work focusing primarily on social intervention. In due course, he, too, had to be terminated from the project.

BOUNDARY ISSUES

Physical boundaries and limitations to the scope of project operations had to be established, with due regard to the functions of the workers from the different component agencies of the project. The target gangs were entrenched in Little Village but were also connected to other gangs and gang problems in other parts of the city. The Latin Kings and Two Six confined most of their gang-crime activity to Little Village. Our concentration was on the two most violent gangs in Little Village and their key violent members. Resources were not available to address the less-violent gang members in the target gangs or the less-violent gangs in Little Village. We could also not do much about gangs from outside the community who invaded Latin King or Two Six turf, or target gang youth fighting gangs outside of the area.

Reduction in rates of serious gang violence for targeted program youth and their gangs, as well as area rates of serious gang-violence reduction, were key objectives. Project staff generally did not operate outside the Tenth District. Project police could not initially extend their efforts even to all of the beats in the Tenth District. The project police could not leave Little Village to intercept Latin Kings or Two Six engaging in criminal gang activities who had traveled to the south or north sides of Chicago and to the suburbs adjoining Little Village (such as Berwyn and Cicero), where the two gangs were also located. However, they could alert other units of the CPD and collaborate with the sheriff's department and local suburban police by providing information about serious criminal activity of target gangs and gang members from Little Village.

Project probation officers were limited by another type of boundary problem. The CCDAP was less clear than the CPD about the territorial focus of the project, at least during the first year of operations. Project probation officers were assigned to address the gang problem in both the Little Village and Pilsen communities. Probation administrators were not clear initially that Pilsen was a "control" area and was not to receive attention for project-related purposes. Project probation officers at first had to deal with both gang and nongang probation youth residing in both areas. Many of the criminal-court judges and

CCDAP administrators also did not fully understand the nature and scope of the project and required the project probation officers to deal with whichever probationers they were assigned. Further, the probation officers were highly individual-case and office oriented, rather than gang-system and street oriented, as were the youth workers and police.

The youth workers had more boundary latitude than the other project workers. They occasionally accompanied gang youth to other communities, where they went to play basketball or football. They were more likely to be aware of gang tensions and gang activities that occurred outside the area that affected target youth in Little Village. Fights between the Latin Kings, Two Six, and (occasionally) other gangs occurred both inside and outside of Little Village, but the youth worker's focus of activity had to remain on Little Village. The youth workers were also required not to focus on other gangs (such as the Two-Two Boys, the Satan Disciples, Latin Disciples, Black Gangster Disciples, and Vice Lords) located in the fringe areas of Little Village, whose members occasionally penetrated the turfs of the Latin Kings and Two Six. The best the youth workers could do was communicate these happenings to project police, who then could address such incidents or alert other police in the Tenth or other districts to address them.

A constraint of the coordinated approach was that different types of team members were not obligated to contact all target youth. Project probation officers had a small target-youth caseload. They did not have jurisdiction over gang youth who were not on probation. The most serious gang offenders were often not on probation or not on parole. Many serious gang offenders had not yet been caught. Project police and outreach youth workers were better able to move about the community to target gang-crime offenders. In addition, only certain sections or branches of the Latin Kings and Two Six in Little Village were contacted by project workers. Despite the project staff's extensive knowledge of gang members and gang situations, not all activities or operations of the gang youth in the target gangs were necessarily known to youth workers or project police. The activities of target gangs, their members, and resulting gang incidents were not entirely predictable; information about gang activities was never complete. Further, while priority effort was directed to the most serious violence-prone youth in sections of the target gangs, there were certain gang sections that were resistive to the project. Youth workers had to be accepted by at least a few key members in each of these sections.

Another set of limitations for youth workers derived from the situation of contacting target gang youth mainly on the streets. Youth workers had to relate to groups of youth, many of whom were not targeted, who hung out on the streets and participated with targeted youth in nonviolent activities. The youth worker also did not have sufficient time to attend to the varied interests and needs of the targeted violent youth. Youth workers were required not to focus on recreation; instead, they were encouraged to contact and encourage youth agencies, schools, and churches in the community to open their facilities to gang youth for various activities. Youth workers could assist with supervision of some in-agency activities that might contribute to violence on the streets in Little Village.

There were limits to the cooperation that project staff could provide to, or expect from, personnel of significant agencies, especially nonproject police. A persistent constraint for youth workers was the actions of zealous police officers in the district, some of whom went out of their way to harass them. Over time, the problem was mitigated by the project tactical officers, the project police sergeant, and the district commander. Nevertheless, it remained a problem throughout the life of the project, particularly as new police officers not familiar with the project were transferred to the district for special gang "sweep activities."

TEAM COLLABORATION

Workers from the four component organizations represented on the project team (later including the Neighbors against Gang Violence [NAGV] neighborhood organizer) were in continual touch with each other, and generally coordinated their actions around targeted gangs, individual gang members, and community gang-crime concerns. They kept in close touch through scheduled weekly or biweekly meetings, as well as through phone and individual field contacts around crisis gang-violence and serious gang-crime situations—when either had occurred or was about to occur. Contacts were made about youth requiring special attention, for example, information to provide a family service, make a job referral, or to achieve a successful arrest. The various fieldworkers often had to take action quickly and contact each other directly. Each of the workers—police, probation, youth workers, and the NAGV organizer—exercised a great deal of discretion as to the kinds of information sought or exchanged, and the decisions made and actions to be taken about specific gang problems in the field.

The most frequent interaction took place between the project tactical officers and the youth workers. Interrelated activity among different project workers might occur, for example, after a target youth's arrest or a probation violation. The youth worker or the NAGV organizer might visit the youth on the street or at the home of a particular shooter to warn him or his family about the consequences if he continued his pattern of behavior. The youth worker might visit the home of a youth arrested after a shooting to explain why the youth was in jail and indicate the likely course of events in the justice system. These visits involved the interaction of various project workers and were carefully planned.

Based on the exchange of views among team members and the collective worker analysis of field situations, decisions could be made that certain target youth would receive extra services or attention during gang crises, including counseling, school or job assistance, surveillance, and intensive probation. Some youth also received extra attention and contact based on the recommendations of other gang members, particularly when their actions became too violent even for their gang sections to tolerate. Such extra project attention produced no negative repercussions from the gang or the specially targeted gang youth. Sometimes the gang members expressed gratitude or relief to a worker. One program youth indicated after he was arrested that he should have been more closely supervised by the project probation officer; he expected to serve his time in jail and then to withdraw from the gang. On one occasion, a youth worker contributed directly to a youth's incarceration. The project's assistant director, an outreach youth worker, and a project probation officer went to court to request that a particular youth be adjudicated in violation of his probation. He was constantly high on drugs and shooting at police cars. The judge accepted the recommendation, and the youth had to complete the rest of his six-month probation at a state correctional institution. The youth worker visited him in the institution several times and helped him complete preparations for a GED. When the youth was released, he no longer hung out with the gang in the community and held no grudge toward the youth worker or other project team members for the action taken. Such collaboration occurred despite different views by the various team members about the reasons gangs and gang members did what they did and how best to control or help them. For example, project youth workers tended to believe that most gang members were personally "messed up": their activities were unpredictable, and they needed help. Youth workers believed that the most important factor in preventing or curtailing the youth's potential for gang crime was the development of a positive relationship with him, and that counseling and mainstreaming him could be achieved through more effective school and job experiences. Project police and probation officers often believed that certain gang members were simply "cold killers," and as much information as possible about the youth and his activities had to be accumulated in order to put him away as quickly as possible. The neighborhood organizer occasionally regarded the police or justice system as more to blame for the youth's arrest and incarceration than the youth's criminal activity.

The different workers often expressed frustration with the project approach and with the efforts of the other types of workers. Worker purposes, actions, and team relationships were not always easy to manage. The project police officers complained at one point that their collaborative efforts with other workers were not successful; some of the gang youth they referred to the youth workers, who helped them to obtain jobs, were still on the streets and getting into trouble. They said that jobs did not necessarily keep "gangbangers" away from the streets but simply meant that the youth "had more money now to buy guns or bullets." They complained that some of the target gang members became too friendly with them and were "getting an attitude. Maybe they should begin locking them up again."

The project youth workers and the NAGV workers were somewhat competitive. They often worked with the same youth and disagreed about what to do with them. A similar service was possibly being provided by both, and ownership of the social service relationship should belong to one or the other, not to both workers. Project-administration and youth-worker supervisory efforts to reconcile these differences were not always successful.

At one time, the project police officers complained that the probation officers were not doing their job. A youth was on general probation, and the project police requested that he be transferred to the Little Village special probation gang unit. The gang probation supervisor agreed and put through the request, but bureaucratic delays occurred in the transfer and the youth got involved in a gang homicide. The tactical officers insisted that if the youth had received intensive supervision by the project probation officers when they requested it, the homicide would not have occurred.

One of the youth workers alerted the project police officers to the presence of several gang drug houses, and as a result one of the drug houses was closed down. Particular gang members became very angry over losing the drug house;

gang youth became suspicious. Some of the youth had been caught in several recent gang "sweeps." The youth worker requested that the officers no longer attend gym practice. The gang members knew that the youth worker and the officers were part of the Gang Violence Reduction Project (GVRP) team. The youth worker was charged with being a "trick" by some members of the group to which he was assigned.

INSTITUTIONAL RELATIONSHIPS

Structural deficiencies in the development of the program were not necessarily or adequately addressed by the project-related agencies. Project police and probation staff remained relatively isolated from their respective agency administrators, who did not understand or know clearly what was going on in the program. Policies and procedures to support the work of police and probation in the project were not quickly or adequately changed or developed. The youth workers, part of the University of Chicago component, were also relatively isolated from existing local community, youth-serving agency staffs and programs. Furthermore, NAGV was a small ad hoc organization formed to cooperate with the GVRP effort, but it was unrelated to any large agency or community organization in Little Village. The lack of established organizational and interagency support for workers' activities and needs interfered with the full development of the project.

While several of the justice-system agencies in Cook County were interested in the project and occasionally sent observers to the weekly and biweekly meetings, few were willing to exchange information about particular youth or to collaborate in joint project initiatives. Representatives of the Cook County state's attorney's office (particularly its juvenile section), the FBI, Drug Enforcement Administration (DEA), and the juvenile section of the Department of Corrections were interested in the project and occasionally called on members of the team for information about local gangs and gang youth of interest to them for their own suppression or control purposes. No reciprocal arrangements were made, however. Efforts to involve Cook County Juvenile Probation, juvenile-court services, the Chicago Public Schools' social services unit, and local area elementary and middle schools in the project's work, especially the exchange of information, did not develop.

The general lack of communication and coordination among agencies at various levels of the so-called criminal justice system created a major contextual obstacle to project operations. For example, the project's Cook County adult probation officer working with older program youth could not obtain information from a Cook County juvenile probation officer about the program-youth's younger brother (also in the project) or his family functioning. Information from the U. S. Justice Department Bureau of Prisons about the father of the same two program youth, in a federal penitentiary, was also not forthcoming. Mobilization of justice-system agencies as well as local social service agencies for joint planning in regard to what should have been common interests and concerns about these youth and their family was not achieved. These issues are further explored in chapters 7 and 16.

At the same time, it could be argued that such nonreciprocation or weak cooperation and limited supervision of street-level staff, especially by the sponsoring agencies, made for rapid development of project-staff interdependency, cohesion, and effective working relationships.

5

Social Intervention: The Outreach Youth Worker

The Gang Violence Reduction Project's team approach depended heavily on outreach youth-work activities in collaboration with those of police, probation, and neighborhood organizers. A distinctive characteristic of the project was its closeness to the grassroots community and the targeted gangs. The outreach youth workers were from the local community, or at least a significant sector of the community. They had been members and influentials in the particular gangs to which they were now assigned. Using such outreach youth workers had advantages. It made for a rapid entry into the gang world and easy targeting of hard-core gang youth by the project team. But it also created a variety of problems. The youth worker was expected to:

- establish contact and positive working relationships with gang youth in their hangouts, mainly on the streets of Little Village;
- identify and assess (with the aid of fellow team members) the hard-core, gang-violent youth the project should target;
- communicate the purpose and scope of the project to targeted gang youth and their peers on the streets, as well as to their parents, local residents, and representatives of agencies and community groups concerned with such youth, with special emphasis on communicating the project's interrelated strategies of social intervention, opportunities provision, and suppression (i.e., socialization and control);
- provide crisis intervention, ongoing advice, brief counseling, and referral for services and access to opportunities to targeted gang youth, and occasionally to their selected gang peers, siblings, and parents;
- gather and provide information about impending gang crises and problems to team members, especially the project police;

- assist project police and probation to carry out their respective law-enforcement, community-protection, and crime-prevention functions;
- prevent and to some extent mediate gang fights, especially between individual youth, through collaboration with other team members;
- assist in the development of local resources for targeted youth, especially educational and job opportunities;
- provide access to local social and recreational facilities and, on a limited basis, organize and supervise recreational or sports activities for targeted gang youth, as a means of implementing other key project objectives;
- assist with project-related community-mobilization efforts involving residents or local organizations addressing the youth gang problem, particularly at the local grassroots level;
- participate in and aid project researchers in the evaluation; and
- participate in staff development to improve skills, especially learning how not to overidentify with gangs, police, or probation officers.

Of special importance was that the youth worker establish positive working relationships with gang youth, with due regard to the safety and protection of community residents, local organizations, businesses, property owners, and others from gang-related criminal activities of these youth. The youth worker was also to do as much as possible to reduce the influence of gang structure (within the constraints of an entrenched local-community, gang-conflict tradition) by assisting target youth to disassociate from the gang and its criminal activities. The youth worker accepted the reality, but not the legitimacy, of the gang and its criminal behavior. He did not regard the gang as necessary for the community's social economy or the social development or day-to-day survival of youth in a chronic gang-problem area such as Little Village.

The youth worker's role, as that of the project police, probation officers, and the neighborhood organizer, was based on a complex understanding that gangs and their sections varied in tradition, structure, cohesiveness, leadership, and patterns of behavior (legitimate and illegitimate), and that these characteristics changed over time. Certain gangs, gang sections, and individual gang members varied in their commitment to violence and other serious criminal behavior, depending on gang-member age and gang structures, processes, and opportunities. These differences needed to be taken into consideration in planning contacts and activities with gangs, especially with their individual members, as well as contacts with local agencies and neighborhood groups related to the gang problem. The youth workers in Little Village were to operate on the assumption that gangs or gang sections were not necessarily highly structured. Leadership and membership characteristics were expected to be fluid and variable. Gang behavior was to be viewed not only as a product of gang structure and process but also of individual gang-member predisposition, interpersonal and family problems, and personal decision making at particular times and places. Individual-gang-member and gang problems, and ways to modify them, were related to pressures from family, school, and girlfriends, as well as to the effects of intergang and internal gang tensions and disputes within and across neighborhoods, the availability of legal and illegal opportunities for income and status, access to weaponry (e.g., guns or vehicles), time of day, local neighborhood culture, social-agency programs, local political activities, and police suppression tactics. All of these factors had to be considered in the assessment of the gang problem and the determination of how the youth workers were to do their job.

The outreach youth workers in the project were mainly in their twenties, a few in their early thirties. They had limited educational and legitimate work backgrounds. They had not yet achieved a fully adequate transition to conventional, mainstream norms and values. A series of procedures had to be fashioned to obtain the most productive and purposeful effort from the youth workers. Their job required that they maintain contact and relationships with gang members within the framework of project goals and objectives. Outreach youth workers, by definition, were marginal and highly vulnerable workers exposed to suspicion, competition, complaint, distrust, and abuse (or even attack) from the gangs, project police and probation officers, local citizens, and community agencies. The role of outreach youth workers had to be carefully structured, protected, supported, and constrained.

The Youth Worker in the Field

- His hours of work were flexible. Generally the youth worker did his job in the field in the late afternoons and evenings from 4:00 p.m. to midnight and worked at least one weekend evening (Saturday or Sunday) per week. He was available in the morning, if necessary, to go to court and to advise a gang youth and his parents on court procedures, provide information to the court on the youth's social adjustment, and also advocate on the youth's behalf. At times he had to meet with a school official, or transport the youth for a job interview. During gang-violence crises he usually worked longer days, well into the early morning hours.

- The goal of the youth worker was to reduce gang violence and serious crime of the program youth, essentially in the gang-demarcated area where he was assigned. He confined his work to a particular part of the neighborhood, where the gang youth and gangs to which he was assigned were located and generally operated. However, gang incidents or precipitating events often occurred outside the immediate neighborhood, and the worker had to be sufficiently mobile to intervene in or prevent some of these incidents. He had to attend some special events relevant to project purposes, for instance, a gang-related wake, a gang member's family celebration, an intergang ballgame, or a special outing of gang youth at the beach. Also, he needed to take special personal precautions when he ventured into an opposing gang neighborhood, when he had reason to believe he might be attacked based on his former gang affiliation or his work with the gang section to which he was assigned. If the gang youth or his gang left the confines and norms of the neighborhood, another set of gang purposes, dynamics, and structures had to be carefully assessed, usually with the project's youth-work supervisor, to determine how the youth worker should operate outside the Little Village area.

- Youth workers were assigned to and focused on a shifting caseload of twenty to thirty active gang youth. Frequency and intensity of contacts with youth were based on the present and potential likelihood of the gang youth being more or less active in violent gang behavior. To the extent possible, contacts with many of the parents/families and girlfriends were also required to assist in the development of a positive or constraining influence on the youth's behavior.

- The worker's contacts had to be focused on those gang sections and their members who were most involved in or at high risk for engaging in violent behavior. The worker was not to contact simply those groups with whom he had "good" relationships or gang members who were particularly responsive to his efforts. He was required to reach out to and work with the more difficult or harder-to-reach, often more hostile, youth.

- Youth workers were in regular, often daily, contact with the youth-work supervisor, other youth workers, and other members of the project team. Direct exchange of information with project police and probation was essential, especially in respect to preventing and controlling violent incidents, and frequently in planning for social intervention with specific gang youth.

- Description and systematic assessment of field situations, especially involving targeted youth, occurred at both regularly scheduled, overall team meetings and at youth-worker staff meetings. Also, rosters and general discussions of program gang youth and their possible associations with and antagonisms toward other, not known, violence-prone gang youth were updated on a project-team basis at least every three or four months, often more frequently. Not all gang youth committing (or about to commit) violent crimes were necessarily known to all of the team members. The youth workers and other team members did not necessarily know all of the gang youth being served or who should be targeted.

- Team members were also required to record significant contacts with gang youth served by the project. For most of the youth workers, who had limited educational background or ability to fill out forms, weekly debriefing sessions took place with project research assistants or office staff members. It was critically important for youth workers to provide a record of what they were doing with particular gang youth and gang situations and with what perceived or observed actual effects. Such information was needed to monitor worker efforts and gang and gang-member situations and problems, to assess program strategy, and ultimately, to determine project effectiveness in reducing gang violence. The information was also important for managing community and interagency relationships.

A variety of aids and constraints were necessary to assist youth workers with their jobs and to hold them accountable for achieving project objectives:

- Beepers were provided to all workers, and cell phones to senior workers.
- Youth workers had to be mobile and use their own vehicles to make contacts and provide services to program youth.
- Legitimate program-related expenses were to be documented and reimbursed, for example, youth-worker transportation costs (based on actual mileage), damage to vehicles (with receipts for repairs), and details of work-related calls made from public or home phones. Reimbursement for food and entertainment with program youth was not provided, except with a supervisor's permission, usually at gang-crisis times.

- Photo IDs were provided indicating the youth worker's affiliation with the project and the University of Chicago. This was essential to protect workers and to prevent and resolve problems that often occurred when the youth workers contacted gang youth on the streets. The workers could be picked up or harassed by police, particularly by those from out of the district and not familiar with the project.
- Medical, accident, and life insurance coverage was provided for youth workers who were employed twenty hours or more per week.
- Protective vests were also available, and the youth workers were encouraged to use them, particularly during periods when drive-by shootings and car rammings were likely to occur.
- Dating girlfriends of gang members, providing temporary shelter to gang youth in the worker's home, letting a gang member use a worker's car, and so forth, were prohibited.
- A variety of administrative devices were established to ensure that the youth worker was in the field and doing his job, attending staff meetings, completing reports or debriefings, and providing adequate documentation for expense accounts. For example, youth-worker staff meetings or field-activity debriefings were scheduled when and where they were to pick up weekly/biweekly paychecks.

GANG-VIOLENCE CONTROL

Gang-problem assessments took place almost on a twenty-four-hour-a-day basis. Outreach youth workers were present on the streets of Little Village not only during assigned work hours but at other times as well, since most lived or had friends and family in the community. Youth workers were expected to know the "hot turf" areas where conflicts were likely to occur. The workers, because of their relationships with the local gang youth, could readily pass through or hang out in particular areas. They had access to information that served law-enforcement and social-intervention purposes. This almost round-the-clock street information was critical for the youth workers to diagnose gang situations. Drive-bys, gang-section disputes, intergang fights, plans and preparations for fights, graffiti forays, torchings of opposing gang members' property (especially vehicles), sporadic non-gang-related batteries, robberies, drug dealing, and other criminal occurrences were known to the youth workers almost as soon as they occurred or were rumored in the community. Street information traveled fast, although often it was not sufficiently accurate and had to be checked with the project police and other youth workers.

Such information had implications for what actions the youth workers, the project police separately, or the project team as a whole would take. Graffiti raids were usually conducted in enemy-gang territory, but sometimes in the territory of another section of the same gang, particularly by younger youth cliques seeking to develop or enhance reputations. The raids usually involved gang members defacing opposing gang or gang-section emblems on a fence or side of a building and marking their own gang's or section's emblem, as well as indicating the artist's own street name or initials. Such graffiti marking in the opposing gang member's turf was taken as a provocation and cause for retaliatory shootings or raids. Violence between or within sections of the same gang was less deadly than between opposing gangs and did not usually involve the use of guns. The intragang conflicts could involve fists; rock, brick, or bottle throwing; and occasionally knifings. The cause of these more limited, intra-gang fights—whether on the streets, at parties, or in chance encounters almost anywhere—could be disputes over drug deals, a girlfriend, antagonisms be-tween individual gang members, or attempts to punish individual gang mem-bers within or across sections for gang-rule violations. The intragang fights resulted usually in minor bruises or injuries, although internal-gang-section or cross-section fights could occasionally result in homicides.

Of greater concern to project workers were the more serious incidents in-volving invasions by members of a particular section of a gang into the territory of a particular section of an opposing gang. Car rammings and walk-up, bicy-cle, or drive-by shootings were common and might occur several times a week, with varying consequences. Gang members were usually on guard at street corners at night, anticipating and ready to counter opposing gang invasions (actual or perceived). The attacks or counterattacks could be against nongang youth who were mistaken for opposing gang members. The attacks could re-sult in serious injury or merely in insults, minor injury, or property damage. The youth worker who was present or happened on the scene was expected to record what happened, make an assessment, describe what he did, and indicate what was important for preventing further gang attacks that might have wider consequences.

The following were excerpted from weekly worker-debriefing-session re-ports of the project research assistant.

Robert [youth worker] noted that three carloads of Latin Kings were cruising their own neighborhood around Twenty-fifth and T Street late one night. They suddenly stopped and busted out the windows of a reputed Two Six girl's car, who lived in the Latin King neighborhood and was in the car with two other persons. The windows were tinted, and the Latin Kings may have thought that Two Six males were in the car with her. The worker heard the attacking youths shout "King Love." The worker expected the Two Six to retaliate within the next day or two.

The Two Six [youth] reported that he saw the Latin Kings come into the Two Six neighborhood in order to shoot at the K Street section; however, the Two Six anticipated their arrival and shot first. No one was hurt, so far as the worker could tell.

Most intergang fights involved gangs and gang youth of the same ethnic or racial background, usually from an adjoining part of the same community, but occasionally major gang fights broke out across racial or ethnic groups involving youth from outside of Little Village.

Frank (youth worker) reported that the Two Six (a Mexican American gang) had been fighting recently with the Vice Lords (an African American gang) from an adjoining neighborhood. This started when members of the Vice Lords had to travel through Two Six territory to return home from Curie High School (which they attended) just south of Two Six territory. The school usually provided special buses to take the African American students directly back to their neighborhood, but because of a sudden lack of such buses, the Vice Lords had to take public bus transportation and transfer on a street in the heart of Two Six territory to get back to their neighborhood.

Frank reported that the Two Six caught a Vice Lord as he waited for the bus. They shot and killed him. He called Gary and Rob [the project tactical officers] right away to give them information on what happened and which Two Six section was involved, but not which specific youth were involved.

This last gang situation caused a furor among citizens in the African American neighborhood about the failure of the school authorities to provide adequate transportation and protection for students. They demanded that arrangements for busing students directly to the African American neighborhood be reinstated immediately. The police also came out in force, both to patrol the Two

Six area where the shooting occurred and to further investigate the situation and find the killers. The youth gangs in Little Village had peripheral and sometimes direct connection with organized-crime operations in the area. Youth in the Two Six at times ran errands or transported drugs for the local Mexican Mafia across the country, that is, between Mexico and the United States or across state lines, usually between Texas and Illinois. Some of the Two Six families were connected to the Mexican Mafia and heavily involved in drug dealing. Nevertheless, most of the youth gang members were not disciplined, organized-crime apprentices. They might attack or rob a local Mexican Mafia drug dealer and take his money. Such an incident occurred when one of the members of a Two Six section robbed twenty thousand dollars from a Mexican Mafia drug dealer on the street. Retaliation by the adult criminal organization was swift and deadly.

> Sammy [youth worker] reported that a member of the same Two Six branch, whose parents were connected to the Mexican Mafia, was ordered to kill the particular Two Six member [a program youth] who robbed the drug dealer, which he did. The assailant [also a program youth] was quickly arrested. Special protection for the assailant was arranged for the youth in Cook County adult detention when threats by other Two Six members who happened to be there were made. The project police were fully informed by the youth worker of various aspects of the situation, including possible threats to the family of the shooter. The Two Six youth worker spent a great deal of time assisting the family of the youth who was killed with funeral arrangements, and also helping the family of the offender to leave the neighborhood for the suburbs. No attacks against the family of the assailant or other gang members occurred.

Injury and death were ever-present dangers for gang youth in Little Village, one of the two most gang-violent areas of the city. However, death did not always come to gang youth from intra- or intergang events.

> Larry [youth worker] reported that he attended the funeral of Sandman, a [Latin King] twenty-year-old youth who shot and killed himself, reportedly over problems with his girlfriend. Larry said that Sandman was a leader of the S Street faction, but he also used a lot of cocaine. Larry said he was surprised by Sandman's death since he seemed happy with his newborn child, to whom he was very attached. Larry planned to spend time with Artie, a close friend of Sandman, who was now moody and depressed because of what happened.

Many of the gang youth who were involved in gang fighting or drug situations were very troubled personally but not willing to seek mental-health treatment. In two cases, the youth worker and a project police officer teamed up to pick up gang youth who were suicidal; these youth had mental-hospital histories and were repeatedly exhibiting self-destructive behaviors. One of the youths, a Latin King, periodically marched into the Two Six territory wearing a Latin King jacket, yelling for the Two Sixer to kill him. The Two Sixer called him "crazy" and usually ignored him. The project police were able to transfer this youth and, on another occasion, a Two Six gang member who periodically slashed his wrists to local mental hospitals. In both cases, the youth were back in the neighborhood within a day or two, since they were classified as voluntary patients and could not be compelled to remain for treatment.

SOCIAL INTERVENTION/SOCIAL OPPORTUNITIES

Because of his identification with gang youth, his imbeddedness in neighborhood relationships, and his strong interests in improving the life chances and welfare of gang youth and their families and neighbors, the youth worker was viewed as a "do-gooder" or social worker in a very basic, if not professional, sense. He did not know much about social work or systematic counseling techniques and the use of agency resources. However, he did generally have easy and nonthreatening access to, and positive relationships with, individual gang youth and their families and friends. Provided with periodic project-staff training and close supervision, the youth worker could be a reasonably effective intervener in social-problem situations. He often had to interrelate control, crisis-intervention, advising, and referral functions. The youth worker was often involved in a range of tense and critical situations. He engaged gang youth individually or in small groups on the street, at home in family contexts, on athletic fields or in recreation centers, in detention facilities, at school, on the job, and elsewhere about a range of problems. A primary concern of the worker was to help the youth stay out of trouble. He counseled the youth to stay off the streets, attend school, find a job, keep his appointments with probation officers, and turn himself in to the police when he was being sought. Parents were constantly calling youth workers to find out where their sons were and to secure help with job referrals or getting them back to school or out of the gang. The youth worker was a proactive communicator and mediator between the youth and other significant persons: his family, his girlfriend or wife, and representatives of social, educational, and criminal justice agencies.

Education

The program youth was generally a high school dropout, who often aspired to complete his basic educational requirements in order to gain entry into a technical training program or community college. He was aware that he could not obtain a decent job or prepare for a good career without a high school (technical or advanced) education. He frequently told the youth worker as well as his family about his interest in obtaining a GED or attending an evening high school program. His family was often willing to support his return to complete his high school education, at considerable expense, even at a private school. The workers enrolled gang youth in a variety of educational programs at youth agencies, parks and recreation centers, the public schools, and community colleges. A few of the older gang youth, who had completed college-level courses in prison, expressed interest in achieving a bachelor's degree. Follow-through by the worker to sustain the youth in these programs was not easy. Early in the project, a special GED evening program was established for one of the gangs in a local church but with hardly positive results. Gang members sporadically left class, diverted by gang business. Attendance was poor, and the GED program eventually had to be abandoned. Subsequently, youth workers referred gang youth to other neighborhood and out-of-the-neighborhood GED programs. At times, youth workers tried to assist youth who had been kicked out of school to gain readmission to the same public high school, or to transfer to another high school. This was not a simple matter. The youth worker often needed help—from the project's assistant director or through a special relationship with a particular principal or official in the rigid Chicago Public School system. Public schools generally wanted to get rid of gang youth and were glad when they did not show up for class.

Yet, there were indirect ways of getting a gang youth back to the public schools. The youth worker at times assisted local high school or local elementary school administrators, and even school security personnel, to resolve tensions and conflicts caused by particular gangs at war with other gangs attending the same school. He extracted promises from gang leaders or particularly violent youth to "cool it." In turn, the youth worker was able to persuade the principal or assistant principal, as a kind of quid pro quo, to permit certain troublesome program youth to return to regular school or help in their transfers to (or from) other schools.

Most gang youth in Little Village were highly ambivalent about returning to regular school programs. There was a preference for getting into a special, non-public-school training or career program (for example, the Army). The youth associated school with the pain of suspension, expulsion, long-term academic failure, hostility from teachers, and their own low self-esteem. Occasionally, the youth worker was able to help the gang youth get out of the neighborhood and the gang by referring him to or supporting his application to a boot camp, Job Corps, or military service (usually the Marines or the Army). However, for a variety of reasons, not many gang youth qualified for admission to these special job-training programs and the military.

Jobs

The program gang youth were almost always more motivated to find a job than to complete high school or pursue further education. Holding a job was an acceptable and appealing symbol of adult status and a recognized means for breaking away from the gang and fulfilling family, neighborhood, and societal expectations. The gang could accept and approve the gang youth holding a job and no longer showing up as often on the street corner or participating in gang events. Gang youth often had a strong commitment to the importance and rewards of work, based on cultural, family, criminal justice, girlfriend, personal-maturation, and even gang pressures. The role of the youth worker as a job broker was very important to gang youth, and they continually approached the workers for help in finding a job—a "good paying" job. The economy was good during the project years, and a variety of jobs—in factories, hotels, restaurants, garages, local stores, and businesses, some paying considerably more than minimum wage—were available for youth even without high school diplomas or GED certificates. Before the project's job developer came on board, the workers had established a variety of contacts with local employers and job agencies. However, the steps involved in connecting particular youth with jobs—let alone sustaining them on those jobs—were not simple. A key first step was to get the gang youth sufficiently motivated—not only to consider a job opportunity but also to follow through with an application to a job agency, employment office, or directly to a workplace. The youth worker, with the aid of project office staff, was prepared to assist the youth with formulating and producing a job resume. The youth worker would sometimes pick up job applications for the gang youth to complete and provide transportation to the job interviews. However, one test of the youth's real motivation and intention was whether he would be out of bed and dressed in the morning by the time the worker showed up to take him to the employment office or the job interview. There were many failures.

The gang youth was often unable to meet certain conditions of work. Some jobs required night hours, others drug tests or the possession of a driver's license. In some cases the youth would have to travel through enemy territory or would need a car (which he often did not have) to get to the suburbs or the farther reaches of the city. In many cases, the youth did not know what kind of job he wanted. A job made sense to him not because of his intrinsic interest in it, or as a step on a career ladder, but because he would then have income, comply with the pressures of his parents or girlfriend, get the probation officer off his back, or simply because it was the appropriate thing at his age to have a job—by neighborhood and even by gang standards. Some youth tried to hold an eight-hour day job and still hang in the streets or party with gang friends for another eight hours a day, and more on weeknights, which meant in due course he had to give up either the job or gangbanging (or partying). A job could also have a gang-related meaning—getting money to buy a gun and bullets to use in gang fights or other criminal activities.

The expressed need for a job was a major basis for communication between the youth worker and the gang youth. It was an acceptable way for the youth and the worker to justify contact with each other. It could open up conversations that led to other issues, such as gang fighting, girlfriends, drug use, problems with parents, and further training or education.

Each of the youth workers developed somewhat different ways of finding jobs for youth—through personal contact with employers, job agencies, reading newspaper ads, talking with neighbors in Little Village who might hear of job openings, or contacts with former gang members now working in places that might need additional workers. Older, former gang members in the neighborhood would often spread the word to younger active gang members about job openings at factories, businesses, hotels, airports, and construction sites. Based on a variety of leads, the youth worker would sometimes take a carload of gang youth to these places for job applications or interviews. Not infrequently, some of the youth would be hired on the spot, with or without resumes.

One worker had good connections with a security-guard agency and was able to place several youth in these jobs. He often accompanied the youth to a construction site for the first day of work, helping him load bricks. He wanted to demonstrate to the youth that he could make a good deal of money if he worked hard at a job for eight hours. (In one case, the youth found the job too strenuous and quit after the first day.) Some gang youth wanted "easy" jobs; some did not want to work during the summer but promised they would look for a job in the fall, or when the weather was cool and there was less action on the streets, and so on.

The youth worker collaborated with girlfriends, parents, and neighbors to find and sustain a youth on a job. A parent or girlfriend might enlist the youth worker to persuade or pressure the youth to find employment. Or on the other hand, the worker might request that the girlfriend or parent keep up the pressure to make sure the youth stayed on the job. There were times when some of the younger youth actively sought and found part-time jobs—cutting grass, painting over graffiti, running errands, and so forth. The workers would circulate handbills or visit neighbors and local shopkeepers seeking jobs for program youth.

MEDIATION

We did not use the term mediation to signify that the worker attempted to settle disputes or arrange "peace" between gang sections or opposing gangs. We emphasized a somewhat different and broader meaning of the term. The youth worker had to broker or mediate between the gang youth and the institutions of the larger society. Gang youth were usually alienated from (yet also partially identified with) family, school, employment, youth agencies, neighbors, opposing gangs, and even parts of their own gang. This social-psychological distance or alienation was inherent in the gang subculture and related to the youth's personality or state of adolescent rebellion. Alienation also developed in response to the rules, actions, and attitudes of the representatives of social and community institutions that dealt with gang youth. The job of the outreach youth worker was to reduce the gang youth's alienation or social distance by facilitating an accommodation between him and representatives of the social and community institutions he had to contact or relate to. In this process, the youth worker had to reorient attitudes not only of the youth but of significant institutional representatives as well.

The traditional role of mediating conflicts between opposing gangs was not often employed by youth workers in Little Village, where the gangs were relatively well established and organized, and hostility between gangs was entrenched. It was extremely difficult to mediate conflicts or establish peace treaties between gangs. It was easier to encourage lulls in fighting and gain agreement from gang leaders or influentials to "get their men to stay in their own neighborhoods." Gang conflict was a way of life that was accepted, encouraged, and perhaps needed for a variety of reasons by gang leaders, gang influentials, "shorties," or "wannabes." Certain neighborhood entrepreneurs, including drug dealers, did not necessarily view gang conflict as a threat to their business; in fact, some viewed it as a means of distracting police attention away from their operations. Gang youth were also useful and available to sell (and use) drugs when they were not fighting. With the widespread, heavy presence of fighting, drug using, and drug dealing at the gang level, it was more feasible for the youth worker to get individual youths and parts of gangs to "cool it," if only temporarily. Brief counseling with a youth to cut down on his use of drugs to perform better at school or to get a job was sometimes effective. It was still necessary for the youth worker to make sure the project police were fully alerted and prepared to deal with specific or potential gang conflicts and even major drug-dealing operations.

Violence between the gangs was essential to the development and survival of the gang as an institution. The leaders of the respective gangs also claimed that a long-term "peace" could not be achieved (although efforts by gang leaders in the community or in prison to call a temporary peace around particular conflicts were sometimes successful). Gang influentials voiced an agreement with the idea of "peace" but stated that if the opposing gang or its members entered their gang territory looking for a fight, they would find it. Gang turf would be defended, and violence would ensue. Contrary to popular and even gang belief, gang leaders had only partial control over gang members' motivations and activities. Certain individual gang members or sections did not observe particular gang leaders' calls for war or truce and prided themselves on being rebels or renegades. It was not so much gang organization or leadership that precipitated gang violence but rather the pervasive influence of gang culture or subculture and sometimes external pressures that could be used by individuals or cliques of gang youth for a whole variety of reasons to attack or not attack other people (who were usually gang related).

Project team members were reluctant to formally mediate conflicts between gangs through gang leaders, since this usually meant recognizing or strengthening the gang leaders' ability and power, and inferring legitimacy to broker or "negotiate" a peace, thereby contributing to gang cohesion and enforcing gang norms. The stated view of project staff, including the youth workers, was that gangs were illegitimate structures, and gang life was destructive and unrewarding. Gang youth had to be persuaded or constrained on an individual basis to leave the gang as soon as possible. The level of violence was so pervasive and extreme in Little Village that on occasion almost *any* means was sought to prevent or neutralize frequent and deadly confrontations between gangs. Police pressure, group recreational distractions, and conditions of "war fatigue" often led to temporary peace or lulls in gang conflict. Project workers could not anticipate, plan for, resolve, and control all of the many daily predictable and unpredictable factors contributing to battles between the two gangs (Short and Strodtbeck 1965).

The project workers were mainly concerned with reducing the level of gang conflict among youth already gang involved. In Little Village, the task of preventing youth from getting into gangs was more difficult and complex than simply getting youth out of gangs or avoiding gang-violent situations. The project's aim was not primarily to address the problem of preventing younger youth from joining gangs or participating in gang activity (although youth workers often counseled younger siblings of target youth to stay out of gangs). Youth workers were occasionally called on by elementary school principals and churches to talk to youth about the perils of gang life, but it was doubtful that such efforts were effective.

The efforts of the youth workers were mainly ameliorative, facilitating social growth and maturation, and attempting to prevent and control gang conflict in specific situations. The youth worker had to depend on his relationships with key gang members, his knowledge of gang dynamics, and the resources available at particular moments.

Larry [youth worker] happened to be present and helped to persuade the Darkside section not to jump in on the side of the K-town and Chi-town sections to fight against the K-town section of the Two Six. In the process, Larry was almost hit by a Darkside member with whom he had a somewhat antagonistic relationship. Luckily, the police came to the scene, and the warring sections were dispersed. No major injuries were reported.

On Tuesday early evening, the Two Six Chi-town section and Latin Kings Twenty-eighth Street section got into a fight at the Boys and Girls Club, regarded as neutral turf. Frank [youth worker] happened to be at the club with the Latin Kings. He was able to separate the warring groups and calmed the situation, mainly because he knew the leader of the King section, who respected him.

The youth worker could be an important mediator between the youth who wanted to leave the gang and the gang itself. At times he could persuade gang leadership to permit the youth to be released from gang membership. Often the gang member, if he had served his time and been a "good soldier," could leave the gang with impunity. He could walk away under certain conditions, for instance, if he obtained a full-time job; if he were involved in college studies; if his wife or his girlfriend were pregnant; or if his brother or uncle had been a senior member or leader of the particular gang section. The worker could sometimes persuade leadership of the gang to agree to arrange for only the mildest punishment for the youth who wanted out of the gang. On one occasion, a gang youth requested the youth worker to get the project probation officer to say that he had been ordered by the court to stay at home in the evenings. The youth was not on probation, but the fiction was agreeable to the project probation officer and the fabrication accepted by the gang members, permitting the youth to stay home and not engage in gang activities.

Changing or neutralizing the destructive or violent behavior of a particular gang section could be a more difficult task and sometimes required the intervention of outside authority. The gang section was unable to control itself in many situations, for example, causing trouble at the gym facilities at a local youth agency, church, or park recreational center. Younger gang members, or those unable to participate or not performing well in basketball games might deface property, smoke "pot" on the premises, or get into fights to "show off" to girlfriends or fellow gang members. Consequently, the entire section might be penalized, "thrown out of the gym," and prevented from returning. In one instance, a fire extinguisher was inadvertently left in a church gym after school by a building staff member who was not present during the game. One of the gang youth on the sidelines was unable to resist the temptation of spraying foam all over the gym floor. The entire section was expelled and no longer permitted to use the gym. In this case, the youth worker arranged for the youth and his gang peers to make amends—clean up and pay for a new extinguisher—but the offer was not accepted by the church school administrators. At times, after a specific disruptive gang incident, it was easier for the youth worker to persuade a particular youth-agency supervisor or church pastor to permit an individual gang member, or several of the more conforming gang members, to make use of the particular facility as "nongang youth." They were to come in individually as regular agency or church members, without gang peers, and obey all rules. This kind of separation of individual youth from the gang was a key project objective. On one occasion, several factions of the Latin Kings—perhaps fifty or sixty youth—were barred from using another church gym because the pastor accused their members of stealing audio equipment from a nearby church meeting room. The gang members in fact were not responsible and, with the intervention of the worker, were able to identify the thieves, who were younger youth unrelated to the gang. The equipment was returned, and the Latin Kings were permitted to continue to use the gym.

Arranging for "peace" or even amicable relations between individuals in gangs (the same gang or different sections of the same gang, or even opposing gangs) was sometimes possible. Youth workers were often able to work out a peace between rival youth who disliked each other personally (gang-section or gang-status issues were not necessarily at stake in these situations). Often the particular youth knew each other from school or lived on the same block but had built up sharp, sometimes long-term, animosities. Youth workers were able to arrange alternate routes and patterns of behavior for the conflicting youths, so that their paths were less likely to cross.

Gang violence was often unpredictable in Little Village, and youth workers had to use their wits to minimize its consequences:

Frank [youth worker], present at the incident, reported that fifteen Latin Kings jumped two guys who suddenly came into their street and beat them severely with parts of a chair. Frank thought they were in danger of killing the victims; Frank urged the Latin Kings to stop the beating. The Kings claimed the two intruders were wearing colors of an opposing gang, the Latin Disciples, from a community just outside Little Village. One of the victims denied he was a gang member. Frank intervened and caused a pause in the fighting. The police also arrived on the scene and apprehended two of the Latin Kings; the other Kings ran away. Frank did not hang around, because he did not know the particular police, and they might assume he was involved in the incident.

THE YOUTH WORKER AND THE COMMUNITY

The youth workers were intimately connected to citizens of the local community. They not only assisted specific gang youth and their families with a range of services and access to opportunities but also tried to assist the local community generally to better address the problems of gangs and gang youth. They did this in various ways. They functioned as gang experts, helping to educate local citizens, block club members, and local school administrators about the reasons particular gang problems arose, and how to deal with them. Much of this occurred as a function of youth workers regularly attending block-club meetings, developing relationships with particular neighbors, and being available to school officials and local citizens to deal with problems of gang loitering, graffiti, littering, and various forms of classroom disruption or citizen annoyance. Because of their relationships with key members of the various gang sections, youth workers were able to persuade gang youth to avoid conflicts at school, disperse from particular street corners, clean up pop and beer cans, avoid street partying, and refrain from marking up buildings, garages, and fences. The gang sometimes volunteered to paint over the graffiti that they themselves had put up to mark their own territory.

Youth workers assisted local residents and block clubs to actively address problems that contributed to gang delinquency. A Two Six faction was hanging out in a local bar, selling drugs, and painting gang emblems on the side of the building. One of the Two Six youth workers spoke with the bar owner and commented that several of the Two Six in the bar were fifteen and sixteen years of age. The owner shrugged his shoulders. He said he was not interested in the problem, and besides, he could not control it. The youth behaved themselves inside the bar, and his business was good. The neighbors continued to express concern, and the youth worker helped them to compose and circulate a petition to the Tenth District police commander to close down the bar. The youth worker discussed the problem with the project sergeant and the two project tactical officers. They also spoke with the district commander. Regular Tenth District police officers were sent to investigate, and within a matter of days the bar was closed down. In another case, one of the youth workers knew that some residents and block-club members were not interested simply in getting rid of gang youth but also genuinely wished to provide services for them. One of the residents and several members of the block club were on good speaking terms with the gang members. The resident knew their families and had watched the gang members grow up. The Latin King worker said that "the guys are very respectful of her; they cleaned up garbage in her yard." With the encouragement of the youth worker, she became the leader of a block effort to find a gym or an indoor facility in the community where they could play ball, especially when the weather got cold.

Youth workers also encouraged parents, neighborhood residents, and block-club members to attend meetings organized by Neighbors against Gang Violence (NAGV), where representatives of various local agencies and community groups came together to address the gang problem. At one community meeting, the youth workers recruited members of the two gangs to participate in the residents' discussions of their concerns about the gang problem. Neighbors pointed out the dangers of children being caught in the cross fire of gangs shooting at each other. The gang members promised to be careful, but they also insisted that members of each of the gangs should stay in their own part of the community. The youth from the two gangs glared at each other during the meeting, but some of the older members gave signs of recognition and some friendliness to older members of the other gang. The meeting had some value for potentially cooling matters between some of the opposing gang members. Youth workers, along with the gang members, were active in assisting parents and neighbors to adjust at times of gang crisis, particularly when shootings occurred and gang members were injured or killed. Youth workers helped gang members raise funds to give to parents to cover the costs of burial of the gang member who had been killed, or to take care of gang members who were seriously injured. Fellow gang members, as well as neighbors, were usually in attendance at wakes and church services for youth on such occasions. One of the youth workers noted,

> The neighborhood is holding a fundraiser for Dillinger, the Latin King who was shot last month. Dillinger was not working at the time of his shooting; he had no medical insurance and left three children for his wife to support. He was receiving medical attention at home, but his condition was getting worse, and he was not expected to live. The neighbors expressed compassion and contributed money to take care of Dillinger and his family.

The youth workers were called upon by schools, colleges, churches, neighborhood-relations police, probation, and the media to describe the Little Village Gang Violence Reduction Project and what they did as youth workers. Organizations requested project youth workers as speakers in Little Village and sometimes in other communities as far away as Aurora, about fifty miles from Chicago. Youth workers responded to these requests, often asking program youth along to these occasions. Youth workers and gang members were provided with food and tickets to ball games, circuses, and theatrical performances by the organizations inviting them.

Two of the Two Six youth workers, who were closely affiliated with evangelical protestant churches, urged gang youth not only to stay in school but also to attend church. One of the youth workers occasionally conducted Bible lessons in addition to providing specific information about the legal (and prison) consequences of gang violence. He regularly took groups of six or more gang youth to an interdenominational church service out of the area, where they sang, studied the Bible, and later played basketball together. What the effects of these particular community-relations and religious-commitment activities on program youth were are not known.

RELATIONSHIPS WITH POLICE

The youth workers and project police officers were partners, along with probation and the NAGV neighborhood organizer, in addressing the gang problem. Yet these relationships were not always characterized by mutual respect and common purpose. The fundamental function of the youth worker was to provide social support and opportunities to project youth; that of the police officer was control or suppression. These functions were traditionally and institutionally opposed; the roles had to be modified and made interactive. It took time for this to occur, at least within the context of project efforts.

The youth worker, who was a former high-status gang member, had been socialized to a gang culture and set of norms that expressed distrust of, and antagonism for, any form of collaboration with the police. In contrast, based on department norms and practices, the police in Chicago were highly committed to harassment and suppression of gangs, by almost any means. Police and gangs were mobilized in opposition to each other. However, during the course of the five years of the project's operations, there was little or no antagonism between project police and youth workers but rather considerable friendliness and cooperation, on and even off the job.

The structured relationship of project police and youth workers may have also rubbed off on the project police in their relationship to the target youth. Despite the fact that many of the program youth were stopped and arrested, the two project police officers established surprisingly positive relationships with the target youth and their families, probably because they gave evidence that they cared about the youth and treated them courteously and respectfully. The project police were often surprised to find themselves welcomed in the homes of gang youth and their families, even though their testimony had contributed to successful prosecution and long sentences for some of the target youth. A youth-work supervisor, newly hired during the last six months of the project, wrote in one of his records,

> One of the most interesting comments made by the [gang] guys was that they appreciated when the police officers in the project would take time out to counsel them instead of just arresting them. The guys seemed to have really felt this was a strong part of the project. They made it clear that even though the officers did arrest the guys in many cases, the fact that they counseled them on the way to custody made a difference in the way they felt about being arrested.

The youth workers collaborated with the project tactical officers in the exchange of information that was vital to their police suppression role. The youth workers also came to depend on the project police for information, assistance, and protection, which was important in the implementation of their own roles: counseling and neutralization of out-of-control gang youth, and also protecting them from "hard-nosed" and sometimes brutal police officers in the district who were not affiliated with the project. The project police were helpful to the youth workers in many respects, sometimes helping them with their own personal or family problems.

Relations of nonproject police with youth workers were generally less than benign. Some district police officers were prone to stop and harass clusters of young people, including gang youth. Much of the harassment was based on the "tough Chicago police" tradition of "bust up" gangs and "lock up" gang youth. This was explicit in Chicago's anti-gang-loitering law, which prohibited five or more gang youth from assembling on the street. The existence of the ordinance served to give license to the police to charge gang (and sometimes nongang) youth with a variety of offenses—if not gang loitering, then mob action, disorderly conduct, and other offenses, some minor, some major. The ban was eventually declared unconstitutional in two separate court decisions, one by the Supreme Court of the United States.

The actions of the nonproject police with gang youth affected how the youth workers performed their role.

Lester [youth worker] reported that the Two Six shot a Vice Lord in Two Six territory on Thursday. Lester voiced concerns over the police response. They were searching the homes of program youth without search warrants and trying to pin the shooting on one of them. Lester spoke to the parents of the target youth in the area and urged them not only to keep their sons off the street but also to avoid the police request to search their home, unless they had search warrants.

Frank [youth worker] went to court with Joey and his father. Joey was arrested for possession of one ounce of marijuana (which Frank believes the police planted on him). The case was dismissed when the arresting officer failed to show up in court.

Frank reported a case of entrapment of a Latin King on a gun-felony charge. The gun was presumed to have been used in a recent homicide. Frank attended a preliminary hearing for José, a fourteen-year-old newcomer to the gang. He was originally caught with a small amount of cocaine, but the police convinced him that they would forget about the cocaine charge if he turned over a gun to them. José managed to obtain a weapon. It had no fingerprints, and the stories of the two police officers did not match each other. José's lawyer said that the gun-felony charge would be thrown out of court.

Another Latin Kings youth worker reported that on Friday evening, as he waited in his car with two target youth, he witnessed Officer L slapping Mario [another target youth] in a nearby police car. [The youth worker] said that the officer, who had been in the neighborhood for many years, hated Mario and was always harassing him. The worker encouraged Mario and his mother to file a report against Officer L.

The youth workers were at times stopped by nonproject police, harassed, abused, arrested, and taken to the Tenth District station for booking. I had to go to court on at least two occasions to persuade judges to dismiss cases of gang loitering against youth workers. The two project police, sometimes in the field or at the Tenth District station when the youth workers were picked up and brought in on a variety of charges, invariably vouched for the youth workers, who were then released and not arrested or booked. Lester indicated that there was a large police presence in the area, including officers of the violent-crime unit from downtown who did not know the neighborhood. On Wednesday, several of the violent-crime officers tried to take him downtown to appear in a police lineup. Lester showed the officers his project identification, but they did not believe him. The two project officers happened to be nearby on the street; they vouched for Lester, and he was released.

Frank reported that Officer S and another officer stopped his car. He had four of the target youth with him. The guys were driving to the YMCA. The officers searched the car and found nothing but made Frank drive to the Tenth District. He was about to lock Frank up, claiming he had no valid driver's license, which was untrue. Officer S also tried to plant a marijuana joint in the car, but one of the target youth saw him. The other officer hit one of the guys in the face and kicked another youth. Frank also discovered that Officer S is presently under investigation based on other citizen charges. Frank said he would go downtown to report the incident to the Office of Professional Standards.

> George [Two Six youth] reported that one officer pulled a gun on him while he was standing with several gang youth on K and Twenty-fifth Street. The police had received a great many complaints about drug dealing on the block. George and the other youth were searched. The police found nothing on them and then walked away.

> Jake [youth-work supervisor] reported that he took one of the Two Six youth to a district lineup because the police were searching for the youth in a robbery case. The victim did not recognize the gang youth as the offender but did claim that Jake, who volunteered to be in the lineup, was the offender in the robbery. Jake had earlier telephoned the two project police that he was taking the Two Six youth down to the lineup. The two project police also came down to see what was going on. They persuaded the other police officers that Jake couldn't possibly have been involved, and he was not arrested.

Resolution of cases of harassment and fake charges against gang youth and youth workers by nonproject police—particularly those from outside the district, who were brought in to do "sweeps" of gang members—took up a good deal of the youth workers' and NAGV neighborhood organizer's time. George, the Latin King worker, in one of his weekly debriefing reports, recorded that most of his time that week was spent taking Latin Kings (younger members) downtown to the Office of Professional Standards on different days to fill out reports concerning police harassment.

On another occasion, Lester tried to prevent a clash between the Darkside and Chi-town sections of the Two Six. It was winter and snow was on the ground. The police arrived and placed twenty of the youth and Lester against the wall. Lester told them who he was, showed the police his project ID card, and explained the workings of the project. The police did not believe him. They checked his hands for spray paint, as they did to all of the gang youth present. Before letting the twenty youth go, the police made them do pushups in the deep snow and slush. Lester tried to read the badge numbers of the police in order to complain. The officers saw this, handcuffed him, and put him into the police car (he, along with Ralphie, leader of the Chi-town group, had refused to do pushups). Both Lester and Ralphie were locked up for about an hour, and then released.

In the next several days, I complained about the incident to the project police sergeant and to the district commander. Lester, as well as the project neighborhood organizer and a priest on the NAGV board, paid a visit to the district commander about this and a series of related harassment incidents. The police-officer offenders—at least those local police who were known to harass youth—were identified. The commander promised to talk to the officers in question. Shortly afterward, the commander transferred one of the officers out of the district.

In another instance, I advised one of the target youth to obtain a lawyer and sue the police department for damages to his car because of negligent police work.

Antonio [former leader of a section of the Two Six] had just been released from a six-month stay in prison on violation of probation. He was working and no longer a gang member. He was stopped for driving without a license on his way to visit his girlfriend in Latin King territory. He was made to park his car and was then taken in the police car to the Tenth District. Antonio pleaded with the officer to let him or have them drive his car out of the area, otherwise the car would be recognized and vandalized by the Latin Kings. He needed the car for his job. The police refused Antonio's request. The Latin Kings torched the car as soon as the police drove off with Antonio. Antonio was quickly released at the station, but he was very upset. He had no objection to the charge of driving without a license but was furious that the police disregarded his claim that his car would be vandalized. Antonio complained to the youth worker and the project coordinator. Antonio was referred to a lawyer with expertise in defending gang youth. The lawyer quickly obtained a judgment against the Chicago Police Department, and Antonio received a satisfactory sum of money for replacement of his vehicle.

PERFORMANCE PROBLEMS

There were problems as well as many benefits to the project in using youth workers who were former members of gangs in the area. Both the limitations and advantages were largely anticipated. Close project administration and supervision of their work were expected to, and did, minimize the negatives and maximize the positives. In the following section we concentrate on problems associated with a wide range of required activities that youth workers were expected to perform but did not always do well. It took time for the project to develop policies and implement procedures for what was appropriate and not appropriate for outreach youth workers to do in many work situations. Some youth workers had to be fired for repeated failures to carry out their duties.

Articulating Project Policy

The assistant director, the youth-work supervisor, and I spent much time explaining the nature and objectives of the project to youth workers, as well as to gang youth, local neighborhood organizations, and citizen groups. Youth workers accomplished initial field-contact objectives reasonably well, but constraints had to be imposed and policy forcefully articulated when certain problems arose, especially in light of the fact that the project was sponsored by the Chicago Police Department.

No effort was made to publicize the project in the first year and a half of operations. After the local media got wind of the project, the youth-work supervisor and youth workers were frequently interviewed by print, radio, television, and even University of Chicago public-relations reporters. Pictures were taken of youth workers with gang members on the street. Gang members appeared with project youth workers and the NAGV neighborhood organizer on radio and television. The youth workers often focused their discussions on the need for more educational and job opportunities for gang youth. Nevertheless, the youth workers and even the gang youth began to be concerned about the large amount of publicity directly involving project gang youth. I had to be clear about how staff should relate to the media and formulated the following policy:

Memo to: Staff
From: Project Coordinator
RE: Staff Relationships with Media
Date: October 1, 1993
It is the policy of the project that all contacts with the media—in which individual gang youth, family, gang locations, or other persons or items related to the particular gang youth or gang situations are identified—are forbidden, except on very special occasions and for specific purposes, which must be approved by me.

This in no way limits or denies project staff the right to establish media contacts and relationships that serve *general* project purposes, but the contact must in no way identify particular youth or gangs.

The primary intent of this policy is to

1. not give publicity to particular youth and gangs and thereby enhance individual gang-member status or affiliation with a gang;
2. protect gang youth from identification by opposing gang members; and
3. avoid competition by gang members and gangs for publicity through negative gang behavior.

Also, please note that the Gang Violence Reduction Project is funded and generally directed by the Chicago Police Department. This fact should be made known to media representatives, who are urged to contact the following:

1. Commander, Tenth District Chicago Police Department (phone #) or
2. Research and development unit (phone #).

At about the same time, a second policy resulted from the participation of the assistant director, several youth workers, a member of the NAGV board, and the part-time project neighborhood organizer in a series of gang-problem summits taking place in Chicago and in a nearby state. The summits involved representatives of several civil-rights, protest, and political organizations primarily concerned with a range of urban problems, including police brutality, housing, poverty, and other agendas not specifically related to gang problems. The key issue was project representation at these meetings, which were politicized and not strictly related to the gang problem.

Memo to: Staff
From: Project Coordinator
Re: Representing the Gang Violence Reduction Project at Political Events and Public Demonstrations
Date: October 15, 1993
Staff members are fully encouraged to participate as individuals in political events and demonstrations, a right guaranteed by the U.S. Constitution. However, the Gang Violence Reduction Project is strictly a demonstration-research program. Moreover, staff, clients, local citizens, and those in the program are *not permitted* to state or imply that they are representing the Gang Violence Reduction Project, the School of Social Service Administration, or the University of Chicago in these activities, when in fact their views and activities represent personal or other organizational and not necessarily project interests.

    If you have any doubt about the distinction between personal and political interests and project purposes and activities, you must clear them with me. In other words, your participation in political events and public demonstrations is on your own time and cost, and in no way should you indicate or imply that such participation is sanctioned by the project.

Both of the above policies were accepted by all the staff, except the assistant director, who shortly afterward decided to run for alderman. He had begun to use time on the job to make contact with a great variety of persons unrelated to the project or its purpose and was no longer sufficiently available for his project responsibilities. The issue of time spent in preparation for his aldermanic race became a key factor in my terminating him from the project. Subsequently, the administrative structure of the project was changed and the combined position of assistant director/youth-work supervisor eliminated.

Another serious problem occurred with the overidentification of one worker with the role of project police. Both overidentification with gang norms and values and overidentification with the police suppression role were contrary to the project model and could (and did) interfere with project operations. Al was the first full-time worker hired to work with the Two Six. He was a big, self-assured man in his mid-twenties, honorably discharged from the Army, with service in the first Gulf War. He was an effective worker during the first year and a half of the project. He established very close relationships with the two project tactical officers, meeting regularly with them to go to dinner in the project neighborhood. He was also frequently observed by program youth sitting in the project police officers' car in Two Six territory. On one occasion he drove with them into Latin King territory. I did not know this until one of the Latin Kings complained that Al was an undercover police officer. Al was directed not to associate so provocatively with project officers and certainly not to ride with them either in Latin King and Two Six territory. He could arrange to have dinner meetings with them outside of Little Village.

Al also took a series of part-time jobs with security firms. He was proud of his work in security, and before coming to a youth-worker staff meeting at SSA one afternoon, he showed off a gun he was carrying. When I confronted him, Al explained that he was licensed to carry the gun on his job as a security guard. He was planning to go to his security job after the staff meeting. I ordered Al to return the gun to the trunk of his car. He was not to show up with it in any of his project work in the future. In a further discussion, Al claimed not to see his youth-worker role as particularly different from that of a law-enforcement officer. This situation resulted in the creation of a third policy clarifying the role of the youth worker and emphasizing that the youth worker was not to perform either as a police officer or a gang member.

Memo to: Staff
From: Project Coordinator
Re: Further Policy Clarification of the Role of Community Youth Worker
Date: December 14, 1994
The outreach youth worker *does not* fulfill the role of *police officer or gang member.*

1. He is an outreach youth worker whose key function is to provide services and access to social opportunities, assist targeted gang youth to control their violent behavior, and to help them make a positive community adjustment. He is expected to work closely and cooperate with other members of the project team, including police, probation officers, and the neighborhood organizer but not perform their roles.
2. To this end, he must not carry a weapon on the job, even if legally permitted to do so elsewhere.
3. Failure to conform to this policy will result in termination of the worker from the project.

Conforming to Project Norms

Supervision of youth workers who were formerly high-status gang members, not long removed from the gang culture, was difficult and challenging. Youth workers were on their own in the community much of the day or night, and there was little hour-by-hour direct supervision of their work. Youth workers had to internalize and operationalize legitimate values and were expected to conform to project norms. Social-agency rules and regulations, and even basic job routines, were not easy for several of the youth workers to follow. The youth workers were expected to complete biweekly time cards, account for field time, respond quickly and cooperatively to communications and requests from other staff or team members, make appropriate use of beepers or cell phones, provide their own job-related transportation (for which they were reimbursed), fill out special reports, complete weekly job debriefings, attend various meetings (especially weekly youth-worker and biweekly team meetings), and also assist project field researchers in locating target youth for interviews.

These expectations were not always satisfactorily met. The problem was not lack of commitment to project goals and objectives, or lapses into criminal behavior, but mainly lack of familiarity with customary agency rules and regulations, and periodic nonobservance of these rules. Specific problems that arose were not showing up on time (or at all) for staff meetings, not responding to beeper calls, and not being out in the field when or where he was scheduled to be. An early administrative problem was failure by youth workers to submit time cards, and worker-tracking forms describing what they had done in the field. Most of the youth workers did not have adequate writing skills. Various recording forms were developed earlier in the project, but they didn't work. The most feasible and effective means of tracking worker effort proved to be regular weekly debriefings by a project researcher or the project secretary, using a standardized worker-tracking instrument.

Youth-worker accountability had to be stressed, and the means to achieve it had to be developed. The youth-work supervisor and I systematically monitored the reliability of youth-worker efforts in the field. But the quality of the youth worker's performance was still difficult to determine. Individual-worker/supervisor meetings were of some help. Group training and staff-development sessions were initiated in the last two years of the project to assist youth workers to better address certain gang, individual-youth, and family problems. These training sessions were useful and should have commenced earlier.

Firing Outreach Youth Workers

A range of problems led to the termination of youth workers more often than had been anticipated. Termination came after frequent warnings and lengthy discussions with the workers about particular issues and problems. When the youth worker's performance problems could not be corrected, I separated the worker from the project but at the same time assisted the worker to find another position and enabled him to collect unemployment insurance, maintain health insurance, and assure that he would remain positively connected to the project. Project and personal contacts were still maintained and job references provided years after the project ended.

In one case, a Latin King youth worker was reluctant to communicate to gang members of the group he was assigned that he was an employee of the University of Chicago and a part of a team that comprised police, probation officers, and a neighborhood organizer. He identified very closely with his gang. I told the worker, "You conceive your role mainly as a kind of gang insider, knowing what's happening but not necessarily trying to effect change in the gang." The worker smiled and admitted this and continued to act as a gang senior member. He moved around the community contacting gang members on warm summer nights, not wearing a shirt. His old gang tattoos were visible on his chest, back, and forehead. He was highly influential and able to resolve many internal gang factional disputes, but he was erratic in his contacts and communications with other team members. After a while it became clear that he was still too closely identified with the gang. After many discussions with the worker, I separated him from the project (but even after termination the worker proved useful to the project police in locating a Latin King charged with a double homicide who had escaped from detention in the Cook County Department of Corrections and was living in another state).

In a second case, a youth worker's performance was deemed unsatisfactory because he had contacted an insufficient number of gang youth and "did not refer youth for jobs or to school programs"; his "travel expenses were very high and out of range, three times as high as for comparable-level and more productive workers"; and his "recording of activity with target youths was thin." In another case, a youth worker was terminated before his ninety-day project probationary period was up because he had not established a "working relationship with senior members or shot callers of the Latin Kings." Unbeknownst to me, he had "several negative experiences with them, in which he was beaten up." The same worker also had "not completed and turned in logs or records of project activities, as requested."

In still another case, the youth worker was well connected with some of the most violent Two Six sections. He appeared positively motivated to help gang youth and share information with project police and probation. Unfortunately, he became substantially disengaged from his job routines, did not show up for meetings or turn in records, and periodically disappeared from the neighborhood. After a while, neither the other workers nor I could keep track of his movements. When he finally did show up, he was fired.

In the case of Al, who was bright and hard working during the first year and a half on the project, there had been a plan to promote him to a new position as assistant youth-work supervisor. However, personal and job-performance problems began to develop. He went through a divorce from his first wife and in the process was twice arrested on charges of domestic violence. Several members of the Two Six gang sections he worked with accused him of "fingering them" for selling drugs. Al lost his relationship with key leaders and members of the gang. "A contract was put out on him," which he said he was able to revoke, but he could no longer work effectively with the most violent and criminal section of the gang. Subsequently, he focused his work on a smaller number of less-violent youth in other Two Six sections. He began to operate alone, not communicating with other youth workers. The project youth-work supervisor and I did not see him regularly in the street any longer.

After Al was terminated, he failed to return his beeper, cell phone, and protective vest to the project. He claimed they were stolen from his car, but the project police and the new youth-work supervisor discovered that his cell phone was still being used. The project police tracked Al down and had him return all of his equipment. There was an interesting follow-up to Al's career. He was able to obtain a managerial position in a security firm, did gang consultation for the state's attorney's office, and later became a coordinator of investigations out of the mayor's office, where he was subsequently involved in a serious corruption case.

GANG STRUCTURE AND THE YOUTH WORKERS

Finally, we note that the characteristics of outreach youth workers, the fieldwork strategies they developed, and the outcomes for program youth they served also varied by the characteristics of the two target gangs. The Latin Kings were a relatively well-structured, hierarchical gang. The youth workers who had effective influence in their assigned Latin King gang sections were older, with backgrounds of gang violence, extensive arrests, and prison experience. They were better connected to the gang's overall top leadership than were the Two Six youth workers. The Two Six sections were part of a more diffuse gang structure, whose overall leadership was not well known. Their program youth, and the outreach youth workers assigned to them, were generally younger than in the Latin Kings. The Two Six were located in a more settled, higher-income part of Little Village. Two Six gang youth and their families were also better connected to elements of the Mexican Mafia (an adult organized-crime structure with primary interest in drug operations). Outreach youth workers represented key former gang leadership breaking away from gang structure in the local community. They had extensive knowledge of gang culture and ongoing gang activities. They were able to contact more gang youth, and more frequently, than other members of the Little Village intervention team. Youth workers could become invested in efforts to socialize gang youth with oversight and support of representatives of other key legitimate institutions of society. The use of (mainly) former gang members as outreach workers with hard-core gangs and their members in Little Village was a risky and controversial methodology. The social-intervention strategy—employing local outreach youth workers (particularly former gang members) in a team arrangement with police, probation, a neighborhood organizer, and other representatives of conventional society—was difficult to implement but probably more efficient and effective than separate institutional approaches of social intervention and suppression, which traditionally have been opposed to each other.

The project-team approach provided its own fail-safe mechanism against unreliability and corruption of youth workers. The actions of a multidisciplinary staff, in a close-knit team working in the same neighborhood with the same youth over time, were highly visible. Problems in youth-worker performance became quickly known. The team structure helped develop and sustain commitment to project goals and objectives and the legitimate values and behaviors needed to achieve them. Project outcome for individual youth indicated that team efforts, including outreach youth-worker services, contributed remarkably to success in reducing program-youth violence and even drug-selling activity (see chapters 12 and 14).

6

Suppression and Social Control

Ideally, the project suppression strategy should be regarded as a variation of community policing and community-based probation, with primary attention paid to the youth gang problem. It should take into consideration the interests of the gang youth (for social control) and the community (for protection, i.e., law enforcement) as well as the need for gang-youth social development. Project police would focus on tactics of preventing and suppressing gang crime, not necessarily "throwing the book at" all gang kids and even referring some for youth-worker services. Project team members, as well as neighborhood residents and staffs of local organizations, would be expected to assist the project officers in this more complex and nuanced gang-targeted community-policing approach. Probation, with ready access to court-processing, criminal, and family-history information, could be useful to project police in need of intelligence about particular youth. Our interest first is in the Chicago Police Department's (CPD) plan and administration of the project, and mainly in the role the two project police tactical officers actually played in addressing the youth gang problem. We pay less attention to the involvement of the Cook County Department of Adult Probation (CCDAP) and the activities of probation officers in the project. Youth workers and the project-related neighborhood organizer also played a complementary role in the implementation of the suppression strategy, which was largely carried out by the CPD.

THE CHICAGO POLICE DEPARTMENT AND THE PROJECT
The research and development (R&D) unit of the Chicago Police Department conceptualized an innovative but vaguely defined approach to the gang problem, to be demonstrated and tested through the Little Village Gang Violence Reduction Project (GVRP). Early on, the R&D unit thought that the project

approach, if successful, could be integrated into its community-policing pro-gram, the Chicago Area Policing Strategy (CAPS), which was in the planning and start-up phase. In the initial proposal submitted by the CPD to the Illi-nois Criminal Justice Information Authority (ICJIA), the following statement appeared: "The police role in the project will be community policing as it tar-gets the gang-violence problem in an outreach, flexible, and comprehensive manner." The CPD proposal spoke of community mobilization and provision of social opportunities directed to hard-core, older gang youth, seventeen to twenty-four years of age, as a means to control gang violence in Little Village. It paid some attention to strategies of social intervention and collaboration with other criminal justice and social agencies and grassroots groups. In the original first-year proposal summary, the CPD stated,

> The strategy of the Gang Violence Reduction Component is based upon the con-cepts of community mobilization and provision of social opportunities. Com-munity mobilization refers to the collaboration and integration of efforts of law enforcement and the criminal justice agencies, grassroots organizations, and local citizens. The provision of social opportunities depends on the availabil-ity and successful use of adequate training, education, and jobs for those gang members most likely to engage in violent behavior.

There was little discussion by the CPD as to how it would implement the project and restructure its various bureaus to facilitate this broader view of the department's mission and support for project operations. Project staff mem-bers were to formulate and implement a plan for mobilizing the community and relevant justice-system agencies within a one-year period. The project was expected to base its gang and gang-member targeting efforts largely on a newly developed, automated early-warning system, which would identify potential neighborhood crisis areas at high risk for spurts of serious street-gang-related violence and homicide. Representatives of the School of Social Service Admin-istration (SSA), University of Chicago, were expected to initiate a process of community-problem assessment and resource planning, and assist with project development and collaborative staff training prior to the actual initiation of field operations. At the same time, field operations were expected to start no later than one month after the project was funded. The entire project was to be under the administration of the commander of the Tenth Police District. The proposed strategies were to represent an elaboration and extension of the department's approach to gang-related problems but now more closely interrelated with criminal justice, community-based, and grassroots efforts to control and reduce the problem. A close relationship with adult probation was to be established: "Members of the CPD's Marquette District (Tenth District) along with members of the Cook County Department of Adult Probation and its Gang Outreach Team are expected to play key collaborative roles. It is expected that team members will be able to fully exchange relevant information with each other."

THE ORIGINAL PLAN
Chicago Police Department

The Chicago Police Department grant application to ICJIA proposed that the commander of the Tenth District would coordinate intelligence, investigations, training, and community-outreach functions. Its neighborhood-relations unit was to be responsible for ensuring that all data necessary to project operations were collected and reported as needed. One additional officer (limited-duty status) was to be assigned to the commander and the neighborhood-relations sergeant. Of special importance was the assignment of two full-time tactical unit officers to the project. They were to act as liaisons to a project advisory council and be responsible for the police component of the project. CPD employees assigned to the project were to analyze all offenses reportedly committed by and against gang members and all incidents where gang members were arrested. The information gathered was to be shared with the project's youth workers and probation officers. While the CPD assignment of officers, especially tactical officers, took place as originally planned, their roles, functions, and support structure developed in quite different ways, to be described below.

University of Chicago

A staff from the School of Social Service Administration and I (a professor, eventually to become the project coordinator) were expected to assist in the development of a prototypical, collaborative effort bringing the CPD, CCDAP, and gang-outreach-services personnel together under the sponsorship of the CPD in a planned program to reduce gang violence, specifically in the Little Village part of the South Lawndale community area. A variety of community contacts, interagency networking activities, a community assessment, training and documentation activities, and gang outreach services were to be the primary means by which the University of Chicago team would assist the project to achieve its goals and objectives in the first twelve months.

Cook County Department of Adult Probation

The CCDAP was expected to assign a supervisor and three full-time probation officers to the project. They were to be experienced field officers who had completed weapons training and who had knowledge of street gangs and their related criminal activities. The supervision of targeted gang youth on probation was to be more intensive, combining close monitoring and compliance to special probation conditions through frequent face-to-face contacts and home visits, curfew checks, and drug testing, in coordination with services such as treatment and counseling. Support and encouragement were also to be provided to gang probationers to assist in their successful reintegration into the community. Adult probation was expected to benefit from a close relationship with the CPD—a relationship that had not previously existed in Chicago. The exchange of information would help probation respond more quickly and effectively when probationers were arrested.

Local Community Organizations

In the original CPD proposal, an advisory group of representatives of local agencies and community organizations as well as local residents (including former gang members) was to be formed to advise and consult with the project staff on the development of programs. Various members of this group would be integrally involved in specific activities in support of project gang control and youth social development. Regularly scheduled meetings were to be held to discuss project issues and activities. How specifically the advisory-group organizations and residents were to be selected, who would sponsor the group, and what benefits would accrue for participation or affiliation with the project (particularly with the police) were not indicated. Only a very general conception of community involvement and support was formulated but not specific responsibility for the project or relation to the CPD.

Basic goals and objectives of the original CPD project proposal were stated in general terms and not easy to achieve. Given the CPD's history of specialized units to suppress gangs, change in their policies and practices could not readily or quickly occur. An oversight administrative or policy group within the CPD and the CCDAP to create the framework for implementation of the project was not identified. The possibility of a larger advisory group, perhaps consisting of representatives of neighborhood, citywide governmental, and nonprofit organizations, was not considered. Focus was on the development of a strictly neighborhood-based project. In the first year, preliminary thought was given by one of the early CPD district commanders to relating the project to the recently established, local Tenth District neighborhood-relations council. Little attention was paid to larger or longer-term potentials of the project.

IMPLEMENTING THE PROJECT
Police

A key initial problem was identifying who in the CPD was to be responsible for the project. Originally, the commander of the gang-crime unit was interested in and expected to be generally responsible for project operations, but the unit was dissolved and the commander retired. The patrol division was now to have some responsibility for administering the project through the local Tenth District commander, although he was only assigned 5 percent of time. The R&D unit was given some administrative oversight, mainly financial. The deputy superintendent's office was to assure there would be intrabureau cooperation to support the project. Specifically, how the organized-crime, youth-division, neighborhood-relations, CAPS, and other units of the department were to be connected to the project was not indicated. In the first three years of project operations, three different commanders in sequence were placed in charge of the Tenth District. The neighborhood-relations sergeant assigned to the project was not clear about his role. He was supposed to serve as liaison to the commander, keeping him informed of project progress and problems. He did not appear regularly at project biweekly team meetings. His major responsibility became the development of the new CAPS effort in the district. About the beginning of the third year of project operations, the neighborhood-relations sergeant decided to take a proactive leadership role in the project. He offered to supervise the youth workers during a transitional period, assuming the project was to be integrated into general police operations. However, R&D and the deputy superintendent's office did not accept his offer, and the sergeant, apparently disappointed, transferred to another district, as did the liaison lieutenant before him. There was also inadequate communication between the R&D unit and the Tenth District commander. The tactical, patrol, community-policing, youth-division, and other units in the Tenth District knew little about the GVRP and made little effort to interrelate their respective operations with those of

the project. The lack of sufficient and authoritative CPD involvement critically
affected the project. I, a University of Chicago professor, filled the role of project
coordinator by default so that the project could not only get started but also
keep going.

Probation

There had been little systemic relationship between adult probation and
the CPD. The GVRP was viewed by CCDAP as an opportunity to build a
specific structure and a systematic relationship with the CPD around the gang
problem, since many probationers seemed to be gang members. The CCDAP
wanted to be the junior partner (with the CPD as the senior partner) in the
project relationship, but a concept of how the probation officers were to relate
to the project and its tactical officers was not formulated. No policy-level or
administrative meetings were held between the two departments to address
this issue. The upper level of CCDAP administration was in the dark as to what
the Little Village probation component of the project specifically should do,
except to carry out some form of regular probation activities in the area. Also
influencing the development of the probation department's participation, it
was in the midst of its own reorganization, under the aegis of a newly appointed
chief probation officer. A deputy administrative officer became interested in
and assumed responsibility for the development of the Little Village probation
unit. Unfortunately, he resigned at the beginning of project operations. The
Little Village gang-probation unit was originally assigned to cover an area larger
than the Little Village community. The decentralized unit was to deal with all
adults on probation from the area, whether they were gang youth or not. It
was not until well into the first year of the project that permission was granted
for the Little Village probation unit to concentrate on gang youth not only in
the Little Village area but specifically in the same beats as the project police.
However, primary attention continued to be on gang probationers who were
arrested for drug offenses.

A further problem was that the supervising probation officer knew little
about gangs and was disposed to apply rigid rules and operating procedures
for the three project probation officers. His lack of understanding of the purpose
of the project and the nature of the gang problem in Little Village, as well as
growing tensions between him and his three project probation officers (who
had more experience and better understanding of the gang problem than he

had), led to a major blowup in the Little Village Project probation unit. All three probation officers requested and obtained a transfer out of the GVRP.

A central CCDAP investigation took place almost immediately. The original supervisor was replaced by one of the original project probation officers. Two new probation officers were added to the project. CCDAP policies and procedures still were not tailored to the needs of the project. The probation officers complained that they could not ride in the same vehicle with project police officers. They were not permitted to invite the project police along with them on home visits or searches. One of the new probation officers submitted a grievance to his union, claiming that facilities and equipment were inadequate for him and others in the office to do the job. In the original funding agreement, the CCDAP had agreed to supply office space in Little Village to be used by probation, police, and youth workers to carry out their tasks and by an affiliated neighborhood organization to conduct a variety of project and community-related activities. This agreement was only partially honored. Space and equipment for the project police officers and outreach youth workers were not provided. However, a computer was installed, and probation officers could provide information to the project police officers and me on the court status and past and present history of all project youth who had been on adult probation. The probation office became the site for most team meetings. At times, the Little Village office was also used by project field researchers to conduct program-youth interviews.

The new probation supervisor continued to voice his frustration with the lack of clear direction and the failure of CCDAP to provide adequate means of supporting the project probation unit and its work. In the fourth year of the project, he recorded his views in a taped conversation:

> I thought our mission was to work effectively with hard-core gang members in the area. We were not viewed as police officers. . . . I felt we'd be able to use the flexibility that probation has to identify the real hard-core guys causing most of the problems. . . . If we can identify those guys for the courts, these guys should be locked up and that may reduce violence. Also, we could identify fringe or marginal members and then we could plug those guys into services, into education or job training or whatever, and slowly pull those guys out of the gang situation.
>
> The team arrangement would give us access to information that the project police officers had, and we would be able to call on the outreach workers for information and access to families and their home situations that we wouldn't

normally have. We didn't achieve all of these objectives well. On a scale of one to ten, I think we achieved a six. If I have criticism, it is that everybody should have been plugged in better. I think a lot of the times one administrative hand didn't know what the other was doing. I think before you even start such a project, you should have clear direction, policy, and procedures, and there should be support by administration. This lack of support by administration held us back. We were always waiting. When was there going to be a structure for us that came from above?

THE PROJECT POLICE OFFICERS

Despite the weaknesses of policy, organizational structure, and support for the roles of project police and probation officers, and perhaps partially because of them, an unusually high degree of cohesion evolved among the members of the project team. A set of effective project-related working relationships emerged in response to the need for interdependent activity among diverse staff thrown together without clear agency direction. Staff developed increasingly common views about the goals and objectives of the project, with great dedication to its work. Much of this was a response to the performance of the two project police officers and their daily interactions with other project team members. The two officers, not bound to traditional tactical-officer routine, were able to create a commonsense, law-enforcement approach as they addressed the complex gang problem in Little Village. They were still very much a part of the police structure, carrying out their own law-enforcement duties and assisting other officers with theirs.

The conversation that follows indicates the extent to which the project police officers could adapt their law-enforcement roles, consistent with the comprehensive community-wide, and especially interdisciplinary, approach to the youth gang problem. It is based on an edited transcript of a discussion between the two tactical officers, Rob and Gary, and me in the fourth year of the project, in which they described the development of their project roles. Both were young officers, each with about two years of CPD experience. Both had just started working with gangs as part of their police tactical work in the Tenth District and did not know much about the traditional CPD approach to youth gangs. Rob said he knew some old patrol officers who had known these kids almost from the time they were born. A few of the beat officers knew the families and had offered to help Rob and Gary get going.

I asked a series of questions in the final year of the project and received the
following responses:

AUTHOR: What happened when you came to the project?

GARY: Part of the problem in the beginning was that there was no direction.
Nobody really knew what they wanted us to do. We looked at it as we're the law
end of it. If one of the kids is the bad apple, we can pull him out. If we pull that
shooter out, or the guy that's doing the stickups, maybe we can quiet the rest of
them down. We're going to go out and find who these guys are, and when they
screw up, we're going to do our job. We're going to try to get them incarcerated. If
we don't get lucky and put them in jail for a long time, then maybe we'll get them
on probation and keep an eye on them twenty-four hours a day. And everybody's
got to work together and figure out what the kids are doing.

ROB: Community policing was just starting, and nobody was paying much attention to us . . . so we kind of went out and did this project with the university
and probation, and . . . set our own rules, our own groundwork without the help
of anybody else—just started, trying different things.

GARY: The first thing . . . we went out there and started talking to these guys.
We let them know who we are and what we're doing. We put out the word that
we are the police, but if you have a problem, talk to us. If we can do something
for you, we'll do it. We're not out there just trying to lock everybody up, because
obviously that didn't work. If you have a problem, like you feel you can't go
to your family, the boys on the street aren't helping you out, maybe we're the
connection. We got some guys like street workers, or the connections which the
university had, that can do something for these guys. Before the project, if a kid
came to a policeman and said, "Hey listen, I got kicked out of school for fighting,
and I need to get back; I screwed up," a policeman couldn't do anything.

ROB: We had a hard time in the beginning because the district police believed we
were going to play babysitter. We got a lot of grief from other policemen. They
thought we were going to stop doing police work and start doing social work.

GARY: You know when we first talked with the gang guys on the street that first
night, a crowd of them gathered. Joe Citizen didn't realize what was going on.
So, immediately they're calling the police district saying it's a gang fight. We had
to get on the radio and say we're just talking to these guys. That's all there is to
it. Well, Joe Citizen doesn't see it that way. A lot of times, people look at us and
they say, "We don't want the police out there just talking to these guys; we want
the police to lock up these guys, and throw the key away."

And a lot of times because of the media, Joe Public in Chicago also gets ideas
that the police are just gangbangers themselves, congregating and making deals

with these guys. But we were just talking with these guys. In the beginning we took a lot of aggravation from our own people. Other policemen got ugly. I told them I talk to those kids the same as I'm talking to you. You know not all these kids are bad kids. Some of these kids are having a lot of problems, and we're trying to help them out. But the other police would say, "We want them locked up. That's our job." I say, "Excuse me, I lock them up, and three hours later they get out. Would that change anything? I lock the kid up for gang loitering, but the kid isn't doing anything—and then I get them all against the police."

AUTHOR: And has that changed much?

ROB: It's changed a lot since we started. The tactical police we work with, they've seen what we've done in four years, how we've developed the information that they didn't have and that they need. Now a lot of them are coming to us for information.

AUTHOR: So, what do you see now as the role of the police?

ROB: We went out, and from day one, we just started talking to everybody. We got to know all the gang sections. We got everybody's name by talking to them. We checked the arrest reports. We pinpointed the violent offenders and the guys who could be shooters, and they usually turned out to be shooters.

GARY: And who they teamed up with to do the shooting was important. It's a pattern. A guy is not going to do a shooting with somebody he doesn't really know well. That guy could be talking to the police. But when he's done something with this guy and nothing's happened before, then he says, "I'm safe with this guy." And so if those guys are arrested together, you have to watch them both.

ROB: You'll see that we didn't make many arrests in the first year. But once we got to the shot callers, we began to solve a lot of homicides, especially in the second and third year.

AUTHOR: How do you men start your day off?

GARY: The first thing we do when we go into the station is start talking to everybody working the same beats as we are.

ROB: We call the detectives to see if they want us to pick up anybody we know, especially for a shooting. We know a lot of the gang guys out there, and the detectives call us for information. We talk to the gang guys on the "tact" team, the rapid response guys. We're still part of the team, too.

AUTHOR: How does your work differ from that of the gang or "tact" team right now?

ROB: Right now, they're starting to do what we're doing. They're getting to know the kids. They're talking to them. They have no choice. The lieutenant is asking them to submit reports. This is all of the stuff we did a long time ago. They didn't know who the guys were who were doing the crime.

GARY: And the other thing is that because we are not tied down to making a certain number of arrests per day or per week, and we don't have a sergeant screaming over us, "I want to see heads on this or that," we're able to concentrate on the gang problem. A lot of times, if a police officer has to make a certain quota of arrests, no matter what it's for, he's going to bring something in, whether it's a drunk, a mob action, a disorderly conduct, anybody with possession of dope or a gun. We don't have that, so we concentrate on gang individuals and gang incidents.

AUTHOR: Because you and the "tact" or gang team are now doing about the same thing, do you sometimes cross wires?

GARY: It's a problem. One of the Two Six [program youth] recently did an armed robbery that we knew about, and one of the gang teams also knew about it. Then the second gang team was on the following day but didn't know anything about the incident. They wondered why we didn't let them have all the facts about the kids. We said we gave the first team all the information and assumed they would be talking to the second team when they came on. They didn't tell the second team because they wanted to get credit for the arrest.

AUTHOR: So you also serve a kind of coordinating function. Officers give or should give the information you have to other officers, but many of the officers don't share the information.

ROB: Right. Now we're at the point where we're playing middleman between the "tact" teams, the gangs, and the other police, because we know a lot of people out there, not just gang kids. We can get information about these kids—whether they're on probation or not.

GARY: The probation guys on the project are great. We call them at home: "Hey, listen, I need a favor: you've got to do whatever you can to help us with this guy." That worked out in a homicide recently. They had a guy under house arrest. He told probation he would talk to us but not in his home. The kid said to us when we picked him up, "Make it look like you're taking me in," and we got the information we needed.

AUTHOR: What are you doing that's different from what the gang or "tact" team is doing now?

ROB: For one, we're talking to probation almost on a daily basis. We also talk to the street workers from the university almost on a daily basis. We're gathering information. Sometimes even when we're not working, the probation or street-worker guys call us about gang kids or incidents.

The regular gang or "tact" teams do an excellent job when it comes to arresting these guys for guns and things like that. That helps us, too. They pinch a kid that we know, and the kid may come to us and say, "They got me.

Maybe there's something you can do for me." We get additional information that way.

GARY: That happens more than you think. It's amazing. These kids get arrested, they grab us on the street, "I got to talk to you. I got arrested with a gun by so and so two days ago. It's like, I'm on probation. I can't take a gun charge. I'll tell you whatever you need to know. Can you help me out?" Also, sometimes the kid complains about a particular officer that's picking on him.

ROB: So we'll go to the police officer and say, "Give the guy some slack. He's talking to us, and he's giving us information. If he gives us anything, we'll give it to you guys. Okay?" And the officer says, "Okay." A couple of days later, we might call that officer and say, "Remember the guy you've been bugging? He just gave us some information on a dope house . . ." and if the officer goes and makes an arrest on the information, he'll say, "Okay, leave it alone for a while." Then the kid's happy. Everybody's happy.

AUTHOR: What about the other members of the project team? Does the team arrangement make sense in doing your law-enforcement thing?

GARY: Oh, definitely. Obviously, we're going to trust other law-enforcement officers pretty much right off the bat. We've started trusting probation. The same with pretrial services.[1] We'll tell those guys anything. We feel like we're talking to our own. But it took longer to develop relationships with the street workers.

ROB: These guys were gang members. If we told these guys something, we didn't know how far it would go. They still have close relationships with the gang.

GARY: It was not only that we didn't trust them—they didn't trust us. There were a few times one of the street workers thought I was wearing a wire. Like we were trying to set him up, and he got really paranoid, and we're like, "Whoa, relax."

ROB: As far as the team in concerned, we probably had the most trouble with the neighborhood organizer. She got too involved with some of these gang guys.

GARY: We locked this one guy up. He was out on bond, and the trial was still pending. He had a record for a whole string of crimes. We said to her, "Don't defend this guy."

AUTHOR: Did the street workers defend this guy?

GARY: No, not the street workers—the neighborhood organizer. The guy commits a homicide and then he says he quit the gang. "Okay, I'm straight. I'm behaving now." But he still has tattoos all over his body. He has the mark of the devil on his face. The police know it. The street workers know it. But the neighborhood organizer doesn't see things that way.

AUTHOR: How did you build the team relationship?

ROB: We spent time together and even socialized. We'd be in our meetings once every other week, and a lot of times we went to eat pizza afterwards. We had a picnic one time, and two or three Christmas parties. You get trust talking about the job to the street workers, and then you talk about other things.

GARY: You get to know the other team members beyond the job.

ROB: You're talking about my family and your family and stuff like that. That's where the trust comes in. I invited most of the people on the program to my wedding two years ago. You know we helped some of the street workers with personal problems, not related to the program at all. We've done stuff that the police would not normally do for them—family problems.

GARY: Some of these guys have our home phone numbers. They call us at home, twenty-four hours a day. I don't know too many policemen who are going to do that with guys from the street. That's a trust thing.

AUTHOR: What about sharing information?

GARY: You know our department is very tight lipped. That's even a problem among the police. You share as much information as you can with other police—more often with officers I know or trust, that I've worked with in the past. Some coppers call on us for assistance. Some don't. Once, there was this gang guy that escaped from Cook County Jail. They couldn't find him. Then they got the bright idea to call us. We found out where he was.

AUTHOR: The reason you were able to get this guy was because you got information from a former youth worker that we fired but who still respected what we were doing.

GARY: That's true.

ROB: He didn't know much about the guy or the escape, but he was a connection. He told us indirectly at first where to go. It was a piece of the puzzle.

GARY: Also, you know his girlfriend ended up getting charged with something. She was in custody, and depending on what's going to happen to her, we got information out of the worker.

ROB: Then, the FBI began to come to us for information. There was a kid killed outside of Little Village that we didn't know, apparently a Two Six. A gang-crime specialist put the FBI in touch with us because everybody was contacting us about gang incidents related to Little Village. As luck would have it, we knew about one of the kids involved. We helped put pieces of that puzzle together for them.

AUTHOR: You share information with the police and probation. So, what kind of information do you share with street workers?

GARY: You know, it depends on the particular street worker.

ROB: With certain street workers, we can say we're looking for the guy for murder. We're not sure he's the right guy. What can you find out about him?

GARY: Sometimes, he'll get the information we need and give it to us. But we are never going to front the street worker as a snitch. We don't want none of the workers to get harmed because of the information they give us. We're not going to jeopardize anybody's life just for a piece of information on somebody's murder or arrest.

ROB: We'll never bring that worker's name up.

GARY: That's where the cellular phone has been a great asset. They can call us on the phone, and nobody knows who talked to us. I'm never going to tell who gave me the information. That's never come up.

But it's not just that kind of information we share. Sometimes, we're out late at night or early in the morning, and we see this kid out. We get his name. He's fourteen years old. We call the street worker; we ask him, "Do you know the kid's family?" Often the worker knows the family. The street worker will talk to the kid and the family about his sneaking out of the house. We say, "He's going to get into trouble with the older guys because he hangs out with them." Either they're going to use him to hold the gun, hold the dope, steal the car, or whatever. They're going to use him. And the kid's not smart enough or he doesn't have enough self-esteem to tell them, "No." He goes along with the flow, to be one of the boys. Maybe his parents don't know what's going on out there. And I don't really have the connection with the parents. But the street worker does.

ROB: Then we got this call from Lester the street worker. The mother found a gun in the kid's bedroom and called Lester. She didn't know what to do with it. She's afraid the police are going to lock up her son. Lester calls us. I asked him, "What kind of kid is he?" He says, "A real good kid. This is the first time he ever did anything wrong. Somebody gave him the gun to hold."

So we went with Lester to the home to see if we could straighten this thing out. The mother made the kid stay home. We went to the house. We took the gun. We said we were not going to arrest the kid. After talking to the kid and to the mother, Lester recommended certain things, especially getting the kid into a different program at school, so he would go more regularly and make different friends.

We realized this kid didn't need to go to jail for his mistake. We also didn't want him to establish a record so that he could say to his gang members that he's been arrested and released. The [juvenile] court isn't going to hold him on a first offense. We didn't want the kid to say, "That's easy. I can do it again."

AUTHOR: Is there anything more on building credibility with the gang members?

GARY: You know, we have to live up to what we say. A lot of times the police officer just wants the arrest, and they'll force the kid to give up information. Then the police officer will go to the other guy and say, "He told me this about you." Not only are they putting that kid in jeopardy, but they are often trying to squeeze the guy to whom they are revealing information. They say, "Okay, now what information can you give on the first guy." We don't do that. We never do that. It puts everybody in jeopardy, and we lose our credibility. The first kid says, "I told you something in confidence, and you turn around and break that confidence. You told me you weren't going to say anything or implicate me. Maybe you said the same thing to the other guy. You're lying and making people rat on each other." If you do that you lose your credibility. We don't do that.

AUTHOR: You've got admirers among the gang kids?

GARY: I remember we stopped one of the gang kids, a while ago. He was one of the Latin King section leaders. We caught him with two bullets. That happens every day. It's no big deal. It wasn't worth our time and trouble to arrest him. Besides, we wanted to establish a relationship with him. He was well connected to the main gang leaders. I said to him, "I think you're smarter than this. We're going to take the bullets. Don't let something stupid like this happen again. Goodbye." The guy looked at us like, "Oh my God, this is incredible. Those cops didn't arrest me." Later the street workers came to us and said, "Man, he thinks you guys are the greatest. You could have put him in jail for a lot of time."

AUTHOR: So, who should be on the team in terms of types of people?

ROB: I'd like to see police and probation involved. But they have to be knowledgeable. It can't just be any policeman or probation officer. I wouldn't take any overly aggressive officer, that's for sure.

GARY: That's part of the problem, you know. When you start talking to these potential police as team members, you have to see their approach. You give them the question, "Okay, you're a police officer, and you have a kid that's caught, let's say, spray painting. What would your decision be? Lock him up for thirty days or maybe have him remove the graffiti, while his parents stand out there and watch—and make sure he goes back to school, and put him on some sort of close supervision or probation?" You have to see how hard a line an officer takes. You cannot just snap the whip on these kids. You have to give them some leeway, because otherwise it doesn't work. I mean, if they don't have the discipline at home, it's not going to change anything. We cannot be the disciplinarians. I would not put an older police officer on a project like this, because he usually doesn't have the right mentality for gang kids: "Lock all these guys up. And let God sort it out." But that does not work!

ROB: One of the bad things about this job is that we get attached to these kids and the families. We interact with the kids' families. It makes it hard sometimes, especially if we know the family well. We've had to lock guys up for murder. We knew the kid and his background. We knew what he was capable of doing, and we were hoping that it would not come to putting him away—sometimes for thirty years.

AUTHOR: What about probation officers? What kind of officers should be on the project?

GARY: They're like us. The same qualifications should apply. They can be more helpful to the kid, but they have to understand and know how tough to be with them.

AUTHOR: And the youth workers or street workers?

GARY: You definitely need them.

AUTHOR: What kind of youth worker do we need for this kind of project?

ROB: You have to check the youth workers out carefully. A good idea would be to have a balance of a former gangbanger and someone from the neighborhood who has a college education, for example, Lester. He was a member of the Latin Kings. He isn't bad. He has some good work experience. He could be a good role model for the kids. Besides, this job helps the youth worker himself go straight. He can get something out of this program that will be useful for his future.

AUTHOR: What about Frankie, the street worker who wasn't confiding in you at the beginning?

GARY: You know, believe it or not, Frankie has come around. In the beginning, he didn't want to talk to us. He didn't trust us, and he was afraid that we were going to "middle" him. It took time to build our relationship. Frankie has come around a lot. We got to help the youth workers as well as the kids.

ROB: He's not active in the gang, the same as Louie. We had to get rid of him.

GARY: You know, I think Frankie is more intelligent than Louie. He came out of prison and realized what he lost, and he decided that he ain't going back there. He would much rather get a job and have a family. His priorities have changed.

AUTHOR: It's hard to pick the right youth workers.

ROB: That's why you have to try to keep a balance, with some former gang guys and some college guys.

AUTHOR: What about the neighborhood organizer in the project?

GARY: You need a neighborhood organizer in the project, not necessarily an activist, but somebody to get the community involved.

AUTHOR: The neighborhood organizer was supposed to have three missions: to get the parents involved, to organize the agencies to work together on the problem, and to develop resources for the kids.

ROB: The neighborhood organizer we have is from Neighbors against Gang Violence. I would think she's supposed to get the neighborhood, the families, together and say, "We're going to stop this. We're going to help the police, probation. We're going to stop the violence."

I guess she could also target certain kids and families for special help. But she has to be careful about which kid she tries to help. She gets too identified with some of them, the wrong ones. We tell her not to help the hard-core guys who have been arrested four times, twice for shootings, two times for a stolen car, and we think he did a murder. That's not the kid she as a neighborhood organizer should try to help. Let's get to this other kid. He's only been arrested once, for disorderly conduct. He's in the gang, but he's on the edge, and figure out how the community can pull him out. The neighborhood organizer should do more prevention and help the community do more prevention.

GARY: She takes it on herself to worry about these kids, but she picks the wrong ones.

ROB: She also believes everything that the kids are telling her against the cops is true. They're using her. She's also trying to do the job of the youth worker and doesn't know how to do it. She's not supposed to do it.

GARY: You need a neighborhood organizer who knows the community, who has relationships with the families, who can get access to resources. She should be in a position to mainly help the street workers. She has to provide information about resources to the youth worker. He [the youth worker] works with the kids directly. She works indirectly with the kids, helping the family, helping the worker get agency resources.

ROB: The neighborhood organizer should teach the parents what to look for in their kid. Maybe their kid has just recently joined the gang, using gang colors. The neighborhood organizer should get the parents together at meetings and teach them about gangs.

GARY: Gang awareness.

ROB: Their sons are starting to join gangs; this guy is wearing his hat cocked or has different color clothes. And he comes up with a tattoo and tells his mom, "Well, that means I love you, Ma." And it's really a gang symbol.

GARY: But above all, you have to get the neighborhood organizer to involve the community, because it's their kids and the kids are the community. The family is part of the community. The neighborhood organizer and the community did not really help us out enough. There were times when we were looking for a particular individual. We were questioning people, and they would say to us, "You know, you guys just work here. But we live here. And our families live here. So, you don't know who you're questioning. There could be times when you're questioning my uncle, my aunt. You think they're going to help you? They're not going to help you. This is my community." They are kind of telling us, "We control the community. We can get away with whatever we want. This is our community."

ROB: Our neighborhood organizer never helped us enough. She gave us a few bits of information. She wanted information for her own purposes. Sometimes it was the wrong purpose, just to get these guys out of jail who should be in jail. Some of her own kids were associating with gangbangers.

GARY: Another thing—resources. The project tried to make resources available, but we caught hell from certain parts of the community and the agencies, and also our own police department. We opened up Piotrowski Park so the gang kids could play basketball. But we never heard the end of that. "These kids are playing basketball. You're doing this and that for these guys but not the good kids."

Then we would say, "What happened when the basketball game was going on? How many crimes were committed? The troublemakers were off the streets that night, and nothing happened. If you leave these kids on the streets, and you say you don't want them here and you don't want them there, they'll find something to do, and it's not going to be what you or I want them to do."

You know our Tenth District is beginning to change. Some of the cops said, "Let's open up a gym and let these kids do some boxing." This project is starting to open up the eyes of the police guys and educate them a little bit. Giving the kids something to do is not such a bad idea.

AUTHOR: Okay, the last thing is how do you organize a project like this? What do you need?

GARY: As we said before, before you get anything off the ground, you have to have resources in place—jobs, school, housing, medical, social activities—every possible thing that these kids are going to need. If you bring in empty promises, you're going to lose your credibility. They'll think you're blowing smoke.

AUTHOR: It took us two years—*two years*—to gain access to resources, so the kids could go back to school, and get jobs for these fellows.

GARY: Basically, what a lot of these kids need is somebody to keep them occupied, whether at school or on the jobs, or somebody to talk to. They could have personal problems, like with a girlfriend. She could be screaming she needs money to pay for their kid's diapers or to pay the rent. The gang guys need someone who can help them with these things. When they don't have the help, they're going to resort to stickups, sell dope, or whatever.

AUTHOR: What should we avoid doing, if the project continues?

GARY: We need a leader from the CPD. You also have to have somebody with "clout." He has to be able to carry things out. We need somebody that has authority to get things done.

ROB: We did a lot of stuff on our own, a lot of stuff.

GARY: Because we were just police officers, and not sergeants, lieutenants, commanders, it was extremely difficult. Nobody wanted to help us, because we were just patrolmen. And there's twelve thousand of us.

ROB: But we found a way to do all that had to be done.

GARY: We wanted it done. But it really has to come from the top command, first. If you don't have their blessing, it's not going to happen, or happen as well as it could. This kind of project needs a long-term commitment. We need somebody that says, "Hey, listen, we've got a long way to go. This looks like it's worth a shot. We're going to stick with it."

The two remarkable project police officers effectively described the purpose, reality, values, and problems of the project in relatively few words. They were very much part of a comprehensive community-wide approach to the gang problem, while still performing their special roles as police officers. The CPD, despite its weak commitment to the model's approach, permitted its officers to operate flexibly and as part of a multidisciplinary team deeply immersed in community-based gang control and youth development.

NOTE

1. Pretrial officers, part of a separate unit of court officers, were briefly part of the project team before they were incorporated into the regular CCDAP. The pretrial service workers were responsible for supervision of chronic and serious offenders before they went to trial or were adjudicated.

7

Community Mobilization

A major weakness of the Gang Violence Reduction Project (GVRP) was the failure to create an effective local and citywide steering committee, with strong involvement and support of the mayor's office, the Chicago Police Department (CPD), and an influential interagency coalition. The successful achievement of the program goal—the reduction of gang violence for the individual target youth, gang-as-a-unit levels, and community levels—was not sufficient to institutionalize the project model. The project was viewed by the CPD as a possible but limited means to improve local policing of gang youth and organize a local citizen or agency group to provide services and resources to help address the problem. How these two efforts were to be achieved and related to each other was not spelled out.

Everyone in Little Village seemed to accept the idea that gang violence was very serious and had to be stopped; even gang members said they were against gang violence. There seemed to be a general readiness to support the project, with its complementary roles of youth worker, police, and probation; various community agencies and community groups also expressed interest in the project. However, the concept of a local interagency or inclusive neighborhood organization to address the gang problem was not necessarily accepted. The need for a neighborhood advisory group to support project efforts was vaguely expressed in the CPD's funding proposal, but little consideration was given to its specific purpose, organizational form, responsibilities, or activities.

Existing neighborhood political and organizational interests affected the project's community-mobilization efforts around the gang problem in Little Village. This determined the nature and sequence of activities carried out (and not carried out) by the advisory committee, the project neighborhood organizer, and me. The support of external and local collaborative organizational interests and leadership interests never essentially materialized. Only limited and fragmented efforts went into the development of the community-mobilization strategy in Little Village. These deficiencies affected the efforts to sustain the project and institutionalize its approach.

CITY AND NEIGHBORHOOD POLITICS

There has been a long and distinctive tradition among established and aspiring leaders in Chicago and perhaps elsewhere of using the gang problem for political, organizational, and moral-interest purposes. Current or former gang members have been employed by local politicians—particularly in segregated or transitional low-income communities of the city—to get the vote out, intimidate opposition candidates, and to justify and promote certain local interests often unrelated to the gang problem. For politicians seeking higher office, gangs often symbolize the basis for the fight of good against evil. Political leaders, especially at election time, tend to promise stronger antigang laws and practices. Increased suppression is the primary, if not exclusive, strategy advocated, with little reference to results in the real world. Before the 1995 aldermanic election, Alderman Medrano of the Twenty-fifth Ward (which included most of Pilsen [the comparison community] but also the eastern part of Little Village) talked about his "successful attacks against the drug-peddling Ambrose gang on Eighteenth Street" (Kass 1995, 1). Ray Frias, the democratic state representative running for aldermanic office in the Twelfth Ward (enclosing the western section of Little Village) talked about "pushing through anti-gang measures in Springfield." (Aldermanic candidate Juan Rangel, in the Twenty-second Ward, said it was "time to stop making excuses for gang behavior." He portrayed the current alderman, Ricardo Munoz, as a supporter of gangs. According to newspaper reports, this was part of Chicago's "new street-gang politics." Alderman Munoz, an opponent of Mayor Daley, was a leader of liberal elements in a long-running feud with conservative Latino political elements from the Southwest Side beholden to the mayor. Both Rangel and Munoz attended the early organizing meetings of Neighbors against Gang Violence (NAGV), which was associated with the Gang Violence Reduction Project in Little Village.

Citywide and local politicians in Little Village and Pilsen were fully engaged during the electoral process. In the

> democratic mayoral primary between Daley [Mayor] and challenger Joseph Gardner, Danny Solis, director of UNO (United Neighborhood Organization) later appointed by Daley as an Alderman, stood next to his candidate, Rangel,

and shouted . . . "We didn't invite Munoz because we don't support the active recruitment of street gangs into politics, as he does." (Kass 1995, 1)

Daley and Munoz both won in their respective elections in 1995. After Medrano was forced to resign because of a conviction of criminal activity, Solis was appointed alderman of the Twenty-fifth Ward by Mayor Daley. Frias was also elected. Alderman Munoz persisted in his interest and support of NAGV and the GVRP during the project period. The aldermen of the other two wards enclosing Little Village did not express any interest in NAGV or GVRP.

The above quotes from a *Chicago Tribune* article noted that "the Rangel-Munoz feud is a blip in a much larger political war between activist Solis and the more liberal Garcia for the allegiance of the growing Latino electorate" (Kass 1995, 1). Mayor Daley consistently made it clear that his first order of business would be to control crime and protect and serve the community. The destruction of gangs would be accomplished almost exclusively through police suppression.

AGENCY INTEREST AND APPROACH

With the exception of criminal justice agencies, few organizations in Chicago in the early and mid-1990s had an interest in the gang problem, other than the use of suppression. Youth agencies were interested in the prevention of delinquency or gang membership for younger youth, mainly through recreational programs. There were no social-intervention or outreach youth-worker programs in Little Village concerned with the gang problem, although they existed in some form in other parts of the city. Schools in gang-problem neighborhoods depended on a "zero tolerance" approach, that is, surveillance, on-call police, weapons screening, school uniform requirements, and drug-free zones, as well as suspensions and expulsions. Schools focused on education for "good kids" and how to protect them from gang members and gang activity. There was little interest in the provision of special education, job training, or social services to keep gang or gang-prone youth in the regular school system.

Some recreation centers and churches in Little Village tolerated individual gang youth. They took precautions to prevent gang fights and keep troublemakers out of their buildings. The priest's or minister's role was to counsel families and youth to avoid gangs, as well as to provide memorial services for gang youth or their victims who died in turf wars. There was no special agency or church program to provide particular gangs or gang youth with a set of interrelated treatment, rehabilitation, social-development services, or controls.

Community-agency and criminal justice leaders seemed to settle on two somewhat connected approaches: (1) partially ignoring the problem, living with it, or during crises, demanding more police presence; and (2) exploiting the problem for political purposes or existing agency-program-enhancing purposes usually not directly related to the gang problem. Politicians and administrators from mental-health, youth-work, media, government, religious, and criminal justice agencies often made use of the gang problem to push their general organizational agendas. The complex nature of the gang problem was not addressed. Solutions proposed were often vague and not meaningfully targeted to specific issues of prevention or intervention. A great deal of promise, fervor, and catharsis usually accompanied sporadic neighborhood and agency pseudo-crime-control activities. Public-relations attention and moral and economic benefits often accrued to organizational leaders of these efforts, with little or no subsequent evaluation of results. The predominant organization in Chicago and Little Village addressing the gang problem was the Chicago Police Department, with its suppression approach.

NEIGHBORHOOD RESIDENTS' CONCERNS

Community groups and neighborhood residents in Little Village concerned with gang crime were not sure what to do, or whether anyone *could* do anything about the problem. Parents were often conflicted over strategies of diversion, social development, suppression, and rehabilitation for their sons (and sometimes daughters) and for the gangs in the community. They were also immobilized or distracted by their other pressing family-survival and community problems. Gang youth were sometimes part of an illegal family-income-providing system, supplementing public aid or assisting the family with drug sales. In some cases, gang membership and the gang problem were intergenerational. Fear and denial of the youth's gang problem were followed by frustration, apathy, and confusion.

A 1990 youth survey conducted by staff and students of Latino Youth (a local youth agency serving Little Village and Pilsen) examined perceptions of youth about local problems that affected their development. In a telephone sample of 353 randomly selected local youth aged fourteen to twenty-one years, many problems were articulated—unemployment, substance abuse, lack of health service, and so on. However, the respondents saw gangs as the most serious of all problems. School dropout rates, teen pregnancy, and family problems were viewed as caused by gangs. Gangs were perceived as a fact of life. At least 15 percent of all Latino youth in the area said they had been injured in gang-related activities. Most youth expected gang activity either to become worse (46 percent) or to remain the same (28 percent); only a few thought the situation would improve (17 percent). More youth in Little Village than in Pilsen thought that gangs were the most serious problem affecting their communities (70 percent and 62 percent, respectively) (Proyecto Intercambio 1990).

A survey conducted by the project's research staff at the beginning of the program in 1992–1993 with heads of households from the worst gang-violence streets in Little Village and Pilsen produced similar findings. Residents most often mentioned gangs as a problem in the community: 92.8 percent in Pilsen and 80.2 percent in Little Village. The second most frequently mentioned problem was general crime and safety: 53.2 percent in Little Village and 41.2 percent in Pilsen. Drugs and lack of services was the third set of problems most often mentioned: 31.3 percent and 28.1 percent, respectively, in Little Village; 26.8 percent and 27.8 percent, respectively, in Pilsen. These problems were mentioned more often than the economy, unemployment, ineffective parenting, alcohol, poor education, or housing (see chapter 15).

Little Village residents' efforts to address the gang problem were limited. Their marches, testimonials, and community meetings were usually sporadic, one-time affairs. Patrols of local residents formed to protect youth on the way to and from school were short lived, as were citizen efforts to aid police in detecting or controlling gang activities. Police instructed parents occasionally in how to determine whether their sons were gang members. Local citizens usually called for more police sweeps, restrictive laws, and more severe penalties for gang offenders.

CONTEXT OF THE PROJECT'S COMMUNITY ORGANIZING

The priority objective at the start of the project was the creation of a street-level team to control gang violence and provide services to target youth. These two objectives would be interrelated and become a basis for community organizing. In initial field contacts, youth were already expressing a strong need for jobs. Neighborhood-organizing activity consisted of meetings with representatives of local community agencies especially to inform them about the purpose and nature of the project, including the expressed need by gang youth for jobs. The assistant director and I spent a great deal of time contacting local employers as well as city agencies, colleges, unions, and youth agencies to inquire about opportunities for training and jobs for program youth. Suburban JobLink, Inc., a relatively new agency in Little Village, happened to be seeking local applicants for jobs in suburban factories and businesses. Special job-training, referral, educational, and social service support would probably be required for gang youth. Several local social service agencies expressed an interest in providing these services, but they did not have the resources to do so.

My requests to fund local agencies to provide services for project youth were not successful. The Illinois Criminal Justice Information Authority (ICJIA) and the CPD would not permit the project to subcontract with local organizations. Such funding arrangements should have been available from the beginning of the project. It would have served to redirect existing gang-youth programs and encourage organizations to become part of the project's interagency, community-wide effort to target the gang problem. Interagency case management directed at program youth was not possible without additional funding. The project was not in a position to serve the interests and needs of target youth and, at the same time, the related needs of local organizations for additional funds and services to be directed, presumably, to the same youth.

Existing Community-Organizations' Interests

When the project began, Little Village resident and organizational constituencies were beginning to form around neighborhood problems such as education, health, sanitation, housing, and economic development but not the gang problem. Local schools had limited interest in the gang problem and claimed they had to contend with other priority problems—poor student attendance, truancy, low educational achievement, pregnancy, drug use, and racial conflicts (African Americans versus Mexican Americans). Youth-agency directors indicated they would participate as part of a network of agencies concerned with the problem but were primarily interested in recreation and gang prevention for younger, possibly at-risk youth. A few local churches were attempting to address the gang problem, mainly through spiritual guidance for youth and their families.

The Alliance for Community Excellence (ACE)—the major local community organization with a broad coalition of local citizens, educational, social and religious organizations, public agencies, and businesses—was concerned with social, economic, educational, housing, and law-enforcement issues in both Little Village and Pilsen but not specifically with the gang problem. A confederation of Catholic churches existed in the larger Little Village and Pilsen area, but it had little interest in the gang problem, although one of the Catholic priests of the confederation established a mission in the nearby Cook County jail to meet the religious needs of prisoners, many of whom were gang members. However, pastors and ministers of three Little Village Catholic churches and a protestant evangelical community church were early and deeply interested in the gang problem and offered to provide facilities for the conduct of some of the project activities. They were willing also to assist in the development of the NAGV advisory board. The Tenth District commander recommended as an advisory group to GVRP the Tenth Police District's Neighborhood Relations Council, made up of local citizens and organizations. However, the council primarily represented the northern part of the district, comprising mainly African American residents. Latino residents and organizations in the Little Village Project area were represented by only one Mexican American, a funeral director. The council was mostly concerned with eliminating drug houses in the northern part of the district.

There appeared to be three options for initiating a community-resident and agency council to advise on the development of the project and perhaps begin to take responsibility for ownership of the GVRP and its approach. They were:

- a long-term, slow process of building interest in the gang problem through one or more of the existing coalitions—ACE, the Catholic Confederation, or the Tenth Police District Neighborhood Relations Council;
- starting up a new grassroots, local citizen, and organization coalition to develop and ultimately take responsibility for the program along with the Tenth Police District; or
- persuading the central police hierarchy to (1) take an active leadership role in the development of a comprehensive community-wide approach to the gang problem in Little Village, incorporating a broad array of agencies and community groups—local or city- and countywide, or (2) adapt and fit the Gang Violence Reduction Project approach into its community-policing program and other citizen-participation arrangements that were underway.

The project pursued all these options in the early months of operations but eventually focused on the second alternative, building a distinctive grass-roots organization around the gang problem. It grew out of the early contacts the assistant director and I had with representatives of organizations interested in the comprehensive approach who would supply services or resources to program youth. It became the feasible way to go, at least in the short term.

THE PROJECT'S ORGANIZING ACTIVITIES

Contacts were made with representatives of social service and health agencies, community groups, businesses, schools, churches, the alderman's office, and other individuals in Little Village, and to some extent outside the community, to explain the project. In this process, the assistant director and I began to identify local leaders and activists who were not only interested but also potentially willing to join in an effort to address the gang problem. Reverend Mike, from a local protestant evangelical community church, offered rooms in his church for GED or continuing-education activities, and for community meetings. The pastor of a local Catholic church indicated that a large gym in his high school could be used. Alderman Munoz recommended and provided contacts with block clubs and citizens that could be helpful.

During the early period of resource development and related community mobilization, a request was made to the Chicago Park District to use a gym in Piotrowski Park in Little Village, in Two Six territory. The request was positively acted upon, and the park recreation center became a place where project police, probation officers, youth workers, and NAGV volunteers engaged Two Six gang youth in basketball activities. At about the same time, the principal of the local high school in the Latin King territory invited project staff to explain the purpose of the project to an assembly of teachers. The session served to provide information to project staff about the scope of gang activities in the school and the immediate school area. In the days that followed, project workers helped high school security guards identify gang leaders and cool tensions, particularly in the mornings and afternoons when youths entered and left school grounds. The relationships the project staff built with school administrators later facilitated the return to school of selected Latin Kings who had been suspended or expelled.

NEIGHBORS AGAINST GANG VIOLENCE (NAGV)

Project administrators met a local community activist, Gloria Lopez, at one of the ACE meetings. At that time, she was employed as a local coordinator of services for a national alternative youth-education organization in the Chicago area. Earlier she had been an organizer for UNO but had a falling-out and was no longer connected to the organization. She had close relations with the families and churches in Little Village concerned with the gang problem. She knew the priests at Epiphany Catholic Church and Our Lady of Tepeyac Church, Rev. Mike of La Villita Community Church (protestant), and the local director of Suburban JobLink, Inc. She volunteered to bring community leaders, residents, and local organizations together to form an association to support the project. She said she could help develop resources and community contacts. With the encouragement of the project's assistant director, she quickly formed a tentative advisory group and selected a name for the potential organization—Neighbors against Gang Violence.

The project research staff, in planning a baseline community-resident and organization survey in Little Village and Pilsen, added questions that might help NAGV with its community-organizing process. The survey included a set of questions about whether Little Village residents and organizations would be interested in participating in an organization such as NAGV. Analysis of survey findings revealed that approximately 50 percent of the one hundred local residents and 25 percent of the representatives of fifty local organizations in Little Village were interested in participating in a community organization to address the gang problem.

By the early spring of 1993, Gloria and Rev. Mike became prime movers in efforts to bring the community (particularly residents and churches) together around the gang problem. A community-wide meeting was planned and extensive phone calls made to local residents and organizations inviting them to attend an open community meeting about the gang problem at La Villita Community Church. Announcements of the meeting were made in several of the Catholic churches at Sunday masses, and flyers were also distributed throughout the area by project youth workers. The spring meeting took place before the first organizing meeting of the NAGV advisory board.

A first community meeting was held at La Villita Community Church in May 1993. Approximately thirty-five people appeared, but they were mainly project police, probation officers, and outreach youth workers, along with representatives of several churches and other agencies; only seven local residents were present. A second community meeting was called and held in June 1993 and drew about sixty people, including forty local residents (six were children). Great concern was voiced at both meetings about the gang problem, especially as it affected children caught in gang cross fires. A number of suggestions were made, including the development of recreational activities for gang youth and ways to organize adult volunteers to support project activities. A small number of residents and agency representatives volunteered to participate in a block-by-block organizing effort with the aid of project police, probation, and youth workers.

Subsequently, I was able to employ Gloria and a clerical assistant from La Villita Community Church part time (twenty hours each), through the project's budget, to manage and coordinate the community-organizing effort for a three-month period, until independent funding from outside sources was obtained. Gloria and I began to solicit local foundations and government sources to obtain funds for the organizing and program-development activities of NAGV. Youth workers and the NAGV clerical assistant together were meeting with block clubs about their neighborhood gang concerns. Project youth workers were also contacting gang youth and community volunteers to assist the youth workers with athletic activities for program youth, for both the Latin Kings (at Our Lady of Tepeyac Church's gym) and the Two Six (at Piotrowski Park's gym).

Tensions quickly developed between Gloria and the clerical assistant, who claimed that most of the residents who showed up at the June meeting had been members of two block clubs that he had organized. He claimed that Gloria and Rev. Mike had no significant relationships with the block clubs. In turn, Gloria raised questions about the reliability and honesty of the clerical assistant. Suddenly, the assistant quit to accept a full-time position at a local health agency.

Meanwhile, Gloria, Rev. Mike, and a priest from Our Lady of Tepeyac had joined to assemble a coalition of representatives of local organizations and community groups who might be prepared to serve as members of the advisory board for NAGV. The first NAGV board leadership meeting took place at one of the two Boys and Girls Clubs in Little Village in late June 1993. Also represented at the meeting were the priest from St. Agnes (who became the Latino bishop of the Catholic church in Chicago), the local director of Suburban JobLink,

Inc., the directors of the two Boys and Girls Clubs, the local alderman, the local area president of UNO, and two local residents, as well as the project's assistant director, several youth workers, and me. Those present from the various organizations and the alderman's office agreed to serve as board members of NAGV. The project police and probation officers were not invited to the meeting. GVRP staff members, although in attendance, were not to be on the board. Gloria stated that NAGV would organize the community block by block to mobilize citizens to address the gang problem and help gang youth obtain various services and resources. NAGV was to be independent of the Tenth District police and the GVRP but would work closely with the project. It would make application for a nonprofit organization charter to the state and apply for funds from the city's Community Development Block Grant (CDBG). In addition, I agreed to assist with NAGV funding applications to the Chicago Community Trust and the Woods Charitable Trust.

In the application to the Woods Charitable Trust, Gloria stated that the goal of NAGV was "to reduce gang violence in the Little Village Community," and its key objectives were to

(1) establish four chapters in target areas of high gang-violence activity; (2) recruit two hundred members from the community; (3) initiate at least three activities in the four target [sub] areas that would bring together community residents, churches, block clubs, gang members, and the police; and (4) also place twenty hard-core gang members on jobs or in educational/training opportunities.

She stated that the organizing strategy was "to establish an open dialogue with community residents and gang members in order to begin the process of working together to develop social/economic opportunities and the establishment of a new consensus of acceptable behavior among all community youth." Moreover, in a special meeting in September 1993, the NAGV mission was further elaborated: "To reassimilate alienated and isolated gang members into the fabric of society by providing opportunities and offering alternatives to a gang lifestyle; to make residents and businesses aware of what they can do to help reduce gang violence; and to coordinate activities with community groups, elected officials, police, and others who are affected by gangs."

The funding applications went forward, but in the next two months there was little organizing effort to involve residents, businesses, or local agencies in any

NAGV activities. Rev. Mike, along with project police and probation officers, frequently attended and participated in basketball games of Two-Six gang youth at Piotrowski Park. At this time, Gloria was almost exclusively interested in the development of the Latin King basketball program at Tepeyac church, which the project youth workers had initiated and conducted over the previous six months. She requested transfer to NAGV of responsibility for supervision of the Latin King basketball games at Tepeyac church, saying she and a volunteer could manage these twice-a-week activities. I accepted the arrangement and directed the youth workers to gradually withdraw from the gym; they were to confine their efforts largely to hard-core gang youth on the streets.

Gloria continued to make applications for funding with various foundations and agencies, most of which were turned down. (I applied to the U.S. Department of Education for funding for both NAGV and project activities but was turned down also.) However, she did obtain $1,400 from a local bank to fund a retreat to bolster NAGV's development as an independent community organization. She visited a variety of social agencies and community groups to stimulate support for NAGV, but the nature of NAGV's collaboration with other local agencies or organizations in regard to the gang problem was not clear.

Attendance was sparse at the NAGV board meetings at La Villita church in October 1993. Gloria, Rev. Mike, and some project youth workers were present, as were the director of the No Dope Express Foundation and the director of an organization called United In Peace, who were both soliciting interest and local organizational participation in a national gang summit to be held in Chicago later in the month. Mainly representatives from African American churches as well as African American gangs and activist organizations on the south side of Chicago were expected to be present at the gang summit. The two directors were seeking the participation of Latino organizations. Gloria, Rev. Mike, and the project's assistant director agreed to attend the summit as observers. Later, according to Reynaldo, the summit focused on issues of poverty, racism, and police brutality. There was no significant discussion about collaboration among Latino and African American community organizations around the gang problem.

At another October NAGV meeting, Gloria reported that she had met with the director of the city's Youth Development Task Force. She was told that the mayor was not supportive of NAGV and what it was doing. The Chicago Department of Human Resources, under instructions from the mayor, was

planning to provide Community Development Block Grant funding for a variety of organizations concerned with the gang problem but only for prevention
programs. NAGV was not included. According to Gloria, the close involvement
of NAGV with the GVRP and Chicago Police Department was not regarded as
consistent with the mayor's approach. Gloria arranged a NAGV overnight retreat at a Catholic seminary in Chicago's northern suburbs in November 1993.
Its purpose was to initiate "a process, structure, and set of programs of community mobilization involving local residents and organizations to deal with
the gang problem." However, only a small group of eleven attended, including Gloria, Rev. Mike, an outside conference facilitator, a Tenth Police District
neighborhood-relations officer, two project youth workers, the project's assistant director, and me, two local citizens, and a target gang youth who was also
a leader of one of the major factions of the Latin Kings in Little Village. Key
Little Village community groups and local agencies were not represented.

In a series of discussions, the conference facilitator helped the attendees
identify NAGV's strengths, weaknesses, and pressing concerns. In her summary
report of these discussions, the strengths of NAGV were identified as "strong
vision," "association with youth workers," "ability to communicate with families," "intermediary with various organizations," and (community) "need for
NAGV services." The pressing concerns were "the perception that NAGV was
too close to gang members, according to the police," "too close to the police,
according to gang members," "lack of economic opportunities for gang youth,"
and "exploitation of the gang issue by various organizations." The weaknesses
of NAGV were viewed as "lack of community involvement," "lack of organizational structure," "lack of a clear mission," and "limited funding and staffing."

At the retreat, a critical issue also discussed was whether NAGV should focus
on developing itself as a separate service organization or a coordinating organization relating the services and programs of various local agencies on behalf
of target gang youth. It was agreed that these issues would be carefully considered. Gloria and Rev. Mike, however, were already moving in the direction of
building a service organization for gang youth and gang families. Gloria emphasized that she wanted to work closely with the pastor of Epiphany Catholic
Church to involve Two Six gang youth and their families in its church-related
activities. In the next six months, several NAGV service and organizing efforts
took place. Gloria obtained two slots for project gang youth to go to a special
leadership-training camp in Boston. The Chicago Community Trust provided

a twenty-five-thousand-dollar grant to NAGV for organizing activities, based on my strong recommendation. One of the senior project youth workers was assigned to work with NAGV to help establish a network of agencies and services directed to the interests and needs of gang youth and their families. Some of the local agencies began to express interest in NAGV and attended a meeting at La Villita church (where the NAGV office was now located). Gloria conducted a series of meetings with parents of the Two Six gang youth to raise consciousness and educate parents about the gang problem. Parents were particularly interested in how the justice system operated and what it meant when their sons were placed on probation.

In early 1994, Gloria, as a part-time organizer on the project's payroll, was requested to emphasize the community-organizing efforts of both NAGV and the GVRP. Gloria's task was specifically to focus on arranging monthly meetings of agency representatives and residents, not only to discuss program and treatment needs for project gang youth, but also to prepare for a proposed mass meeting of community residents and gang youth about the work of NAGV and the GVRP. She arranged a press release (dated July 13, 1994) about a planned memorial service and community mass meeting on July 14. The press release encouraged "all residents who have lost family, friends, or acquaintances to gang violence, including current gang affiliates, to attend.... 'We want the gang members to feel like members of the community.... We want other residents to respect their neighbors. We don't necessarily want to get rid of the gangs—just the gang-related violence,' explained [Gloria]."

The meeting developed into a large community event. The memorial service took place at St. Agnes church. Approximately two hundred community residents attended, including parents and gang youth, mainly Latin Kings (St. Agnes was in Latin King territory). Two members of the Two Six gang were also present, protected by project youth workers, police, and probation officers who were stationed both inside and outside the meeting hall. Some of the older Latin King leaders attempted to disrupt the meeting because the Two Six youth were present, but the Latin King youth workers and police intervened to prevent a melee and any violence. Reporters of several major city and Spanish-language newspapers were present. An account of the memorial service appeared in the English and Spanish press in the following days.

Subsequently, Gloria and the project youth workers were invited to participate in radio and television programs. Reports of the work of the project and NAGV began to appear in the national media. NAGV board meetings increased in frequency in the fall of 1994, and board attendance improved. Epiphany Catholic Church (located in Two Six territory) was particularly active in preparations for the Day of the Dead marches in the western part of the neighborhood in early November. Many Two-Six gang youth, along with their families, were involved in the community march, which ended up at the church. Again, project youth workers, police, and probation officers were present.

In the early winter of 1994, the governor of Illinois visited Little Village and publicly announced the award of a forty-thousand-dollar State Drug Prevention Agency grant to NAGV. The Woods Charitable Trust, however, turned down the NAGV application for funds because it claimed that NAGV represented essentially a one-person agency, had little citizen involvement, and was primarily concerned with the development of a service agency rather than community organizing (a requirement of the trust). At about the same time, a nonprofit organization charter was granted to NAGV by the state of Illinois, with Gloria as chairperson and Rev. Mike as cochair.

Gloria hired an assistant to provide family services, and she continued to develop her mothers' group meetings. There were few NAGV board meetings in the winter and early spring of 1994–1995. I pressured Gloria to call an interagency meeting, and it finally took place at La Villita church in April 1995. Representatives of five local organizations concerned with the Little Village gang problem attended—Piotrowski Park, Latino Youth, Farragut High School, Catholic Charities, and Mujeres Latinas (a Latina mothers and girls organization providing day care)—as well as representatives of the Tenth Police District Neighborhood Relations Unit, and project police, probation officers, and youth workers. Each of the representatives of the community agencies offered information about programs and services that they could make available to gang youth. The organizations agreed to continue meeting to exchange information about target and problem gang youth in their own programs. Many of the project youth were known to the agencies, and joint or collaborative programming was recommended. Progress toward an interagency program effort in regard to the gang problem seemed to be developing. However, NAGV made no additional planning or follow-up calls for meetings, and no mechanism was created for sharing information about gang youth for specific service collaboration.

NAGV Crises

A series of crises occurred in June 1995, which had long-term consequences for the development of NAGV. Gloria focused more and more on the delivery of services to families and individual gang youth. She referred neighborhood youth for jobs; a few were project target youth. Tensions developed between Gloria and some of the project youth workers; she believed that the youth workers should refer more youth to the NAGV program. The Tepeyac church gym program (now conducted by the NAGV) was suddenly closed down by the pastor, due to lack of adequate supervision by Gloria and her volunteer staff. Apparently, Latin King vehicles were parked illegally near the church and they created a good deal of noise; neighbors complained to the church and the police about a possible gang meeting in the church.

Gloria, without consulting me, suddenly decided to conduct a graffiti paint-out involving Latin Kings. She inappropriately selected a "hot" border street between the Latin Kings and Two-Six turfs for the paint-out. The youth participating were provided with T-shirts with an NAGV logo. The event was to be a way of advertising the work of NAGV to the community. A young, inexperienced project probation officer (a friend of Gloria's) assisted with paint-out preparations. project youth workers, the two project police officers, and the two other probation officers were not involved in the planning or implementation of the event. Gloria herself was not present, although her volunteers were. In the course of the paint-out, two of the Latin King youth broke away from the group, jumped into a car, and "did a drive-by" at a nearby school yard in Two Six territory. A Two Six youth was shot and wounded. Another youth (not a gang member) standing next to a Two Six was killed.

I complained about the lack of preparation by NAGV for the event and insisted that there had to be close supervision by Gloria of her NAGV staff and volunteers, and coordination with project personnel. Project police and youth workers had to be present at any further graffiti paint-outs; the buildings and streets selected for the paint-outs had to be well within the territory of a particular gang and not on the borders or the flash points of the two opposing gangs. Further, I demanded that the number of gang members selected for any paint-out be small—no more than ten to fifteen youth, and not the forty or fifty present on that day.

Shortly after the tragic incident, the mother of the youth killed sued NAGV and La Villita Community Church. The state's attorney required NAGV staff to testify in court against several of the Latin Kings who were involved. At the same time, NAGV began to have increased funding difficulties. The state grant was not renewed, largely because Gloria did not submit reports of NAGV's activities or an accounting of how funds had been used. The NAGV board was also suddenly concerned that Gloria had been drawing substantial funds from both the state grant and her project part-time job, without board clearance. Questions were raised about "double dipping."

Tension began to develop between Gloria and Rev. Mike because of the graffiti paint-out incident. Nevertheless, they continued their collective NAGV fundraising and organization-building efforts. A breakfast meeting at the end of July 1995 brought together a variety of local organizations, including representatives of Catholic and Protestant churches, Suburban JobLink, Inc., Latino Youth, Mt. Sinai Hospital, Ridgeway Boys and Girls Club, Mujeres Latinas, Farragut High School, and the Santa Fe Corporation, which had a large transportation center in the area. Local agency and community concerns about gangs and the gang problem were discussed. The representative of the Santa Fe Corporation indicated interest in providing funds to NAGV, but apparently did not follow through.

Violence between the gangs was high during the summer of 1995. Efforts by the project youth workers to bring the leaders of the two gangs together to arrange a peace were only partially successful. Joint meetings between NAGV and GVRP staff were held. Members of the two gangs expressed interest in coming together with community residents to discuss their needs for training and jobs. Such a meeting would be an opportunity for the community residents again to talk and complain to gang youth about their violent activities and the property damage they caused, as well as to make offers to them for training and job help. Where to hold such a meeting—when the community gang situation was so volatile—was a problem. Requests to meet at the nearby Cook County Criminal Court building were denied by the presiding judge.

By the end of the third year of project operations, the organizing efforts of NAGV continued to be few and sporadic. Gloria apparently had little interest in interagency coordination and broadscale community organizing. Her expressed concern was now to establish her own service agency. Her ties, initially stronger with the Two Six than Latin King youth and families, began to weaken. A group of Two Six youth accused her of "ratting" to the police. At the same time, tensions between project police and Gloria increased. She charged that the project police were falsely accusing a (nonproject) gang youth of a shooting he had not committed. The project police were also becoming distrustful of some of Gloria's efforts; they claimed she was organizing neighbors against the police.

Gloria began to expand her gang-related and youth-development activities across a variety of social agencies and churches elsewhere in the city. She developed close relationships with a YMCA program of outreach recreational activity for gang youth on the north side. She also took a part-time job at the Juvenile Detention Center of the Cook County Juvenile Court. Still, Gloria continued to conduct local community meetings at La Villita church. In December of 1995, a meeting to discuss the needs of gang youth for education, training, and jobs—and also the reduction of gang activity, especially violence and graffiti—was finally held. The gang youth present (mainly older gang youth) were almost exclusively interested in vocational training and job opportunities. Gloria and several citizens present promised to find an instructor to provide basic vocational carpentry training. Gang youth also said that they were concerned about the graffiti problem, particularly since it was a stimulus to gang violence, which they were trying to control. There was little overt hostility expressed between the Latin Kings and Two Six, who sat opposite each other, but there were angry and suspicious looks between gang members and community residents. Concerns about gang violence and the issue of a specific peace between the two gangs were muted; focus was on the needs of youth for training and jobs. Gloria said she would involve both gang youth and residents in planning for a vocational training project.

At a follow-up meeting at La Villita church in late February 1996, representatives of several agencies were in attendance, including Latino Youth and Suburban JobLink, Inc., and a large group of older gang youth (seventeen Latin Kings and eight Two Six). Each of the agencies indicated that they could provide training and job opportunities, but the main interest of the gang youth was in Gloria's plan to invite an instructor to La Villita church to conduct a half-year carpentry training session that would lead to some form of apprentice licensing. In March, the carpentry instructor began to hold sessions, but attendance dwindled after two meetings. At the third session the instructor refused to continue because his wallet had been stolen. In early June 1996, Gloria declared that because of lack of funding from foundation and government sources, she could no longer continue efforts to organize the community. I began to use youth workers to enlist selected storekeepers and residents in the area (where

frequent gang shootings were occurring) to provide job and recreational opportunities, as well as offering to coordinate their concerns with project police
efforts to control gang-youth violent activities. In late June 1996, I sent a letter
to Gloria notifying her that project funds for her employment would terminate
in July 1996. I stated that I hoped to transfer the project to a community agency
or network of organizations, or to have the CPD take over. I asked Gloria to
provide her views about the strengths and weaknesses of GVRP's and NAGV's
related organizing efforts.

Gloria stated in her report that

> the churches continued to offer night basketball at Our Lady of Tepeyac, St. Agnes,
> and La Villita Community Church. The Epiphany Catholic Church attempted to
> offer group discussion services to the Two Six, but this was discontinued because
> there was little attendance. Parents of Two Six, however, did continue attending a
> support group at the Epiphany church. However, their commitment was stronger
> to the church than to any community organization....
>
> The community continued to have a tough time coming to grips with the
> gang problem and creating alternatives for gang youth. Basically, they still were
> afraid of gang youth and viewed them as troublemakers....
>
> Two agencies were providing additional services to gang youth. Mt. Sinai
> Hospital was offering a tattoo-removal program with counseling for gang youth.
> Latino Youth remained involved, mainly through its alternative high school.
> However, the Boys and Girls Clubs and Piotrowski Park were still mainly in-
> terested in younger youth, five to thirteen years old—they provided no special
> programming for gang youth—and Farragut High School, under its new prin-
> cipal, was expelling more gang members than ever.

INSTITUTIONALIZING THE PROJECT

In late 1996, I announced I would be leaving at the end of August 1997 to
take another assignment. I urged the CPD to continue the project as part of
ongoing police operations with the assistance of a consortium of agencies.
The CPD was noncommittal but decided to renew the University of Chicago
contract and continue the project for another six months, to give itself more
time to decide what it wanted to do. The present round of funding was available
for another three years, if the CPD wanted to sign on.

In late October 1996, Rev. Mike offered to replace Gloria as part-time community organizer for the project; he would also sustain NAGV activities. He

agreed to draw together a group of community leaders and organization representatives to assist with the project transition, to work with neighborhood groups at the block level to support project operations, and to assist in the development of project resources, especially training and job opportunities for project youth. He indicated that he would attend all project meetings and became intimately involved in its day-to-day operations.

Rev. Mike contacted the NAGV board to explain his new role. However, like Gloria, he seemed to be less interested in contacting and coordinating community groups and agencies than in supervising and ultimately taking responsibility for the project's outreach youth workers. He did arrange one community meeting of agencies and local groups to develop a more active and coordinated approach to the gang problem but suddenly could not attend. He had to leave town, and I conducted the meeting. At the meeting were the alderman, representatives of Victory Outreach (a religiously oriented drug-rehabilitation program), Mt. Sinai Hospital, the Little Village Community Chamber of Commerce, Spry School, a regional evangelical protestant church youth director, and project staff. None of the Catholic church's priests or their representatives attended. Project police and probation officers were not present, although two youth workers were. Various agency and organization representatives did not know much about what the others were doing in regard to gang-related services. The meeting was used mainly to introduce the representatives of the agencies and groups to each other. They described their respective programs and offered to provide services to program youth. Plans for a follow-up meeting were to be developed by Rev. Mike upon his return. This did not happen.

Community-organization efforts thereafter were mainly concerned with issues and options for transferring the project to a local agency (see chapter 16). A final citizens meeting was arranged by Rev. Mike in the spring of 1997 to protest the Chicago Police Department's possible termination of the project. The meeting was poorly attended. Only Rev. Mike's small church staff, twelve local residents, and three project youth workers were present. An organized protest effort did not materialize.

In the final analysis, the efforts of the GVRP and NAGV were insufficient to develop an effective, coordinated local agency and neighborhood-organizing effort to address the gang problem. The priority concerns of established community leadership were other basic social problems such as education, business development, health, and sanitation. Local citizen-group and local agency coordination efforts were weak. The community-mobilization strategy should have been better developed by NAGV organizers. Both NAGV and GVRP lacked the support and direction of influential local community and citywide leaders. The fragmentation of local political and county/city criminal justice–system leadership contributed to the weakness of local community-mobilization efforts in respect to the gang problem.

My decision to base community mobilization efforts mainly on the capacity and motivation of a grassroots group was not a good one. Local community and agency leaders struggled to develop resources and support for their ongoing programs or other local community interests. Often these struggles were related to the enhancement of personal leadership status or additional income. Fierce competition among local groups and agencies and politicians to develop their own distinctive programs made it very difficult to achieve collaboration around a common set of gang-program objectives unless outside community resources, direction, or influence were provided.

City or community-wide leadership might have been in a position to provide resources and direction to develop and support a local community, comprehensive gang-program initiative but only if the interest of outside leadership such as the mayor's office, the city council, the catholic archdiocese, the public school system, the Welfare Council, and the criminal justice system were engaged. Substantial outside leadership interest was never achieved. The community-organizing and organizational-change-and-development strategies of the Little Village comprehensive gang-program model were only partially realized.

Evaluation: Program Analysis and Project Outcome

8

The Project Evaluation Model

We do not attempt to review the evaluation literature on gang (or gang-violence) prevention, intervention, suppression, or comprehensive programs. A growing list of such reviews exists (Curry 1995; Decker 2003; Howell 2000; Klein 1995; Mihalic et al. 2001; Reed and Decker 2002; Sivilli, Yin, and Nugent 1995; Spergel 1995). Gang programs in earlier decades have emphasized mainly single-strategy approaches to gang prevention or intervention. Evaluations of these programs suggest negative, indeterminate, or in a very few cases, limited positive results (Howell 2000). Community-based gang programs have failed for a range of reasons: poor conceptualization, vague or conflicting objectives, weak implementation, goal displacement, and politicization (Klein 1971; Spergel 1972). The evidence that a particular approach does or does not work, however, may be due not only to failures of program design or implementation but also to failures of public policy and the limitations of evaluation-research methodologies (Curry 1995; Decker 2003). Most gang-program approaches viewed as successful by community leaders, politicians, and policy makers may, in fact, not be successful but continue due to prevailing community myth and agency interests. Evaluation research that shows negative or no results usually has had little or no impact on ongoing policy or gang-program development. This may be due not only to the complexities of public policy and organizational interests but also to the complexities and difficulties of designing and implementing effective community-based gang-program evaluations, especially of comprehensive programs.

EVALUATION ISSUES

Models for evaluations of gang-intervention programs have not been clearly developed or adequately tested. Key questions remain about the nature and effectiveness of gang projects, including the strategies employed and the roles of detached gang (or community) youth workers, criminal justice, social-agency, and community-group personnel and their collaborative arrangements for addressing the youth gang problem. Process-and-outcome elements of gang programs have not been adequately identified and analyzed. The following are some of the program-process questions that continue to exist, particularly relevant to the development of comprehensive gang programs:

- What is the specific gang problem addressed?
- Who has taken primary responsibility for developing and conducting an interagency, community-wide, and grassroots approach to the problem?
- How closely are criminal justice agencies involved with youth agencies, community groups, and former gang members in addressing the gang problem?
- Are former gang members effective in dealing with gangs?
- To what extent are police and other suppression workers themselves engaged in social-intervention practice?
- Are schools engaged in interagency programs in dealing with gang youth, other than through "zero tolerance," suspension, and expulsion practices?
- Are training and job programs targeted to gang youth effective?
- And to what extent is counseling, suppression, or a combination of the two effective with gang youth and, if so, under what conditions?

Problems of Research Design

Gang program researchers generally have not addressed basic characteristics of gang youth and gang programs, which is essential for evaluation purposes. They have not fully specified relevant demographic, family, gang, social-space, and criminal-background factors of youth. They have not developed procedures for gathering information about these factors from multiple data sources (e.g., police, court, local citizens, and gang members themselves). Appropriate comparison groups may not have been found, selected, or developed. Particular program services, strategies, and worker activities directed to youth have not been identified and carefully measured. Multivariate analyses of the interrelationship of critical variables have not usually been emphasized. Findings of what street workers and police do with different kinds of gang youth, and with what results, have not been developed (Schubert and Richardson 1976; Sivilli, Yin, and Nugent 1995; Eccles and Gootman 2002).

There are special policy issues related to how, and which, gang youth are selected for inclusion in gang programs, as well as for the program evaluations: Who is a gang member, based on what definition? What is the specific nature of the crime or criminal pattern of the gang member? How equivalent—based on key demographic, gang-membership, gang-identification, and prior-arrest histories—are youth in the comparison and program groups? (There is a tendency in gang-program evaluations to select less-delinquent comparison youth, since more equivalent or serious-delinquent comparison youth may not be "knowable" or accessible to the researcher.) How representative are program gang youth of the community's gang population? And how representative of the program youth sample are the youth in the actual evaluation? There are many types of policy, program, and data-gathering problems connected with answering these questions.

The evaluations have not been characterized by strong research design. Early and even recent gang-program evaluations do not necessarily determine whether the gang programs succeed in reducing gang crime at the individual-youth level (Berleman 1969; Berleman, Seaberg, and Steinberg 1972), let alone at the gang or community levels, or between or among these levels. Only gross measures of change in patterns of delinquency, and sometimes of serious crimes such as homicides, have been used. Different types and combinations of types of youth gang crime usually have not been adequately assessed. Multivariate analyses, when conducted, have lacked controls for different types of gang offenders for whom different worker-strategies might have been more or less effective. Differential organizational and interorganizational, policy, and community effects possibly contributing to individual program-youth outcomes have not been explored.

The present examination of the Little Village Gang Violence Reduction Project addresses many complex dimensions of gang-program development. We inquire into the specifics of the activities and strategies of the project outreach youth workers, police, probation officers, and neighborhood organizers and their relation to outcomes for particular types of gang youth. A range of carefully constructed measures of police arrest and self-report variables is used. The influence of important intervening variables—such as changes in gang membership, family, school, job, peer, and community factors—are introduced into the analyses. We describe and analyze factors that determined

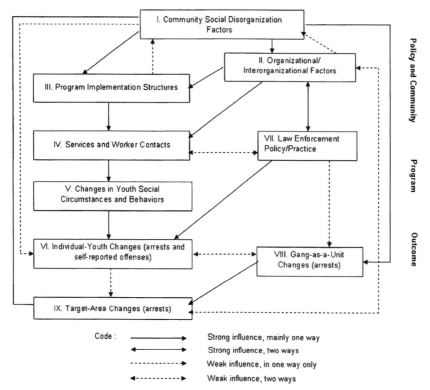

FIGURE 8.1
Project evaluation model: Interactive and feedback levels of effort (top down).

success or failure—not only of the comprehensive gang program but also of its institutionalization in Chicago.

COMPONENTS OF THE EVALUATION MODEL
The project evaluation model (figure 8.1) was based on the relationship of general community-disorganization and policy factors that interact with and affect factors at the local community level, including organizational and interorganizational relationships, program structure, worker and service contracts, normative changes in youth life-space/life-course behaviors, and law-enforcement policies and practices. Program activities are viewed as directly affecting the outcome behavior of individual youth and, probably less directly, gang- and community-level gang-crime changes.

A variety of assumptions are made and suppositions proposed, particularly about program effects on individual youth. Our analysis is more rigorous at the program-effects level, yet program statistical findings cannot be understood without consideration of policy and community-level conditions and constraints that we have described, mainly in narrative terms.

Community Social Disorganization (Assumption)

Certain economic, social, cultural, and political conditions and policies over time create the community circumstances favorable to the development of the gang problem, including family crises and groups of youth engaged in violence, drug selling, and other criminal activities. The generating circumstances include

- rapid movement, expansion, or shift of population (particularly of low-income minority groups) into a relatively segregated and class-segmented area, as a stable, middle-class, or nonminority population declines;
- concentration of a large, adolescent-male, minority population weakly integrated into formal socialization, educational, and employment systems in the community; and
- development of substructures and subcultures providing alternate criminal opportunities.

Organizational and Interorganizational Factors (Assumption)

Local social organizations, agencies, and institutions are unable adequately to accommodate the interests and needs of low-income, minority, unstable populations that require increased access to services, social (including educational) and economic (job) opportunities, and controls on youth who are in gangs or at high risk for gang membership. Key city, county, and local governmental and nongovernmental agency leadership and interests do not coalesce to address these problems. The nature and extent to which key organizations are included in the development of the program and agree on strategies determines program structure-and-process development and any eventual success in reducing gang crime, especially violence.

Program-Implementation Structures (Hypothesis)

An advisory or steering committee is established, comprising key leaders of government and local organizations (including criminal justice and social agencies, grassroots and community-based groups, businesses, and religious groups), which advises on policy and generally supports the program. The program structure is based on an interrelated set of strategies of community mobilization, outreach youth services, provision of social opportunities, suppression and social control, and relevant organizational change and development. A key component of the program structure is an interagency street team to serve gang youth.

Worker Contacts and Services (Hypothesis)

A team of police, probation officers, and (particularly) outreach youth workers and neighborhood organizers is established to target eligible youth. The team members are expected to collaborate and provide a range of services, opportunities, and controls for the targeted youth. Training and especially jobs, school, and treatment resources have to be available to the team in their work with youth.

Changes in Youth Behaviors and Circumstances (Hypothesis)

Key objectives for the workers are to influence the attitudes and behaviors of program youth and to modify their social circumstances, including their relationships to other gang members and nongang youth, family, girlfriends or wives, school, jobs, and their community, and also their life-space/life-course aspirations and expectations. Activities on behalf of program youth involving family, neighbors, social agencies, schools, employment sources, and criminal justice authorities are provided by workers in coordination with each other (to the extent possible).

Individual-Youth Outcome (Hypothesis)

Changes in the attitudes and behaviors of program youth are expected to result in a reduction of criminal behavior, particularly violence and drug use or drug selling, relative to reductions for similar, nonserved youth. Different worker contacts and services are also expected to impact program gang youth differently, depending on demographic factors (especially age), length of exposure to the program, and arrest history.

Law-Enforcement Policy and Practice (Hypothesis)

The project police unit is expected to modify its single-minded suppression approach to include a commitment to social intervention and improved neighborhood and family relationships. The effects of the modified police-team approach are expected to feed back and contribute to changes in district tactical police practices in regard to the youth gang problem and result in improved understanding, better intelligence, and more effective but not necessarily increased numbers of arrests.

Gang-as-a-Unit Crime Change (Hypothesis)

While the program is expected to directly influence program-youth behavior, it will also contribute to change in criminal behavior at the gang-as-a-unit level. Not only violence arrests of program youth but also to some extent violence arrests of the target gangs are expected to be reduced.

Community-Area Crime Change (Hypothesis)

Based on the perceptions of citizens and organizations, as well as on official crime statistics, gang-violence rates are expected to be reduced in the target community relative to violence rates in the comparable, nonserved gang-problem communities over the same program period.

RESEARCH DESIGN

Ideally, comprehensive gang-program evaluations should be designed to assess program process, individual outcome, and the program's impact on the gang and the community—and their interrelationships—based on an explicit (hopefully well-developed) model that is theoretically relevant and operationally practicable. The program evaluator's primary purpose, however, is not to test gang causal, developmental, or control theory but rather to test a program model, which usually contains references to elements of several theories. Effective gang programs in the real world may also not be based on one set of gang prevention, intervention, or suppression theories or policies. Program evaluation is a particularly difficult challenge for social scientists, including criminologists, who are often more interested in testing basic theoretical propositions than in describing the specific nature and determining the effects of an intervention model, especially a comprehensive gang-program model.

Program goals, objectives, structural components, and activities that may reduce gang-delinquent or criminal behavior, especially violence, need to be specified and understood by the program operator, key influentials (including funders and community leaders), and especially the evaluator; for example, which key-agency services and worker contacts are to be provided, and which project activities are expected to produce what intended results, for which youth. Research variables, that is, independent, mediating, outcome, and controlling factors (e.g., youth demographics, gang-membership status, and delinquency or crime characteristics), must be articulated and related to the program model, as well as conditioned by the reality of program structure and operations. Ultimately, the main job of the evaluator is to know not only what the intended program goals, objectives, structural components, and activities are but also what they really do in the program and what the results are.

Ideally, gang-program research should be experimental, with random selection of subjects and random assignment of treatment modalities, in which intervention or independent and mediating variables are controlled. This is very difficult, if not impossible, to achieve in certain kinds of community-based gang program research. At best, the Little Village gang-program evaluation was to be prospective and quasiexperimental, with room for limited change in research design and tactics within the constraints of program-development procedures, community conditions, and access to gangs and their members. Some criteria of quasiexperimental gang-program research were met: appropriately defined and targeted program youth; use of nonserved comparison gang youth; and comparable gangs and gang-violent communities. Random selection of subjects and random assignment of different program-service or control activities were not possible in the open community.

Sampling

An assessment of a community's actual gang problem should be the basis for determining the violence and violence-prone universe from which to select the gang-program youth sample. Specific characteristics of the universe of gangs, and their location in a particular community, should be established based on police data; surveys/observations of gang youth; other criminal justice, school, youth-agency, and media information; and occasionally community resident and organization surveys. The program manager, funder, and evaluator should know that youth in the program are representative of gang youth who are violent or are at high risk for violent gang behavior.

An essential task of the evaluator in quasiexperimental gang research is to select a comparison-group sample, that is, nonserved youth with characteristics similar or equivalent to the program youth. Finding, selecting, and interviewing appropriate comparison youth may not be easy. Police, probation, and youth agencies often have insufficient information about the gang youth selected for the program, and even less information about who appropriate comparison gang youth are and where or how to find them. Probably the best solution to the problem of obtaining or developing similar, let alone equivalent, samples in the open community is to use several types of comparison groups. Co-arrestee gang members from the same gangs often have similar characteristics; youth from the same-named gangs in an equivalent gang area in the same city may be sufficiently comparable; and a comparison gang from a comparable city may create special problems for analysis, unless community-context factors are controlled. The selection of comparison youth from the same or other equivalent gangs or local communities assumes that gang patterns, local community contexts, and police practices have been comparable during the preprogram and program periods, which may or may not be the case. Appropriate measurement and multivariate analytic techniques with controls can, within limits, compensate for differences between program and comparison youth, gangs, and communities.

Data Sources

Multiple sources of data and different units or levels of analysis have to be considered in community gang-program research. The individual youth's self-report and arrest data, gang- and community-level gang incident or arrest data, as well as ethnographic observations of field situations have to be gathered, as they are necessary for interpreting the findings of program research, particularly in respect to individual-youth change. Field observations and police arrest or individual-youth-interview data alone may not be sufficient for program evaluation. The use of either field observations or police or self-report data as a primary basis for determining program effects—unrelated to what the worker specifically does with a particular youth—is also not adequate for policy or program-development purposes, although such has been the tradition in gang-program evaluation (Miller 1957; Klein 1971; Short and Strodtbeck 1965; Decker 2003).

Worker-service or program-tracking records have to be created to describe the key program activities or worker contacts provided to (received by) program youth. Existing agency records (whether police, probation, or social-agency) may be inadequate or insufficient for purposes of testing the program model. Evaluators of comprehensive gang programs must develop commonly understood terms for use among different types of project-related agency workers—terms that also take organizational missions and worker roles into consideration. Common definitions across program-worker activities must be established, since services or contacts may have different meanings and purposes in different agencies and across different worker disciplines. Data from multiple agency and worker sources have to be meaningfully integrated for analysis.

The definition of collaboration or coordination among workers and agencies in the provision of services and controls is important in assessing the effects of a comprehensive gang program. Patterns of coordination are important measures of program objectives that contribute to program outcome. Data on program effects also have to include the types and dosages of services provided by the different workers to different gang youth. Measures are needed to determine changes over time in the youth's identification with the gang, his gang-membership status (rank in the gang, level of gang participation, and time spent with gang or nongang friends), gang victimization, gang involvement of parents or siblings, and so forth. Finally, a typology of gang youth may be important in discovering which kinds of services are most effective with which kinds of gang youth, for example, youth with different offense histories.

Analysis Considerations

The effectiveness of a comprehensive community-wide gang program must be determined and judged within a framework of changing public policy, community structures, and interorganizational relationships, as well as the contributions of program strategy, staffing arrangements, and service effects to the reduction of gang crime, especially violence. Not only must the program predict a reduction in violence for program gang youth but also for the target gangs and the community as a whole. Further, the program, if successful, is expected to lead to institutional change in which the components of the comprehensive community-wide program are sustained, if not elaborated.

In the following chapters we discuss a sequence of analyses and how they were constructed. First, a process of change in the life space and life course of program youth during the five-year program period is described. The extent to which these specific changes are related to a reduction in certain types of gang deviant or criminal behavior is examined, using both self-reported offense and arrest data. A more systematic and rigorous multivariate analysis is used to account for the effects of the program in changing the level of arrests between the matched preprogram and program periods for program and comparison youth, controlling for age, program exposure time, and preprogram-period arrests. How contacts by different workers contributed to life-course changes of program youth is also discussed. Further, we analyze the effects of different service patterns on reducing criminal behavior, especially violence, for different kinds of program youth, depending on their patterns of career arrest.

Finally, we describe gang-crime pattern changes of the target gangs compared to the nontarget gangs in Little Village and gang-crime pattern changes in Little Village, overall, compared to changes in similar gang-problem communities in Chicago over the same time periods. The consequences and implications of these changes for action by community organizations and the Chicago Police Department in controlling the program and institutionalizing the comprehensive, community-wide gang-program model are considered. Certain lessons are learned. A summary of the analyses is provided.

9

Changes in Social Context of Program Youth

We were interested in the gang youths' perceptions of changes in their relationship to community, family, gang, school, job, girlfriend or wife, and other relationship factors associated with possible changes in their behavior during the five-year program period. We viewed program youth as undergoing a series of life-space and life-course changes that might or might not have been influenced by the program. In the next chapter, we will focus on those factors specifically predictive of self-reported deviancy pattern changes.

PROGRAM YOUTH INTERVIEWS

We discuss findings relevant to 127 program youth from the Latin Kings and Two Six who were interviewed three times (time I, time II, and time III) at approximately one-year intervals during the program period. Of the original total of 195 targeted program youth, 68 were not interviewed at time III. Focus in the analysis is on the three large groupings of youth (cohorts I, II, and III) who were contacted and entered the program in sequential and overlapping periods. The initial time I interview was conducted shortly after the youth in each of the cohorts entered the program. Time II and time III interviews were conducted usually when the youth was still present in the program, sometimes when he was out of the community. (We did not interview comparison gang member co-arrestees from the respective gangs for various reasons, including lack of resources, although we did obtain their arrest histories, a process that we describe in chapter 11.) We were interested primarily in changes in community and social characteristics that could be related to changes in deviancy patterns between time I and time III, comparing characteristics of program youth from the two target gangs over time. We make no specific claims in this chapter that the project was responsible for changes in the youth's behavior, attitudes, and relationships, but we will make this claim later, in chapters in-corporating statistical controls and data from program services and contacts and police arrest reports. Our preliminary analysis will suggest only that there was a natural progression of gang youth both into and out of the gang world and that their behaviors were associated with a variety of personal-maturation, social-context, and possibly, program effects.

The analysis is based on certain constructs of social control, cohesion, anomie, lack of opportunities, differential association, and differential gang organization, as elements of a general theory of social disorganization con-tributing to delinquent gang behavior. We emphasize ideas of social disorga-nization and limited opportunity systems as the basis for understanding the project's purpose of planning change to interactively affect individual, gang, and community behaviors in respect to the youth gang problem (Shaw and McKay 1942; Bursik and Grasmick 1993; Spergel 1995). These multiple con-structs provided a basis for the development of a set of comprehensive strategies of intervention, prevention, and suppression regarding the gang problem.

OBTAINING DATA: THE INDIVIDUAL GANG-MEMBER SURVEY

Each individual gang-member survey was administered by project field-research staff in an approximately one-hour interview session, using a ques-tionnaire containing mainly closed-ended questions. The following question categories were used in sequence to discover:

- program-youth views about Little Village community institutions and agency programs relevant to the gang problem;
- individual gang-membership characteristics, gang structure and process, and peer relationships;
- family life;
- employment;
- educational experience;
- household and individual income sources (legal and illegal); and
- income and occupational aspirations and expectations.

Self-reports of deviant behaviors and justice-system involvement were also in-cluded in the survey, and those findings are discussed in chapter 10. There was no formal program registration or intake process. Gang youth contacted by field staff members who met the criteria of violent activity (based on field-staff observations, police data, and other gang member information) were included in the program and assigned for interviews. Informed consents for the interviews were signed by the youth (and a parent, if the youth was under seventeen), giving the project research staff permission not only to interview him but also to examine his justice-system records. A sum of twenty dollars was paid to the youth for each interview he gave. There was no exchange of information between the youth worker and interviewer in regard to program contacts or interview findings.

The project youth workers usually arranged for the interviews. They accompanied the project field researcher to the place where the planned interview was to take place, then left. The field researchers were often from the program-area neighborhood and were likely to be college students or older residents. There was little resistance by youth to taking the interviews, probably due to the youth worker's positive relationship already established with the youth. The major problems initially were finding suitable interview locations offering privacy and specific times convenient for both the gang youth and the researcher. Interviews were generally conducted in local churches, libraries, fast-food restaurants, parks, recreation centers, the backs of cars, and in the homes of program youth themselves. The key data-collection problem was finding and reinterviewing program youth for the time II and time III interviews. Youth interviewed were sometimes on the run from police, in a local jail, or in a downstate prison during the program period. Three program youth joined the armed forces, one was killed in a gang fight in the community, and several left for either short or longer periods to locate in other places in Illinois, Minnesota, Florida, Texas, and Mexico. Time II and time III interviews were sometimes conducted by long-distance telephone.

Youth were often located for reinterviews through information provided by a network of gang peers, family, youth workers, and other members of the project team. The reinterview rate at time III for those interviewed at time I was 65.5 percent—relatively high, considering the nature of the hard-core, violent gang population, their unpredictable routines, and their mobility in and out of the neighborhood. Inability to locate program youth, rather than any resistance to being reinterviewed, was the major reason for failure to obtain a higher percent of reinterviews after time I.

We note that there were violent peripheral program youth from the two gangs who were not interviewed but were provided with limited worker contacts and services, and there were comparison youth co-arrestees of program youth who were not interviewed and not provided with any contacts or services. These groups were labeled the quasiprogram and the comparison samples, respectively, and matched with program youth in the analyses using arrest data.

REPRESENTATIVENESS OF THE INTERVIEW SAMPLE

The 127 youth in the time I through time III interview analysis were a good representation of all 195 youth in the program who were interviewed at time I (approximately at program initial contact). Latin King youth were on average a year older (18.4 years) than Two Six youth (17.4 years). Almost all of the youth were of Mexican American ethnicity. To determine the representativeness of the analysis sample, we compared it to the remaining group of program youth (n = 68)—the nonanalysis sample—who were excluded (those interviewed at time I only, or at times I and II only).[1] Using time I interview data (including self-reported offenses), we found non–statistically significant differences between youth in the analysis sample and nonanalysis samples in the distributions of the following sets of variables:

- gang (Latin Kings and Two Six)
- program cohort (I, II, III)
- age group (sixteen years and under, seventeen and eighteen years, and nineteen years and older)
- residence in or out of Little Village
- education (grade level)
- household and individual-youth income (legal and illegal)
- gang-membership status (active or former gang member)

There were only two statistically significant differences: (1) the Two Six cohort I youth in the nonanalysis sample (mean age = 17.2) were older than the Two Six cohort I youth in the analysis sample (mean age = 14.6) ($p \leq 0.001$); and (2) fewer youth in the nonanalysis sample (76.1 percent) were residents of Little Village at time I, compared to 86.2 percent of youth in the analysis sample ($p = 0.031$). The program youth who did not reside in Little Village at time I, whether Latin Kings or Two Six, were more difficult to find at time III.

Self-report offense patterns for the analysis sample and the nonanalysis sample were almost identical at time I, using the following offense variables:[2] total offenses, total violence offenses, serious violence offenses, property offenses, drug use and drug selling,[3] and alcohol use. Self-report arrest patterns of the analysis and nonanalysis samples were essentially identical.

Thus, we concluded with some confidence that the characteristics of the analysis sample were representative of all the program youth.

FINDINGS

We were interested in changes in certain community and social characteristics of program youth in the two gangs during the program period. The interview items included the youth's perceptions of his neighborhood; household and family background; gang-membership status; peer relationships; education, job status, and income and occupation aspirations; and changes between the time I and time III interview periods. We did not control for age, gang-membership status (or position), or family relationships. Some of these relationships and changes were statistically significant in the bivariate analyses using categorical, nonparametric (sign), means (t), and variance (F) tests but were no longer significant in the statistically controlled multivariate analyses. In this section, we describe change factors at a simple, descriptive level rather than through more rigorous analysis, which we conduct in the next and later chapters.

NEIGHBORHOOD

The Latin Kings and Two Six in Little Village were largely neighborhood bound and hung out in certain gang territories—"turfs"—which they defended as their own and sought to expand. One of our assumptions was that if neighborhood social, economic, and community-organizational conditions improved, gang-youth behavior would improve. Reciprocally, if the behavior of gang youth grew more positive (i.e., less violent or delinquent), neighborhood conditions would be perceived as improved. The gang was an integral part of the social, economic, cultural, and organizational world—the ecology—of the local community. We expected changes in gang-youth behavior to be associated over time with certain perceived changes in neighborhood characteristics.

We asked the youth about any changes they saw in the quality of life in the neighborhood and in the activities of neighborhood institutions and local community groups, and whether such changes might be related to the gang problem. Based on the responses at time III compared to time I, the youth felt the community was a somewhat better place to live. For example, while twelve youth at time I thought the community had gotten better, forty said it was about the same, and seventy-one thought the community had gotten worse. At time III, twenty-four regarded it as better, fifty-two thought it was about the same, and fifty-six regarded it as worse. Thus, while the majority of program youth still did not regard the community favorably at either time I or time III, there was a perceived improvement (sign test of forty-three individual-youth positive changes and eighteen negative changes indicated statistical significance at p ≤ 0.001). Also, the youth were relatively more satisfied with living in the community; seventy-one were satisfied and fifty-three dissatisfied at time I, but eighty-one were satisfied and forty-three dissatisfied at time III (sign test of forty-three individual-youth perceived positive changes and thirty negative changes indicated almost statistical significance, p = 0.08).

Of interest was whether perceptions of gang-related crime in the neighborhood had changed for better or worse, that is, gang-related crime had decreased or increased between time I and time III. The dominant view at time I was that the gang problem was a "serious" or "very serious" problem (n = 104) compared to "little" or "no problem" (n = 21). At time III, the gang problem was still considered as "serious" or "very serious" (n = 95) compared to "little" or "no problem" (n = 30). This constituted a significantly improved view about the problem (p ≤ 0.001). Similarly, the nongang crime problem was viewed as less serious. At time I, seventy-one youth saw it as "serious" or "very serious," and fifty-three saw it as "no problem" or a "little problem"; at time III, only thirty-one saw it as a "serious" problem, and ninety-three saw it as a "little problem" or "no problem" (p ≤ 0.001). Program youth saw neighborhood crime (gang or nongang related) as significantly less serious at time III. (These perceptions were somewhat consistent with those of Little Village adult residents and local organization respondents—see chapter 15.)

On the other hand, there was no statistically significant change in respect to perceptions of specific gang-crime-related characteristics of the community. Program youth were still afraid of gang attacks and of walking alone in the neighborhood; they were also *not* doing fewer things to avoid gang crime. There was also no perception that local institutions, community groups, or adults in general had significantly affected the community's gang problem. At time III, youth did not think the police were doing more to deal with gang crime than they did at time I, and local residents or organizations were not perceived as doing much to help reduce gang crime. There was no perceived change in the activity of criminal adults who used gang youth as accomplices. There was evidence, however, that probation was more likely to be perceived as dealing with the gang problem. Program youth did not see any community changes or improvements that they could attribute to the activities of police, local organizations, or community residents. To some extent this may have reflected or confirmed the final inability of the project to mobilize community support or directly modify local institutional conditions that were associated with or may have contributed to the gang problem.

FAMILY AND HOUSEHOLD

We were not sure how family factors as they existed during the program period influenced gang-youth development. The youth in our sample were older adolescents and young adults, with already weakened ties to their families of origin. Nevertheless, we thought it was possible that changes in family structure and relationships between the time I and time III interviews could account for, or predict, changes in youth behavior. Gang youth mostly still lived in the same neighborhood as their families and had some contact with them. Many youth had steady girlfriends, and some were married and setting up new family arrangements.

Household Size and Age

There was little difference in household structure between time I and time III for the sample as a whole or for each of the gangs. The average size of the households dropped from 3.5 to 3.3 members; the average age of the household members increased from 20.7 years to 27.3 years. Much of this change was due to the increase of age in the Two Six households, where program youth were more rapidly leaving their families of origin than were the Latin Kings (who were generally older and had already left their original family households). None of these differences were statistically significant across time or between gangs.

Household Employment

Household employment increased but not significantly. At time I, 46.8 percent of household members over fourteen years of age were employed, compared to 54.5 percent at time III. The level of employment was slightly higher for the Two Six households (50.0 percent at time I; 59.1 percent at time III) than for the Latin King households (43.7 percent at time I; 50.6 percent at time III). General increases in the levels of employment for members of the households might have been due to the general upswing in the economy in Chicago during the project period.

Household Income

Of special interest were the findings for average household income, from legal and illegal sources. Average total income per household for the entire sample increased from $23,644 to $24,173, hardly a significant rise over a three-year period. There were differences between the Latin King and Two Six households. While average Two Six household income increased significantly, from $25,104 to $29,649 ($p \leq 0.05$), average Latin King household income decreased from $22,407 to $19,297, but this change was not statistically significant. The difference between groups at time I and time III was significant ($p \leq 0.05$).

We were able to obtain information differentiating legal and illegal household income. Yearly legal household income increased slightly for the sample as a whole, from $20,700 to $21,033; for the Latin King households it increased from $15,555 to $15,703, and for the Two Six families from $26,739 to $27,018, which was statistically significant ($p \leq 0.05$). Again, the difference between legal household income in the two gangs was significant ($p \leq 0.05$).

We were also able to calculate differences in sources of income (legal and illegal) per household. At time I, the total sample of respondents ($n = 121$) reported that 67.0 percent of household income was from legal sources; at time III it was 71.0 percent. The percentage of Latin King legal household income did not essentially change (62.0 percent to 63.0 percent), but the percentage of Two Six legal household income increased significantly, from 72.0 percent to 80.0 percent ($p \leq 0.05$). Again, there were statistically significant differences between the Latin King and Two Six households ($p \leq 0.05$) over time.

Interestingly, we found that illegal household income comprised a relatively small proportion of total income. Annual illegal household income for the total sample increased from an average of $2,727 to $3,140 over the three-year period. Illegal income increased for the Latin King households—from $1,666 to $5,370, and for the Two Six households—from $454 to $2,045. However, the percentage of the total sample reporting illegal household income was only

9.0 percent at time I (n = 5) and 12.0 percent at time III (n = 15). It was 16.0 percent for the Latin Kings at time I and about the same (15.0 percent) at time III; it was 1.0 percent for the Two Six at time I and 10.0 percent at time III. Illegal income comprised a small but probably important source of reported household income, more for the Latin Kings than for the Two Six. Thus, total household income rose somewhat for the Two Six households but not for the Latin King households, which appeared to depend relatively more on income from illegal sources.

Criminal Character of Households

Excluding the youth themselves, the criminal character of households—as measured by household members' gang affiliations, arrests, incarcerations, and probation status—lessened between time I and time III. Whereas 12.1 percent of household members were currently gang members at time I, only 3.8 percent were at time III. The reported decline was greater for the somewhat more criminally identified Latin King households (16.7 percent to 4.6 percent) than for the Two Six households (4.2 percent to 2.8 percent). The decline in household arrests was statistically significant, from 13.5 percent to 5.9 percent (p ≤ 0.01) and occurred mostly in the Latin King households. The percentage of total sample household members on probation also declined, from 7.7 percent to 3.7 percent, and the decline occurred more in the Latin King households (10.7 percent to 2.6 percent) than in the Two Six households (5.1 percent to 4.9 percent).

Family Relationships

The quality of the youth's relationships with family members was reported to be very positive. The most positive family relationships were with mothers; between 86.0 percent and 91.0 percent of the youth said they got along well most of the time with their mothers. There was little change over time. The pattern was somewhat different for their relationships with their fathers, with whom they seemed to get along a little less well. While there was evidence of a slight decline in positive relationships with their fathers for the Latin Kings (67.4 percent to 57.1 percent), there was an increase for the Two Six (60.0 percent to 75.9 percent). None of these changes across time, or between the gangs, was statistically significant. Positive relationships with siblings, while greater than with fathers, generally declined for both gangs: Latin Kings from 81.3 percent to 77.4 percent, and Two Six from 87.9 percent to 78.3 percent. These differences were also not statistically significant. We shall see that some of these relationships were quite significant, in perhaps unexpected ways, in explaining changes in deviant behavior and arrests when we examine the findings of our multivariate models.

Wives or Steady Girlfriends and Gang Friends

The pattern of change in the relationships between program youth and their wives or steady girlfriends was also interesting. Some of the changes could be accounted for by the average age differences between the youth of the two gangs. The Latin Kings were older than the Two Six, and more of the Latin Kings had wives or steady girlfriends, both at time I (75.4 percent) and time III (84.6 percent), than did the Two Six at time I (66.1 percent) and at time III (64.5 percent). There was a slight decrease in such relationships for the Two Six. While the differences between time I and time III were not statistically significant for the sample as a whole or for each of the gangs, the changes were statistically significant between the gangs ($p \leq 0.01$).

On the other hand, the quality of relationships between program youth and their wives or steady girlfriends (i.e., getting along well most of the time) was only moderately good at time I, and had deteriorated by time III. The rate of deterioration of relationships between time I and time III was greater for the Latin Kings (61.2 percent to 44.4 percent) than for the Two Six (68.4 percent to 57.7 percent).

Time spent with wives or steady girlfriends increased significantly ($p \leq 0.01$) for the whole sample between time I and time III. The increase was statistically significant ($p \leq 0.001$) for the Latin Kings but not for the Two Six. It could be that as gang youth matured, they were spending more time with their wives and steady girlfriends, but surprisingly, the relationships were increasingly conflictual during this maturation period, as gang youth were probably transitioning out of the gang. Gang members in the sample as a whole, and in each of the gangs, were spending significantly less time with gang friends: total sample ($p \leq 0.001$); Latin Kings ($p = 0.038$); and Two Six ($p \leq 0.001$). Gang members could be spending less time, reluctantly or ambivalently, with fellow gang members. Wives and girlfriends of gang youth could have been facilitating this process, accompanied by some tension and appropriate persuasion.

Household Crises

There was strong evidence of an increase in household or family crises between time I and time III, such as death, illness, physical abuse, income-related problems, drug abuse, and gang-violence victimization and arrests. These crises were classified as either family related or crime related, and increases in both types of crises were statistically significant: family-related crises ($p \leq 0.01$) and crime-related crises ($p \leq 0.01$). The increase in crime-related crises was slightly less in the Two Six households than in the Latin Kings households. However, the increase was statistically significant in each of the two gangs for both types of crises: Latin Kings family-related crises ($p \leq 0.01$) and crime-related crises ($p \leq 0.01$); and Two Six family-related crises ($p \leq 0.01$) and crime-related crises ($p \leq 0.05$). Household crises would prove to be an important variable in our multivariate models predicting changes in gang activity.

THE TARGET GANGS

The gang itself obviously was a key context directly affecting the youth's identity and criminal activity during his period in the gang (Thornberry et al. 2003). The project's objectives included modifying the behavior of program youth, and possibly the gang, so that the youth's and his gang's crime patterns (especially of serious violence) would be reduced. Whether this meant that the institution of the gang (i.e., the tradition, structure, and processes of ganging in Little Village) would consequently change was not clear. It was possible that a complex gang system could not change until changes occurred in local community and larger social, political, economic, and cultural conditions (e.g., poverty, access to jobs, segregation of low-income minority groups, low quality of education, and gun-control laws). The project did not address these larger issues, but some reduction in gang-as-a-unit violent-crime patterns could possibly occur as a result of program-youth changes.

Individual youth were asked specific questions relevant to gang structure and behavior: whether changes occurred in the size of the gangs—for both female and male sections—and whether gangs grew less violent over time.

Gang Size

Based on the time I through time III interview responses, we found no evidence that the target gangs were substantially changing in size or shifting emphasis in respect to violence or other criminal activities over the five-year project period. (We did find a shift in emphasis of gang-crime activities, based on police incident and arrest data; see chapter 15.) Perceptions of the size of gangs was not statistically significantly different at time III compared to time I. Latin King respondents indicated that their gang was either larger (52.9 percent) or about the same (39.2 percent) at time III, compared to estimates that it was larger (62.1 percent) or about the same (24.1 percent) at time I or earlier. The Two Six respondents viewed their gang as larger (63.2 percent) or about the same (17.5 percent) at time III, compared to larger (56.0 percent) or about the same (24.5 percent) at time I or earlier. It was also possible that the individual youth's perception of differences in the size of his gang could be related more to his own identification with the gang and his gang-membership status and criminal activity than to changes in actual characteristics of the gang.

The size of the female sections of their gangs, as perceived by the male youth in the samples, was changing. The Latin King males saw their female associates, the Latin Queens (an identifiable, organized group) as increasing in numbers. This change was statistically significant ($p \leq 0.01$). The Two Six males also saw their female associates (not formally organized or as closely-related to the male organization) as increasing in numbers ($p \leq 0.01$).

Fighting between the Gangs

Fighting between the males in the two gangs was almost continuous. Hardly a day passed without a confrontation between individuals or sections of the two gangs. Certain sections of each of the gangs had a reputation for being more violent than other sections; also, each section seemed to go through phases or cycles of more or less violence. There were fashions and degrees of violence in the sections of the two gangs, from bottle throwing, knifings, and car ramming to drive-by, bicycle, and walk-up shootings. The Latin Queen and the Two Six females were clashing with each other more often but only in periodic fist and knife fights. Gang-violent incidents—whether involving males or females—were more often unplanned rather than planned, depending on situational opportunities and the moods of the gang youth.

Fighting was an essential component of the active gang tradition in Little Village. It served to sustain or develop the status and reputation of the individual gang member and the gang. The Latin Kings generally were an older, more established, and larger gang than the Two Six, with sections (not necessarily closely related) throughout Chicago, the Midwest, and the rest of the country. The Latin Kings in Chicago had a reputation for violent and extensive criminal activity. The Two Six were also a large gang, although its sections were smaller than those of the Latin Kings. The Two Six were somewhat younger and had recently expanded into the Chicago suburbs, to Indiana, and as far away as Texas. The Two Six were more volatile and mischievous, and prone to attacking the Latin Kings, who would then retaliate, usually with greater force and violence. The project team worked with about fifteen sections each from the Latin Kings and the Two Six in Little Village.

A key question was whether the youth felt that their gangs or gang sections had modified their violent behavior between time I and time III. To the question, "Has your gang been in a fight with other gangs in the last three months?" the responses were very similar at time I and time III (Latin Kings "yes" 93.7 percent at time I and 92.2 percent at time III; Two Six "yes" 95.2 percent at time I and 89.5 percent at time III). The fights generally involved weapons (guns) and were perceived as not changing in frequency (Latin Kings 80.7 percent at time I and 85.1 percent time III; Two Six 87.5 percent at time I and 90.2 percent at time III). None of these changes were statistically significant. The program youth claimed there was some decline in lethality of gang violence, that is, death from fighting with the other gang (Latin Kings 58.2 percent at time I and 37.0 at percent time III; Two Six 48.9 percent at time I and 33.3 percent at time III). These perceived changes of gang-level violence were not statistically significant for either gang.

Fighting between Sections of the Same Gang

The different sections or branches (aggregations of street sections) of the gangs were perceived as continuing to fight other sections or branches of the same gang (Latin Kings 48.3 percent at time I and 44.9 percent at time III; Two Six 36.0 percent at time I and 47.4 percent at time III). These differences were also not statistically significant. The youth stated that the confrontations between sections of the same gang were generally less violent than confrontations across the two gangs, although occasionally a weapon such as a gun (more often a bottle or knife) was used. The fights between sections were more likely to occur at weekend parties, as part of drunken brawls, or to test the machismo or reputation of the youth from different sections. Nevertheless, sample youth reported that fights between sections of the same gang were becoming more serious, with death or serious injury increasing.

Fighting within the Same Gang Section

Fighting among members of the same gang section did occur periodically, often at parties and usually over personal conflicts, girlfriends, drug deals, and so forth. These fights were rarely lethal, although occasionally a death did result. Youth workers reported during the program period that two such deaths occurred within particular Latin King sections over "bad" drug deals, and one death occurred within a Two Six section, again over a drug deal. There were unstable, complex connections between the youth gangs and the adult criminal organizations in the area. The presence of adult criminal organizations was more often reported in the Two Six area.

In sum, patterns of fighting by gang youth could be lethal but did not seem to change much over time; they continued to be very serious between gangs and less serious (although still at times lethal) between and within particular gang sections. Youth who were drawn to gang activity may have been relatively more disposed to violence than youth not drawn to gangs, although the commitment of gang members to different types and levels of violence varied within the gangs, across gang sections, and by individuals in the gang (chapters 13 and 14). The youth were also asked about their awareness of the possibility that their death could result from gang violence. They clearly understood that gang fighting could result in death, and there was little change in their awareness over time (Latin Kings "yes" 67.1 percent at time I and 71.2 percent at time III; Two Six "yes" 80.4 percent at time I and 76.8 percent at time III).

INDIVIDUAL-YOUTH CHARACTERISTICS
Mobility

In our earlier discussion, we observed that most of the youth who were not reinterviewed at time III had probably left the area. Mobility was a factor, even for youth who were reinterviewed and continued to be active in Little Village and involved in the program. The number of program youth who did not live in the area but still hung out in Little Village increased over the course of the program. The mobility of reinterviewed program youth was similar in the Latin Kings and the Two Six: 87.7 percent of the Latin Kings lived in Little Village at time I but only 70.8 percent at time III; similarly, 88.7 percent of the Two Six lived in Little Village at time I but only 68.9 percent at time III. Fewer members of each gang (p ≤ 0.01) were living in Little Village at time III than at time I, but they still occasionally hung out in the area.

Gang Membership

All youth were asked to indicate whether they were active or former gang members. While most claimed to be active gang members at time I and time III, a few already had identified themselves as former gang members at time I. Former gang membership increased for the Latin Kings—from 4.6 percent to 29.7 percent—and for the Two Six—from 3.9 percent to 18.0 percent. The drop in active gang membership for the Latin Kings was statistically significant (p ≤ 0.01), as it was for the Two Six, to a slightly less significant degree (p ≤ 0.05).

Position in the Gang

Gang members who stated they were active gang members at time I tended to say they had become leaders and core members by time III. This pattern was expected. If gang members stayed in the gang long enough, their status would rise. The pattern was similar and statistically significant for the Latin Kings (p ≤ 0.05) and the Two Six (p ≤ 0.01), with the increase in gang status more characteristic of the Two Six (comprising younger youth) than of the Latin Kings. On the other hand, those who claimed they were former gang members at time I tended to classify themselves still as former gang members at time III. As we shall see in our later analyses, older youth in both gangs tended to say they were former gang members (and had reduced arrest frequencies).

Education

Most youth in both gangs improved their educational standing between time I and time III. The dropout rate was reduced, and more youth returned to school—graduating from high school, achieving their GED, or entering community college. The percentage of dropouts declined between time I and time III for the Latin Kings (from 52.3 percent to 35.4 percent) and for the Two Six (from 43.6 percent to 25.8 percent). Between time I and time III, the percentage of youth who returned to school or graduated increased significantly for the Latin Kings (p ≤ 0.05) and for the Two Six (p ≤ 0.05). The total number of Latin Kings and Two Six who were in school, had a GED, or graduated high school increased from sixty-six (52.0 percent) at time I to eighty-eight (70.0 percent) at time III.

Employment

More program youth were employed at time III than at time I: 35.7 percent of the Latin Kings reported employment at time I and 48.2 percent at time III, while 30.9 percent of the Two Six reported employment at time I and 63.3 percent at time III. The increase of employed Two Six youth was statistically significant ($p \leq 0.05$). More program youth had access to, and were using, both educational and employment opportunities at time III than at time I. How these opportunity factors were related specifically to the youth's continued gang membership, increased position in the gang, and any reduction in his patterns of gang crime and violence are assessed in later chapters.

Individual Income

Most of the gang youth in the sample were seventeen years of age or older and no longer completely dependent on the family for income. Some youth were working legitimate jobs, others were "hustling" or engaged in illegal enterprises. A series of questions was asked about the source and amount of the youth's annual income. We found a barely significant increase in total individual income for the sample as a whole ($p \leq 0.05$). Mean total annual income for the Latin Kings increased from $9,730 at time I to $12,787 at time III; the increase for the Two Six was from $9,268 to $11,797.

Mean total income was computed based on two types of income—legal and illegal—considered separately and together. The increase in annual legal individual income for the Latin Kings was hardly impressive, from $7,036 at time I to $7,969 at time III. The increase for the Two Six was more substantial, from $5,927 to $9,393. However, between time I and time III the Latin Kings showed an increase in annual illegal income from $2,564 to $4,720, while the Two Six showed a decrease in illegal income from $3,438 to $2,332. These changes were not statistically significant, since only a small percentage of youth (particularly at time I) stated they were obtaining income from illegal sources. The number of Latin Kings who said they were engaged in illegal enterprise increased from twelve at time I to twenty-four at time III; the number of Two Six from eight to thirteen. Illegal income as a proportion of total income rose for the Latin Kings—from 15.0 percent at time I to 23.0 percent at time III; it remained at 12.0 percent for the Two Six. Thus, combined legal and illegal income increased for members of both gangs, but the increase in income for the Latin Kings came mainly from illegal sources.

ASPIRATIONS AND EXPECTATIONS

We asked a series of questions based on concepts of anomie, or alienation, both at time I and time III. We asked the youth to state what their aspirations or wishes were for future occupation and income and then to state what their realistic expectations were. We then computed the gap, or disjunction, subtracting expectation from aspiration responses for each youth. Based on anomie theory, we proposed that the greater the disjunction (i.e., the greater the interpreted anomie or alienation), the greater the potential for participating in crime or violent activity. We anticipated that as the youth aged, matured, and had access to additional or improved opportunities—or was exposed to the influence of the program—his level of alienation and related criminal activity would decrease, especially his involvement in violent crime.

Occupation Aspirations and Expectations

Occupational aspirations declined for gang youth over time. While at time I a high proportion of Latin Kings and Two Six aspired (perhaps unrealistically) to be professionals, own their own businesses, or become managers, by time III a greater number aspired (more realistically) to clerical, trade, and factory positions. The changes were consistent, but not statistically significant, within and between gangs. On the other hand, rather low expectations for future jobs (such as clerk, trade, or factory worker) were typically reported at time I, but they substantially increased (to managerial and clerical-level jobs) at time III. The increased occupational expectations were statistically significant for the total sample ($p \leq 0.05$).

In other words, by time III members of both gangs had lowered their occupational aspirations but raised their occupational expectations. The decrease in disjunction for the total sample was statistically significant ($p \leq 0.05$), as was the decrease for the Latin Kings ($p = 0.016$), who were older, but not for the Two Six, who were younger. Perhaps by time III older gang members had become more realistic about their future careers (Merton 1957).

Income Aspirations and Expectations

The results were somewhat different using income as the variable. At time I, members of both gangs aspired to future income levels between thirty and forty thousand dollars per year; these aspirations rose to between forty and fifty thousand dollars at time III. The increases were similar and statistically significant for members of both gangs (Latin Kings, $p \leq 0.01$; Two Six, p ≤ 0.01). However, income expectations declined only slightly, from the high-thirty-thousand-dollar range at time I to the low-thirty-thousand-dollar or upper-twenty-thousand-dollar range at time III. There were minor differences in these patterns between the two gangs. The gap between income aspirations and expectations, similar to that using the occupation variable, declined for the Latin Kings but increased slightly for the Two Six. The disjunction or degree of alienation, using income as a criterion, was possibly greater for the younger Two Six than for the older Latin Kings between time I and time III, but these differences were not statistically significant.

SIGNIFICANT YOUTH SOCIAL-CONTEXT CHANGES

A great many changes—some possibly related to program effects—were occurring for program gang youth between the time of their first and third interviews. The changes were important, often statistically significant, and would predict changes in self-reported patterns of deviant behavior. The community was perceived as getting better—a better place to live in. The youth were relatively more satisfied living in Little Village. Community gang and nongang crime were generally seen as reduced. Gang youth were less concerned about family victimization through gang crime. However, the youth did not see local organizations, residents, or police as changing during the program period, or doing much to address the gang problem.

While there was little change in household composition, household income increased slightly and was higher in the Two Six than in the Latin King households. While illegal income was a smaller proportion of household income than legal income—ranging from 9.0 percent to 16.0 percent—it became a bigger proportion in the Latin King households. Mean total household income for the total sample increased from $23,644 to $24,173.

Some of the household members or families had and continued to have contacts with the criminal justice system but at a declining rate. Gang membership of household members declined from 12.1 percent to 3.8 percent; arrests of household members declined from 13.5 percent to 5.9 percent; household members on probation declined from 7.7 percent to 2.7 percent.

Relationships of youth with mothers, fathers, and siblings were reported as positive at both time I and time III. The quality of relationships between gang youth and their wives or steady girlfriends was only moderately positive (deteriorating by time III) but would be important to the reduction of gang violence, as we show later in multivariate analyses. There were some increases in health and mental-health crises in the households. Household environments, economically and socially, continued to be marginal, although some improvement was occurring. The gang itself was a key context directly affecting the level of the youth's criminal activity, especially violence. The male sections of the gangs were perceived as not changing in size between time I and time III, but the size of female sections (or clusters), which were related to or hung around with gang males, was viewed as growing larger. Fighting between the males of the two gangs was continuous, serious, and often lethal. Less-serious fighting occurred between sections and within sections of the same gang, although fights among individuals in the same section over drug deals could occasionally be lethal. There was no evidence that violence at the gang level was perceived as changing between time I and time III, although a reduction in violent activity for individual program youth would become evident in analyses of police data (described in later chapters) that would cover a preprogram and program period and include comparison and quasiprogram youth.

More program youth declared they were no longer active members of the gang toward the end of the program period. The drop was particularly marked for the Latin Kings. Also, those who said they were former gang members at time I still said they were former gang members at time III. Similarly, those who said they were peripheral or regular gang members at time I were likely to report they were core or leadership members at time III.

Educational levels and employment increased for members of both gangs. At time III, the number of Latin King school dropouts decreased from 52.3 percent to 35.4 percent, and the number of Two Six dropouts decreased from 43.6 percent to 25.8 percent. At time I, 35.7 percent of the Latin Kings reported they were employed; this jumped to 48.2 percent at time III. At time I, 30.9 percent of the Two Six reported employment, jumping to 63.3 percent at time III. The increase in employment for the Two Six was statistically significant ($p \leq 0.05$). Access to educational and economic opportunities was opening up for program youth. Most of the gang youth in the sample were seventeen years of age or older at time I and no longer completely dependent on the family for income. There was an increase in the youth's individual income from approximately $9,200 per year to $12,000 per year. The increase in legal income was greater for the Two Six than for the Latin Kings, while the increase in illegal income was greater for the Latin Kings than the Two Six. The level of illegal income for the Latin Kings, as a proportion of total income, rose from 15.0 percent to 23.0 percent; it remained at 12.0 percent for the Two Six.

Realistic occupational expectations rose over time for members of both gangs, but aspirations fell. However, income aspirations and expectations remained relatively high for members of both gangs. The gap or disjunction between income aspirations and expectations declined more for the Latin Kings than for the Two Six, possibly because of the age factor. Aging out of the adolescent period appeared to be correlated with many of the community and social changes perceived as occurring.

The extent to which these differences predicted a change in self-reported deviant behavior and arrest patterns, and the extent to which project workers and the services and controls they provided influenced these changes, as well as outcome factors, are described in the following chapters.

NOTES

1. Twelve youth who were interviewed at time I but not reinterviewed at time II were later located and reinterviewed at time III. They are included in the analysis sample.

2. The specific components of these offense categories are further described in chapter 10.

3. We computed drug use and drug selling based on a different set of interview questions. Although these data were normed and compared with the other self-report deviancy data, we did not include them in the total offenses category.

Life-Course Factors Related to Self-Reported Offense and Arrest Changes

We next explore whether certain life-course and life-space factors, such as neighborhood, gang context, family relationships, household crises, relation to the gang, school and jobs, and aspirations and expectations, might affect offense-change patterns during the program period. These data provide a rich and complex picture of the various influences that could contribute to or predict change in gang-youth delinquency patterns. An analysis of the effects of the program—based on police arrest–change data—is provided in later chapters, when we introduce life-space and life-course changes.

First, we examine changes in criminal or deviant activities reported by 127 program youth between the time I and time III interviews. We compare changes in the mean frequencies of self-reported offenses (and self-reported arrests) for the total program sample, the two gangs separately, the three cohorts (groupings of youth based on the time they entered the program), and various age groups. We wondered whether program youth were changing their patterns of violent activities and to what extent they were also changing their patterns of using or selling drugs and using alcohol. We wondered whether some of these activities took place differentially with gang or nongang peers. Next, we looked at whether changes in self-reported offenses were related to social and community-context findings. Finally, we employed multiple-regression modeling to predict the possible effects of the program on change in self-reported offenses during the program period, using social and community-context variables.

The program youth were asked whether they had committed any of sixteen offenses,[1] and how many times they had committed and been arrested for them. The self-report list of offenses was short but useful,[2] focusing on crimes likely to be committed by gang youth in Little Village—particularly violence. The offenses, which were characteristic and traditional among gang youth in Chicago, and probably elsewhere, were as follows:

1. writing nongang graffiti;
2. writing gang graffiti;
3. destroying property worth three hundred dollars or less;
4. breaking and entering a building to commit theft;
5. shoplifting;
6. stealing a car for joyriding;
7. breaking into a car and stealing parts;
8. robbery, by force or threat of force, without a weapon;
9. robbery with a weapon—gun or knife;
10. gang intimidation;
11. threat to attack a person, without a weapon;
12. threat to attack with a dangerous weapon;
13. battery without a dangerous weapon;
14. battery with a dangerous weapon;
15. drive-by shooting; and
16. homicide.

In a separate set of questions, respondents were asked about their use and sale of each of the following drugs: marijuana, cocaine, crack, heroin, "wicky stick" (marijuana soaked in PCP), LSD, and "other" drugs. These represented the range of drugs used by gang members in the Little Village community during the project period.

We calculated offending rates by frequency of offenses and arrests in four categories over the six-month period prior to the time I and time III interviews:

1. total offenses and arrests;
2. serious violence offenses and arrests—robbery with a weapon, battery with a weapon, threatened someone with a weapon (gang motivated), threatened someone with a gun (not gang motivated), participated in a homicide, or participated in a drive-by shooting;
3. less-serious violence offenses and arrests—robbed someone of property without use of a weapon, threatened to attack someone without a weapon,

or beat up or battered someone without using a weapon (i.e., other than fists); and

4. property offenses and arrests—wrote nongang graffiti, wrote gang graffiti, destroyed property worth three hundred dollars or less, entered a building or store to commit a theft, broke into a building to commit a theft, stole a car for joyriding, or broke into a car and stole auto parts.

A separate index of drug-selling offenses (but not arrests) was also created, based on frequency of selling drugs, per week, per six-month period.

The analysis using self-report data of program youth was not statistically controlled for preprogram criminal records, length of time in the program, and other characteristics, as it was in the later multivariate analyses using arrest data. However, the data were important in determining which specific life-course and life-space variables played a special role in the increase, decrease, or lack of change in the youth's self-reported criminal activities during the program period.

SELF-REPORTED OFFENSE AND ARREST CHANGES: TIME I THROUGH TIME III

We found extensive, if not extraordinary, reductions in mean frequencies of self-reported offenses and arrests by all youth in the sample between time I and time III (table 10.1).

Most of these reductions were highly statistically significant using t-tests. There were substantial reductions in frequencies of self-reported total offenses, from a mean of 52.7 at time I to 9.4 at time III; in total violence offenses, from a mean of 28.7 to 6.6; in serious violence offenses, from a mean of 18.5 to 3.6; in property offenses, from a mean of 24.0 to 2.8; and in drug-selling offenses, from a mean of 4.1 to 2.8 per week (but this reduction was not statistically significant). There were also non–statistically significant declines in the use of drugs and alcohol. The rate of decline in self-reported total violence, serious violence, and property offenses was in the range of 77.0 percent to 88.0 percent. These are very highly significant declines from a youth-development or policy perspective, even assuming considerable exaggeration by youth in their reporting.

Youth were also asked to self-report frequencies of arrests for these same types of offenses. There were far fewer arrests than offenses self-reported. However, the pattern of declines (nonsignificant) in self-reported arrests was similar

Table 10.1.   Mean frequencies and changes of self-reported offenses and arrests for youth
(n = 127) at time I and time III

Offense/arrest categories	Time I		Time III		Difference		
	Mean[a]	N	Mean	N	Mean	N	t[b]
Total offenses[c]	52.68	127	9.40	121	−42.56	121	−6.91***
Total violence offenses[d]	28.72	127	6.57	121	−21.54	121	−5.26***
Serious violence offenses[e]	18.53	127	3.55	121	−14.49	121	−4.97***
Property offenses[f]	23.95	127	2.83	121	−21.02	121	−6.26***
Drug-selling offenses[g]	4.11	126	2.80	121	−1.12	120	−1.54
Total arrests[h]	2.00	127	0.31	121	−1.64	121	−2.62**
Total violence arrests	1.02	127	0.22	121	−0.74	121	−1.84
Serious violence arrests	0.59	127	0.13	121	−0.47	121	−1.53
Property arrests	0.98	127	0.09	121	−0.49	121	−2.77**

Source: individual gang-member survey.
Notes
a. Means of total offenses, total violence offenses, serious violence offenses, property offenses, as well
   as total arrests, total violence arrests, serious violence arrests, and property arrests are calculated on a
   six-month basis, as self-reported, prior to the time I and time III interviews. Mean self-reported
   drug-selling offenses (based on a different set of questions) are calculated on a weekly basis during
   the six-month periods prior to the time I and time III interviews.
b. For differences between time periods: * $p \leq 0.05$; ** $p \leq 0.01$; *** $p \leq 0.001$.
c. Includes violence offenses and property offenses, but not drug-selling offenses.
d. Includes robbery with and without a weapon, threats with and without a weapon, gang intimidation,
   battery with and without a weapon, homicide, and drive-by shootings.
e. Includes robbery with a weapon, threats with a weapon, gang intimidation, battery with a weapon,
   homicide, and drive-by shootings.
f. Includes writing gang and nongang graffiti, destroying property worth three hundred dollars or less,
   entering or breaking into a building to commit a theft, stealing a car for joyriding, and breaking into a
   car and stealing parts.
g. Includes selling marijuana, cocaine, crack, heroin, "wicky stick," acid, and other drugs.
h. Includes both total violence arrests and property arrests, but not drug arrests.

to that of self-reported offenses between time I and time III. The reduction in
frequencies of self-reported total arrests was from a mean of 2.0 to 0.3; total
violence arrests, from a mean of 1.0 to 0.2; serious violence arrests, from 0.6 to
0.1; and property arrests, from 1.0 to 0.1, that is, arrests for property offenses
were reduced almost to zero. The patterns of declines were similar to those
found in later analyses using official police arrest histories for violence and
drug offenses, when we used multivariate statistical models (chapter 12).

Gang

There were also declines in total self-reported offenses between the interviews (time I and III) when the unit of analysis was the gang, that is, using
individual-youth self-reports aggregated by gang. Similar sharp declines in
frequencies of various types of offenses occurred in the Latin Kings and Two
Six samples. The reductions were statistically significant for all types of self-
reported offenses in each gang, except for drug selling, which declined, but not

Table 10.2. Mean frequencies and changes of self-reported offenses and arrests for the Latin King (LK) and Two Six (26) gangs at time I and time III

Offense/arrest categories[a]	Gang	Time I		Time III		Difference		
		Mean	N	Mean	N	Mean	N	t[b]
Total offenses	LK	57.26	65	10.60	62	−45.61	62	−5.12***
	26	47.87	62	8.14	59	−39.36	59	−4.61***
Total violence offenses	LK	32.22	65	7.05	62	−23.24	62	−4.17***
	26	25.07	62	6.07	59	−19.75	59	−3.27**
Serious violence offenses	LK	19.40	65	4.07	62	−13.81	62	−3.96***
	26	17.61	62	3.02	59	−15.20	59	−3.19**
Property offenses	LK	25.05	65	3.55	62	−22.37	62	−4.79***
	26	22.81	62	2.07	59	−19.61	59	−4.03***
Drug-selling offenses	LK	5.28	65	3.96	63	−1.11	63	−0.92
	26	2.87	61	1.54	58	−1.13	57	−1.46
Total arrests	LK	2.57	65	0.39	62	−2.03	62	−2.12*
	26	1.40	62	0.22	59	−1.22	59	−1.53
Total violence arrests	LK	1.15	65	0.27	62	−0.73	62	−1.80
	26	0.87	62	0.15	59	−0.76	59	−1.06
Serious violence arrests	LK	0.42	65	0.15	62	−0.26	62	−2.05*
	26	0.77	62	0.12	59	−0.69	59	−1.12
Property arrests	LK	1.42	65	0.11	62	−1.31	62	−2.21*
	26	0.53	62	0.07	59	−0.46	59	−2.05*

Source: individual gang-member survey.
Notes
a. Same offenses and arrests as in table 10.1 (c–h).
b. For differences within group between time periods: * $p \leq 0.05$; ** $p \leq 0.01$; *** $p \leq 0.001$.

significantly. The percentages of declines were somewhat greater for the Latin Kings than the Two Six (table 10.2).

Some of these differences were attributable to the difference in age of the Latin Kings, who were older and, perhaps, aging out of criminal behavior more rapidly. (We control for age differences in the multivariate analyses based on police arrest data in later chapters.)

Cohort

It was complicated comparing the three youth cohorts because of the variations in the size of each cohort and the youth-age distributions within each cohort. The first cohort contained more than twice the number of youth as either the second or third cohorts. Cohort I youth tended to be a little older and were in the program for a longer period. Cohort III youth were younger and had the least program exposure. In general, all of the cohorts self-reported declines in offenses and arrests over time (table 10.3).

Table 10.3. Mean frequencies and changes of self-reported offenses and arrests for cohorts I, II, and III at time I and time III

Offense/arrest categories[a]	Cohort	Time I		Time III		Difference		
		Mean	N	Mean	N	Mean	N	t[b]
Total offenses	I	56.38	72	10.22	67	−47.52	67	−5.41***
	II	46.88	24	7.26	23	−38.65	23	−3.10**
	III	43.94	31	9.19	31	−34.74	31	−2.96**
Total violence offenses	I	31.97	72	7.21	67	−23.60	67	−4.32***
	II	27.54	24	5.22	23	−23.13	23	−2.11*
	III	22.10	31	6.19	31	−15.90	31	−2.20*
Serious violence offenses	I	20.17	72	3.67	67	−15.54	67	−4.80***
	II	22.88	24	2.96	23	−20.70	23	−1.96
	III	11.36	31	3.74	31	−7.61	31	−1.73
Property offenses	I	26.40	72	3.02	67	−23.93	67	−4.72***
	II	19.33	24	2.04	23	−15.52	23	−2.34*
	III	21.84	31	3.00	31	−18.84	31	−3.51**
Drug-selling offenses	I	4.97	72	3.20	67	−1.47	67	−1.28
	II	1.96	24	2.58	23	0.53	23	0.53
	III	3.77	30	2.10	31	−1.60	30	−1.40
Total arrests	I	2.79	72	0.45	67	−2.27	67	−2.24*
	II	0.04	24	0.00	23	−0.04	23	−1.00
	III	1.68	31	0.23	31	−1.45	31	−1.36
Total violence arrests	I	1.51	72	0.34	67	−1.09	67	−1.57
	II	0.04	24	0.00	23	−0.04	23	−1.00
	III	0.61	31	0.10	31	−0.52	31	−1.03
Serious violence arrests	I	0.99	72	0.19	67	−0.84	67	−1.52
	II	0.04	24	0.00	23	−0.04	23	−1.00
	III	0.10	31	0.10	31	0.00	31	0.00
Property arrests	I	1.28	72	0.10	67	−1.18	67	−2.30*
	II	0.00	24	0.00	23	0.00	23	0.00
	III	1.07	31	0.13	31	−0.94	31	−1.59

Source: individual gang-member survey.
Notes
a. Same offenses and arrests as in table 10.1 (c–h).
b. For differences between time periods: * $p \leq 0.05$; ** $p \leq 0.01$; *** $p \leq 0.001$.

The level of decline was statistically greater in the first cohort than in the other two cohorts. There were two minor exceptions to the general reduction of offenses and arrests across the cohorts: cohort II showed a slight increase in drug-selling offenses at time III, and its property arrests remained unchanged (but they were already at zero at time I, and remained at zero at time III).

Age Group

We wondered whether changes in the patterns of self-reported offenses and arrests might be mainly a result of age differences. Our knowledge of age-related gang participation suggested that older youth, nineteen years and over, would experience lower rates of gang offending (both at time I and time III) because they were already at the end of their gang-involvement cycle. Youth seventeen and eighteen years old were expected to be at a peak age for gang crime, especially violence, and therefore would show a greater relative decline in offenses; youth sixteen years old and under, who were just entering the gang-crime cycle, probably would show the least decline, or even an increase. These expectations were largely, but not completely, met.

Most importantly, all age groups showed a decline in the sixteen offense and arrest items used in the gang-member survey. The oldest group, nineteen years and over, already had almost the lowest mean level of self-reported offenses and arrests at time I. The seventeen- and eighteen-year-olds had the highest level of offenses and arrests in six of the nine offense and arrest categories at time I, but they also had the highest level of reduction in these six categories by time III. The youngest age group (fourteen to sixteen years) did not have the highest level of offenses and arrests at time I, except for serious violence, and showed the least decline in self-reported offenses and arrests between time I and time III, especially for serious violence. Nevertheless, this age group experienced consistent as well as some statistically significant declines in offenses (table 10.4).

DIFFERENCES IN YOUTH REPORTING NUMBER AND TYPE OF OFFENSES AT TIME I AND TIME III

While most youth self-reported committing a variety of offenses, not all of the youth in the program reported committing all of the different types of offenses. Some who reported property, violence, or drug-selling offenses did not report any of the other types of offenses, either at time I or time III. Also, there were six youth who self-reported they had committed *no* offenses, including drug selling, at time I and time III. (One youth did not respond to the drug-selling question at time III.) It is possible that these particular youth were not involved in offending in the reporting period, were in jail, or lied. Some of the youth in the program in fact had no police arrest records. (I explore these issues in later chapters.)

The number of youth reporting offenses at time I (n = 107) declined at time III (n = 69), a drop of 35.5 percent. The number of youth reporting violence and (particularly) property offenses dropped sharply at time III. For those

Table 10.4. Mean frequencies and changes of self-reported offenses and arrests for three age categories at time I and time III

Offense/arrest categories[a]	Age category	Time I		Time III		Difference		
		Mean	N	Mean	N	Mean	N	T[b]
Total offenses	16 & under	47.53	34	16.12	33	−31.03	33	−2.80**
	17 & 18	67.22	54	9.06	52	−59.33	52	−5.36***
	19 & over	37.03	39	3.72	36	−28.92	36	−3.88***
Total violence offenses	16 & under	29.09	34	11.36	33	−18.61	33	−1.77
	17 & 18	31.44	54	6.50	52	−25.15	52	−4.41***
	19 & over	24.64	39	2.28	36	−19.00	36	−3.41**
Serious violence offenses	16 & under	21.71	34	6.76	33	−15.61	33	−1.84
	17 & 18	18.50	54	3.06	52	−15.56	52	−4.57***
	19 & over	15.80	39	1.33	36	−11.92	36	−3.30**
Property offenses	16 & under	18.44	34	4.76	33	−12.42	33	−4.24***
	17 & 18	35.78	54	2.56	52	−34.17	52	−4.87***
	19 & over	12.39	39	1.44	36	−9.92	36	−3.81***
Drug-selling offenses	16 & under	3.62	34	3.38	33	−0.35	33	−0.23
	17 & 18	4.56	54	2.91	52	−1.42	52	−1.22
	19 & over	3.92	38	2.11	36	−1.40	35	−1.21
Total arrests	16 & under	2.09	34	0.73	33	−1.36	33	−1.06
	17 & 18	2.74	54	0.19	52	−2.60	52	−2.18*
	19 & over	0.90	39	0.08	36	−0.50	36	−2.59*
Total violence arrests	16 & under	1.38	34	0.52	33	−0.91	33	−0.71
	17 & 18	1.09	54	0.14	52	−0.98	52	−2.00*
	19 & over	0.59	39	0.06	36	−0.25	36	−2.17*
Serious violence arrests	16 & under	1.18	34	0.30	33	−0.91	33	−0.85
	17 & 18	0.46	54	0.12	52	−0.37	52	−1.64
	19 & over	0.26	39	0.00	36	−0.22	36	−2.09*
Property arrests	16 & under	0.71	34	0.21	33	−0.45	33	−2.33*
	17 & 18	1.65	54	0.06	52	−1.62	52	−2.22*
	19 & over	0.31	39	0.03	36	−0.25	36	−1.95*

Source: individual gang-member survey.
Notes
a. Same offenses and arrests as in table 10.1 (c–h).
b. For differences between time periods: * $p < 0.05$; ** $p < 0.01$; *** $p < 0.001$.

youth who still reported offenses at time III, the rate of offending dropped sharply. Few youth reported more offenses at time III than at time I.

Of special interest was that self-reported drug selling, drug use, and alcohol use did not drop as sharply as violence and property offenses. At both time I and time III, fewer youth were selling drugs than using drugs, but more youth were using alcohol. Frequencies of drug selling, drug use, or alcohol use for those still involved in these activities also declined at time III (table 10.5).

Table 10.5. Numbers[a] and percent declines of youth committing offenses (n = 121),[b] means (standard deviations)[c] of offenses at time I and time III

Offense categories[d]	Time I		Time III		Differences[e] # of youth $N_d = N_1 - N_3$	Decline Percent $N_d/N_1 \times 100$
	Youth N_1 (%)	offenses Mean (S.D.)	Youth N_3 (%)	offenses Mean (S.D.)		
Total offenses	107 (88.4)	60.4 (67.5)	69 (57.0)	16.1 (18.4)	38	35.5
Total violence offenses	95 (78.5)	36.8 (47.3)	61 (50.4)	12.8 (15.3)	34	35.8
Serious violence offenses	85 (70.2)	26.6 (36.1)	44 (36.4)	9.6 (11.6)	41	48.3
Property offenses	93 (76.8)	32.0 (39.5)	42 (34.7)	7.9 (6.7)	51	54.8
Drug-selling offenses	50 (41.3)	10.4 (7.5)	45 (37.2)	6.9 (4.8)	5	10.0
Drug use	95 (78.5)	5.1 (4.6)	78 (64.5)	4.5 (3.0)	17	17.9
Alcohol use	112 (92.6)	5.0 (3.8)	105 (86.8)	3.6 (2.6)	7	6.3

Notes
a. Note that N1 and N3 indicate the numbers of youth who self-reported having committed the offenses listed in the tables at time I and time III, respectively. Percents (%) are calculated using the total of all youth committing offenses, N = 121.
b. One hundred twenty-one (121) youth (males, aged twelve to twenty-four years) said they committed offenses and completed both a time I and time III interview. One hundred eighty-two (182) youth completed a time I interview only. The attrition rate of youth interviewed between time I and time III was 33.6 percent. Youth who did not complete a time III interview were mostly nineteen and older (they were also generally the most serious offenders at time I).
c. Means and standard deviations (S.D.) are calculated only on the number of youth who self-reported having committed offenses at time I and time III.
d. Same offenses as in table 10.1 (c–h). Means of youth committing offenses are calculated for total offenses, total violence offenses, serious violence offenses, and property offenses on a six-month basis; mean offenses are calculated for drug-selling offenses, drug use, and alcohol use on a weekly basis during the six-month periods prior to the time I and time III interviews.
e. Nd indicates difference in number of youth between time I and time III.

Nevertheless, there was evidence that although fewer youth were selling drugs, there was some increase in youth who were both using and selling drugs between time I and time III, from 38 to 45 out of the sample of 120. One implication of this finding was that program youth were probably not highly specialized to drug selling or preparing to be entrepreneurial drug sellers (table 10.6).

OFFENSES COMMITTED WITH PEERS

Program youth were much more involved with gang peers than nongang peers in committing certain types of offenses—particularly violence, property

Table 10.6. Distribution of changes in self-reported drug-use and drug-selling offenses
for youth (n = 120) between time I and time III

Combined drug-use and drug-selling offense category[a]		Time III				Total at time I
		Do not use/sell	Sell only	Use only	Use & sell	
	Do not use/sell	8	1	4	3	16
	Sell only	3	1	2	4	10
	Use only	16	1	18	21	56
Time I	Use & sell	8	0	13	17	38
Total at time III		35	3	37	45	n = 120[b]

Notes
a. Some of these youth were only occasional drug sellers and offended less than once per week in the previous six months.
b. Test of marginal homogeneity indicates that the difference in the distributions of drug-use and drug-selling offenses between time I and time III are statistically significant, with Chi-square = 17.31 (df = 3, p = 0.0006).

offenses, and alcohol use—and less involved with gang peers in drug selling and drug use. This was especially the case at time I and slightly less at time III. The offense most likely to occur without gang peers was drug use; most gang youth used alcohol rather than drugs in the company of gang peers. Drug selling was about as likely to take place with or without gang peers. In other words, violence, property crime, and alcohol abuse were more likely to occur with gang peers, but drug selling was as likely to occur with or without gang peers. Drug selling, and certainly drug use, did not appear to be as integral to gang activity as other types of offenses. Drug selling and drug use were not frequent activities for certain gang youth and may not have required the presence of gang peers or the gang structure. Alcohol use was more likely to occur with gang peers than without gang peers at time I and especially at time III (table 10.7).

Gang youth who engaged in acts of violence were probably more likely to be high on alcohol than on drugs. Latin Kings and Two Six gang norms did not condone the use of drugs, particularly drugs that were highly addictive (especially heroin). This would be consistent with the findings of classic research on "fighting gangs." A youth who was high on drugs, or an addict, was not likely to be a good gangbanger. However, traditional gang norms against selling drugs appeared to have been modified in recent decades. More than 40 percent of program youth were occasionally engaged in selling drugs—an increasingly important source of income.

Finally, we note that the drug used and sold was mainly marijuana. At time I, 76.9 percent of the youth used marijuana, while 40.5 percent sold marijuana;

Table 10.7. Numbers (percents) of youth (n = 121) who reported committing offenses with and without gang peers at time I and time III[a]

Offense categories[b]	Time I			Time III		
	Youth reporting offenses	With gang peers	Without gang peers	Youth reporting offenses	With gang peers	Without gang peers
Total offenses[c]	107 (88.4)	101 (83.5)	6[d] (5.0)	69 (57.0)	55 (45.5)	14 (11.6)
Total violence offenses	95 (78.5)	85 (70.3)	10 (8.3)	61 (50.4)	48 (39.7)	13 (10.7)
Serious violence offenses	85 (70.3)	75 (62.0)	10 (8.3)	44 (36.4)	39 (32.2)	5 (4.1)
Property offenses	93 (76.8)	88 (72.7)	5 (4.1)	42 (34.7)	36 (29.8)	6 (5.0)
Drug-selling offenses	50 (41.3)	26 (21.5)	24 (19.8)	45 (37.2)	23 (19.0)	22 (18.2)
Drug use	95 (78.5)	33 (27.3)	62 (51.2)	78 (64.5)	32 (26.5)	46 (38.0)
Alcohol use	112 (92.6)	74 (61.2)	38 (31.4)	105 (86.8)	85 (70.5)	20 (16.3)

Notes
a. One hundred twenty-one (121) youth (males, aged twelve to twenty-four years) who said they committed offenses completed both a time I and time III interview. One hundred eighty-two (182) youth completed a time I interview only. The attrition rate of youth interviewed between time I and time III was 33.6 percent. Youth who did not complete a time III interview were mostly nineteen and older (they were also generally the most serious offenders at time I).
b. Same offenses as in table 10.1 (c–h).
c. Total offenses include only total violence offenses (i.e., serious and less-serious violence offenses) and property offenses.
d. Indicates those gang peers with whom the program youth said they committed both violence and property offenses.

28.9 percent used, and 31.7 percent sold, powdered cocaine. Relatively more youth used than sold marijuana, while slightly more youth sold than used cocaine (table 10.8).

LIFE-SPACE AND LIFE-COURSE CHANGES RELATED TO SELF-REPORTED OFFENSES AND ARRESTS

We inquired whether there was a correlation between the reductions of self-reported offenses and arrests and any changes in life-course or life-space factors—such as characteristics of the neighborhood, household and family, household crises, gang structure, relations to school and jobs, income and occupation aspiration or expectation levels—either at or between time I and time III. We were also particularly interested in findings that would give us

Table 10.8. Percent of youth (n = 121) using and selling various types of drugs, and alcohol use at time I and time III

	Time I		Time III	
	% used	% sold	% used	% sold
Drugs				
Marijuana	76.9	40.5	63.8	36.5
Cocaine	28.9	31.7	18.1	19.1
Crack	2.5	4.1	0.0	0.0
Heroin	0.8	5.6	0.0	0.0
LSD	10.7	5.0	12.9	3.4
Other	8.3	0.9	1.8	0.0
Alcohol				
Beer	90.0	N/A	96.5	N/A
Wine	19.8	N/A	13.9	N/A
Hard liquor	44.6	N/A	38.3	N/A

insight into the reasons for decreases or changing patterns in offenses and arrests between time I and time III. We identified correlations that were statistically significant, but we did not yet control for the effects of other key and interaction variables—for example, age and preprogram offenses and arrests—or for other factors.

Neighborhood

The youth's increased fear of gang-related problems in the neighborhood between time I and time III was highly correlated with decreases in the youth's self-reported drug-selling offenses, total self-reported arrests, total violence arrests, and serious violence arrests at time III. Concern with suppression efforts also emerged as an important neighborhood-level effect. Two community-level police variables were correlated with self-reported arrest variables. At time I, if the youth did not perceive the police patrolling in squad cars, he self-reported higher rates of total violence arrests at time III and even higher rates of serious violence arrests. A perception of less police patrolling in the neighborhood and increased harassing of youth at time I was correlated with increased self-reported total offenses at time III. The youth's perceptions of probation officers addressing the gang problem were similarly correlated with total self-reported offenses and arrests. If the youth knew a specific probation officer at time I who dealt with the gang problem, there was a correlation at time III with lower self-reported total offenses (excluding drug offenses), serious violence offenses, total violence offenses, property offenses, and drug use. A strategy of suppression was very important in the reduction of self-reported total offenses.

Household and Family

Larger household size was correlated with an increase in self-reported property arrests at time I ($p \leq 0.01$) and time III ($p \leq 0.01$). In other words, as household membership increased, the likelihood of the youth reporting that he had been arrested for property offenses increased. Annual household illegal income was correlated with higher arrests for serious violence at time I but not at time III. However, annual household illegal income was highly correlated with an increase in drug-selling offenses both at time I *and* at time III. The higher the level of household illegal income, the higher the probability that the youth reported he was selling drugs.

Program youth reported positive relationships with members of their families, particularly with their mothers. At time I, these positive relationships with mothers were highly correlated with lower levels of self-reported offenses and arrests. The more positive the relationship with mothers at time I, the more likely the youth self-reported fewer total offenses, property offenses, total arrests, and property arrests, and also fewer total violence offenses, serious violence offenses, and less drug use. Nevertheless, all of these relationships were no longer statistically significant at time III. There were also no significant correlations of relationships with fathers and self-reported offenses or arrests, either at time I or at time III. Positive relationships with siblings were related to decreased property offenses at time I and decreased drug use at time III. However, these parental and sibling relationships were no longer present (or showed opposite effects with the frequency of certain offenses) in the multivariate analyses below.

One surprising correlation was the nature of the youth's relationships with wives or steady girlfriends and self-reported offenses. A negative relationship with a wife or steady girlfriend at time I was correlated with a reduction in self-reported total offenses, violence offenses, and property offenses at time III. Unlike the youth's relationships with mothers, fathers, and siblings, problematic relationships with wives or steady girlfriends appeared to result in reduced levels of offending over time. This could be explained by pressures from wives or steady girlfriends on gang youth to reduce their level of involvement with the gang. Furthermore, an increase in the amount of time spent with wives and steady girlfriends at time I was significantly correlated with a reduction in self-reported total offenses, violence offenses, and serious violence offenses at time III. Also, youth who spent more time with wives or steady girlfriends at time III than they did at time I, despite or because of tension and conflict with spouses, showed reduced total offenses and violence offenses at time III.

Household Crises

The greater the number of personal problems of household members, the greater the increase in the youth's self-reported offending. Household drug-abuse problems at time I were strongly correlated with increases in self-reported drug use and drug selling at time III. Drug abuse by household members was correlated with self-reported total violence offenses and serious violence offenses at time I, but at time III it remained associated only with an increase in the youth's reported drug selling. Gang-crime-related problems of household members at time I were also correlated with higher levels of self-reported violence arrests (p ≤ 0.01), total arrests, and drug offenses at time III.

Personal and family problems reported by youth at time III (now including physical abuse) were highly correlated with self-reported increases in violence offenses and serious violence offenses, and self-reported total arrests, violence arrests, and serious violence arrests. Arrests of household members were highly correlated with the youth's self-reported total offenses, violence offenses, drug use, and serious violence offenses at time III. Victimization of household members due to gang violence at time I was correlated with higher levels of youth self-reported total offenses, violence offenses, and property offenses, and self-reported violence arrests and serious violence arrests at time III. A death in the family at time I was correlated with an increase in total offenses and property offenses reported by the youth at time III. Thus, household or family problems were strongly associated with increased levels of self-reported offending, although the character of these household or family problems varied somewhat between time I and time III.

At time I, a small number of youth reported they received treatment for mental-health problems. Such treatment was highly correlated at time I with lower self-reported property offenses, total offenses, total arrests, property arrests, drug use, and violence arrests. Treatment for alcohol problems at time I was also associated with reduced levels of self-reported drug-selling and property arrests. However, none of these treatment effects was related to the level of self-reported offending at time III. In sum, a range of serious family and household problems at time I was highly correlated with self-reported patterns of offending for many of the youth, and there was some evidence that treatment was useful in the reduction of some of the youth's offending problems at time III.

Gang Structure

A variety of questions were asked in the interviews that permitted analysis of possible changes in the youth's perceptions of his gang's structure, patterns of fighting, and reasons for fighting. Surprisingly, there were few gang-level change characteristics correlated positively or negatively with the youth's self-reported offense or arrest levels. There was also little to distinguish between the perceptions of the Latin Kings and Two Six regarding gang structure and fighting.

The one generally meaningful or interpretable relationship was that the youth's perception of the size of his gang section was associated with his offense or arrest level. If the youth perceived that his section had become smaller between time I and time III, this was associated with a reduction in his total self-reported offenses, violence offenses (including serious violence offenses), and self-reported property arrests at time III. In other words, the smaller the perceived size of the gang section over time, the less likely the youth self-reported that he was involved in gang offending. This could be interpreted in several ways: the youth was withdrawing from the gang section; others in his group were also withdrawing; or gang-section membership might have become less "tight" (or cohesive). If the gang section was perceived as smaller, then the youth might no longer value the gang or be attracted to the gang's criminal norms or activities (Klein 1971).

The literature on gangs has indicated that a youth's involvement with the gang, or his holding high status or position in the gang, affects his involvement in criminal activities (Thornberry et al. 2003). Our findings support these observations. At time III, youth who declared they were still active in the gang, compared to the youth who said they were no longer active in the gang, self-reported higher levels of total violence offenses, serious violence offenses, and drug use. The higher the youth's rank in the gang (e.g., core member or leader rather than regular or peripheral member), the more often he self-reported higher levels of total offenses, total violence offenses, serious violence offenses, property offenses, total arrests, violence arrests, and serious violence arrests.

At time I, the amount of time the youth spent with gang friends was positively correlated with increased self-reported total offenses and property offenses. The more time the youth spent with gang friends at time I was also highly correlated with increasing frequency of offenses and arrests at time III. The less time youth spent with gang friends at time I, the lower the level of time III self-reported total offenses, drug use, drug selling, property offenses, total violence offenses, serious violence offenses, total arrests, violence arrests, and serious violence arrests.

Further, if the youth said he was thinking of leaving the gang (or considering leaving in the future), he was more likely to self-report lower levels of offenses and arrests, both at time I and time III. This correlation was particularly significant at time I for total offenses, violence offenses, serious violence offenses, property offenses, drug use, drug selling, total arrests, total violence arrests, and serious violence arrests.

There was also a correlation between more time spent with parents and relatives and fewer self-reported offenses and arrests. At time I, this was true for total offenses, violence offenses, serious violence offenses, property offenses, total arrests, and property arrests. However, the direction of the correlation was different at time III. The more time the youth spent with parents or relatives, the more he increased his involvement in drug use or drug selling. The different patterns between time I and time III possibly indicated the varying influence of parents and relatives in controlling the youth's involvement in certain types of illegitimate behaviors. It was possible that parents and relatives were more concerned with the youth's involvement in gang fighting than drug activities, particularly at time I.

School and Jobs

We were particularly interested in the youths' use of legitimate social opportunities that could lead to a reduction of gang crime. We examined the youths' access to education, employment, and income (legal and illegal) in relation to self-reported offending at time I and time III. We looked first at the relationship of the youth's self-reported offenses to changes in educational status. Almost all youth had prior or current negative experiences in the public school system. Educational achievement was weakly correlated with self-reported offenses at time I. The higher the educational level, the more likely the youth was to self-report lower levels of total arrests or property arrests. This pattern remained unchanged at time III but was not statistically significant.

Employment was associated with a general reduction in self-reported arrests. Employment was strongly correlated at time I with lower levels of total offenses, violence offenses, property offenses, drug use, and drug selling. At time I, employed youth were more likely to self-report fewer property arrests. Generally, youth who were employed at both time I and time III reported fewer total arrests and property arrests. The more time the youth spent in some form of legitimate employment, the lower the level of self-reported total offenses, serious violence offenses, total violence offenses, drug use, and drug selling. Employment appeared to be much more strongly associated than educational achievement with lower levels and fewer categories of self-reported offenses and arrests.

Legally derived income was correlated with a reduction in offenses (arrests) at time III. The higher the level of legal income, the lower the level and fewer the categories of self-reported total offenses, violence offenses, serious violence offenses, property offenses, and drug use. If the youth had a legitimate job or access to legal sources of income, his offending patterns were also reduced at time III. We look more closely at access to legal and illegal income as predictors of reductions in offenses in the multivariate models in the next section.

Aspirations and Expectations

Finally, we briefly examined the relationship of the youths' income and occupational aspirations and expectations to their self-reported offending patterns. Levels of income and occupational aspirations, per se, were not correlated with offense variables. However, the relationships between income aspirations and expectations, and between occupation aspirations and expectations, were significantly correlated with offense variables, particularly at time III. The larger the income aspiration and expectation gap, or "disjunction," the greater the association was with increased property offenses at time III but not at time I. A larger gap or disjunction between occupational aspirations and expectations was correlated with greater drug use at time III. In our multivariate analysis below, when other variables are statistically controlled, we found that as the gap decreased between aspirations and expectations, especially for occupation, the level of self-reported total offenses lowered. In a later chapter, we will find that a higher dosage of services predicted a smaller gap between income aspirations and expectations (chapter 14).

MODELS
Predicting Change in Self-Reported Offenses between Time I and Time III

We selected multiple regression modeling as the method by which to predict the effects on change in self-reported offenses using the neighborhood, family, gang, and individual-youth characteristics we identified as statistically significant in the correlation analyses above. We also used certain control variables (the youth's age at program entry and the gang with which he was affiliated) and covariates (time I total offenses and time I violence offenses). These control variables and covariates entered our models as predictors of change in three independent equations. The dependent variables in the different equations were change in total offenses, change in total violence offenses, and change in drug-selling offenses between time I and time III. Since the values of some of the variables were missing for six program youth, the sample size for the models in this analysis was 121.

Total Offenses

The best model for predicting change or reduction in total self-reported offenses between time I and time III included six variables: age category at time I (under nineteen, nineteen and older); time spent with wife or steady girlfriend at time I (few hours or most of the day, no time); has known probation officers who dealt with the gang problem at time I (yes, no); gang size at time III (larger, about the same, smaller); number of major household crises at time III (ranging from zero to eleven); and difference between occupational aspirations and expectations at time I (large difference, small difference, missing response, no difference).

This model explained 43.0 percent of total variance in change in total offenses between time I and time III. The factors that best accounted for variance, in order of significance, were as follows: having known probation officers addressing the gang problem at time I; spending more time with wives or steady girlfriends at time I; and a younger age of the youth (under nineteen years). Although younger youth reported higher levels of offenses at time III in our earlier prediction model above, they were likely to show more positive change, or a greater reduction in total offenses, than older youth, particularly when we did not distinguish differences between the younger age groups (sixteen and under and seventeen and eighteen) and the nineteen-and-over youth. This age finding would be reversed in general linear and logistic regression models when we examined all three age categories separately for explaining arrests.

Those youth with less gap or "disjunction" between occupational aspirations and expectations at time I were more likely to decrease their offending levels between time I and time III, while those with a larger gap or "disjunction"

Table 10.9. Best multiple regression model[a] predicting change in self-reported total offenses[b] between time I and time III

Youth Variable	Beta	F[c]
Age at time I: under nineteen (= 1); nineteen and older (= 0)	−19.88	4.14*
Time spent with wife or steady girlfriend at time I: few hours/most of the day (= 1); no time (= 0)	−26.22	6.06*
Has known probation officers who dealt with the gang problem at time I: yes (= 1); no (= 0)	−39.58	7.54**
Gang size at time III: larger (= 1); about the same (= 0); smaller (= −1)	15.35	3.42
Number of major household crises[d] at time III: (0–11)	6.15	3.99*
Difference in occupational aspirations and expectations[e] at time I: large difference (= 2); small difference (= 1); missing response (= 0); no difference (= −1)	13.44	4.09*

Notes
a. Overall R square for the model = 0.43, N = 121, df = 6.
b. Same total offenses as in table 10.1 (c).
c. For differences between time periods: * $p \le 0.05$; ** $p \le 0.01$; *** $p \le 0.001$.
d. Eleven problem categories: death in the family; serious illness in the family; drug abuse; physical abuse; crime-related problems; victim of gang violence; arrest in the household; family-relationship problems; job-related problems; income-related problems; and other problems.
e. Eight aspiration and expectation categories: professional/executive; managerial; clerical; mechanical; semiskilled and unskilled positions; own business; and not working.

were likely to increase their offending levels. The presence of fewer household and family crises at time III resulted in a significant decrease in self-reported total offenses. Finally, the youth's perception at time III that his gang size was smaller was almost statistically significant in predicting positive change or a higher reduction in total offenses (table 10.9).

Knowledge of or contact with a probation officer at time I was the strongest predictor of a reduction in total offenses between time I and time III. The youth spending more time with his wife or steady girlfriend, the younger youth (sixteen and under, seventeen and eighteen), and the youth with closely aligned occupational aspirations and expectations indicated less alienation and contributed to a reduction in self-reported total offenses. The perception of a smaller gang size at time I was somewhat predictive of a reduction in self-reported total offenses. Finally, a household with fewer health and criminal justice crises at time III predicted a reduction in self-reported total offenses between time I and time III.

Consistent with the project model, a closely related suppression and social-control approach appeared to play a key role in successfully addressing the gang problem of program youth, at least based on the findings of interview and self-report data. Monitoring and supervision of the youth's behavior, as well as guidance about social norms and behaviors and realistic occupational opportunities were important. Counseling youth to spend more time with their wives or steady girlfriends rather than with the gang, and helping youth and their families cope with a variety of social, health, and criminal justice problems were also important.

Total Violence Offenses

Our initial efforts to predict change, or reduction, in self-reported violence offenses in the total program sample between time I and time III were only mildly successful. We couldn't find a strong model to predict change in total violence offenses using the sample (N = 121). Consequently, we decided to divide the sample into the seventy-five youth who committed fewer violence offenses at time III than at time I—possibly representing the youth with whom the project was successful—and the forty-six youth who committed the same number or even more violence offenses between time I and time III. Best models were selected to predict change in violence offenses for each of these two subsamples.

The best model for predicting change in total self-reported violence offenses of youth who *reduced* their total violence offenses between time I and time III included seven variables. No control variables (e.g., age or specific gang) entered significantly into this equation. The variables used in our model were as follows:

- number of gang-crime avoidance actions at time I (ranging from zero to five), including turning down a job because of unsafe location, not keeping a gun or other weapon at home, arranging to go out with someone so the youth would not be alone, selecting a residence because it was safe, and not going to a school with gang problems;
- satisfaction with the community at time I (very/somewhat satisfied, very/somewhat dissatisfied);
- number of treatments for problems (drug, alcohol, physical, mental health) at time I (ranging from zero to four);

- youth's total monthly illegal income at time III (zero to eight thousand dollars);
- knew probation officers who dealt with the gang problem at time I (yes, no);
- total household yearly legal income at time I (eight income levels); and
- got along with father in the past year at time III (always/most of the time, sometimes/never).

This change model explained 60.0 percent of total variance in the reduction of total violence offenses between time I and time III. The factors that best accounted for variance, in order of degree of influence, were avoiding actions that exposed the youth to gang crime; satisfaction with living in the community; undergoing treatment for personal problems; lower level of illegal income; and not knowing (or having had contact with) probation officers who addressed the gang problem. Also, higher legitimate household income and *not* having a positive relationship with the father were important factors in predicting lower levels of violence offenses but just missed statistical significance (table 10.10).

The most powerful factors contributing to a reduction of the youth's violent activity were simply avoiding violent situations and being satisfied with conditions in the community. Also important were the youth's undertaking treatment for his various personal problems, as well as not engaging in illegal activity (such as selling drugs) and not being placed on probation.

These commonsense considerations would seem not difficult for the youth to handle with some external guidance, support, and control. Individual counseling, provision of opportunities for legitimate jobs, and curtailment of sources of illegitimate income for the youth appeared to be useful approaches for program and policy development.

Our best model for predicting change in total self-reported violence offenses for youth who *increased* (or experienced no change in) total violence offenses between time I and time III also included seven variables:

- number of gang-crime avoidance actions at time III (but not time I, as in the previous model for total violence offenses; ranging from zero to five);
- gang size at time III (larger, about the same, smaller);
- total household yearly illegal income at time III (eight income levels);
- total youth monthly illegal income at time III (zero to eight thousand dollars);
- total youth monthly legal income at time III ($0 to $3,900);

- gets along with siblings at time III (always/most of the time, some-times/never); and
- number of days per week carrying a gun at time III (ranging from zero to seven).

Table 10.10. Best multiple regression model[a] predicting change in self-reported total violence offenses[b] for youth who *reduced* their total violence offenses between time I and time III

Youth variable	Beta	F[c]
Satisfaction with his community at time I: satisfied (= 1); dissatisfied (= 0)	−37.49	13.93***
Number of actions taken to avoid gang-crime situations at time I:[d] (0–5)	−11.89	23.66***
Knew probation officers who dealt with the gang problem at time I: yes (= 1); no (= 0)	22.71	4.57*
Total household yearly legal income at time I:[e] (0–7)	− 0.47	3.45
Number of treatments for problems at time I:[f] (0–4)	−39.70	6.33*
Total youth monthly illegal income at time III[g]	0.01	5.00*
Got along with father in the past year at time III: always/most of the time (= 1); sometimes/never (= 0)	16.05	2.84

Notes
a. Overall R square for the model = 0.60, N = 75, df = 7.
b. Same total violence offenses as in table 10.1 (d).
c. For differences between time periods: * p ≤ 0.05; ** p ≤ 0.01; *** p ≤ 0.001.
d. The five gang-crime-avoidance actions are as follows: turned down a job at an unsafe location; didn't keep a gun or other weapon at home; arranged to go out with someone; selected a safe residence; and didn't go to a school with gang problems.
e. The eight income categories are as follows: $0; $1–$10,000; $10,001–$20,000; $20,001–$30,000; $30,001–$40,000; $40,001–$50,000; $50,001–$60,000; and $60,001 and over.
f. The four treatment problems are as follows: drug, alcohol, physical, and mental health.
g. The two income sources are as follows: selling drugs and other illegal activities. Range = $0–$8,000.

This change model explained 68.0 percent of total variance in the model. The characteristics of youth who showed no change, or got worse, in terms of an increase in total violence offenses were as follows: not avoiding activities or situations that exposed them to gang crime; perceiving an increase in gang size or viewing and identifying with the gang or gang section as a growing and powerful entity; having limited access to both illegal and legal income; getting along well or identifying with siblings who might be gang members; and often carrying a gun (table 10.11).

The addition of two more variables in this model—fear of walking alone because of gang concerns and gap between occupation aspirations and

Table 10.11. Best multiple regression model[a] predicting change in self-reported total violence offenses[b] for youth who *increased* (or experienced no change in) their total violence offenses between time I and time III

Youth variable	Beta	F[c]
Number of actions taken to avoid gang-crime situations at time III:[d] (0–5)	−4.60	18.56***
Gang size at time III: larger (= 1); about the same (= 0); smaller (= −1)	10.407	19.09***
Total household yearly illegal income at time III:[e] (0–7)	12.28	19.80***
Total youth monthly illegal income at time III[f]	−0.01	14.06***
Total youth monthly legal income at time III[g]	−0.01	8.37**
Got along with siblings at time III: always/most of the time (= 1); sometimes/never (= 0)	13.89	23.48***
Number of days per week carrying a gun at time III: (0–7)	8.52	23.40***

Notes
a. Overall R square for the model = 0.68, N = 46, df = 7.
b. Same total violence offenses as in Table 10.1 (d).
c. For differences between time periods: * $p \leq 0.05$; ** $p \leq 0.01$; *** $p \leq 0.001$.
d. The five gang-crime avoidance actions are as follows: turned down a job at an unsafe location; didn't keep a gun or other weapon at home; arranged to go out with someone; selected a safe residence; and didn't go to a school with gang problems.
e. The eight income categories are as follows: $0; $1–$10,000; $10,001–$20,000; $20,001–$30,000; $30,001–$40,000; $40,001–$50,000; $50,001–$60,000; $60,001 and over.
f. The two income sources are as follows: selling drugs and other illegal activities. Range = $0–$8,000.
g. The nine income sources are as follows: jobs/regular employment; odd jobs/self-employment; public aid; unemployment compensation; parents/family; girlfriend/spouse; friends; and other. Range = $0–$3,900.

expectations—would have produced a more powerful (but perhaps less-efficient) model, contributing 74.0 percent of the total variance in the model for predicting changes in total violence offenses of youth.

This model indicated that hard-to-change, violent gang youth did not avoid high-risk gang situations, were highly fearful, and frequently carried a gun; they saw the gang as growing larger and got along with their siblings who might have been gang members or involved in criminal activities. These youth were exposed to a double failure of opportunities—they were not successful at gaining income from legitimate or illegal sources (Cloward and Ohlin 1960).

All of these factors were highly significant predictors of a program's having difficulty in addressing the problems of violence-prone gang youth. Not only were they prone to personal and social failure, but also their families might be criminally oriented and socially and psychologically disorganized during the period of the youth's gang involvement. A highly integrated set of strong controls, intensive counseling, and the provision of social opportunities—both for youth and for their families—was extremely important.

Drug-Selling Offenses

It was difficult to find variables to predict change or reduction in drug-selling offenses among program youth. Several of the youth sold drugs occasionally at time I. More and different variables were needed than were used in the previous three multiple regression models. We were interested in whether the pattern of predictors might indicate a relationship between gang violence and days per week selling drugs. We excluded drug use from this model, since we already knew it was highly correlated with drug selling. Age was also not a significant predictor in the best ten-variable model we could find.

The ten predictor variables used in our model were as follows:

- afraid to walk alone in the neighborhood because of gang-related concerns at time I (yes, no);
- knew a probation officer who dealt with the gang problem at time III (yes, no);
- serious gang fighting with another gang that might result in his serious injury at time III (yes, less-serious injury or don't know);
- bothered that he could be killed because of a gang fight at time III (yes, no);
- his section of the gang had changed at time III (better, same, worse);
- number of relatives in jail at time III (ranging from zero to two);
- total youth monthly illegal income at time III (zero to eight thousand dollars);
- received a GED or graduated from a job-training program at time I (yes, no);
- most of the day spent at work at time III (a few hours or more, no time); and
- marital status at time III (married, other).

This change model explained 62.9 percent of total variance in the reduction of days per week of selling drugs between time I and time III.

The factors that best accounted for an increase in self-reported drug selling, in order of influence, were as follows: the presence of serious gang fighting in the neighborhood; viewing his gang section as less involved in violence than it used to be; high illegal income; spending little time at a legitimate job; having earned a GED or graduated from a training program; knowing a probation officer who dealt with gang problems; and being afraid to walk alone in the neighborhood because of gang activity.

Table 10.12. Best multiple regression model[a] predicting change in self-reported drug-selling offenses[b] between time I and time III

Youth variable	Beta	F[c]
Self-reported total change in drug using	0.32	4.43*
Afraid to walk alone in neighborhood because of gang-related concerns at time I: yes (= 1); no (= 0)	2.88	3.52
Knew probation officers who dealt with the gang problem at time III: yes (= 1); no (= 0)	3.45	3.60
Serious gang fighting might result in his (very) serious injury at time III: yes (= 1); less-serious injury/don't know (= 0)	1.87	17.87***
Is bothered that he could be killed because of a gang fight at time III: yes (= 1); no (= 0)	−4.51	8.72**
Gang section has changed at time III: better (= −1); same (= 0); worse (= 1)	2.80	6.14*
Number of relatives in jail at time III: (0, 1, 2)	−4.67	5.37*
Total youth monthly illegal income[d] at time III	2.79	7.95**
Received a GED certificate or graduated from a job training program at time I: yes (= 1); no (= 0)	7.85	6.56*
Spends most of the day at work at time III: a few hours or more (= 1); no time (= 0)	−3.69	5.20*
Marital status at time III: married (= 1); other (= 0)	−3.16	7.29**

Notes
a. Overall R square for the model = 0.65, N = 75, df = 11.
b. Same drug-selling offenses as in table 10.1(g). Several youth were only occasional drug sellers.
c. For differences between time periods: * $p \leq 0.05$; ** $p \leq 0.01$; *** $p \leq 0.001$.
d. The two income sources are as follows: selling drugs and other illegal activities. Range = $0–$8,000.

The factors that contributed to a decrease in self-reported drug selling, in order of degree of influence, were as follows: the youth was concerned that he might end up dead because of a gang fight; he was married; several of his relatives were already in jail; and he spent most of the day at work (table 10.12).

There appeared to be an inverse relationship between gang violence and drug selling. Gang violence may have become too extreme and deadly; the youth may have been very concerned with the possibility of getting killed; and he was now making a good deal of money selling drugs. In other words, the youth was transitioning to drug selling because of the high risks of gang violence and the pull of making money selling drugs, particularly as others in the gang were also doing it. He had obtained a fairly adequate education and calculated that drug dealing provided better rewards than gang fighting.

On the other hand, pressures to reduce his involvement in drug dealing came from his wife or girlfriend. He was also spending considerable time at a legitimate job, and he had a number of relatives already in jail, possibly because of drug dealing. In a later chapter, we develop the proposition that different types of gang members may be more predisposed to either violence or drug selling, or a combination of the two, and that the project might have been more effective with one type of gang youth than another.

VARIED EFFECTS OF COMMUNITY AND SOCIAL FACTORS ON YOUTH GANG CRIME

Interview and self-report offense data were available for program youth and permitted a preliminary but rich analysis of the wide range of community, social, and personal factors that contributed to changes in gang-youth-offense behavior. The analysis was limited, however. We did not have interview and self-report data for comparison gang youth, and our analysis of changes was limited to the project period. Also, the effects of project-worker contacts and services that predicted these changes were not yet introduced.

The analysis is useful, nevertheless, because it reports the array of factors of community, family, gang, relationships with wives or girlfriends, school, jobs, and aspirations and expectations that can influence gang youth. These are the project workers' targets for change, in relation to the youths' specific deviant behavior. Of special interest is identification of the different types of social situations that influence gang youth for better or worse. Gang youth are not all the same in their responses to situations and project staff.

In the self-report data collected from program youth in three successive interviews during a three- or four-year-program period, the youth stated they were less involved in all types of gang offenses. They reported significantly less involvement in violence offenses and fewer drug arrests, although not significantly fewer. The Latin King youth reported greater declines than the Two Six, particularly in violence offenses, but the Two Six reported fewer drug-selling offenses. Cohort I youth (who were contacted by program workers for longer periods of time than cohort II and cohort III youth) reported the greatest declines in offenses.

While violence appeared to be more often gang- or peer-group related, drug use and drug selling were more often reported to be non-gang-related activities. Alcohol use was reported most often to occur with gang peers.

Based on multiple regression analyses, certain life-course and life-space factors seemed to be the best predictors of reductions in the different types of self-reported offenses. The best-model predictors of reduced total offenses included the youth's contact with or knowledge of a probation officer dealing with the gang problem, more rather than less time spent with a wife or steady girlfriend, and being an older youth (nineteen years or older). The best-model predictors of reduced-violence offenses were the youth's satisfaction with the community, his avoidance of gang situations, and more rather than less involvement in treatment for different personal problems. The best-model predictors of reduced drug-selling activity were having a greater number of relatives in jail, having a wife or steady girlfriend, and spending more rather than less time at a job.

In later chapters we explore the extent to which the project and certain specific worker services and activities contributed to these reductions in offenses, using comparison samples and arrest changes between preprogram and program periods in controlled, multivariate statistical models.

NOTES

1. There is a seventeenth offense category, "other." It was not frequently used, and when it was, we were usually able to reclassify the offense into one of the sixteen categories. The crimes that were not reclassifiable were included only in the analysis of total self-reported offenses (arrests).

2. This list is not necessarily equivalent to the larger listing of official criminal justice offense codes (chapter 12).

Project-Worker Contacts, Services, and Strategies

What did the Little Village Project workers do? Surprisingly, key elements of gang projects, for example, what specific workers do with different youth in gang programs and how effective they thought their efforts were, have not been generally identified in gang-program evaluations (Bickman 2000). In earlier chapters, we provided a glimpse of the project workers' specific activities. In this chapter, we more systematically describe the nature of the contacts made and services provided to program youth by project outreach youth workers, police, probation officers, and the neighborhood organizer and the strategies they employed. We do this first through use of summary reports (worker tracking) collected on an annual basis from all of the project workers for 191 program youth. Second, we focus on the network of services or activities developed, using weekly worker-debriefing records, which also included contacts with other persons regarding the services provided. Debriefing records were completed for only 65 of the 191 program youth. Both types of records describe in detailed, quantitative terms the specific efforts and roles of the different workers. The findings of the worker-tracking and debriefing records prove to be reasonably consistent.

WORKER-TRACKING RECORDS

Worker-tracking forms were completed three times, at yearly intervals during the course of the five-year program period—in the second, fourth, and fifth years. We used worker-tracking data collected for 191 program youth to look at the characteristics of worker service contacts in terms of the dosage—that is, duration, frequency, and intensity—of the following specific types of activities: individual-youth brief counseling (advice), family contacts, school and job-related services, and suppression efforts. We determined what services were provided by which workers to which gang youth, with what frequency of contacts per youth per month, over how many months. Contacts for services or activities encompassed different strategies: social intervention, social opportunities provision, and suppression.

Contacts by workers were directed to hard-core gang youth who were exhibiting high rates of violence and other kinds of criminal behavior. The more serious a youth's involvement in these behaviors, the more project workers were expected to sustain or intensify contacts with the youth. We expected that the nature and frequency of services and contacts, along with the particular combination of workers involved, would contribute to the project's goal—the reduction of the youth's gang activities, particularly violence, and possibly other crimes.

The Worker-Tracking Youth Sample

The number of program youth with worker-tracking records was not exactly the same as the number of program youth who were interviewed, or for whom we had police arrest data. Of the 195 youths in the program who were interviewed, only 164 had worker-tracking data. Youth workers, for various reasons, failed to provide tracking data for thirty-one youths. These thirty-one youths were not included in the present analysis, although most did, in fact, receive some services and contacts. In addition, there were twenty-seven youths who should not have been targeted for services who nevertheless were tracked by the workers and received some services. These twenty-seven youths *are* included in the present analysis—yielding a worker-tracking sample of 191 youths.

Of the 164 interviewed youths in this sample who had worker-tracking records, eighty-five (51.8 percent) were in cohort I[1] (those youths who entered the program in its first two years of operations); thirty-eight (23.2 percent) were in cohort II, some of whom began receiving services at about the same time as cohort I youth but did not complete a first interview until the second year of the program; and forty-one (25 percent) were in cohort III, who came into the program and were interviewed at the beginning of the fourth program year. Relatively more of the older program youth, mainly nineteen years and older and seventeen and eighteen years, were in cohorts I and II, respectively, and relatively more of the younger youth (mainly fifteen- and sixteen-year-olds) were in cohort III. More of the youth who were interviewed two or more times had worker-tracking data (91.4 percent), compared to those who were interviewed only once (50.0 percent).

Scope of Worker Contacts

The scope of worker contacts is based on the amount of time (expressed in months) that contacts were provided, the frequency of contacts per month, and the intensity of contacts, that is, total frequency of contacts with youth divided by total months of contact. We examine the characteristics of the contacts provided by the different types of project workers separately, and together in various combinations. We first describe worker activities over the five-year project period by total sample (N = 191), cohort (I, II, and III), and gang (Latin Kings and Two Six).

Duration of Contacts

Not all project workers were in continuing contact with each program youth; that is, the same worker or worker team did not necessarily provide contacts for services to a particular youth over the period of time the youth was in the program. On average, contacts were made by 2.4 different types of workers over a period of 29.2 months. Each youth was contacted by one or more different types of workers over an average of almost two and a half years.

Project outreach youth workers were in touch with and served the largest number of youth of any of the other types of project workers. An average of 1.7 different youth workers served 179 youth over 17.5 months. (Note that the average stay of outreach youth workers with the project was approximately two years.) Usually, two youth workers were assigned to each gang—the Latin Kings and the Two Six—including different sections of each gang at any given time period. The assigned youth workers contacted members of different sections of their particular gang but never of both gangs. The project police, probation, and to some extent the neighborhood organizer were generally able to work with, or at least contact, youth across all sections of both gangs.

The pattern of project police contacts was different from that of the youth workers: an average of 1.6 project police officers served or contacted fifty-eight youth from both gangs for a longer period—an average of 32.6 months per youth. The same two police officers usually worked together during the entire five years of the project. This consistency was not the case with the youth workers, the probation officers, or the neighborhood organizer. The project experienced greater turnover of youth workers than other types of workers.

Five adult probation officers were assigned to the project in two overlapping three-year periods; an average of 1.8 different probation officers served twenty program youth during an average 15.5-month period. Probation officers reported contacts only with those program youth who were currently on adult probation through the Little Village office. The data in this chapter do not include program-youth contacts with other Cook County adult probation officers. We have no tracking data regarding youth on juvenile probation during the program period. We know that a small number of program juveniles, that is, less than seventeen years of age, were either on probation or in juvenile detention at some point during the program period. Cook County Juvenile Court Probation, as an organization, did not formally join or collaborate with the project, although project workers did contact individual juvenile probation officers on a case-by-case basis.

The neighborhood organizer provided services to program youth over a period of two and a half years, mainly advice or brief individual or family counseling, job referrals, and occasionally supervising athletic activities. The organizer was in contact with twenty-five youth for an average of 10.2 months per youth.

Most tracked youth in the first cohort were exposed to more workers and had longer periods of service but were not necessarily provided a greater frequency of contacts. On average, eighty-five cohort I youth were served by three workers over thirty-seven months; sixty-five cohort II youth were served by two workers for an average of 27.3 months; and forty-one cohort III youth were served by 1.7 workers for an average of 15.9 months. While the number of workers varied by cohort, frequency of monthly contact did not; it depended mainly on the nature of the youth's troublesome gang activity, especially his violent behavior. Frequency of contact usually diminished once the youth "settled down."

Based on worker-tracking data, the project served more Latin Kings (n = 102)—the older and more violent of the two gangs—than Two Six (n = 89). The Latin Kings were served, on average, by more workers (2.6) and for a longer period of time (32.5 months) than the Two Six, who were served by 2.1 workers for 25.3 months. Nevertheless, the Two Six were provided with more frequent contacts, as explained below. Also, more of the program youth who were both tracked and interviewed were in contact with more workers (2.6), and longer (31.7 months), than program youth who were tracked but not interviewed. The twenty-seven youth for whom we had tracking data only were served essentially by one worker for a period of 13.4 months. There was also a relationship between the number of times a program youth was interviewed and the length of time the youth was served. Youth interviewed two or more times were provided with 23.2 months of contacts, while youth who were interviewed only once were provided with 16.7 months of contacts. Youth for whom we had more tracking records (and who were interviewed more often) were more serious violent offenders.

Frequency of Contacts

Frequency was computed based on the number of youth contacts per month made by each worker. An average of 2.4 project workers were in contact with program youth an average of sixteen times per month over the entire time the youth were in the program. In other words, program youth were provided with a great deal of contact by a variety of workers, on average almost four times a week. An average of 1.7 youth workers served 179 youth and were in contact with each youth thirteen times per month; 1.6 project police served fifty-eight youth and had contact with each youth 7.7 times per month; and 1.8 project probation officers served twenty youth and contacted each youth 7.4 times per month. One neighborhood organizer, with a twenty-five-youth caseload, contacted youth an average of 5.6 times per month.

The 164 worker-tracked youths who were interviewed were provided with considerably more worker contacts, more frequently—seventeen times per month—than the twenty-seven worker-tracked youths who were not interviewed. These twenty-seven youths were contacted exclusively by youth workers an average of 9.7 times per month. The program youth who were interviewed once and those who were in the program for a short period of time were not necessarily provided fewer contacts per month during the period they were in the program than youth interviewed two or more times.

The pattern of contacts varied slightly for the Latin Kings and the Two Six. The Latin Kings were contacted on average by a few more workers (2.7), but they received contacts somewhat less frequently—an average of 15.7 times per month. The Two Six were contacted by fewer workers (2.1) but a little more frequently—an average of 16.3 times per month. Also, there was some difference in numbers of contacts with youth based on different age categories. Overall, there were more contacts per month with seventeen- and eighteen-year-olds (19.3) than with those sixteen and younger (16.6) and nineteen and older (15.3). Outreach youth workers, police officers, and probation officers focused more on contacting seventeen- and eighteen-year-olds—the heavy gangbangers. The neighborhood organizer concentrated on contacting youth sixteen and younger.

Intensity of Contacts

We developed a measure of intensity of contacts. The computation of the intensity score was based on the total number of contacts made with a youth by a particular worker, divided by the number of months the youth was in the program. The score took into consideration the length of time the youth was in the program overall and the frequency of contacts by all of the workers and by particular types of workers. For the total 191 youth in this analysis, the average intensity score was 8.9 contacts per month and represented mainly the intensity of contacts established by the youth workers with 179 youth—8.8 contacts per month. Contacts by the project police, who served fewer youth (n = 58), were less intense—5.4 contacts per month, the same as that established by the neighborhood organizer, who served even fewer youth (n = 25). The intensity score for project probation officers, who served the fewest number of youth (n = 20), was 4.3 contacts per month. In other words, the intensity of contacts with program youth made by the youth workers, even though they served more youth, was greater than that of other team members.

The intensity of contacts varied depending on the needs of youth for controls and services, as well as their response to worker efforts. Youth in cohort II were provided with the greatest intensity of contacts per month (10.3), compared to youth in cohort I (8.4) and in cohort III (7.8). The Two Six were provided with a greater intensity of contacts per month (10.1) than the Latin Kings (7.9). As indicated above, we found that youth seventeen and eighteen years of age, who were probably at the peak period of their gang activity and gang violence, were provided with the greatest intensity of contacts over the longest period of time compared to the other age categories, particularly by project youth workers and project police.

Types and Perceived Effectiveness of Service Contacts

Our discussion in this section is based on findings of the worker-tracking records. Not all youth were provided with every type of service. The key services provided by the various types of project workers included the following: gang or individual counseling and advice (brief rather than extended);

family-related services; school referrals or assistance; job training, job referral, or job placement; suppression (arrest, probation violation, supervision, warning, etc.); athletic activities; and other kinds of services (e.g., hospital visits, assistance for girlfriends, and camping trips). The actual services were provided in different social and physical contexts, and with different purposes in mind. These are elaborated in the findings of the debriefing records discussed below.

All types of workers were also asked to estimate their effectiveness, or success, in the provision of particular types of services or activities. They could respond that a pattern of particular services provided to a particular youth over a worker-tracking period was either not effective (1 = none), little effective (2 = little), somewhat effective (3 = some), or very effective (4 = very much). The perception of varying degrees of effectiveness or success of the worker's specific service efforts were partially related to arrest outcomes (see chapter 14).

Individual Counseling

An average of 2.4 workers provided advice or brief counseling to 86.4 percent of all youth in the sample (N = 191). An average of 1.7 youth workers provided these services to 91.2 percent of the youth (n = 179); 1.6 project police officers to 64.4 percent of the youth (n = 58); 1.6 project probation officers to 78.0 percent of the youth (n = 20); and the neighborhood organizer to 92.0 percent of the youth in her caseload (n = 25). While all types of workers provided a certain level of brief counseling and advice, this did not preclude the project police and probation officers from arresting and violating some of the same youth when the occasion warranted.

The third cohort, comprising the larger proportion of youth sixteen years of age and under, was provided with the most contacts for brief counseling (92.0 percent). The first cohort, comprising the largest proportion of older youth (nineteen and over), was provided with the least brief counseling contacts—85.6 percent. The corresponding percentages for the second cohort were between those of the first and third cohorts (88.59 percent). A somewhat higher percentage of the Two Six (n = 89) were provided with counseling—89.2 percent—than were the Latin Kings (n = 102)—83.9 percent. However, slightly more workers (2.6) provided counseling to the Latin Kings than to the Two Six (2.1). The twenty-seven noninterviewed, worker-tracked youth (90.7 percent) were provided brief counseling or advice exclusively by youth workers.

A slightly higher level of effectiveness perceived by workers who provided brief counseling was reported for cohort III (the youngest) than for cohorts I and II, and for the Two Six than for the Latin Kings. Youth workers reported a slightly higher level of success with brief counseling than did the other types of workers.

Family-Related Services

About half of all youth tracked (52.8 percent) were provided with some form of family-related services consisting of brief counseling or advice to parents, usually in the youth's home. Youth workers made more family-related contacts than the other workers, but this was still only for 51.3 percent of the families of youth in their caseloads. The neighborhood organizer and the project probation officers reported the highest proportion of family-related contacts, 78.0 percent and 71.0 percent, respectively, but each had smaller caseloads than the youth workers. The project police were also in contact with a substantial number of families (46.3 percent) in their caseload.

More of the youth—61.0 percent—in cohort III (generally comprising younger youth) were provided with family-related services, compared to 52.9 percent of youth in cohort I and 47.7 percent in cohort II. A higher proportion of family-related contacts was made with Two Six families (59.1 percent) than with Latin King families (47.2 percent). Also, a slightly higher proportion of noninterviewed youth received family-related contacts than did interviewed youth. Overall, workers reported a slightly higher level of brief-counseling success, or effectiveness, with families than with individual youth. The youth workers, and especially the neighborhood organizer, perceived relatively higher levels of effectiveness for their family-counseling efforts than did project police or probation officers.

School-Related Services

About 38.0 percent of the tracked program youth (N = 191) were provided with school contacts or referrals (e.g., helping the youth to get back to their school or transfer to another school, and resolving a variety of school-related problems including suspensions, conflicts with teachers and students, and absences). The highest proportions of contacts around school issues, per caseload, were made by the neighborhood organizer (86.1 percent) and the project probation officers (65.3 percent). Fewer youth were contacted in regard to school issues by youth workers (35.7 percent) and project police (31.6 percent). What is remarkable is that project police had even this high a proportion of school referrals or school problems. More of the Two Six (45.0 percent) than Latin Kings (31.7 percent) were provided with school-related contacts or referrals. Also, youth who had been interviewed were provided with slightly more school-related contacts (38.7 percent) than noninterviewed youth (33.0 percent).

The level of success or effectiveness perceived by workers in regard to school issues was slightly lower, in the "little" to "good" range (scales 2–3), than the level of success claimed for individual or family counseling, which was closer to "good" (scale 3). There was little variation in claims of worker success for youth across the three cohorts. A somewhat lower level of school-related success was claimed by workers for youth in cohort III (younger youth who had more school problems than older youth). The level of perceived effectiveness was slightly lower for the Two Six workers than for the Latin King workers, and for the interviewed youth than for the noninterviewed youth.

Job Training, Referral, and Placement

A higher proportion of youth were contacted, and a higher level of effectiveness was reported, for job training, job referral, and job placement (mainly by outreach youth workers and the neighborhood organizer) than for school referrals and assistance. Nevertheless, individual- and family-counseling efforts were rated at a slightly higher level of perceived effectiveness than they were for job training, referral, and placement, most of which were made by youth workers, who reported that they attempted to place about half of all youth in their caseloads in jobs. The neighborhood organizer, working with a smaller number of youth, reported job-related contacts for the highest proportion of youth in her caseload (75.0 percent); no job-related referrals were made by project police or probation officers.

More project workers provided job-related contacts to the Latin Kings (1.9) than to the Two Six (1.4). A slightly higher proportion of interviewed youth were contacted around job-related services (51.0 percent) than were noninterviewed youth (48.1 percent). The proportion of youth contacted for job training, referral, and placement services was about equal across the three cohorts.

Job-related efforts were rated as slightly more successful for cohort I than for cohorts II and III. Job-training, referral, and placement efforts were rated at slightly higher levels for the Latin Kings than for the Two Six, and for interviewed youth than for noninterviewed youth.

Suppression

The second highest proportion of contacts for a particular service (66.3 percent) was for suppression, that is, surveillance, warning, arrest, probation violation, and so forth. This was the second highest proportion after individual counseling (86.4 percent). However, all of the suppression contacts were reported either by the project police (64.9 percent—with a caseload of fifty-eight youth) or by probation (85.8 percent—with a caseload of twenty youth). Youth workers and the neighborhood organizer reported no suppression contacts with youth, but this was because there were no questions about suppression on their particular worker-tracking forms. In fact, based on field observations, the youth workers and neighborhood organizer were involved in suppressing program-youth activity. They recommended arrest or probation violation to project police and probation officers for about 10 percent of youth in their respective caseloads. Advice and counseling efforts by youth workers, particularly on the streets, often included warnings about avoiding criminal behavior, particularly violent acts. The suppression-related aspects of the youth worker's contacts are described in more detail in the analysis of debriefing records discussed below.

Relatively more youth (73.3 percent) in cohort II than in cohort I (68.2 percent) or cohort III (50.0 percent) had suppression contacts by project police and probation officers. A slightly higher proportion of Two Six (68.5 percent) than Latin Kings (62.7 percent) was contacted for suppression activities. Almost all youth contacted for suppression were interviewed youth; only one of the noninterviewed youth was provided with a suppression contact—by a probation officer. The noninterviewed youth with tracking records were more likely to be younger, fringe gang members, who were provided with services (particularly brief counseling or job training and referral services) by outreach youth workers, mainly with prevention in mind. Project police and probation rated their suppression efforts as somewhat successful.

Athletics

Lower program priority was given to group athletic activities (e.g., basketball, baseball, and football) than other types of services.[2] The level of youth response to athletic services was not measured. Project workers reported that they provided sports-related services to 35.7 percent of program youth. Youth workers provided athletic activities to 42.5 percent of the youth in their caseloads; probation—38.7 percent; the neighborhood organizer—38.0 percent; and project police—24.4 percent. Cohort I was provided with slightly more athletic activities than cohorts II and III, while both gangs were provided with an equal proportion of these activities. Interviewed youth were provided with more athletic-related services (38.1 percent) than were noninterviewed youth (20.0 percent).

In sum, individual and family counseling, job and school referral, and suppression were the primary activities of project workers. They provided these contacts for services to a varying number of youth. Regardless of the type of worker in contact with a program youth, the youth could be provided with a variety of services or controls. The youth workers were involved in provision of some suppression services, and police and probation with a range of social services. All workers generally claimed a modest level of positive response by youth to their particular service or control efforts.

Youths' Perceptions of the Project

In a series of open-ended questions about the purpose of the project in the individual gang-member survey at time III, almost half (48.2 percent) of the 135 youth responding said the main purpose of the project was the reduction of gang activity. Counseling was mentioned second most often, by 21.9 percent of youth, followed by the project's purpose of reduction of violence and general crime—11.3 percent. Less often perceived by youth as a purpose of the project were the following: helping the community deal with gang problems—8.0 percent; jobs or job training—4.7 percent; and athletics—1.8 percent.

Youth who had been interviewed three times and had worker-tracking records viewed the project as very helpful with going "straight." About three-quarters (77.5 percent) of the total sample responded that the project helped them to deal with "one or more personal problems," and 71.9 percent said that the project "helped him get involved" in a range of legitimate activities.

WORKER DEBRIEFING RECORDS
The Debriefing Youth Sample

In addition to worker-tracking summary records, more detailed process information was obtained by project researchers through debriefing interviews of eleven youth workers regarding their activities with sixty-five youth (a subsample of the 164 interviewed and worker-tracked youth).[3] Youth workers were street based and spent less than 10 percent of their time on office or administrative tasks. (Youth-worker supervisors also spent the majority of their time on the streets, in frequent contact not only with street workers but also with gang youth.) Youth workers were expected to be debriefed once a week, although this did not always occur. A total of 284 debriefing forms were completed by the end of the project. The debriefing process was standardized, based on several questions the research assistant asked the youth worker regarding the most important things that happened in his work, including whom he contacted, for what purpose, and around what specific issues. The research assistant conducted the debriefing interviews at the project research offices at the University of Chicago School of Social Service Administration. The debriefing discussion was guided by specific sets of topics and questions but was relatively open ended so that the youth workers would feel free to bring up other related things they had done or observed during the week.

The debriefing format was originally intended as an administrative method of monitoring what youth workers were doing on the job, but the recorded interviews also proved useful for gathering detailed information about the nature of what the worker did and whom he contacted. The analysis reflected a bias in favor of the worker who was debriefed more often. In fact, a productive worker in the field might have completed fewer debriefing interviews but have done a more effective job with program youth. Nevertheless, the debriefing interviews provided information that was generally consistent with field observations and summary worker-tracking records.

All project youth workers were former members of the two targeted gangs in Little Village—the Latin Kings and the Two Six—except for one youth worker who was not a gang member but lived in Little Village and had an extensive history of contacts with gang youth. (He left the project for a job as a probation officer with the Cook County Department of Adult Probation.) Youth workers generally were assigned to youth in the same gang or gang section they had originally been affiliated with (and those sections of the same gang they had some positive, if not influential, relationship with). Six out of the eleven youth workers whose debriefing records are described in the analysis worked with Two Six sections and completed 57.0 percent of the total 284 debriefing interviews; the five Latin King workers completed 43.0 percent. The Latin King workers contacted more program youth than did the Two Six workers, and their work was at least (if not more) effective than that of the Two Six workers.

Table 11.1. Types of services (activities) provided by outreach youth workers

Service (activity) type	Description
Gang-related issues	Mostly counseling regarding gang-related activities, such as gang feuding, violence, and drug dealing
Job-related services	Counseling regarding job search, placement, and development
School-related services	Counseling regarding staying in (or returning to) school; help with school placement
Recreation-related services	Facilitating participation in sports, such as basketball and baseball
Criminal justice–related services	Counseling regarding legal issues; accompanying youth and family members to court
Family-related services	Services directed specifically to family members (or girlfriends); counseling gang youth regarding their relations with family members or girlfriends
Community-related services	Services such as graffiti paint-outs, attendance at community meetings; contacts with representatives of other community organizations and agencies
Spiritual-related services	Advising youth and family members in regard to religious matters
Surveillance	Any form of contact (or field observation) of the worker with youth providing information about actual or potential gang-violence crises
Other	Organization or agency activities that could not be included in any of the above categories, such as staff meetings, facilitating special events, and other administrative work

There were thirty specific services or activities (statements) identified but not the person contacted for the services or activities. Each statement in the completed record was coded. The service or activity, and to whom it was made or provided, were identified in 1,299 of the 3,043 total statements. The specific person contacted was identified in 887 statements, but the service activity was not. An additional 827 statements did not include a specific service or activity, or identify the person contacted. Totals in the tables at the end of this chapter vary, depending on whether the analysis focused on types of service or activity provided and types of persons contacted by the youth worker.

Types of Services and Contacts by Project Youth Workers

Data were classified and aggregated in ways relevant to the underlying strategies of the program and the kinds of participants involved. The types of services provided by the youth workers were classified into nine major categories and one residual category (table 11.1).

The types of persons the youth workers contacted for direct and coordinated services were classified into eight categories (table 11.2).

Table 11.2. Types of persons contacted by outreach youth workers

Persons contacted	Description
For direct services	
Individual youth	Individual program youth
Groups of gang youth	Any group of program youth
Families and girlfriends	Family members or girlfriends of program youth
For coordination and development of services	
Other project youth workers	Other youth workers in the project
Project police officers	Police officers assigned to the project
Project probation officers	Probation officers assigned to the project
Project neighborhood organizers	Workers from Neighbors against Gang Violence (NAGV)
Community leaders, agency personnel, and residents	Members of NAGV advisory board (priests, aldermen, and youth-agency administrators), school personnel, and a few community residents and businesses

Coding the types of persons the worker contacted for direct services was not a simple process. For example, although the categories of "individual youth" and "a group of gang youth" are logically separable, it was often difficult for the coder to make a clear distinction about whom the worker was primarily addressing. When a specific youth was clearly identified as a recipient of a service or contact, it was coded as a service contact with an individual; when focus seemed to be on a section of the gang, or gang-member associates of the program youth, it was coded as a service to a group. In some cases, neither the person contacted nor the services provided were clearly identified.

Table 11.3 summarizes the types of youth-worker services (activities) and to whom they were provided ($N = 1,299$, the sum of services and persons contacted). Youth workers had contacts with a wide range of individuals or groups. The plurality of services (activities) was directed to individual program youth (41.5 percent), but substantial numbers of contacts were also made with family members (13.9 percent) and groups of gang youth (12.1 percent). Significant numbers of field contacts were made for purposes of information exchange and to facilitate provision of services to program youth by project probation officers (8.0 percent), project police officers (6.2 percent), other project youth workers (6.0 percent), the project neighborhood organizer (3.9 percent), and community leaders, agency personnel, and residents (6.3 percent). It was clear from the debriefing records that youth workers were not strictly oriented to

Table 11.3. Types of services (activities) by outreach youth workers, by type of persons contacted[a]

Services/activities	Persons contacted								Total
	For direct services			For coordination and development of services					
	Individual youth	Groups of gang youth	Families/ girlfriends	Other project youth workers	Project police officers	Project probation officers	Project neighborhood organizer	Community leaders/agency personnel/residents	
Gang-related issues	64 (4.9%)	15 (1.2%)	20 (1.5%)	4 (0.3%)	43 (3.3%)	10 (0.8%)	2 (0.2%)	1 (0.1%)	159 (12.2%)
Job-related services	283 (21.8%)	2 (0.2%)	31 (2.4%)	4 (0.3%)	2 (0.2%)	2 (0.2%)	10 (0.8%)	9 (0.7%)	343 (26.4%)
School-related services	140 (10.8%)	2 (0.2%)	25 (1.9%)	1 (0.1%)	0 (0.0%)	1 (0.1%)	4 (0.3%)	8 (0.6%)	181 (13.9%)
Recreation-related services	3 (0.2%)	136 (10.5%)	11 (0.8%)	16 (1.2%)	7 (0.5%)	14 (1.1%)	10 (0.8%)	17 (1.3%)	214 (16.5%)
Criminal justice–related services	34 (2.6%)	0 (0.0%)	24 (1.8%)	2 (0.2%)	0 (0.0%)	23 (1.8%)	0 (0.0%)	0 (0.0%)	83 (6.4%)
Family-related services	16 (1.2%)	0 (0.0%)	7 (0.5%)	0 (0.0%)	0 (0.0%)	0 (0.0%)	0 (0.0%)	0 (0.0%)	23 (1.8%)
Community-related services	4 (0.3%)	0 (0.0%)	1 (0.1%)	5 (0.4%)	6 (0.5%)	3 (0.2%)	14 (1.1%)	21 (1.6%)	54 (4.2%)
Spiritual-related services	19 (1.5%)	2 (0.2%)	9 (0.7%)	0 (0.0%)	1 (0.1%)	0 (0.0%)	1 (0.1%)	3 (0.2%)	35 (2.7%)
Surveillance	1 (0.1%)	0 (0.0%)	47 (3.6%)	4 (0.3%)	17 (1.3%)	40 (3.1%)	0 (0.0%)	0 (0.0%)	109 (8.4%)
Other	15 (1.2%)	0 (0.0%)	6 (0.5%)	29 (2.2%)	4 (0.3%)	11 (0.8%)	10 (0.8%)	23 (1.8%)	98 (7.8%)
Total	579 (41.5%)	157 (12.1%)	181 (13.9%)	65 (6.0%)	80 (6.2%)	104 (8.0%)	51 (3.9%)	82 (6.3%)	1,299[b] (100.0%)

Notes
a. Percentages are calculated based on the 1,299 total services (contacts) provided to sixty-five youth and other persons related to the program.
b. The 1,299 contacts for services (activities) in this table differ from the 3,043 total services provided and persons contacted, which include unidentified services (activities) to identified persons, identified services (activities) to unidentified persons, and unidentified services (activities) to unidentified persons.

working with groups of gang youth. Their primary objective was working with individual program youth within a multiworker context. More than three times as many contacts were made with individual youth as with groups of gang members.

More than 40 percent of youth-worker activities were career-development issues, mainly job services (26.4 percent) and education services (13.9 percent). Recreation (16.5 percent) and criminal justice (6.4 percent) contacts were also made. The services focusing mainly on individual youth were as follows: job related (21.8 percent), education related (10.8 percent), gang-related counseling (4.9 percent), and criminal justice related (2.6 percent). The bulk of services provided on a group basis were for recreational or athletic activities (10.5 percent), and only a relatively few addressed gang-related issues (1.2 percent). Gang-related issues were primarily addressed at the individual-youth level (4.9 percent).

The essence of the youth worker's role with individual program youth was counseling around jobs, school issues, and gang control and crime. A variety of contacts with others—particularly family, probation, and police—were made in support of these primary individual-youth–related concerns and problems. Of importance to gang-violence control was that group or gang-related recreational activities involving members of opposing gangs usually included the presence of project probation and police officers, as both observers and participants. (Certain community-related activities such as citizen meetings and graffiti paint-outs also involved the police and probation officers.) Information from field surveillance activities of youth workers about criminal and potentially criminal youth gang activities was shared with project probation and police, and also with the youth's family.

Gang-Related Issues

Although they comprised only 12.2 percent of total youth-worker services, gang-related issues were discussed most with individual program youth (40.3 percent), project police (27.0 percent), and families of youth (12.6 percent). The specific gang-related topics varied with the particular persons contacted. In regard to issues of serious violence, youth workers mainly contacted project police (17.6 percent). Quitting the gang was discussed mainly with individual youth (12.6 percent) and families and girlfriends (5.0 percent). Stopping gang feuding was discussed mainly with individual youth (9.4 percent), as was drug selling and drug use (5.7 percent). These four topics (issues of serious violence, quitting the gang, stopping gang feuding, and drug-related activities) comprised 67.3 percent of all gang-related issues discussed. Other gang-related topics of discussion included relations with project police (7.5 percent), weapons (5.0 percent), robbery committed by program youth (3.8 percent), and youth not coming home (3.1 percent) (table 11.4).

The discussions around gang-related issues were not necessarily initiated by the youth workers; often they were initiated by project police or the program youth himself. Project police and youth workers frequently interacted with each other in discovering details of a youth's involvement in particular crimes, especially gang-related fighting. The youth worker continually advised the individual youth not to be involved in gang activities. Program youth in turn initiated contact with youth workers to seek advice about quitting the gang. The youth worker shared information openly with project police about gang violence (or threats of gang violence), both at staff meetings and frequently through telephone calls or field contacts with the officers. However, information about other types of gang-related activities, such as vandalism, disorderly conduct, or drug dealing, was not necessarily shared at staff meetings; rather it was discussed informally with individual project police officers, particularly after staff meetings or on the phone. Youth workers as a rule did not meet openly with project police in the gang territories.

Job-Related Services

Job-related services, the primary overall service (26.4 percent) provided by youth workers, were directed mainly to individual program youth (82.5 percent). The worker's job contacts were usually specific and concrete: driving the youth to apply for a job (37.0 percent), searching newspapers or agency advertisements for jobs, and contacting other job-resource personnel, including neighborhood adults and even former gang members (32.7 percent). The youth worker interacted with the youth directly in such efforts most of the time (25.9 percent). The youth workers also advised youth to go on their own to specific employment agencies or business locations for jobs (11.4 percent). In addition, the workers handled requests for general information about jobs, or specific help with finding them, from the youths' family members and girlfriends (7.9 percent). The neighborhood organizer was also a resource for job information and job placement (2.9 percent) (table 11.5).

Table 11.4. Gang-related issues raised by outreach youth workers, by type of persons contacted

| | Persons contacted | | | | | | | | |
| | For direct services | | | For coordination and development of services | | | | | |
Gang-related issues	Individual youth	Groups of gang youth	Families/ girlfriends	Other project youth workers	Project police officers	Project probation officers	Project neighborhood organizer	Community leaders/agency personnel/residents	Total
Serious violence (e.g., gang homicide and gang shooting)	3 (1.9%)	2 (1.3%)	0 (0.0%)	2 (1.3%)	28 (17.6%)	2 (1.3%)	0 (0.0%)	1 (0.6%)	38 (23.9%)
Quitting the gang	20 (12.6%)	2 (1.3%)	8 (5.0%)	0 (0.0%)	0 (0.0%)	0 (0.0%)	0 (0.0%)	0 (0.0%)	30 (18.9%)
Stopping gang feuding	15 (9.4%)	3 (1.9%)	1 (0.6%)	1 (0.6%)	1 (0.6%)	0 (0.0%)	0 (0.0%)	0 (0.0%)	21 (13.2%)
Drug-related activities	9 (5.7%)	1 (0.6%)	3 (1.9%)	0 (0.0%)	2 (1.3%)	3 (1.9%)	0 (0.0%)	0 (0.0%)	18 (11.3%)
Relations with project police	4 (2.5%)	1 (0.6%)	7 (4.4%)	0 (0.0%)	0 (0.0%)	0 (0.0%)	0 (0.0%)	0 (0.0%)	12 (7.5%)
Weapons	1 (0.6%)	0 (0.0%)	0 (0.0%)	0 (0.0%)	4 (2.5%)	3 (1.9%)	0 (0.0%)	0 (0.0%)	8 (5.0%)
Robbery	0 (0.0%)	0 (0.0%)	0 (0.0%)	0 (0.0%)	4 (2.5%)	2 (1.3%)	0 (0.0%)	0 (0.0%)	6 (3.8%)
Not going home	5 (3.1%)	0 (0.0%)	0 (0.0%)	0 (0.0%)	0 (0.0%)	0 (0.0%)	0 (0.0%)	0 (0.0%)	5 (3.1%)
Other	7 (4.4%)	6 (3.8%)	1 (0.6%)	1 (0.6%)	4 (2.5%)	0 (0.0%)	0 (0.0%)	2 (1.3%)	21 (13.2%)
Total	64 (40.3%)	15 (9.4%)	20 (12.6%)	4 (2.5%)	43 (27.0%)	10 (6.3%)	0 (0.0%)	3 (1.9%)	159 (100.0%)

Table 11.5. Job-related services provided by outreach youth workers, by type of persons contacted

| | Persons contacted | | | | | | | | |
| | For direct services | | | | For coordination and development of services | | | | |
Job-related services	Individual youth	Groups of gang youth	Families/ girlfriends	Other project youth workers	Project police officers	Project probation officers	Project neighborhood organizer	Community leaders/agency personnel/residents	Total
Talking about getting a job	17 (5.0%)	1 (0.3%)	27 (7.9%)	2 (0.6%)	0 (0.0%)	0 (0.0%)	0 (0.0%)	0 (0.0%)	47 (13.7%)
Helping with job preparation (vocational training, etc.)	9 (2.6%)	0 (0.0%)	0 (0.0%)	0 (0.0%)	0 (0.0%)	1 (0.3%)	0 (0.0%)	0 (0.0%)	10 (2.9%)
Job referral	39 (11.4%)	0 (0.0%)	3 (0.9%)	0 (0.0%)	1 (0.3%)	0 (0.0%)	0 (0.0%)	0 (0.0%)	43 (12.5%)
Job search, placement, and development	89 (25.9%)	1 (0.3%)	0 (0.0%)	2 (0.6%)	1 (0.3%)	1 (0.3%)	10 (2.9%)	8 (2.3%)	112 (32.7%)
Taking youth to apply for a job	125 (36.4%)	0 (0.0%)	1 (0.3%)	0 (0.0%)	0 (0.0%)	0 (0.0%)	0 (0.0%)	1 (0.3%)	127 (37.0%)
Taking youth to a job interview	2 (0.6%)	0 (0.0%)	0 (0.0%)	0 (0.0%)	0 (0.0%)	0 (0.0%)	0 (0.0%)	0 (0.0%)	2 (0.6%)
Taking youth to work	2 (0.6%)	0 (0.0%)	0 (0.0%)	0 (0.0%)	0 (0.0%)	0 (0.0%)	0 (0.0%)	0 (0.0%)	2 (0.6%)
Total	283 (82.5%)	2 (0.6%)	31 (9.0%)	4 (1.2%)	2 (0.6%)	2 (0.6%)	10 (2.9%)	9 (2.6%)	343 (100.0%)

Table 11.6.   School-related services provided by outreach youth workers, by type of persons contacted

| | Persons contacted | | | | | | | | |
| | For direct services | | | | For coordination and development of services | | | | |
Education-related services	Individual youth	Groups of gang youth	Families/ girlfriends	Other project youth workers	Project police officers	Project probation officers	Project neighborhood organizer	Community leaders/agency personnel/residents	Total
Advice about returning to/staying in school	42 (23.2%)	1 (0.6%)	23 (12.7%)	1 (0.6%)	0 (0.0%)	0 (0.0%)	4 (2.2%)	2 (1.1%)	73 (40.3%)
Secondary school placement (return, transfer, and conflict mediation)	22 (12.2%)	0 (0.0%)	0 (0.0%)	0 (0.0%)	0 (0.0%)	0 (0.0%)	0 (0.0%)	2 (1.1%)	24 (13.3%)
GED program placement	18 (9.9%)	0 (0.0%)	1 (0.6%)	0 (0.0%)	0 (0.0%)	0 (0.0%)	0 (0.0%)	1 (0.6%)	20 (11.0%)
College placement	4 (2.2%)	0 (0.0%)	0 (0.0%)	0 (0.0%)	0 (0.0%)	0 (0.0%)	0 (0.0%)	0 (0.0%)	4 (2.2%)
Trade school placement	10 (5.5%)	0 (0.0%)	0 (0.0%)	0 (0.0%)	0 (0.0%)	0 (0.0%)	0 (0.0%)	0 (0.0%)	10 (5.5%)
Junior college information	14 (7.7%)	0 (0.0%)	0 (0.0%)	0 (0.0%)	0 (0.0%)	1 (0.6%)	0 (0.0%)	3 (1.7%)	18 (9.9%)
Information about other education/training	23 (12.7%)	1 (0.6%)	0 (0.0%)	0 (0.0%)	0 (0.0%)	0 (0.0%)	0 (0.0%)	0 (0.0%)	24 (13.3%)
Other	7 (3.9%)	0 (0.0%)	1 (0.6%)	0 (0.0%)	0 (0.0%)	0 (0.0%)	0 (0.0%)	0 (0.0%)	8 (4.4%)
Total	140 (77.3%)	2 (1.1%)	25 (13.8%)	1 (0.6%)	0 (0.0%)	1 (0.6%)	4 (2.2%)	8 (4.4%)	181 (100.0%)

School-Related Services

School-related services were also directed primarily to individual program youth (77.3 percent). The key issue or topic discussed was the youth's return to or staying in school (40.3 percent). Mostly the youth himself was contacted (23.2 percent), but family members or girlfriends were also involved (12.7 percent). A good deal of worker effort was spent assisting youth in their contacts with school officials, arranging their return or transfer to another school, and occasionally mediating a conflict between them and the school staff (12.2 percent). Other school-related services included placing the youth in a GED program (9.9 percent), providing information about trade schools (5.5 percent), and providing youth with special educational programs available through Job Corps, public-school summer sessions, and boot camps (12.7 percent). It was not unusual for the youth workers to respond to requests for information about programs at junior colleges (7.7 percent) (table 11.6).

Nevertheless, only about half as many services were directed to school-related issues as to job-related issues. This was due in part to the fact that most youth were over sixteen years of age, out of school, highly alienated from the public-school educational system, and had far greater interest in the rewards of status and income (legitimate and illegitimate) that went with a job. Most of the youth worker's efforts in regard to school or education issues were directed to youth under sixteen years of age; most of the job-related contacts were directed to youth seventeen and older. We shall see later that job-related contacts proved to be more successful than school contacts and were more likely to be associated with a reduction in arrests during the program period.

Criminal Justice–Related Services and Issues

Most contacts by youth workers regarding justice-system issues involved not only individual program youth (41.0 percent) but also families (28.9 percent) and project probation officers (27.7 percent). Youth workers accompanied the youth (21.7 percent) and his family (13.3 percent) to court, providing social support and facilitating communication between parents, the youth, and court personnel. They explained court procedures to family members (8.4 percent) and helped them to understand the specific probation requirements the youth had to meet (4.8 percent). The youth worker was concerned with the interests of both the youth and the probation officers, helping youth remember appointments and accompanying them to the probation office (7.2 percent).

Table 11.7. Criminal justice–related services provided and issues raised by outreach youth workers, by type of persons contacted

| | Persons contacted | | | | | | | | |
| | For direct services | | | | For coordination and development of services | | | | |
Criminal justice–related services/issues	Individual youth	Groups of gang youth	Families/ girlfriends	Other project youth workers	Project police officers	Project probation officers	Project neighborhood organizer	Community leaders/agency personnel/residents	Total
Accompanying youth (and family) to court	18 (21.7%)	0 (0.0%)	11 (13.3%)	0 (0.0%)	0 (0.0%)	0 (0.0%)	0 (0.0%)	1 (1.2%)	30 (36.1%)
Presence at time of arrest	0 (0.0%)	0 (0.0%)	0 (0.0%)	0 (0.0%)	0 (0.0%)	3 (3.6%)	0 (0.0%)	0 (0.0%)	3 (3.6%)
Monitoring criminal justice relationships	0 (0.0%)	0 (0.0%)	0 (0.0%)	0 (0.0%)	0 (0.0%)	3 (3.6%)	0 (0.0%)	0 (0.0%)	3 (3.6%)
Discussing probation-related responsibilities	6 (7.2%)	0 (0.0%)	4 (4.8%)	0 (0.0%)	0 (0.0%)	13 (15.7%)	0 (0.0%)	1 (1.2%)	24 (28.9%)
Taking youth to probation office	1 (1.2%)	0 (0.0%)	0 (0.0%)	0 (0.0%)	0 (0.0%)	1 (1.2%)	0 (0.0%)	0 (0.0%)	2 (2.4%)
Missing probation appointments	0 (0.0%)	0 (0.0%)	0 (0.0%)	0 (0.0%)	0 (0.0%)	2 (2.4%)	0 (0.0%)	0 (0.0%)	2 (2.4%)
Discussing court proceedings	0 (0.0%)	0 (0.0%)	7 (8.4%)	0 (0.0%)	0 (0.0%)	0 (0.0%)	0 (0.0%)	0 (0.0%)	7 (8.4%)
Discussing legal rights	2 (2.4%)	0 (0.0%)	0 (0.0%)	0 (0.0%)	0 (0.0%)	0 (0.0%)	0 (0.0%)	0 (0.0%)	2 (2.4%)
Helping obtain legal assistance	2 (2.4%)	0 (0.0%)	2 (2.4%)	0 (0.0%)	0 (0.0%)	0 (0.0%)	0 (0.0%)	0 (0.0%)	4 (4.8%)
Advice about surrendering to authorities	3 (3.6%)	0 (0.0%)	0 (0.0%)	0 (0.0%)	0 (0.0%)	0 (0.0%)	0 (0.0%)	0 (0.0%)	3 (3.6%)
Other	2 (2.4%)	0 (0.0%)	0 (0.0%)	0 (0.0%)	0 (0.0%)	1 (1.2%)	0 (0.0%)	0 (0.0%)	3 (3.6%)
Total	34 (41.0%)	0 (0.0%)	24 (28.9%)	0 (0.0%)	0 (0.0%)	23 (27.7%)	0 (0.0%)	2 (2.4%)	83 (100.0%)

Table 11.8.   Persons contacted by outreach youth workers, by gang assignment

| | Gang assignment of youth worker | | |
Persons contacted	Latin King n and (%)	Two Six n and (%)	Total
For direct services			
Individual youth	240	563	803
	(33.0%)	(38.6%)	(36.7%)
Gangs/groups of gang youth	48	131	179
	(6.6%)	(9.0%)	(8.2%)
Families/girlfriends	73	200	273
	(10.0%)	(13.7%)	(12.5%)
For coordination and development of services			
Project police and probation officers	193	262	455
	(26.5%)	(18.0%)	(20.8%)
Other project youth workers/	85	168	253
neighborhood organizer	(11.7%)	(11.5%)	(11.6%)
Community leaders/agency	89	134	223
personnel/residents	(12.2%)	(9.2%)	(10.2%)
Total	728	1,458	2,186
	(100.0%)	(100.0%)	(100.0%)

He provided information to the probation officer about where a youth might currently be living and his current job and school status, and often arranged special meetings between the probation officers and the youth, particularly when the youth missed probation appointments (15.7 percent) (table 11.7).

Youth-Worker Contacts and Services to the Target Gangs

The youth workers generally developed different patterns of contacts for services depending on the gang to which they were assigned. The Two Six workers were relatively more oriented than the Latin King workers to direct-service contacts with individual program youth, groups, and families (Two Six = 61.3 percent; Latin Kings = 49.6 percent). The Latin King workers were relatively more oriented to work with project police and probation officers and community leaders (Latin Kings = 38.7 percent; Two Six = 27.2 percent) (table 11.8).

The Latin King workers spent more time in contact with project police and probation officers regarding criminal justice issues, while the Two Six workers spent more time on social control (i.e., advice and counseling efforts with younger delinquent youth). The Two Six workers generally made more family contacts than Latin King workers. Nevertheless, both sets of workers spent most of their time in direct contact with individual program youth, their families, and the gangs. The different distribution of contacts by youth workers with each of the gangs was a function mainly of the project model but also of the specific needs, interests, and life-course problems of the Latin Kings and Two Six, particularly conditioned by such factors as the youth's age and criminal history.

Scope, Range, and Nature of Worker Contacts and Services

Many contacts and services were provided intensively to target youth by project workers in close coordination with each other, on a team basis, over a substantial period of time. Most contacts and services, however, were provided by the youth workers, focusing on youth seventeen years and older. All workers were engaged variably in both social-intervention and suppression contacts or services. Youth workers and the neighborhood organizer were primarily involved in providing access to job opportunities and school contacts.

Contacts and services were directed mainly to individual youth and secondarily to gangs or groups of gang youth as units. Nevertheless, the nature of contacts and services to the youth was determined in part by the different characteristics of the two gangs. Latin King youth were older and had more extensive and serious criminal backgrounds. Two Six youth were generally younger, with less extensive criminal records. Our analysis of the effects of the program model had to control for age and background of youth across the two gangs.

On average, contacts were made by 2.4 different project workers (youth workers, police, probation, and the neighborhood organizer) with 191 program youth over a period of 29.2 months. Project youth workers served the largest number of youth. Based on worker-tracking data, the project served more Latin Kings (n = 102)—the older and more violent of the two gangs—than Two Six (n = 89). Project workers were in contact with program youth an average of sixteen times per month over the entire time the youth were available in the community during the project period.

Overall, more contacts per month per youth were made with seventeen- and eighteen-year-olds (19.3) than with youth sixteen and under (16.6) and nineteen and older (15.3). Project youth workers, police officers, and probation officers focused more on contacts with seventeen- and eighteen-year-olds; the neighborhood organizer on contacts with youth sixteen and under. The most intense contacts (contacts per month) to these age groups were provided by youth workers and project police.

A range of service-and-contact activities were addressed to the youth. All workers were asked to estimate the success or degree of effectiveness of the particular pattern of services provided to each youth during the worker-tracking period. While youth workers provided brief counseling to the most youths and their families, the police, probation officers, and neighborhood organizer were also providing individual and family counseling and advice. About half of all program youth were provided with family contacts for counseling services. Youth workers considered that brief counseling was slightly more effective than the other types of services they provided.

About 38 percent of youth were provided with school-related contacts and referrals, such as helping the youth get back to school and resolving a variety of school-related problems. The highest proportion of contacts per youth around school issues was made by the neighborhood organizer and probation officers. Mostly the Two-Six (who were younger than the Latin Kings) were provided with these services.

Most contacts for job training, referral, and placement were made by youth workers, who attempted to place about half of all youths in jobs. Relatively more Two Six (59.6 percent) than Latin Kings (43.0 percent) were involved in job-related efforts.

After individual-youth counseling, the highest proportion of contacts made by all of the project workers was for suppression, mainly by probation officers (85.8 percent) and police (64.9 percent). Based on field observations, it was estimated that youth workers were directly involved in suppression efforts in at least 10 percent of contacts with youth in their caseloads.

Outreach youth-worker debriefing forms were developed for a subsample of sixty-five youth. Our interest was in the types of contacts the youth workers had, both with the individual program youth themselves and with other types of persons in the field. Most contacts were made with individual program youth (41.5 percent). Of this percentage, most were in regard to job-related services (21.8 percent), school-related services (10.8 percent), and gang-related issues (4.9 percent). Most contacts made with the gang as a focus (12.2 percent) were made in regard to recreation activities (10.5 percent).

The youth workers developed different patterns or concentrations of services and contacts, depending on the gang they served. The Two Six workers were relatively more oriented to direct-service contacts within individual program youth, gang groups, and families (61.3 percent) than were the Latin King workers (49.6 percent). The Latin King workers were relatively more oriented to working with project police, probation, and community leaders (38.2 percent) than were the Two Six workers (27.2 percent).

NOTES

1. Program youth were grouped into three cohorts (I, II, III), based on the time they entered the program.

2. In all cases where both gangs together were provided with athletic activities at a site, the youth workers, project police, and probation officers were also involved, usually as a team.

3. The debriefing interviews were conducted during the last half of the program period, and while they did not represent all of the youth workers, they provided a fuller, more open-ended report of the persons contacted and activities carried out than did the summary worker-tracking records. On average, debriefing information from youth workers was obtained for 46.1 percent of the weeks during the time they were in the project. On the other hand, summary worker-tracking forms were completed during the entire five-year project—three times, one and a half years apart—and provided more systematic but less detailed information on specific services and other workers contacted.

Arrest Changes for Program and Comparison Youth

Our most rigorous analyses of the effectiveness of the Little Village Gang Violence Reduction Project were based on Chicago Police Department arrest data. This was of special importance from a policy perspective in assessing the value of the program and the model on which it was based, since the Little Village Project was sponsored by the Chicago Police Department. Changes in arrest patterns, rather than changes in self-reported offenses, were the coin of law-enforcement operations and policy decision making. Yet the two types of data and program information were both critically important for determining why, and how, these outcomes occurred.

Using arrest data, we introduced two comparison groups of gang youth for program samples: a "quasiprogram" group of ninety youth who were provided with some limited (mainly recreational) services and a "true" comparison group of 208 youth who were provided with *no* services or contacts from project workers.[1] We matched youth from each of the comparison samples respectively with their program-youth co-arrestees by gang (Latin Kings, Two Six), cohort, and age. The youth in the comparison samples were gang co-arrestees of program youth,[2] involved in the same arrest incidents occurring at about the same time the program youth were contacted and entered into the program.

We did not have comparison-youth interview data to determine whether changes in self-reported offenses would have been similar to those of program youth. We did have complete Chicago arrest histories and Cook County Court criminal histories for all of the youth—program and comparison, interviewed or not—over the entire matched program and preprogram periods.[3]

There were advantages to using official arrest data over self-report data. Arrest data for program and comparison youth covered the entire five-year preprogram period (time I) and five-year program period (time II) for all youth.[4] Self-report data were collected only during the program period for those youth in the project. Also, the range of offenses in the police arrest records was far greater than in the set of self-reported offenses used in the gang-member survey, which stressed crimes typically committed by Little Village gang youth—violence, drugs, and property crime. In the next chapter, we establish the consistency of crime patterns and changes in crimes for program youth, using self-reported offense and official police arrest data.

SAMPLING METHOD

The findings of the self-report data discussed in chapters 10 and 11 were based on most of the program youth in the repeatedly interviewed (time I and time III) sample (N = 127). In this discussion, we describe and compare a total of 493 youth: the total target, or time I–interviewed program sample (N = 195); the quasiprogram sample (N = 90); and the "true" comparison sample (N = 208). The process by which we developed the comparison and the quasiprogram samples was as follows:

In a violent gang-crime community setting such as Little Village, it was extremely difficult, if not impossible, to find and randomly select highly gang-involved, violent youth and provide some with social services or special controls, and others not. The large universe of Latin King and Two Six youth in Little Village involved in gang crime was not necessarily known either to project workers, project police, other agencies, or even to program youth themselves. In 1995 we began collecting police arrest histories and court-processing data for all targeted youth in the program. As we searched and examined justice-system records, we noted that program youth were usually arrested with others from the same gangs. These gang co-arrestees were not interviewed or part of the program, so we decided they could serve as a nonprogram *comparison* sample.[5] Subsequently, we obtained special court permission to examine the co-arrestees' criminal histories, along with those of program youth.

The initial group of approximately three hundred co-arrestees, mainly from cohorts I and II, were identified first through criminal-court records and contained no juveniles. Several problems arose in putting together the juvenile component of the comparison sample. We soon discovered that there were not sufficient numbers of juveniles arrested along with adults listed in the adult criminal-court records, and there were also not enough juvenile co-arrestees of program juveniles to form a meaningful juvenile comparison-youth sample. (In addition, the records of juvenile co-arrestees in the Chicago Police Department's Youth Division were often expunged before we could get to them.) We finally developed the juvenile component of the comparison sample based on the co-arrestees of the adult program youth when *they* were juveniles, using data from juvenile-court records. We also extended the risk period of program juveniles as far back as necessary to obtain a sufficient number of juvenile co-arrestees. In due course, we obtained a sample of seventy-three juvenile co-arrestees, including fifty-two juvenile co-arrestees from the earlier-time-period sampling frame. After extensive analysis, we discovered that the juvenile co-arrestees did not differ significantly from program juveniles, based on preprogram-period arrest, detention or incarceration, and age distributions.

Another problem arose when we classified youth into the program and comparison samples. After reviewing the comparison-youth sample with project youth workers and police and probation officers, we found that some project contacts and services had indeed been provided to ninety of the youth. We decided to call this group the *quasiprogram* sample. These youth had been neither targeted nor interviewed, nor tracked through program records. They were often on the fringes of the program, participating occasionally in recreational activities, yet proved to be the most delinquent or criminal of the youth in the three samples. The project may have some effect on them, but they were not specifically targeted for project-team contacts and services.

DATA COLLECTION

The task of collecting accurate and reliable (and sometimes *any*) criminal justice data for youth and adults in Chicago was formidable. This was true not only because of inaccuracies and inconsistencies in record keeping, both within and across components of the justice system, but also because gang youth who were arrested often gave false or contradictory information to police, the courts, and correctional officials. Youth frequently falsified their real names and deliberately changed their family names, birth dates, and addresses. One of the key ways the justice-system researcher identified and checked program- and comparison-youth names and addresses was to compare the records of both program youth and their co-arrestees over time. Because of the peer and network character of gangs, the same youth were often arrested together in several gang incidents over time. New, confirming data were found at each record search. In almost all cases, we were able to identify the youth's criminal record, even though false or inaccurate names and addresses might have been given. Because of this continued, network-type checking procedure, we believe our arrest data are both reliable and valid.

DEMOGRAPHIC CHARACTERISTICS OF YOUTH

So far as we knew, all youth in our samples were documented United States citizens. There were hardly any statistically significant differences in race or ethnicity, gender, and age across the three samples: program, quasiprogram, and comparison.

Race and Ethnicity

The ethnicity and race of program, quasiprogram, and comparison youth (N = 493) was predominantly Latino, mainly Mexican American. Only 4.2 percent (n = 8) of the program sample was of European origin; there were no Asian youth and only one African American youth. The quasiprogram sample was even more predominantly Latino or Mexican American; only 2.3 percent (n = 2) were non-Latinos. The comparison sample, although predominantly Mexican Americans or Latinos, was a little different. Twenty-five youth (11.5 percent) in this sample were non-Latino or non–Mexican American, including nineteen youth of middle-European origin; five additional youth were African American and one was Asian. The proportion of Latino youth in the comparison sample is probably an underestimate, since most of these youths had at least one parent of Mexican background, and they may not have identified themselves as Latino.

Gender

We examined only males in our arrest-change analyses, although there were a small number of females in each of the samples (program = 4, quasiprogram = 3, comparison = 4). The sample selection was a function of the project's focus on youth identified and arrested as offenders in serious gang-violent situations. They were almost exclusively males. Our field observations indicated that females affiliated with the Latin Kings and Two Six were not directly involved in serious violent-gang situations. Some data on the nature and changing patterns of female gang delinquency and criminality in Little Village are provided in a later chapter, using community-level gang-crime statistics.

Age

There were no significant age differences among the matched youth in our three samples.[6] The mean ages of all youth in each of the samples at time I (the preprogram period) were almost identical: program sample = 17.98 years; quasiprogram sample = 17.86 years; and comparison sample = 17.95 years. There was also no significant statistical difference between the ages of the Latin Kings and the Two Six comparing the total program samples. However, the Latin Kings were older than the Two Six in the first cohort but younger in the third cohort. The age range of youth in our samples at the time of program entry was twelve years to twenty-nine years. One program and two comparison youth were almost thirteen years of age. Twelve youth were between twenty-five and twenty-nine years of age (program sample = 5, quasiprogram sample = 3, comparison sample = 4). We excluded these twelve older youth from the analysis.

We classified our samples into three age groups. The categories seemed appropriate and consistent across legal and justice-system processing definitions in Illinois, gang-violence research findings, and youth-development and maturation theory, at least in Little Village. Gang youth under sixteen in Little Village were largely wannabes, looking for gang status and increasing their gang-related delinquent activity. Youth seventeen and eighteen were probably at the peak of their participation in gang activity and crime, especially gang-motivated violence. Youth nineteen and over were decreasingly involved in violent activity and were leaving the gang, often obtaining legitimate jobs, raising families, and settling down—or moving into more sophisticated crime (for economic reasons). The project was engaged in modifying or accelerating program youth out of and away from these age-related crime and gang developmental stages, especially those involving violence.

DETENTION AND INCARCERATION HISTORIES

In the preliminary-analysis phase we focused on criminal histories of youth not only with respect to types of arrests but also to patterns of detention and incarceration during the preprogram period within each of the different cohorts, in all three samples. All of the youth in the quasiprogram and the comparison samples had criminal histories in the preprogram period. While 83.1 percent (n = 162) of the program youth had preprogram criminal histories, 16.9 percent (n = 33) of program youth had no preprogram or program-period arrests or court appearances (and therefore no detention or incarceration record); some of the program youth, however, developed criminal justice records during the program period. In our arrestee analyses, we used program youth who had records of arrests either in the preprogram or program period. Our samples were well matched on characteristics of preprogram-period detention and incarceration: 14.2 percent of the program youth had records of preprogram secure confinement (n = 23), compared to 12.2 percent of the quasiprogram youth (n = 10), and 10.6 percent of the comparison youth (n = 26). These proportions do not represent statistically significant differences. Almost none of the sixteen-and-under youth in the three samples had preprogram-period detention or incarceration records. Older youth were more likely to have been in secure confinement. For the seventeen- and eighteen-year-olds, more of the quasiprogram youth (45.5 percent) than the program youth (30.4 percent) and the comparison youth (19.1 percent) had preprogram detention or incarceration histories. The nineteen-and-over comparison youth had detention or incarceration experience more often (76.2 percent) than the nineteen-and-over program youth (65.2 percent) or the nineteen-and-over quasiprogram youth (54.6 percent). When we examined the number of days in detention and incarceration, the comparison youth spent more preprogram-period time in detention or incarceration (mean = 62.98 days) than either the quasiprogram youth (mean = 49.84 days) or the program youth (mean = 49.84 days). These differences across samples were not statistically significant when controlling for age group.

During the program period, all of these secure-confinement percentages and figures went up drastically for each of the samples and in all age categories, in large measure because of more stringent laws and a hardening of the justice-system sentencing procedures for gang offenders. Time in detention or incarceration went up, particularly for younger youth. The average increase for program youth was from twenty to eighty-nine days; quasiprogram youth from eleven to fifty-seven days; and comparison youth from sixteen to seventy-three days.

ARREST HISTORIES
Preprogram-Period Arrests (Time I)

In the analysis of preprogram-period arrest patterns, we excluded not only youth who were over twenty-four years of age at program entry, females (because of small numbers), and those youth in the program sample without preprogram or program-period arrests but also those in the three samples who were serving long prison sentences imposed after the first three months of program-period contact, since they were essentially no longer at risk for arrest in the community. This reduced the total size of the combined samples to 418: 154 program youth, 84 quasiprogram youth, and 180 comparison youth. A fairly equal distribution of age groupings remained in each sample: about a third nineteen and over, a third seventeen and eighteen, and a third sixteen and under. The sixteen-and-under age group in the program sample (36.8 percent) was slightly larger than in the quasiprogram sample (39.3 percent) and the comparison sample (40.6 percent).

To determine whether preprogram arrest patterns differed for the samples, we examined mean arrests for each youth for different juvenile and adult arrest categories together: total arrests; serious violence arrests (including homicides, aggravated batteries, aggravated assaults, and armed robberies—most involving use of a firearm); total violence arrests (including serious and less-serious violence arrests—simple battery, simple assault, and weapons violations); property arrests; drug and alcohol arrests; and arrests for "other," less-serious crimes (e.g., mob action, gang loitering, disorderly conduct, obstruction of law enforcement—all reflecting a good deal of police discretion—and status offenses).

We attempted to discover whether arrests in the preprogram period varied across the samples by types of arrests and age categories, controlling for equivalent program and preprogram periods. We found no statistical differences in total arrests within the respective age categories between program and comparison samples; they did exist relative to total arrests in the quasiprogram sample, whose youth generally had more extensive histories of total and different types of arrests. In the preprogram period, total mean arrests were 4.57 for the program sample, 4.01 for the comparison sample, and 7.75 for the quasiprogram sample. The difference between the quasiprogram and each of the other two samples was statistically significant ($p \leq 0.05$) but not between the program and comparison samples. When we examined serious violence arrests (homicide, aggravated assault, aggravated battery, and robbery), we found no statistically significant differences in the preprogram period between program youth (mean = 0.79) and comparison youth (mean = 0.82), but the quasiprogram sample (mean = 1.35) had a significantly greater history of serious violence arrests compared to each of the other samples ($p \leq 0.05$).

The same patterns of differences occurred using a more expansive list for violence offenses, which included (in addition to the serious violence offenses listed above) simple assault and simple battery as well as illegal possession of a weapon, mainly a gun. The means were as follows: program youth = 1.04, comparison youth = 1.16, and quasiprogram youth = 1.95.

The patterns of differences among the samples were about the same using mean property arrests: program youth = 1.44, comparison youth = 1.29, and quasiprogram youth = 2.36. When it came to mean drug and alcohol arrests, there were again no statistically significant differences among youth in the three samples in the preprogram period: program sample = 0.43, comparison sample = 0.34, and quasiprogram sample = 0.56. For other types of crime (particularly mob action, disorderly conduct, obstruction of an officer, and also for status offenses) we found similar patterns as above, that is, the quasiprogram sample had significantly more arrests than either the program or comparison sample. There were no statistically significant differences between program and comparison samples in the analysis for different preprogram offenses. Based on arrest data in the preprogram period, our samples seemed to be relatively specialized to violent behavior. For the three samples together, there were a total of 8 arrests for murder, 19 for armed robbery, 40 for aggravated battery, and 107 for aggravated assault during the matched preprogram periods. The total of all serious and less-serious violence arrests was greater than the total for all property arrests. Only 5 percent of preprogram arrests were for drug-law violations, almost exclusively for possession of marijuana or cocaine. We had selected program and comparison samples of gang youth who had extensive, if not dominant, backgrounds of arrests for violence.

We appeared to have well-matched samples (particularly for program and comparison youth, less so for quasiprogram youth) on all key demographic, arrest, and detention and incarceration variables. However, in the analyses that follow in the next chapter, when we matched specific career or "specialization" patterns of arrests (or self-reported offenses)—violence, no drug; drug, no violence; no violence, no drug; and violence and drug—we found differences in subtypes of offenders in each of the three samples. The offense careers of youth in each of the samples diverged somewhat.

Program-Period Arrests (Time II)

The following discussion is based on the results of a general linear model (GLM) statistical procedure—the analysis of variance. The seven models presented each employ a different dependent arrest-change variable—the mean number of arrests at time II (the program period) versus the mean number of arrests at time I (the matched preprogram period)—for each youth in each model: total arrest change; serious violence arrest change; total violence arrest change (including serious and less-serious violence arrests); property arrest change; drug arrest change; and "other" arrest change, including change in special police-activity arrests such as mob action, gang loitering, and disorderly conduct. The values of all the arrest variables are adjusted for the youth's at-risk time in the community. Four independent variables and control factors are entered into each equation to explain the different dependent variables: the particular time I arrest level (none, low, medium, high); the three age categories (nineteen and over, seventeen and eighteen, sixteen and under); the three samples (program, comparison, quasiprogram); and four particular time I and time II detention or incarceration levels (none, low, medium, high). There are two interaction terms in each model: age category × sample, and level of time I arrest category × sample. Only the types of arrests differ in each of the seven models in the analysis.

The length of time in detention or incarceration had significant effects on the dependent variables (arrest changes), but the direction during the program period tended to be positive, while it tended to be negative in the preprogram period. In other words, most youth who increased their number of arrests, regardless of the category of the arrest, had relatively short stays in confinement in the preprogram period but considerably longer stays in the program period. This was particularly true for violence arrests. In general, length of time in confinement did not have a differential effect on outcomes for the program, comparison, and quasiprogram youth.

In the following discussion we describe the findings of the seven GLM analyses in some detail, but our tables present only summary results and differences (LS means) between program, comparison, and quasiprogram samples.[7] The specific numbers of program, quasiprogram, and comparison youth vary by levels and types of arrests in the preprogram period (table 12.1).

MODEL I: TOTAL ARRESTS

In the first model, level of total arrests at time I, age category at time I, and time in secure confinement at time II were each highly significant ($p \leq 0.001$) in explaining variance in the dependent variable, change in total arrests between time I and time II. Level of detention or incarceration at time I, and the

Table 12.1. Distribution of arrests in the three samples (N = 418) levels and types of arrests in the preprogram period

Levels of arrests for the three samples	Subsample size		Total arrests	Serious violence	Types of arrests				
	n	%			Total violence	Property	Drug	Other	Special—Police
None—program	30	19.5	490	95	83	69	112	63	68
None—comparison	63	35.0	573	119	106	91	145	100	112
None—quasiprogram	14	16.7	210	37	29	34	57	24	29
Low—program	46	29.9	212	33	36	36	28	54	55
Low—comparison	46	25.6	213	28	32	36	23	50	44
Low—quasiprogram	15	17.6	135	21	21	18	15	31	29
Medium—program	46	29.9	129	14	19	34	12	32	18
Medium—comparison	37	20.6	97	8	11	29	9	27	18
Medium—quasiprogram	27	32.1	69	11	6	15	10	20	7
High—program	32	20.8	63	12	16	15	2	5	13
High—comparison	34	18.9	97	25	31	24	3	3	11
High—quasiprogram	28	33.3	90	15	28	17	2	9	19

Table 12.2. An analysis of variance of change in total arrests between time I and time II program, comparison, and quasiprogram samples

(12.2a) ANOVA summary table (R square = 0.436)

Source	Adjusted df	Adjusted MS	F	Pr > F
Total arrests at time I: none, low, medium, high	3	1567.49	47.96***	0.001
Age: 16 & under, 17–18, 19 & over	2	562.44	17.21***	0.001
Total incarceration at time I: none, low, medium, high	3	111.70	3.42*	0.018
Total incarceration at time II: none, low, medium, high	3	1009.14	30.87***	0.001
Sample: program, comparison, quasiprogram	2	1.28	0.04	0.962
Sample × age	4	83.28	2.55*	0.039
Sample × total arrests at time I	6	24.91	0.76	0.601
Within error	394	32.69	—	—
Total	417	—	—	—

(12.2b) Adjusted mean change in total arrests (and standard error) and pairwise t-test for the sample main effect

Sample	Adjusted mean	Std err	i/j	Pr > |T| Ho: adjusted mean (i) = adjusted mean (j) 1	2	3
Program	0.60	0.82	1	—	0.857	0.788
Comparison	0.48	0.84	2	0.857	—	0.898
Quasiprogram	0.38	0.96	3	0.788	0.898	—

For differences between groups: *p ≤ 0.05; **p ≤ 0.01; ***p ≤ 0.001.

interaction term age category × particular sample were also statistically significant, respectively at $p = 0.018$ and $p = 0.039$. This model explained 43.6 percent of the variance in the dependent variable (table 12.2a).

In terms of detailed results, we found that the level of total arrests at time I had a strong statistical regression effect, adjusting for all other variables in the equation. The greater the level of total arrests at time I, the greater the reduction in total arrests at time II; the lower the level of total arrests at time I, the greater the increase in total arrests at time II. But the statistical regression effect was present in all of our model results and affected the different sample and subsample comparisons in equal fashion.

Most important for this analysis, when we compared the three samples overall (program, quasiprogram, and comparison) using total arrest changes between time I to time II, we found increases but no statistical differences among the samples (table 12.2b).

However, when we compared outcomes within age categories, we found several differences, some statistically significant. In each of the samples, youth nineteen and older and seventeen and eighteen reduced their total arrests at time II, but youth in the youngest age category (sixteen and under) increased their total arrests. The difference between the two older age categories was not statistically significant, but the differences between both nineteen-and-older youth and the seventeen- and eighteen-year-olds, compared to the sixteen-and-younger age group, were statistically significant ($p \leq 0.001$).

Significant differences existed when we compared total arrest changes for the same age categories across the three samples. The seventeen- and eighteen-year-olds in the program sample reduced their total arrests, while the comparison-sample seventeen- and eighteen-year-olds increased their total arrests, but the difference was not statistically significant. However, there was a significant difference ($p \leq 0.05$) for this age group between the comparison and quasiprogram samples. The quasiprogram seventeen- and eighteen-year-olds had a significant decrease (LS mean $= -2.47$ arrests), while the comparison sample had a slight increase (LS mean $= 0.75$ arrests). It was noteworthy that the increase for the program-sample sixteen-and-under youth (LS mean $= 3.7$ arrests) was greater than that for the comparison-sample equivalent-age youth (LS mean $= 1.6$ arrests). The difference was almost statistically significant ($p = 0.056$).

From the first model, we concluded that there was little to distinguish the three samples regarding differences in changes in total arrests between time I and time II, controlling for other factors. There was an overall increase in arrests in each sample. Older youth across the samples generally reduced their levels of arrests, while younger youth, especially those sixteen and under, increased theirs. The seventeen- and eighteen-year-olds in the program sample did better than those in the comparison sample and also better than any other age category in the program sample. The program-sample sixteen-and-under youth did worse than the equivalent comparison-sample age group.

MODEL II: SERIOUS VIOLENCE ARRESTS

In this model—probably the most important for determining program effectiveness—the variables for level of arrests for serious violence at time I

Table 12.3.   An analysis of variance of change in serious violence arrests between time I and time II program, comparison, and quasiprogram samples

(12.3a) ANOVA summary table (R square = 0.454)

Source	Adjusted df	Adjusted MS	F	Pr > F
Serious violence arrests at time I: none, low, medium, high	3	123.49	52.94***	0.001
Age: 16 & under, 17–18, 19 & over	2	5.21	2.23	0.109
Total incarceration at time I: none, low, medium, high	3	29.83	12.79***	0.001
Total incarceration at time II: none, low, medium, high	3	76.31	37.71***	0.001
Sample: program, comparison, quasiprogram	2	10.09	4.32*	0.014
Sample × age	4	3.52	1.51	0.199
Sample × serious violence arrests at time I	6	6.36	2.73*	0.013
Within error	394	2.33	—	—
Total	417	—	—	—

(12.3b) Adjusted mean change in serious violence arrests (and standard error) and pairwise t-test for the sample main effect

Sample	Adjusted mean	Std err	i/j	Pr > |T| Ho: adjusted mean (i) = adjusted mean (j) 1	2	3
Program	−1.59	0.23	1	—	0.010**	0.014*
Comparison	−0.94	0.25	2	0.010**	—	0.981
Quasiprogram	−0.95	0.25	3	0.014*	0.981	—

For differences between groups: *p ≤ 0.05; **p ≤ 0.01; ***p ≤ 0.001.

and the level of detention or incarceration at time I and time II were highly statistically significant ($p \leq 0.001$) in explaining total variance of the dependent variable, serious violence arrests comparing time I and time II. There were also significant differences in serious violence arrests for the three samples ($p = 0.014$), as well as in the interaction term level of serious violence arrests at time I × sample ($p = 0.013$). The model explained 45.4 percent of variance in the dependent variable (table 12.3a).

Again, we observed a regression effect comparing youth with different levels of arrests for serious violence between time I and II. The group with no history of arrests for serious violence at time I increased its arrests for serious violence at time II. In all the samples, youth with histories of arrests for serious violence reduced their levels of arrests, with the greatest reduction for youth with the most serious violence-arrest histories at time I. However, program youth with the highest numbers of preprogram serious violence arrests had a significantly greater reduction of these arrests during the program period than did comparison youth ($p \leq 0.01$).

Each sample reduced its level of serious violence arrests between the pre-program and program periods (time I and time II). However, program youth achieved the greatest level of decrease (LS mean $= -1.59$). The differences between the program and comparison samples (LS mean $= -0.94$; $p \leq 0.01$) and between the program and quasiprogram samples (LS mean $= -0.95$; $p = 0.014$) were statistically significant (table 12.3b).

All age categories in each of the three samples reduced their levels of arrests for serious violence. The greatest reduction was for the nineteen-and-over category (LS mean $= -1.40$), followed by the sixteen-and-under category (LS mean $= -1.11$), and the seventeen- and eighteen-year-old category (LS mean $= -0.96$). While the size of the decrease between the nineteen-and-over and sixteen-and-under groups was not statistically significant, it *was* significant between the nineteen-and-over group and the seventeen- and eighteen-year-olds ($p = 0.044$).

When we examined differences by age categories across the three samples, the program sample reduced its level of serious violence arrests more for each age category compared to the comparison and quasiprogram samples. The difference was highly statistically significant between the program and comparison sample in the nineteen-and-older age category ($p \leq 0.001$). The program-sample seventeen- and eighteen-year-olds also did significantly better than the comparable quasiprogram age group in reducing levels of serious violence arrests ($p = 0.04$). However, while the sixteen-and-under youth reduced their levels of serious violence arrests more than those youth in the comparison and quasiprogram samples, this difference was not statistically significant.

In sum, the program sample and its various age categories did much better in lowering levels of serious violence arrests than did the comparison and quasiprogram samples and subsamples. The reduction in serious violence arrests was more than *60 percent greater* for program than for comparison seventeen- and eighteen-year-olds, especially for the highest-rate offenders in that age group, controlling for other variables in the equation. The findings suggest that the project had a *considerable* across-the-board effect in reducing the levels of arrests for serious violence among program youth in relation to the comparison youth and the quasiprogram youth.

MODEL III: TOTAL VIOLENCE ARRESTS

The variable for change in total violence arrests in this model included not only the more serious violent crimes (homicide, aggravated battery, aggravated assault, and armed robbery) but also the less-serious violent crimes (simple battery, simple assault, and weapons violations). The results of this analysis were about the same as those of model II. Similar control variables were significant. The model explained 43.7 percent of variance in the dependent variable (table 12.4a).

Again, program youth reduced their levels of total arrests for violent crime more than the comparison youth ($p = 0.03$; table 12.4b). The program sample had a greater reduction of total arrests for violence at all age levels compared to the other samples. The differences were significant for the nineteen-and-over program sample in relation to the quasiprogram sample ($p \leq 0.01$) and the comparison sample ($p = 0.02$). Again, the program subsample with the greatest history of preprogram arrests for violence did significantly better than the comparable quasiprogram ($p \leq 0.001$) and comparison ($p = 0.003$) subsamples. Based on police arrest data, and using various statistical controls, the effects of the project in reducing total violence arrests as well as serious violence arrests were highly noteworthy.

MODEL IV: PROPERTY ARRESTS

The same procedures were used in this model as in the previous models, except that the dependent variable was change in property arrests between time I and time II, and the key control variable was property arrests at time I. Only three variables were statistically significant in this model: property arrests at time I, detention or incarceration at time I, and detention or incarceration at time II. Sample, age, and the interaction terms age category × sample and property arrests × sample were not significant. The variables in this equation accounted for 44.3 percent of variance in the dependent variable (table 12.5a).

Once more, we found that a regression effect explained the relation between levels of time I and time II property arrests. Youth who had lower numbers of

Table 12.4.   An analysis of variance of change in total violence arrests between time I and time II program, comparison, and quasiprogram samples

(12.4a) ANOVA summary table (R square = 0.437)

Source	Adjusted df	Adjusted MS	F	Pr > F
Total violence arrests at time I: none, low, medium, high	3	182.77	52.54***	0.001
Age: 16 & under, 17–18, 19 & over	2	4.13	1.19	0.306
Total incarceration at time I: none, low, medium, high	3	30.83	8.86***	0.001
Total incarceration at time II: none, low, medium, high	3	108.88	31.30***	0.001
Sample: program, comparison, quasiprogram	2	17.32	4.98**	0.007
Sample × age	4	1.09	0.31	0.868
Sample × total violence arrests at time I	6	9.75	2.80*	0.011
Within error	394	3.48	—	—
Total	417	—	—	—

(12.4b) Adjusted mean change in total violence arrests (and standard error) and pairwise t-test for the sample main effect

Sample	Adjusted mean	Std err	i/j	$Pr > |T|$ Ho: adjusted mean (i) = adjusted mean (j) 1	2	3
Program	−1.48	0.27	1	—	0.030*	0.003**
Comparison	−0.89	0.29	2	0.030*	—	0.268
Quasiprogram	−0.53	0.34	3	0.003**	0.268	—

For differences between groups: *$p \leq 0.05$; **$p \leq 0.01$; ***$p \leq 0.001$.

property arrests at time I accounted for a higher increase in property arrests at time II. The reverse was also true: the youth with more property arrests at time I accounted for a higher reduction in property arrests at time II.

The differences for the samples and subsamples were not significant, although the reduction in property arrests was greatest in the quasiprogram sample. The patterns of reduction were almost identical in the program and comparison samples (table 12.5b).

The reduction of property arrests among youth in the different age categories across the samples was also similar: there were no statistically significant

Table 12.5. An analysis of variance of change in property arrests between time I and time II program, comparison, and quasiprogram samples

(12.5a) ANOVA summary table (R square = 0.443)

Source	Adjusted df	Adjusted MS	F	Pr > F
Property arrests at time I: none, low, medium, high	3	349.49	63.84***	0.001
Age: 16 & under, 17–18, 19 & over	2	8.81	1.61	0.201
Total incarceration at time I: none, low, medium, high	3	33.79	6.17***	0.001
Total incarceration at time II: none, low, medium, high	3	87.27	15.94***	0.001
Sample: program, comparison, quasiprogram	2	2.58	0.47	0.625
Sample × age	4	4.87	0.89	0.470
Sample × property arrests at time I	6	3.30	0.60	0.727
Within error	394	5.47	—	—
Total	417	—	—	—

(12.5b) Adjusted mean change in property arrests (and standard error) and pairwise t-test for the sample main effect

Sample	Adjusted mean	Std err	i/j	$Pr > \lvert T \rvert$ Ho: adjusted mean (i) = adjusted mean (j) 1	2	3
Program	−0.83	0.33	1	—	0.876	0.357
Comparison	−0.88	0.35	2	0.876	—	0.417
Quasiprogram	−1.17	0.38	3	0.357	0.417	—

For differences between groups: *p ≤ 0.05; **p ≤ 0.01; ***p ≤ 0.001.

differences. The project apparently had no effect on the level of property arrests of program youth that was different from that which occurred for comparison and quasiprogram youth. All samples showed similar declines in property arrests between time I and time II.

Also, the youngest age group (sixteen and under) at time I showed the least reduction in property arrests at time II. The nineteen-and-over group had the greatest reduction in property arrests at time II, followed by the seventeen-and eighteen-year-olds. None of these differences were statistically significant, except that the difference between the oldest and youngest groups did approach statistical significance (p = 0.077).

MODEL V: DRUG ARRESTS

The project did not primarily target drug-crime behavior among program youth, but project workers were concerned about it and attempted to some extent to address the problem. Drug use and drug-selling activities were pervasive among gang and nongang youth in Little Village, although perhaps not directly related to the intergang violence problem. Drug selling in Little Village was organized, with a great deal of control exercised by the Mexican mafia, particularly with respect to the Two Six. Nevertheless, drug selling by program youth was generally on a small scale. Drug-crime arrests were mainly for possession of small quantities of marijuana or cocaine. There was evidence that youth in the three samples were involved on a limited basis in illegal drug transport and deliveries of substantial amounts of marijuana and cocaine. More extensive and somewhat specialized drug dealing was confined to a small subsample of youth in each of our samples (chapter 13).

Based on aggregate gang and community-level arrest data, gang-related drug crime in Little Village increased markedly over the program period. We expected a significant increase in drug arrests for program youth if gang-violence activity went down. To our surprise, the findings indicated that arrests for drug crime *decreased* in the program sample during the program period, while they increased in the comparison and quasiprogram samples.

The drug-arrest-change model was constructed the same way as the other models. Again, the control variable was level of drug arrests at time I, and the dependent variable was change in drug arrests between time I and time II. Drug arrests were not as frequent as violence and property arrests for Little Village program youth. The drug-change model was not as powerful as the other models. Only drug arrests at time I and detentions or incarcerations at time II were highly significant predictors ($p \leq 0.001$). The difference between the samples was almost significant ($p = 0.053$), and the interaction term drug arrests at time I $\times$ sample was significant ($p = 0.021$). The model accounted for 17.1 percent of variance in the dependent variable (table 12.6a).

The regression effect—that is, youth with fewer drug arrests at time I increasing their drug arrests at time II, and those with more drug arrests at time I decreasing their drug arrests time II—did not completely pertain for the category of youth with the most serious histories of drug arrests. These youth showed an increase rather than a decrease in drug arrests at time II.

Table 12.6. An analysis of variance of change in drug arrests between time I and time II program, comparison, and quasiprogram samples

(12.6a) ANOVA summary table (R square = 0.171)

Source	Adjusted df	Adjusted MS	F	Pr > F
Drug arrests at time I: none, low, medium, high	3	25.92	8.82***	0.001
Age: 16 & under, 17–18, 19 & over	2	5.59	1.90	0.150
Total incarceration at time I: none, low, medium, high	3	0.61	0.21	0.892
Total incarceration at time II: none, low, medium, high	3	33.77	11.49***	0.001
Sample: program, comparison, quasiprogram	2	8.73	2.97	0.053
Sample × age	4	2.12	0.72	0.579
Sample × drug arrests at time I	6	7.41	2.52*	0.021
Within error	394	2.94	—	—
Total	417	—	—	—

(12.6b) Adjusted mean change in drug arrests (and standard error) and pairwise t-test for the sample main effect

Sample	Adjusted mean	Std err	i/j	$Pr > |T|$ Ho: adjusted mean (i) = adjusted mean (j) 1	2	3
Program	−0.33	0.39	1	—	0.015*	0.186
Comparison	0.81	0.36	2	0.015*	—	0.327
Quasiprogram	0.34	0.39	3	0.186	0.327	—

For differences between groups: *$p \leq 0.05$; **$p \leq 0.01$; ***$p \leq 0.001$.

Comparing the samples and controlling for other variables, we found that only the program sample had a drop in drug arrests at time II, while the comparison sample had a substantial increase and the quasiprogram sample had a modest increase. This difference was statistically significant between the program and comparison samples ($p = 0.015$) (table 12.6b).

Each of the age categories in the program sample reduced their drug arrests, while each of the age categories in the comparison and the quasiprogram samples increased their drug arrests, except for the seventeen- and eighteen-year-old quasiprogram subsample, which nevertheless did not decrease as much as the equivalent-age program subsample. The decrease in drug arrests was statistically significant for the program-sample compared to the comparison-sample sixteen-and-under group ($p \leq 0.011$), and the seventeen- and eighteen-year-old program group ($p = 0.024$) compared to the equivalent-age comparison group.

We were very pleased but cannot adequately explain why the project was so consistently effective in reducing gang-related drug crime, when this was not the priority objective of the project. Possibly the program was effective with those program youth who were only partially committed to drug dealing and were in the process of transitioning out of the gang and away from criminal behavior generally. The program was also more effective in reducing drug arrests for younger youth, particularly the Two Six (chapter 14). In our analysis of different types of offenders in the gang (chapter 13), we find that youth who were probably not highly committed to both violence and drug crime did better in reducing different types of arrests than youth who were more specialized to either violence or drug crimes.

MODEL VI: "OTHER" ARRESTS

"Other" arrests included arrests for all other offenses committed by the youth in the three samples: status offenses, violations of probation, and especially crimes such as mob action, disorderly conduct, gang loitering, and obstruction of a police officer, which typically reflected special police activity regarding gang youth. We focus on this latter subset of "other" offenses in model VII.

Our analysis procedure for model VI was the same as for previous models, except that our key control variable was now the level of "other" arrests at time I, and the dependent variable was the change in "other" arrests between time I and time II. In this model, level of "other" arrests at time I, age category, and detention or incarceration at time II were highly statistically significant ($p = 0.002$). Also statistically significant was the interaction term age category × sample ($p = 0.02$). Together, the variables accounted for 40.6 percent of the variance in the dependent variable (table 12.7a).

Again, we observed a strong regression effect for "other" arrests at time I compared to time II. For example, the youth who had very high levels of arrests for these crimes at time I experienced very sharp reductions at time II. All three samples generally showed highly similar reductions in "other" arrests between time I and time II (table 12.7b).

Table 12.7.   An analysis of variance of change in "other" arrests between time I and time II program, comparison, and quasiprogram samples

(12.7a) ANOVA summary table (R square = 0.406)

Source	Adjusted df	Adjusted MS	F	Pr > F
"Other" arrests at time I: none, low, medium, high	3	348.8	44.49***	0.001
Age: 16 & under, 17–18, 19 & over	2	276.92	35.32***	0.001
Total incarceration at time I: none, low, medium, high	3	16.54	2.11	0.099
Total incarceration at time II: none, low, medium, high	3	121.28	15.47***	0.001
Sample: program, comparison, quasiprogram	2	0.11	0.01	0.986
Sample × age	4	23.10	2.95*	0.020
Sample × "other" arrests at time I	6	11.73	1.50	0.178
Within error	394	7.84	—	—
Total	417	—	—	—

(12.7b) Adjusted mean change in "other" arrests (and standard error) and pairwise t-test for the sample main effect

Sample	Adjusted mean	Std err	i/j	$Pr > \lvert T \rvert$ Ho: adjusted mean (i) = adjusted mean (j) 1	2	3
Program	−1.35	0.48	1	—	0.926	0.867
Comparison	−1.30	0.53	2	0.926	—	0.957
Quasiprogram	−1.27	0.47	3	0.867	0.957	—

For differences between groups: *p ≤ 0.05; **p ≤ 0.01; ***p ≤ 0.001.

There was generally little difference in pattern of arrests for "other" crimes across program, quasiprogram, and comparison samples when comparing specific age categories, although there were increases in arrests for "other" crimes for sixteen-and-under youth at time II, while the older-age youth were experiencing a reduction in these arrests. The differences were highly statistically significant among the sixteen-and-under youth and the seventeen- and eighteen-year-olds (p = 0.001), compared to nineteen-and-over youth (p ≤ 0.001). Comparison sixteen-and-under youth did much better in reducing arrests for "other" crimes than did program and, especially, quasiprogram sixteen-year-olds.

The key finding in respect to arrests for "other" crimes was that the youngest age subsample did worse than the older subsamples across all three samples at time II. There may have been some offense-substitution effect in increased "other" arrests, at least in regard to decreased gang violence and drug arrests for youth in the program sample, particularly for the youngest age group.

MODEL VII: SPECIAL POLICE-ACTIVITY ARRESTS

Certain relatively minor crimes, such as disorderly conduct, mob action, gang loitering, and obstruction of a police officer were typically charged against gang youth. Our final model addressed the issue of whether law enforcement was more suppressive at time II than at time I, in particular arresting more gang youth for these minor crimes, especially the younger program youth. Did the project, because of its existence, result in more arrests for these minor crimes for program youth than comparison youth during the program period?

We used the same GLM analysis of variance and the same variables in this model as in the model for "other" arrests, with the exception of the control variable for level of special police-activity arrests at time I (which now included only the distinctive police suppression arrests), and the dependent variable change in special police-activity arrests between time I and time II. The time I control variables—special police-activity arrests, age category, and level of detention or incarceration—were significant at time II ($p \leq 0.001$), suggesting special police activity influencing these arrests. Initially, this notion seemed to be confirmed by the statistical significance of the two interaction terms in the equation: age category $\times$ sample ($p \leq 0.01$) and special police-activity arrests at time I $\times$ sample ($p = 0.045$). The contribution of all of these variables to explain total variance in the dependent-variable change in special police-activity arrests between time I and time II was 40.37 percent. This was suggestive, but a detailed examination of the specific effects of these variables led to a conclusion favoring a positive project effect (table 12.8a).

We found a strong and consistent regression effect as in all of the models. The category of youth with the fewest arrests for police suppression-type activities at time I had the most increase in these arrests at time II. Those youth who had the most arrests for crimes of this type at time I had the greatest decrease at time II.

Each of the samples showed a decrease in special police-activity arrests between time I and time II. The Chicago police in Little Village, overall, made

Table 12.8.   An analysis of variance of change in special police-activity arrests between time I and time II program, comparison, and quasiprogram samples

(12.8a) ANOVA summary table (R square = 0.403)

Source	Adjusted df	Adjusted MS	F	Pr > F
Special police-activity arrests at time I: none, low, medium, high	3	320.37	43.57***	0.001
Age: 16 & under, 17–18, 19 & over	2	254.55	34.62***	0.001
Total incarceration at time I: none, low, medium, high	3	9.99	1.36	0.255
Total incarceration at time II: none, low, medium, high	3	86.22	11.73***	0.001
Sample: program, comparison, quasiprogram	2	17.92	2.44	0.089
Sample × age	4	24.66	3.35*	0.010
Sample × special police-activity arrests at time I	6	15.91	2.16*	0.045
Within error	394	7.35	—	—
Total	417	—	—	—

(12.8b) Adjusted mean change in special police-activity arrests (and standard error) and pairwise t-test for the sample main effect

Sample	Adjusted mean	Std err	i/j	$Pr > \|T\|$ Ho: adjusted mean (i) = adjusted mean (j) 1	2	3
Program	−1.22	0.41	1	—	0.030*	0.564
Comparison	−0.31	0.43	2	0.030*	—	0.180
Quasiprogram	−0.96	0.46	3	0.564	0.180	—

For differences between groups: *p ≤ 0.05; **p ≤ 0.01; ***p ≤ 0.001.

fewer arrests for these types of crimes. Moreover, the differences across samples favored the program sample. The program sample showed the greatest decrease in these arrests at time II compared to time I, and the comparison sample showed the least decrease (table 12.8b).

The difference between the program and comparison sample was statistically significant (p = 0.03). In general, the youngest age group (sixteen years and under) in all three samples was relatively more likely to be arrested for special police-activity offenses than the other age groups. While the changes between time I and time II showed a decrease in the seventeen and eighteen and nineteen-and-over age groups, they showed an increase in the sixteen-and-under group. These differences were highly statistically significant, respectively at $p \leq 0.001$. Furthermore, the seventeen- and eighteen-year-old program group did better than the comparison seventeen- and eighteen-year-olds ($p = 0.028$), and the nineteen-and-over program group did better than the nineteen-and-over comparison group ($p \leq 0.01$). Although there was an increase in police suppression-type arrests for the sixteen-and-under youth in each of the three subsamples, there were no statistically significant differences between them. Also, the program youth with the two highest time I levels of arrests (medium and high) for these types of arrests did better than the equivalent comparison ($p = 0.043$) and quasiprogram youth ($p \leq 0.05$).

There appeared to be no evidence of an increase in special police-activity arrests for any of the samples at time II compared to time I. There was a decrease in these arrests, and the decrease was significantly greater in the program sample than in the comparison sample. The police did not single out program youth for special arrest attention and were not targeting program gang youth in particular for arrest at time II. It was also possible to view the significantly greater reduction of program-youth arrests than comparison-youth arrests for disorderly conduct, mob action, gang loitering, and obstruction of police officers as related to youth engaged in or about to be engaged in violent activity. The sharp reduction of such activity by program youth was probably a positive program effect.

SUCCESS IN REDUCING VIOLENCE ARRESTS

Using arrest data (as well as self-report data; see chapter 10), it was clear that the Little Village Gang Violence Reduction Project was successful in achieving its primary objective of significantly lowering violence rates of program youth compared to comparison youth. We matched the program sample ($N = 195$) with a comparison (no services) sample ($N = 208$) and a quasiprogram (limited services) sample ($N = 90$) in order to examine the effects of the project on changes in different types of arrests between the preprogram and program periods: total arrests, serious violence arrests, total violence arrests (serious and less serious), drug arrests, property arrests, other (minor) arrests, and special police-activity arrests (mob action, disorderly conduct, gang loitering, and obstruction of a police officer).

Using general linear modeling statistical analysis of variance, we found that program youth generally lowered their total violence, serious violence, and drug arrest levels during the program period significantly more than the comparison youth, and often more than the quasiprogram youth. Program youth also showed greater reductions in arrests for the types of minor crimes usually typical when the police are dealing with gang youth who are engaged in or contemplating violence. Program youth in two age groups—nineteen and over and seventeen and eighteen—generally did better than the equivalent-age comparison youth in reducing their arrest levels. The project had no significant effect on changing (i.e., lowering or raising) levels of total arrests, property arrests, or other (minor-crime) arrests.

The project appeared to be particularly successful with the most serious violence offenders, who were the prime targets for program attention. The project was also somewhat more effective in controlling or reducing arrests for younger program youth (sixteen and under) than for the equivalent-age comparison and quasiprogram youth.

NOTES

1. The quasiprogram sample (n = 90) comprised youth originally identified as belonging to the larger comparison sample (n = 298). Project workers were later able to identify a subsample of these 298 youth as indeed having received some project services, mainly recreation, that is, a "quasiprogram" sample. Each youth in the quasiprogram sample was identified as a member of either the Latin Kings or the Two Six.

2. We were able to obtain RAP sheets and police arrest reports that provided arrest histories of the comparison youth. The arrest reports explicitly indicated that 85 percent of comparison youth either identified themselves (or the arresting officer identified them) as members of the Latin Kings or the Two Six. We believed there was an extremely high probability that the remaining co-arrestees were also members of these two target gangs, based on community-gang dynamics.

3. The program-exposure period was defined on a cohort basis. Program youth from cohorts I and II and their corresponding co-arrestees (comparison and quasiprogram youth) were defined as exposed to the project six months after it started, for an average of four and a half years of possible program exposure. Program youth in cohort III and their corresponding co-arrestees (comparison and quasiprogram

youth) were defined as exposed or at risk at the end of the third to most of the fifth year of the project, or an average of two years. The arrests of the cohort III youth were then multiplied by a factor of 2.25 to make project effects equivalent for all cohorts.

4. The time I and time II arrest periods are not equivalent to the time I and time III self-report periods.

5. We did not have the resources to interview comparison youth in other, similar gang-crime communities, and it was not feasible to interview co-arrestee comparison youth in the same target gangs because of gang dynamics in Little Village.

6. Youth in the quasiprogram and comparison samples were matched with program youth based on the program youth's age when he entered the program (i.e., at program entry).

7. More extensive findings and detailed tables and reports of the project evaluation may be obtained from the Illinois Criminal Justice Information Authority (www.icjia.state.il.us) or iaspergel@uchicago.edu.

13

Arrest Changes for Different Types of Gang Youth

We continue our analysis of arrest changes for program youth compared to those for comparison and quasiprogram youth, focusing on the effects of the project on different subgroups of youth. Youth gang members may be differentially disposed to or engaged in certain types or sets of offenses—violence, drug selling, property, and other types of crime. Gang youth may be chronic offenders, yet certain youth may be more disposed to violent, drug, or other delinquent or criminal behavior than other youth in the same gang.

The goal of the project was to reduce violence by gang youth. Staff were expected to target shooters and potential shooters with special services, opportunities, and controls. They were continually making distinctions between shooters and potential shooters, and those who were less interested in violence or more interested in drug or other criminal activities. It was important, therefore, to determine whether the program was more effective with one type or subgroup of gang youth, particularly those youth more engaged in or disposed to violence, than other subgroups. Arrest and court records, as well as field observations of gang members, were useful in determining which youth to target.

A current debate in criminology is whether trajectories of crime exist and can be predicted from early childhood to old age (Sampson and Laub 2005). We make no such claim. We sought to discover whether some gang youth had special commitments to certain kinds of offending than other gang youth, and especially whether the program was more effective with certain types or categories of gang youth than other types or categories of gang youth from the same gangs.

We center attention on changes among youth who had different configurations of arrests, that is, for violence but not drugs, violence as well as drugs,

drugs but not violence, and neither violence nor drugs (but for other types of crimes). It was possible that the program generally was more effective in lowering certain types of arrests for certain types of gang youth; specific worker contacts and services may have had different effects on the different types or categories of gang youth.

RELATION BETWEEN VIOLENCE AND DRUG CRIME

With the development of youth gangs and gang problems in many locales throughout the United States and other countries, most recently in Central America, there has been increased concern with the connection between violence and drug crimes by gang members. The prevailing view among law-enforcement authorities and the media has been that most large urban gangs are now engaged in a great deal of both violence and drug crime, and that these crimes are interconnected. While there is growing evidence that street-gang members are engaged in both types of activities, the precise relationship, or causal connection, between these behaviors has not yet been made (Block et al. 1996; Howell and Decker 1999; Moore 1990; Skolnick 1992). Valdez and Sifaneck (2005) recently indicated that there are different dimensions of drug dealing and drug using among American Mexican gang members and that the connections between drug dealing and violent behavior are complex and fluid.

Certain gangs and their cliques in Little Village had developed reputations as drug gangs or violent gangs, or both. It was not clear that all members of the gangs in our program samples were engaged to the same extent in the same patterns of criminal behaviors. We thought there might be different configurations of antisocial behaviors, particularly violence, among youth in the various sections of the target gangs in the Little Village Project. We operated on the assumption that most program youth were primarily oriented to violent gang behavior—these were the specific youth we wanted to target. (This was not to say that gang youth arrested for violence did not also commit and get arrested for other crimes, such as drug use or selling, property crime, disorderly conduct, obstruction of a police officer, mob action, loitering, etc.) But if gang youth in the samples were differentially committed to violence (based on their arrest and self-report offense records), the question then was whether the project was more effective in reducing violent behavior for those program youth especially committed to violence than for other program youth less committed to violence. Comparisons would have to be made with similar subsamples of comparison and quasiprogram youth.

CONSTRUCTING THE ARRESTEE TYPOLOGY

One of the first things we wanted to know was to what extent gang youth in the different samples were involved not only in a range of crimes but especially in violence crimes, drug crimes, or both, that is, those crimes that most distinguish youth or street gangs from other kinds of delinquent or criminal youth groups, especially in Little Village and Chicago. We examined data on arrests of individual youth in the three samples over both the preprogram and program periods. (Self-report data were not as adequate for the preprogram period.) Our focus was on individual gang youth with arrest records, not necessarily on whether youth had been arrested together, that is, in subgroups or cliques for the same kinds or patterns of crime, although this most likely occurred.

The total 418 youth in our three samples who had arrest histories were classified by particular arrest charges using data derived from Chicago Police Department RAP sheets, which summarized charges for individuals originally listed in the arresting officer's arrest reports. We were unable to gain access to all arrest reports for the youth, but we had a complete set of RAP sheets. Our analysis of RAP sheets, and of the several hundred police arrest reports we did have, indicated that in 95 percent or more of the cases the original arrest charges for individuals were listed exactly the same in both records. When two or more charges were listed in the original arrest report, usually only one charge (the more serious charge) appeared on the RAP sheet. A charge for a minor crime (e.g., disorderly conduct) appearing on the arrest report may not have appeared on the RAP sheet. Because of the very close association of data in the arrest reports as a whole and the RAP sheets, we felt that information derived from RAP sheets alone was reliable for classifying arrest charges of individual youth, particularly the more serious charges. Our analysis was based on 4,153 arrests involving 4,277 charges for the 418 youth in the three samples, over the five-year preprogram and five-year program periods.

Youth in each of the samples were involved in many arrest incidents over the combined preprogram and program periods: program youth had 9.7 mean arrests; comparison youth 8.3 mean arrests; and quasiprogram youth 13.9 mean arrests. In the great majority of cases, only one charge per arrest was listed on the RAP sheet for youth in each of the samples: 89.0 percent of program youth;

91.7 percent of comparison youth; and 78.8 percent of quasiprogram youth. Quasiprogram youth were relatively more likely to have two charges listed per arrest than either program or comparison youth.

Youth were arrested for a wide range of crimes. For our analyses, we classified each youth in our samples into one of four major arrestee categories, or subsamples, based on all arrest charges: violence, no drug; drug, no violence; violence and drug; and "other." The category of "other" arrestee included youth with no record of violence or drug arrests but who still had arrests for property crimes, disorderly conduct, mob action, status offenses, and so forth. Our classification task was to assign youth from each of the samples with similar types of arrest charges into one of the four subsamples: (1) violence exclusive of drug charges; (2) drug exclusive of violence charges; (3) both drug and violence charges; and (4) "other" types of charges (but not violence or drug). It was clear from our analyses in the previous chapter that youth in all the samples (and probably in the subsamples) were likely to be arrested more often for "other," no violence, no drug crimes. However, our focus was on the extent to which youth might be "quasispecialized" to violence or drug crime. Our primary interest was in youth arrested for these different categories of crime, and only secondarily in the frequencies of arrests for the different types of crimes.

The largest proportions of youth in all three samples were in the following arrestee subsamples: violence, no drug (program = 41.6 percent, comparison = 38.3 percent, and quasiprogram = 40.5 percent); and violence and drug (program = 35.0 percent, comparison = 22.8 percent, and quasiprogram = 45.2 percent). The next largest proportions of youth were those in the "other" or no violence, no drug subsamples (program = 16.9 percent; comparison = 32.8 percent; and quasiprogram = 13.1 percent). The remaining and smallest proportions of youth were in the drug, no violence subsample (program = 6.5 percent; comparison = 6.1 percent; quasiprogram = 1.2 percent). There were few gang members in any of the samples who were "quasispecialized" to arrests for drug crimes but not violence (table 13.1). Of interest was the relative distribution of the subsample arrestee types within the samples.

The notions of "arrest" and "arrestee" constituted different units of analysis. Although frequency of arrests of the program and comparison youth appeared to be similar when we looked at mean yearly arrests by particular offenses committed in the preprogram period (see chapter 12), the arrestee subsamples (possibly influenced by different career crime interests) were now somewhat different. While youth in the program, comparison, and quasiprogram samples

Table 13.1. Distribution of program, comparison, and quasiprogram samples by arrestee typology

	Youth samples—n and (%)[a]		
Arrestee typology	Program	Comparison	Quasiprogram
No violence, no drug	26(16.9)	59 (32.8)	11 (13.1)
Violence, no drug	64 (41.6)	69 (38.3)	34 (40.5)
Drug, no violence	10 (6.5)	11 (6.1)	1 (1.2)
Violence and drug	54 (35.0)	41 (22.8)	38 (45.2)
Total	154 (100)	180 (100)	84 (100)

Notes
a. The number and percent of youth for the type of arrestee are computed for each sample separately.

were reasonably well matched in our earlier analyses using separate categories of arrests in the preprogram period, they were not as well matched in this analysis using arrestee types over both preprogram and program periods. For example, the size of the no violence, no drug subsample of comparison youth (32.8 percent) was considerably larger than the no violence, no drug subsamples of program youth (16.9 percent) and quasiprogram youth (13.1 percent). The size of the violence and drug subsample of quasiprogram youth (45.2 percent) was greater than for the equivalent subsamples of program youth (35.0 percent) and comparison youth (22.8 percent). This suggested different career crime interests and patterns of arrests for sizable numbers of youth in the different samples, especially between both the program and quasiprogram samples and the comparison sample.

The program and quasiprogram samples contained relatively higher proportions of both violence, no drug, and violence and drug arrestees (76.6 percent and 85.7 percent, respectively) than the comparison sample (61.1 percent). Although there were somewhat different proportions of youth in each of these arrestee subsamples in the three samples, the greatest proportion of gang youth still was in the violence, no drug, and violence and drug subsamples. Nevertheless, it should be clear that the Latin King and Two Six youth in each of the samples were arrested primarily for crimes other than no violence, no drug crimes.

DIFFERENT FREQUENCIES OF ARRESTS BY ARRESTEE SUBSAMPLE

All youth in the arrestee subsamples did not have had the same frequency of arrests. Mean levels of yearly total arrests of youth were generally highest

Table 13.2. Means and standard deviations of yearly arrests[a] by arrestee subsamples for program (N = 154), comparison (N = 180), and quasiprogram (N = 84) youth samples

Arrestee typology	Arrest category	Preprogram period			Program period			Mean change		
		P	C	Q	P	C	Q	P	C	Q
No violence, no drug	Total arrests	0.46 (0.92)	0.25 (0.39)	0.51 (0.69)	0.39 (0.37)	0.57 (0.79)	0.92 (1.15)	-0.07 (1.01)	0.33 (0.88)	0.41 (0.57)
Violence, no drug	Total arrests	1.28 (1.36)	1.15 (1.61)	1.16 (1.60)	1.78 (1.38)	1.22 (1.08)	2.20 (2.09)	0.50 (1.96)	0.07 (2.04)	1.04 (2.49)
	Serious violence	0.22 (0.33)	0.23 (0.38)	0.21 (0.27)	0.41 (0.57)	0.24 (0.41)	0.38 (0.53)	0.19 (0.66)	0.01 (0.51)	0.17 (0.63)
	Total violence	0.31 (0.38)	0.36 (0.60)	0.33 (0.40)	0.55 (0.58)	0.42 (0.46)	0.59 (0.55)	0.24 (0.68)	0.06 (0.71)	0.26 (0.64)
Drug, no violence	Total arrests	0.39 (0.41)	0.20 (0.33)	1.11 (—)	0.82 (0.80)	1.91 (1.71)	0.49 (—)	0.43 (0.91)	1.71 (1.64)	-0.62 (—)
	Drugs	0.16 (0.30)	0.05 (0.15)	0.22 (—)	0.28 (0.18)	0.49 (0.45)	0.00 (—)	0.12 (0.46)	0.45 (0.52)	-0.22 (—)
Violence and drug	Total arrests	1.77 (1.52)	2.56 (2.02)	3.52 (2.77)	2.62 (2.50)	3.17 (2.66)	3.27 (2.33)	0.85 (3.09)	0.63 (2.79)	-0.25 (2.72)
	Serious violence	0.32 (0.45)	0.55 (0.54)	0.59 (0.55)	0.42 (0.52)	0.50 (0.62)	0.62 (0.79)	0.10 (0.79)	-0.04 (0.72)	0.03 (0.84)
	Total violence	0.39 (0.51)	0.79 (0.74)	0.87 (0.69)	0.52 (0.57)	0.77 (0.78)	0.91 (0.79)	0.12 (0.89)	-0.02 (0.97)	0.05 (1.05)
	Drugs	0.14 (0.25)	0.20 (0.32)	0.18 (0.27)	0.56 (0.63)	0.72 (0.82)	0.58 (0.55)	0.42 (0.73)	0.52 (0.85)	0.39 (0.61)

(—) indicates standard deviation cannot be computed due to one observation only.
P = program; C = comparison; Q = quasiprogram.
Notes
a. The top and bottom (in parentheses) numbers are the mean and standard deviation of yearly arrests.

for the violence and drug subsamples, and lowest for the no violence, no drug subsamples, except in the quasiprogram sample, where mean levels were higher for the no violence, no drug subsample than for the drug, no violence subsample (table 13.2).

The tendency to a "quasispecialization" effect existed by subsample. The proportions of mean serious violence arrests or mean total violence arrests to total arrests was higher in the violence, no drug arrestee subsample than in the violence and drug subsample, across the three samples and particularly in the program period. The proportion of mean drug arrests to mean total arrests for the drug, no violence subsample was higher than for the violence and drug subsample, except for quasiprogram youth in the program period.

Mean Change in Numbers of Arrests

There were different patterns of change in mean arrests for the different arrestee subsamples, within each sample and across all the samples between the preprogram and program periods. Without multivariate statistical controls, we found a substantial increase in violence arrests, mainly in the program and quasiprogram violence, no drug subsamples. However, the increase in violence arrests was less marked in the program and quasiprogram violence and drug subsamples. There was less of an increase in violence arrests in the comparison violence, no drug subsample, and also a slight decrease in violence arrests in the comparison violence and drug subsample.

Drug arrests increased substantially more in the comparison drug, no violence subsample than in the equivalent program subsample, and not at all in the equivalent quasiprogram subsample (which showed no arrests for drugs). There was an increase in drug arrests in all of the violence and drug subsamples. Mean violence arrests increased in the program violence and drug subsample, stabilized in the equivalent quasiprogram subsample, and actually decreased in the comparison subsample. Nevertheless, total arrests—particularly no violence, no drugs arrests and, especially, property-crime arrests—increased more sharply in the program and quasiprogram violence, no drug subsamples, relative to the equivalent comparison subsample.

In other words, based on mean arrests between the preprogram and program periods, we observed a "quasispecialization" effect toward violence arrests, especially serious violence arrests, in the program and quasiprogram samples; and a "quasispecialization" effect toward drug arrests and no violence, no drug (mainly property) arrests in the comparison sample. While the quasiprogram sample was the most delinquent or criminal subsample in terms of total arrests, its frequency of violence arrests abated somewhat for several of its arrestee subsamples. All of the arrestee subsamples continued their specialized patterns of delinquent or criminal behaviors. Violence arrests were increasing (or stabilizing), but drug arrests relatively decreasing (or not increasing) in the program and quasiprogram subsamples. However, a reverse effect was occurring in the comparison subsamples, particularly in terms of a decline in serious violence and total violence arrests, and an increase (or stabilization) in drug arrests.

The changes in mean arrest frequencies indicated the increasing "quasispecialization" of arrest configurations in the three samples and their arrestee subsamples. Mean total arrests declined in the program no violence, no drug subsample but increased in the equivalent comparison and quasiprogram subsamples. While total arrests increased in all three of the violence, no drug subsamples, they increased more in the program and quasiprogram subsamples. Total arrests increased more sharply for youth in the comparison drug, no violence subsample than for youth in the equivalent program subsample, and actually declined for youth in the equivalent quasiprogram subsample. Increases in total arrests in the program violence and drug subsample were greater than in the equivalent comparison subsample. Mean arrests for violence increased for youth in the program violence and drug subsample, abated in the equivalent quasiprogram subsample, and declined in the comparison subsample.

The largest increase for drug arrests was in the violence and drug subsamples of all three samples. The highest rate of increase in drug arrests was in the quasiprogram violence and drug subsample; it was slightly lower in the program violence and drug subsample than in the comparison subsample. Nevertheless, youth in the comparison violence and drug subsample still had the highest mean drug arrests, compared to equivalent subsamples in the program and quasiprogram samples, during both the preprogram and program periods.

Similarity of Change Patterns in Arrests and Self-Reported Offenses

The tendency to "quasispecialization" existed across the three samples. This was the case whether we used arrest or self-report data. A comparison of arrest and self-report offense data for the program sample suggested a similar tendency to "quasispecialization,"[1] although arrests and self-reports were not matched by the same preprogram and program periods. The project focused on the gang-violence problem; contacts were primarily made with those gang members who were more violent and less drug-crime oriented, rather than those who were relatively more active in drug and property crime. These latter types of offender/arrestee subgroups were more likely to be in the comparison sample and, to a lesser extent, in the quasiprogram sample.

We compared changes in arrests and self-reported offenses of youth (excluding those with only time I interviews) included in the arrestee typology, that is, no violence, no drug; violence, no drug; drug, no violence; and violence and drug (table 13.3).

However, most (N = 108) but not all of the program youths interviewed at time I and time III who self-reported offenses (N = 119) also had arrests. Youth in the four program arrestee subsamples could be classified in equivalent fashion based on self-reported offenses, despite the fact that the interview sample (N = 119) was smaller than the arrest sample (N = 154), and the interview data covered approximately a three- to four-year program period only, while the arrest data covered approximately a six-year (three-year preprogram and three-year program) period, on average, for each of the youth. We identified a fifth self-reported offense subsample: eleven youth (9.5 percent)[2] who did not have arrests in either the three-year preprogram or three-year program period but who self-reported a variety of offenses committed during their program periods. We called this the no-arrest-history offense subsample.

Most program youth with self-reported offenses were either in the violence, no drug subsample (36.2 percent) or in the violence and drug subsample (29.3 percent). Most program youth with arrests were in the violence, no drug subsample (41.6 percent) and the violence and drug subsample (35.0 percent). Each arrestee subsample was somewhat larger than the equivalent self-reported offense subsample. The subsample with the highest percentage of drug-selling offenses (6.9 percent) was almost equivalent to the drug, no violence arrestee subsample (6.5 percent). The no violence, no drug offense subsample (18.1 percent) was also almost equivalent to the arrestee subsample (16.9 percent). The no-arrest-history offense subsample (9.5 percent) had lower levels of self-reported offenses in respect to total offenses and violence offenses than the no violence, no drug; violence, no drug; and violence and drug offense subsamples at the time I interview but not the drug, no violence subsample. The no-arrest-history offense subsample had a higher mean level of

Table 13.3. Change in patterns of self-reported offenses[a] (N = 119) and yearly police arrests[b] (N = 154) by arrestee typology

Arrestee typology	Crime[c] category	Preprogram period[d] Self-reported offenses	Preprogram period[d] Police arrests	Program period[e] Self-reported offenses	Program period[e] Police arrests	Mean change Self-reported offenses	Mean change Police arrests	Sample size[f] N_{SR} (%$_{SR}$)	Sample size[f] N_{PA} (%$_{PA}$)
No arrest history[g]	Total crime	19.57	—	9.0	—	-10.57	—	11 (9.5)	0 (0.0)
	Serious violence	7.50	—	4.86	—	-2.64	—		
	Total violence	12.00	—	8.07	—	-3.93	—		
	Drug	4.38	—	3.21	—	-0.92	—		
No violence, no drug	Total crime	32.86	0.46	6.95	0.39	-25.90	-0.07	21 (18.1)	26 (16.9)
	Serious violence	13.62	—	2.19	—	-11.43	—		
	Total violence	17.48	—	4.52	—	-12.95	—		
	Drug	3.43	—	2.79	—	-0.64	—		
Violence, no drug	Total crime	70.26	1.28	9.93	1.78	-60.33	0.50	42 (36.2)	64 (41.6)
	Serious violence	21.71	0.22	3.31	0.41	-18.40	0.19		
	Total violence	39.50	0.31	6.50	0.55	-33.00	0.24		
	Drug	4.38	—	2.05	—	-2.03	—		
Drug, no violence	Total crime	16.38	0.39	7.75	0.82	-8.63	0.43	8 (6.9)	10 (6.5)
	Serious violence	5.63	—	1.38	—	-4.25	—		
	Total violence	8.88	—	4.63	—	-4.25	—		
	Drug	5.13	0.16	2.50	0.28	-2.63	0.12		
Violence and drug	Total crime	61.68	1.77	11.09	2.62	-50.59	0.85	34 (29.3)	54 (35.0)
	Serious violence	22.59	0.32	4.74	0.42	-17.85	0.10		
	Violence	30.21	0.39	7.91	0.52	-22.29	0.12		
	Drug selling	4.12	0.14	3.51	0.56	-0.61	0.42		

Notes

a. Self-reported offenses (SR) data are derived from three gang-member-survey interviews obtained from program youth during the program period.

b. Police arrest (PA) data are derived from Chicago Police Department arrest records.

c. Total crime for self-reported offenses excludes drug selling. Total crime for police arrests includes all drug-related arrests.

d. The preprogram offense period covers a six-month period prior to the youth's time I interview. The preprogram arrest period for youth in cohorts I and II covers arrests in a four-and-a-half-year period (1987–1992); for youth in cohort III, a two-year period (1993–1995).

e. The program offense period covers a six-month period prior to the youth's time III interviews. The program arrest period for youth in cohorts I and II covers a four-and-a-half-year period (1992–1997); for youth in cohort III, a two-year period (1995–1997).

f. NSR (percentSR) and NPA (percentPA) represent subsample sizes (percents) of two unmatched samples of youth over time—self-reported offense sample (N = 119) and police arrest sample (N = 154).

g. The eleven interviewed youth with no arrest history were not included in the police arrest data analysis.

selling drugs than two of the three arrestee subsamples at the time I and time III interviews.

The patterns of self-reported offenses of program youth in the subsamples was similar to their arrest patterns, at both time I and time III. Mean offenses for violence were highest for program youth in the violence, no drug and the violence and drug subsamples. Mean self-reported offenses for drug selling were not always high in the drug, no violence subsample; the youth in the no-arrest-history subsample had a fairly high level of self-reported drug selling.

However, it was difficult to be sure about the meaning of changes in specific patterns of offenses among program youth between the time I and time III interviews (approximately three years apart) during the program period, compared to changes between the four-and-a-half-year preprogram and the four-and-a-half-year program arrest periods. Also, the range of self-reported offenses (twenty-six items in the gang-member survey) was more limited than the range of arrest charges in the RAP sheets (one hundred–plus crime categories). The self-report offense questions in the program-youth interviews focused relatively more on violence arrests; the official arrest charges included all types of offenses. Further, it was possible to question the reliability of self-report responses; program youth reported a very high number of offenses at time I but an extremely low number at time III.

Based on self-report offense data, program youth were engaged in a great deal of delinquent or criminal behavior, far greater than their arrest histories would indicate. Nevertheless, while the self-report offense-change data may have been less reliable than arrest-change data, there were still striking similarities in the patterning of categories of arrests and self-reported offenses within and across the youth subsamples (table 13.3).

SUBSAMPLE ARREST CHANGES

To understand whether the program had a differential effect on arrest changes, we conducted a similar analysis as in chapter 12 using GLM, including the subsample arrestee typology variable. The dependent variables in the models, again, were changes in total arrests, serious violence arrests, total violence arrests (serious and less serious), drug arrests, and "other" arrests (i.e., nonviolence and nondrug arrests, including property arrests, alcohol arrests, etc.) between the preprogram and program periods. The following control variables were entered into the models: age category (sixteen years and under, seventeen and eighteen years, nineteen years and over); gang (Two Six and Latin Kings); subsample arrestee typology (no violence, no drug; violence, no drug; drug, no violence; and violence and drug); level of preprogram yearly arrests (none, low, medium, and high); and project (whether the youth was in the program, comparison, or quasiprogram sample).

In the following analyses exploring changes in arrests we focused on the two main effects—program sample and subsample arrestee typologies—and their interactions with other variables. In each model the strongest effects were levels of preprogram yearly arrests (a regression effect) and age category (the older the youth the greater the reduction in arrests). There were no significant effects of the gang (Latin Kings versus Two Six) variable. In general, program youth still showed more positive changes, or reduced levels of arrests—particularly for violence and drugs—than comparison and quasiprogram youth. Nevertheless, there were differences in respect to subsample changes within and across samples, which were of particular interest.

Total Arrests

In the model with the dependent variable change in yearly total arrests, the subsample arrestee typology variable was highly significant as a main effect ($p \leq 0.001$). The LS mean varied for the different arrestee subsamples across the three samples: no violence, no drug (-2.28); drug, no violence (-1.46); violence, no drug ($+1.25$); and violence and drug ($+33.84$). The youth in the no violence, no drug subsample generally did best in reducing total arrests compared to the violence, no drug subsample ($p = 0.001$) and the violence and drug subsample ($p < 0.001$). In all the samples, the drug, no violence subsample did better than the violence and drug subsample ($p = 0.041$), and the violence and drug subsample did worst, with a large increase in total arrests.

There were no statistically significant differences in change patterns for yearly total arrests for any of the subsamples across the program, comparison, and quasiprogram samples. We found that while youth in the program and quasiprogram drug, no violence subsamples reduced their total arrests in the program period, youth in the equivalent comparison subsample increased their total arrests. In contrast, while the youth in the comparison violence, no drug subsample reduced their total arrests, the equivalent program and quasiprogram subsamples increased their total arrests.

With regard to the project main effect and the project × age category interaction effect, the pairwise comparisons were insignificant, although in all cases the program-sample age categories had smaller increases in total arrests than equivalent comparison-sample age categories: older program youth (nineteen and older) decreased their total arrests, while older comparison youth increased theirs.

Serious Violence Arrests

Although youth in the program sample did almost significantly better (p = 0.07) in reducing yearly serious violence arrests than youth in the comparison sample, and the comparison sample did significantly (p = 0.04) better than the quasiprogram sample, the subsample arrestee typology variable was not a significant main effect. However, the program violence, no drug and the violence and drug subsamples did better in the reduction of serious violence arrests than the equivalent comparison and quasiprogram subsamples. In terms of reductions in serious violence arrests, the program violence and drug subsample did almost significantly better (p = 0.095) than the equivalent comparison subsample, and significantly better (p = 0.015) than the equivalent quasiprogram subsample. Again, with regard to the project main effect and the project × age category interaction effect, most of the pairwise comparisons were insignificant. In all subsamples, the program sample did better than the comparison and quasiprogram samples, although the differences were not always statistically significant.

Total Violence Arrests

The program sample reduced its level of yearly total violence arrests (serious and less serious) while the comparison and quasiprogram samples increased theirs. Differences were almost statistically significant between the program and the comparison samples (p = 0.09) and statistically significant between the program and the quasiprogram samples (p = 0.002). We found somewhat similar results in the violence, no drug and the violence and drug subsamples. The program youth in the violence and drug subsample reduced their levels of yearly total violence arrests compared to youth in the equivalent comparison and quasiprogram subsamples.

As with serious violence arrests, the program sample did better than the comparison and quasiprogram samples in reducing total violence arrests in all age groups. The seventeen- and eighteen-year-old program youth did significantly better (p ≤ 0.01) than the seventeen- and eighteen-year-old quasiprogram youth. The nineteen-and-over program youth did significantly better (p ≤ 0.05) than the nineteen-and-over quasiprogram youth.

Drug Arrests

Overall, youth in the program sample reduced their levels of drug arrests, while the comparison and quasiprogram youth increased theirs. The differences were not statistically significant. Also, program youth in the drug, no violence and the violence and drug subsamples reduced their levels of drug arrests compared to the equivalent comparison and quasiprogram subsamples, but again these differences were not statistically significant.

We knew that youth in the various samples and subsamples had very few drug arrests in the preprogram or program periods. Nevertheless, the LS means reduction in yearly drug arrests was six times greater for youth in the program drug, no violence subsample than for youth in the equivalent comparison subsample. While youth in the program violence and drug subsample decreased their LS mean yearly drug arrests by more than one-third, youth in the equivalent comparison subsample increased theirs by more than 50 percent. Across the different age categories, the program youth did better (but not significantly) than the comparison youth.

"Other" Arrests

The subsample arrestee typology variable was a significant (p = 0.012) main effect in the GLM equation with "other" arrests (nonviolence/nondrug arrests, including property, alcohol, etc.). Youth in each of the samples reduced their levels of yearly "other" arrests. The main differences were between arrestee subsamples within each of the samples, rather than across the three samples. The most significant difference (p = 0.002) was the large reduction of "other" arrests for youth in the no violence, no drug subsamples compared to youth in the violence and drug subsamples. The youth in the violence, no drug subsamples did significantly better (p = 0.029) than youth in the violence and drug subsamples in reducing their levels of "other" arrests. Across the samples, the youth in the program and comparison violence, no drug subsamples did better than the youth in the equivalent quasiprogram subsample.

SPECIFICITY IN IDENTIFYING ARRESTEE SUBGROUPS

The Little Village Gang Violence Reduction Project attempted to target youth in the two gangs—Latin Kings and Two Six—most engaged in violent behavior. In the course of the five-year project, we found that program youth were committed or "quasispecialized" to different patterns of criminal behavior, including violence. It was possible to establish a similar arrestee typology of gang youth for the subsamples of program, comparison, and quasiprogram youth. Further, whether using their arrest or self-report offense histories, an equivalent typology was established using the same program youth. The arrestee typology had four categories of youth with different combinations of arrests in their backgrounds: no violence, no drug; violence, no drug; drug, no violence; and violence and drug. In all of the arrestee subsamples, youth were also arrested for a variety of "other" crimes, such as theft, property crime, mob action, disorderly conduct, graffiti, alcohol use, obstruction of justice, and so forth.

The arrestee typology confirmed the specification and verified the project's process of identifying and targeting subgroups of youth in the program, quasiprogram, and comparison samples who were likely to increase their arrests for violence between the preprogram and program periods. The arrestee typology variable was significant as a main effect in several of our GLM analyses. Program youth did better in lowering their levels of violence arrests than comparison or quasiprogram youth in almost all cases, particularly in the violence, no drug subsample and the violence and drug subsample. Again, there was no statistical difference between the program, comparison, and quasiprogram samples in respect to reducing "other" arrests.

The arrestee typology demonstrated that there were different subgroups of gang youth in each of the samples—program, comparison, and quasiprogram—based on their career arrest and possibly career self-reported offense patterns. Not all gang members had the same patterns of delinquent or criminal behavior. The arrestee typology confirmed that the project targeted violent youth in the gangs and that the program was most effective in reducing violence arrests for those youth who had the highest commitment, or potential, for violence.

In the next chapter we identify those worker contacts and services that specifically contributed to a reduction of violence, drug, or a combination of violence and drug arrests for youth in the different arrestee subsamples of the program sample.

NOTES

1. Interview and self-report data were not obtained for quasiprogram or comparison youth.

2. Fourteen of the youth interviewed at time I through time III had no arrest histories. The other 105 youth were part of the program arrest sample (N = 154); 49 of the arrested program youth had only a time I but no time III interview. The no-arrest-history subsample did in fact have self-reported offenses.

14

Services and Outcome

Finally, we come to a discussion of which specific parts of the program were effective. We describe what the project workers did that accounted for reductions in violence arrests, and also drug-crime arrests, of program youth. First, we ask whether the right youth were targeted and provided with sufficient worker contacts, and what the results were in terms of change in arrests patterns. Next, we examine the nature and quality of worker contacts and services that may have contributed to positive changes in the youth's relationship to his social environment, and led to improved arrest outcomes. We then determine what specific worker services or activities predicted a reduction of arrests for different youth arrestee types. In the analyses we use data drawn from worker-tracking records, police arrest histories, and interviews of program youth.

TARGETING

The first task was to determine whether project workers targeted the more violent delinquent or criminal gang youth, as intended in the program design. The number of worker-tracking forms completed for individual youth became a key independent variable to discover which kinds of program youth, that is, with what arrest backgrounds, were contacted and provided with services. During the course of the program, a total of 479 tracking records were completed for 184 program youth:[1] 315 (65.8 percent) by outreach youth workers, 134 (28.0 percent) by police and probation, and 30 (6.3 percent) by the neighborhood organizer. We considered that the varying numbers of tracking forms completed by workers could reflect different levels of attention to different types of youth who were (or should have been) provided with services. The project objective was to pay most attention to violent or potentially violent gang youth. Such youth were to be provided with the most contacts and services. This should be evidenced by the existence of more tracking records per youth.

Table 14.1. Means and standard deviations (S.D.) of preprogram-period arrests for youth (N = 153) with different numbers of worker-tracking records[a]

Arrest category	Zero tracked (n = 17)		One-time tracked (n = 45)		Two-or-more-times tracked (n = 91)	
	Mean	S.D.	Mean	S.D.	Mean	S.D.
Total arrests	2.8	2.87	4.70	5.33	4.86	5.23
Serious violence arrests	0.53	0.72	0.83	1.09	0.82	1.75
Total violence arrests	0.59	0.87	1.07	1.53	1.12	1.99
Property arrests	1.06	1.30	1.68	2.55	1.39	2.17
Drug/alcohol arrests	0.35	1.06	0.23	0.43	0.55	0.96
"Other" arrests	0.82	1.33	1.71	2.45	1.78	2.22

Notes
a. The total preprogram period was the equivalent of four and a half years prior to the youth's entry into the program.

The sample for this analysis consisted of 153 out of the 154 youth who had arrest histories, and for whom we had clear evidence that a tracking record had or had not been completed. The categories of youth with varying numbers of tracking records were as follows: "zero tracked" = 17 (11.1 percent); "one-time tracked" = 45 (29.4 percent); and "two-or-more-times tracked" = 91 (59.4 percent). Worker-tracking records were completed for each youth up to three times, usually at one- or one-and-a-quarter-year intervals, over a three- or four-year period. The analysis revealed that, at program entry, the zero-tracked youth had considerably fewer arrests for every category of offense than the one-time or two-or-more-times tracked youth. The youth who were tracked only once had slightly fewer arrests than youth who were tracked two or more times. Youth tracked one time and those tracked two times had similar arrest patterns, except that youth tracked two or more times had slightly more total arrests and total violence arrests. The youth tracked one time had somewhat more property arrests (table 14.1).

The program group with zero tracking forms contained disproportionately younger youth (58.8 percent) than the group with one tracking form (31.1 percent) and the group with two or more tracking forms (37.4 percent). Usually, younger youth had fewer arrests in the preprogram period.[2] The zero-tracked group had the smallest percentage of seventeen- and eighteen-year-olds (11.8 percent, the age group at peak levels of violent crime) compared to the one-time tracked (33.3 percent) and the two-or-more-times tracked (34.1 percent) groups. Also, the zero-tracked seventeen- and eighteen-year-olds had no records of arrests for violence, drug, or alcohol offenses. The proportions of youth nineteen and over in the different tracking groups were as follows: zero tracked = 29.4 percent; one-time tracked = 35.6 percent; and two-or-more-times tracked = 28.6 percent. Youth in the zero-tracked group were *not* targeted, or targeted only for a brief period of time, because they were less violent, less gang involved, and less delinquent or criminal.

EFFECTS OF TARGETING

The second task was to conduct a multivariate analysis using a general linear model (GLM) procedure to determine whether there might be different patterns of yearly arrest changes in the three different tracking groups between the preprogram and program period. Our dependent or outcome variable in each model was change in yearly arrests for specific types of offenses between the preprogram and program period. Our key independent or program variable was tracking group: zero, one, and two or more tracking forms; the control variables were age category (sixteen and under, seventeen and eighteen, nineteen and older) and preprogram-level of yearly arrests (none, low, medium, high) for youth in each of the different arrest categories—total arrests, serious violence arrests, total violence arrests, property arrests, and drug arrests. Our interaction terms were age category × tracking group, age category × preprogram-period yearly arrests, and preprogram-period yearly arrests × tracking group. The results were as follows:

Yearly Total Arrests

The tracking group variable was not statistically significant when the outcome variable was change in yearly total arrests. None of the types of tracking groups did significantly better than the others in respect to change in total arrests, although the youth in the zero-tracked group slightly reduced their frequency of total arrests, while the one-time and two-or-more-times tracked groups slightly increased theirs. Age category (younger youth increased their arrests; $p = 0.005$) and preprogram-period yearly arrests (regression factor; $p \leq 0.001$) were significant predictors in the model, which accounted for 49.0 percent of total variance.

Yearly Serious Violence Arrests

However, when the dependent variable was change in yearly serious violence arrests, the tracking group variable was significant ($p = 0.042$), as was preprogram-period yearly arrests for serious violence (p ≤ 0.001). The two-or-more-times tracked group predicted a significantly greater reduction in level of serious violence arrests compared to the one-time tracked group (p = 0.05). We could not estimate a change score for the zero-tracked group; not enough zero-tracked youth had serious violence arrests. The highest serious violence–arrest subgroup in the two-or-more-times tracked group also did significantly better (p = 0.013) than the comparable subgroup in the one-time tracked group. This model accounted for 56 percent of total variance.

Yearly Total Violence Arrests

The pattern of results here was almost identical to the previous model, when the dependent variable was change in yearly total violence arrests. The tracking group variable was significant (p = 0.04), as was preprogram-period yearly total violence arrests (p ≤ 0.001). The two-or-more-times tracked group did better (but not significantly) than the one-time and zero-time tracked groups. All age categories showed declines in yearly total violence arrests, as did all of the tracking groups. There were no significant differences by particular age categories based on preprogram-period arrest levels of violent offenders. The model again accounted for 56 percent of variance.

Yearly Property Arrests

There were interesting differences in the three tracking groups regarding property arrests during the program period, particularly between the zero-tracked and the one-time and two-or-more-times tracked groups. All variables except the interaction term age category × tracking group were significant in the model. The most significant factors were age category (p ≤ 0.001) and preprogram-period arrests for property offenses (p ≤ 0.001). The tracking group variable significantly predicted (p = 0.02) the level of property arrests. The zero-tracked group showed a significant decline, compared to the one-time tracked group (p = 0.005) and the two-or-more-times tracked group (p < 0.01). This model accounted for 48 percent of total variance. Across all tracking groups, only the youngest age category (sixteen and under) increased its level of property arrests, compared to the two older age categories (whose property-arrest levels generally declined). The differences were highly significant (p ≤ 0.001) when comparing the youngest group to either of the two older groups. The declines for the zero-tracked seventeen- and eighteen-year olds were significantly greater (p = 0.04) than for the one-time tracked group.

Yearly Drug Arrests

In our model predicting changes in yearly arrests for drug crimes, only the preprogram-period yearly drug arrests variable entered the general linear model at a significant statistical level ($p = 0.04$). We could not estimate differences among age categories, tracking groups, or tracking subgroups with high drug-arrest levels. However, the zero-tracked group showed a small (nonsignificant) decline in mean yearly drug arrests during the program period, compared to the other two tracking groups. The model accounted for 25 percent of total variance.

These findings strongly indicated that the zero-tracked group was indeed less violent, and also generally less delinquent or criminal, and that the project workers appropriately did *not* target this group. The relatively small number of zero-tracked youth reduced their arrests more than one- or two-or-more-times tracked youth during the program period, in spite of the fact that they were provided with the least amount of worker contacts and services. The zero-tracked group probably should not have been targeted in the first place. We believe that 88.9 percent ($n = 136$) of the youth in the program analysis sample *were* appropriately targeted for worker contacts and services.

CONTACTS AND SERVICES RELATED TO LIFE-SPACE AND LIFE-COURSE CHANGES

We assumed that changes in the individual program youth's delinquent or criminal behavior might be a function largely of changes in his relationship to his social circumstances, which might be influenced by project workers. In other words, the project workers sought to affect certain mediating factors or conditions that predicted the youth's involvement in antisocial activity. In the course of suppression or counseling contacts, the youth might decide to leave the gang, obtain a legitimate job, and spend more time with a wife or girlfriend rather than with gang peers; lower his job and income aspirations to realistic levels; and come to perceive the community as a good, or satisfactory, place in which to live. The quantity and quality of the workers' services or controls could bring a change in these mediating circumstances or relationships resulting in a decline in criminal behavior.

We were interested in what specific types of service contacts induced youth to give up certain dysfunctional attitudes and behaviors. We used individual-level data from the gang-member surveys, worker-tracking records, and the youths' police arrest histories to determine whether certain worker contacts and services contributed to life-space and life-course changes.

Program data collected through the worker-tracking instrument and the life-space and life-course factors measured in our survey data were both of a categorical nature. We employed logistic regression analysis to determine which service or control contacts were particularly useful in predicting successful life-space and life-course changes, which could subsequently contribute to higher proportions of youth with reduced arrests. We included the youth's age as a covariate in the following change models, and it was always the older-age category—nineteen and over—that made the most significant, positive life-space and life-course changes.

First, we found that four types of contact and service variables were statistically significant in predicting success in contributing to positive life-space and life-course changes for 148 program youth:[3] suppression (particularly by police); job referrals by youth workers and the neighborhood organizer; school referrals (mainly by youth workers); and program dosage, that is, contacts by all workers together—youth workers, police, probation, and neighborhood workers (but especially by youth workers). Project-worker success was defined in perceptual terms, that is, the worker's perceived effectiveness of a particular service or contact in getting the youth to change his attitudes, relationships, and certain life-space and life-course behaviors. Levels of effectiveness are categorized in a later section.

Suppression

Suppression was associated with more youth reducing their gang-membership status from leader to core, regular, or peripheral gang member, or to a nongang youth. The odds ratio of success to failure was 1.99 ($p = 0.044$), regardless of age. Suppression could make for changes in the youth's degree of attachment to the gang. Suppression was also useful in getting more youth to reduce the gap between income aspirations and realistic income expectations, so more youth had realistic income-level aspirations; the odds ratio of success to failure was 2.71 ($p = 0.006$). Suppression powerfully aided more program youth, particularly older youth, to more realistically face the world of making a legitimate living. Law enforcement, through threat of arrest, probably had a deterrent and socially maturing effect, which could then serve to reduce the gang youth's (particularly the older gang youth's) attachment to the gang and help him more realistically approach a conventional income lifestyle.

Job Placement and Referral

Job placement and referral, particularly job placement, predicted more youth spending less time with gang friends. The odds ratio of success to failure was 0.707 (p = 0.064) and was more characteristic of older than younger youth. In addition, job placement and referral contributed to the probability that youth would spend more time with wives or steady girlfriends. In earlier analyses, we found that time spent with a wife or girlfriend was a strong predictor of fewer arrests for almost all types of crime, including violence and drug crime, across all age categories. A good deal of tension often developed in these relationships, as the wife or girlfriend encouraged (or nagged) program youth to get a job and spend less time (or no time) with gang friends (chapters 9 and 10).

School-Related Contacts

School-related contacts produced a slightly positive but nonsignificant effect on the odds ratio of success to failure 1.74 (p = 0.150) of youth graduating from high school or achieving a high school equivalency certificate. School-related discussions with youth and contacts with educational institutions on their behalf were more effective with older youth than younger youth. Older youth belatedly became aware that further education was important to obtaining a job or pursuing a better-paying job.

Program Dosage and Mediating Variables

The higher the number of service contacts with the youth during the total program period, the greater the odds ratio of success to failure (1.31; p = 0.044) in reducing the gap between the youth's income aspirations and expectations (usually by lowering aspirations and raising expectations). Similarly, the higher the total number of service contacts per month, the greater the odds ratio of success to failure (1.34; p = 0.039) in reducing the gap between income aspirations and expectations.

Program dosage had a significant effect in reducing the youth's contact with gang friends. The higher the number of service contacts during the total program period, the greater the odds ratio (1.59; p = 0.004) of reducing the youth's ties with gang friends; also, the more contacts per month with the youth,

Table 14.2. Worker contacts and services predicting arrest outcomes

Logistic model[a]		Model A			Model B		
Predictor → Outcome[b]		Contact dosage yes vs. no			Service effectiveness "very effective" vs. "less than very effective"[c]		
Type of service	Change in arrests	Odds ratio[d]	p[e]	Std. err.	Odds ratio	p	Std. err.
School →	Violence	1.032	0.645	0.461	0.666	0.492	0.591
	Violence & drug	0.529	0.166	0.460	0.364	0.122	0.652
	Drug	0.377	0.164	0.701	0.515	0.577	1.193
Job →	Violence	2.665	0.037*	0.470	2.558	0.066	0.511
	Violence & drug	1.923	0.141	0.444	1.426	0.472	0.493
	Drug	1.299	0.681	0.638	0.816	0.790	0.762
Opportunity →	Violence	2.097	0.137	0.498	2.468	0.060	0.479
	Violence & drug	1.148	0.766	0.462	1.263	0.614	0.463
	Drug	1.069	0.922	0.681	0.735	0.687	0.764
Family →	Violence	0.923	0.861	0.458	1.315	0.560	0.470
	Violence & drug	1.149	0.753	0.441	1.786	0.209	0.461
	Drug	1.368	0.634	0.657	1.494	0.561	0.690
Counseling →	Violence	2.831	0.115	0.660	2.608	0.042*	0.471
	Violence & drug	1.325	0.619	0.565	2.150	0.094	0.456
	Drug	0.411	0.259	0.789	1.354	0.637	0.643
Suppression →	Violence	1.108	0.645	0.224	1.668	0.307	0.504
	Violence & drug	0.893	0.801	0.448	0.990	0.985	0.514
	Drug	0.693	0.594	0.687	0.478	0.387	0.851

Notes

a. All logistic regression models included a service predictor and three additional control variables—age (nineteen and over; eighteen and under), gang (Latin King; Two Six), and arrestee typology (violence, no drug; violence and drug; drug, no violence).

b. Three arrest outcomes for youth (N = 128) are as follows: violence, no drug; violence and drug; drug, no violence.

c. Service effectiveness was categorized by the degree of successful response to the service as perceived by the worker: "very effective" and "less than very effective" (i.e., "somewhat," "little," and "not at all").

d. The odds ratio of failure to success is the reciprocal of the odds ratio of success to failure.

e. *p < .05.

the greater the odds ratio of success to failure (1.52; p = 0.011) in reducing his ties with gang friends. This latter effect occurred across all age categories.

WORKER CONTACTS, SERVICES, AND ARREST OUTCOMES

All the youth (N = 184) in the program sample—whether interviewed or not, whether they had police records or not, and whether they had worker-tracking records or not—were contacted by workers. However, not all program youth were provided with a full range of services during the period they were in the program. Data from the worker-tracking records indicated that certain services were more likely to be provided than others. The percentages of all youth provided with the specific services were individual counseling (93.5 percent); brief family advice or counseling (60.3 percent); and job services (59.3 percent). Fewer youth were provided with school-related services—45.7 percent—or suppression services—26.1 percent.

The workers were expected to indicate in the tracking records of each youth whether they—the youth workers—considered that the particular service provided was "very effective," "somewhat effective," "a little effective," or "not at all effective," based on their observations of the youth's activities in response to the particular service. The workers did not necessarily have knowledge of the youth's previous arrest history and did not know whether the contacts or the services they provided were related to a change in the youth's subsequent arrests.

The specific services provided to youth were categorized as relating to school, jobs, opportunity provision (a combination of school and job services), individual counseling, family counseling, and suppression. The outcome variables were change in yearly total violence arrests (serious and less serious), violence and drug arrests, and drug arrests. Logistic regression models were used to determine (1) whether contacts that included a particular type of service contributed to a higher ratio of success to failure in reducing a particular category of arrests than contacts that lacked the particular type of service (table 14.2, model A); and (2) whether contacts that provided a particular "very effective" service contributed to a higher ratio of success to failure in reducing a particular category of arrests than contacts that provided the same but "less than very effective" service (table 14.2, model B).

The two sets of logistic regression models controlled for the age categories (nineteen and over, eighteen and under), gang (Latin King, Two Six), and arrestee typology (violence, no drug; violence and drug; drug, no violence).

The findings generally showed that when contacts included the provision of job-related, opportunity-provision, family-counseling, and individual-youth-counseling services, the odds ratios of success to failure in reducing arrests, particularly for violence, were higher than if the contacts did not provide these particular services. Similarly, "very effective" job-related services, opportunity provision, family counseling, and individual-youth counseling predicted higher odds ratios of success to failure in reducing violence arrests than if the services were perceived by workers as "less than very effective."

Across all types of services, the highest odds ratios of success to failure almost always predicted the reduction of violence arrests and almost always the lowest odds ratios of success to failure in the reduction of drug arrests. The probability of success to failure of job services versus no job services lowering violence arrests was odds ratio 2.67 ($p = 0.037$), and of "very effective" versus "less than very effective" individual-youth-counseling services lowering violence arrests, odds ratio 2.61 ($p = 0.042$).

Frequency of Services and Their Perceived Effectiveness

The worker's perception of the effectiveness of the particular services he provided was related to the frequency with which those services were provided. We had worker-tracking records for each of the three tracking periods indicating whether workers made contacts and provided particular types of services to particular youth. We were able to compute the overall level of effectiveness for the different services, based on the number of tracking records in which a type of service was specified.

We proposed that if the quality of the particular service was classified as "very effective" in at least one tracking period, it indicated a superior possibility of lowering arrests than if "less than very effective" service was provided. We found that "very effective" services from all the service categories were provided to some but not all youth. It became evident that the more a youth was provided a particular service, the more likely the service would be classified as "very effective." Also, a youth provided with a particular type of service across all three tracking periods was more likely to be perceived as having been provided with a "very effective" service than a youth who was provided with a particular type of service in only one or two tracking periods.

We also found that school-related services, which were less often provided to youth, were less likely to be perceived by the worker as "very effective," compared to any other types of services, across all tracking periods (table 14.3).

Table 14.3. Numbers and percentages of youth (N=184) contacted for services, and services perceived as "very effective"

| Type of service | Number of contacts[a] (C) | Youth contacted for services | | "Very effective" services | |
| | | | | Within # of contacts | |
		All youth N (%)	Excluding no service %[b] of C ≥ 1	N[c]	%[c] = Ne[d] × 100 N
School	0 contacts	100 (54.3)	—	—	—
	1 contact	65 (35.3)	77.3	18	27.7
	2 contacts	15 (8.2)	17.9	8	53.3
	3 or more contacts	4 (2.2)	4.8	3	75.0
Job	0 contacts	75 (40.7)	—	—	—
	1 contact	78 (42.4)	71.6	22	28.2
	2 contacts	23 (12.5)	21.1	15	65.2
	3 or more contacts	8 (4.4)	7.3	8	100.0
Family	0 contacts	73 (39.7)	—	—	—
	1 contact	70 (38.0)	63.1	21	30.0
	2 contacts	35 (19.0)	31.5	27	77.1
	3 or more contacts	6 (3.3)	5.4	6	100.0
Counseling	0 contacts	12 (6.5)	—	—	—
	1 contact	105 (57.1)	61.0	33	31.4
	2 contacts	51 (27.7)	29.7	27	52.9
	3 or more contacts	16 (8.7)	9.3	13	81.3
Suppression	0 contacts	136 (73.9)	—	—	—
	1 contact	24 (13.0)	50.0	9	37.5
	2 contacts	13 (7.1)	27.1	9	69.2
	3 or more contacts	11 (6.0)	22.9	10	90.9

Notes
a. All youth (N = 184), with or without interviews and with or without arrests, were classified by four categories of contacts (0, 1, 2, or 3+) for the specific services recorded during the three worker-tracking periods.
b. % = percentage of youth contacted for a particular type of service (excluding no service).
c. % = percentage of youth provided with "very effective" services for the particular category of contacts.
d. Ne is the number of youth provided with "very effective" services. Ne/N is the ratio of youth with "very effective" services to youth who were contacted for both "very effective" and "less than very effective" services. A "less than very effective" service included a "somewhat," "little," or "not at all" successful contact.

That school services were in short supply could have been due to the fact that most program youth were no longer in public school, interested in attending or returning to school, or participating in GED programs.

The implication of these findings was that "very effective" job-related services and "very effective" individual-youth counseling (particularly by outreach youth workers in an interdisciplinary team context) predicted higher odds ratios of success to failure in reducing arrests for violence than other types of "very effective" services. There was also some evidence of higher odds ratios of success to failure of these two types of services reducing a combination of violence and drug arrests. School and suppression services had the lowest odds ratios of success to failure in reducing violence arrests, violence and drug arrests, and especially, drug arrests (i.e., school and suppression services were generally least likely to reduce drug arrests).

ARRESTEE TYPES AND EFFECTIVE SERVICES

We examined the impact of "very effective" services in the reduction of particular types of arrests, taking into consideration differences in age, gang affiliation, and especially, arrestee typology. Again, we used logistic regression models to predict odds ratios of success to failure in arrest changes. Successful outcomes were defined as a youth reducing his level of yearly total arrests for violence only, a combination of violence and drug arrests, or drug arrests only. Unsuccessful outcomes were defined as a youth increasing his level of a particular category of arrests or remaining at the same level. Youth who were not in the arrestee types of violence, no drug; violence and drug; and drug, no violence (i.e., youth who were arrested for crimes other than violence or drugs) were excluded from the analysis. We used the variable "very effective" service reported by the project worker as the independent or program variable.

Each logistic regression model now contained the "very effective" service variable and three control variables: age category (nineteen and over, eighteen and under); gang (Latin King, Two Six); and arrestee typology (violence, no drug; drug, no violence; violence and drug). The dependent variables in the model were as follows: change in yearly (total) violence arrests, change in yearly (total) violence and drug arrests, or change in yearly drug arrests between the preprogram and program period. We compared the odds ratios of success to failure of each of the service types in reducing violence-only (no drugs) arrests for the violence and drug arrestees versus the violence, no drug arrestees. Similarly, we compared the odds ratios of success to failure of the service types in reducing drug-only arrests for the violence and drug arrestees versus the drug, no violence arrestees. Summaries of the results of these analyses are presented in table 14.4.

"Very Effective" Contacts for School Services

School services, even when perceived as "very effective," did not help the large majority of program youth in any of the youth-arrestee categories reduce their levels of violence arrests, drug arrests, or violence and drug arrests.

For change in violence arrests, the workers' school-related services were associated with a 50 percent greater odds ratio of failure to success,[4] particularly

Table 14.4.   Odds ratio of success to failure in predicting arrest outcomes by "very effective"services, age category, gang, and arrestee type

| Successful outcome[b] | Service items | Logistic model predictors[a] | | | |
		"Very effective" services[c]	Age[d]	Gang	Arrestee type
Violence arrests	School	0.67	0.29***	0.59	1.19
	Job	2.56	0.30***	0.76	1.26
	Opportunity	2.47	0.30***	0.77	1.40
	Counseling	2.61	0.28***	0.81	1.25
	Family	1.32	0.30***	0.68	1.24
	Suppression	1.67	0.29***	0.67	1.22
Violence and drug arrests	School	0.38	0.33***	0.71	1.24
	Job	0.38	0.33***	0.89	1.21
	Opportunity	1.29	0.33***	0.88	1.22
	Counseling	2.10	0.32***	1.02	1.18
	Family	1.72	0.32***	0.93	1.18
	Suppression	0.94	0.33***	0.83	1.23
Drug arrests	School	0.52	0.66***	1.24	1.50
	Job	0.82	0.67***	1.33	1.37
	Opportunity	0.74	0.29***	1.29	1.38
	Counseling	1.35	0.68***	1.49	1.29
	Family	1.49	0.68***	1.53	1.20
	Suppression	0.48	0.69***	1.34	1.57

Notes
a. All logistic regression models included a service predictor and three additional control variables—age (nineteen and over = 0; eighteen and under = 1), gang (Latin King = 0; Two Six = 1), and arrestee typology (drug, no violence = -1; violence, no drug = 0; violence and drug = 1).
b. Three arrest outcomes included youth who were arrested for violence, no drug (n = 118); violence and drug (n = 128); or drug, no violence (n = 64). The odds ratio of failure to success is the reciprocal of the odds ratio of success to failure.
c. Service effectiveness was categorized according to the degree of success perceived by the worker: very effective (i.e., "very much") and less than very effective (i.e., "somewhat," "little," and "not at all").
d. ***$p < 0.001$.

for the younger compared to the older age groups and the Two Six compared to the Latin Kings. Nevertheless, the violence and drug arrestees had an 18.9 percent better odds ratio of success to failure than the violence, no drug arrestees in reducing violence arrests.

For change in violence and drug arrests, the workers' school-services contacts were associated with a more than two-and-a-half-times greater odds ratio of failure to success in reducing both violence and drug arrests during the program period, again for the younger versus the older youth and the Two Six versus the Latin Kings. But, the violence and drug arrestees had a 23.8 percent better odds ratio of success to failure than the violence, no drug arrestees in reducing their arrests for violence.

The pattern was different in regard to drug arrests. The workers' school-services contacts were associated with a 94 percent greater odds ratio of success to failure for older youth compared to younger youth; the Two Six drug, no violence arrestees had a higher odds ratio of success to failure compared to the Latin Kings. However, across all types of arrestees, the violence and drug arrestees still had a 45 percent better odds ratio of success to failure than the drug, no violence arrestees in reducing drug arrests.

"Very Effective" Contacts for Job Services

In contrast to the general failure of worker efforts at helping youth with school problems, help with jobs resulted in higher odds ratios of success to failure in youth reducing arrests. The majority of youth in the program were seventeen years of age and older and were far more interested in jobs than in school achievement. However, the success-to-failure odds ratios of youth provided with job services reducing their levels of violence arrests, drug arrests, or violence and drug arrests, varied by the type of arrestee.

For change in violence arrests, the worker's job-related efforts were associated with a greater odds ratio of success to failure (2.6 times greater) than when providing no job services. In particular, the older age group did much better than the younger age group in reducing their violence arrests during the program period, and the Latin Kings did better than the Two Six. However, the violence and drug arrestees had a 25.7 percent higher odds ratio of success to failure in reducing their violence arrests than the violence, no drug arrestees.

For change in violence and drug arrests, the workers' efforts around jobs were associated with a 37.8 percent greater odds ratio of success to failure in youth reducing their levels of these arrests. Again, the older age group did much better than the younger age group, and the Latin Kings did somewhat better than the Two Six. Nevertheless, both age categories had higher success-to-failure odds ratios in response to job services. The violence and drug arrestees had a 20.6 percent greater odds ratio of success to failure in reducing violence arrests than the violence, no drug arrestees.

For change in drug arrests, job-services efforts were associated with a 22.5 percent greater odds ratio of failure to success in reducing drug arrests. The worker's probabilities of success in reducing drug arrests by delivering job services were again greater for the older than the younger youth, and for the Two Six than the Latin Kings. The violence and drug arrestees had a

37.0 percent higher odds ratio of success to failure than the drug, no violence arrestees. However, project workers did relatively better in reducing drug arrests for older rather than younger youth, and for Two Six than for Latin Kings.

"Very Effective" Contacts for Opportunity-Provision Services

Opportunity-provision services included "very effective" school services and "very effective" job services for youth. The logistic regression model determined the success-to-failure odds ratio of a combination of both types of services in contributing to the youth's reduction of various types of arrests.

For change in violence arrests, the workers' opportunity-provision efforts were associated with a greater odds ratio of success to failure, 2.5. The difference was almost statistically significant ($p = 0.06$). The older age group and the Latin Kings were associated with higher success-to-failure probabilities of reducing their violence arrests. The violence and drug arrestees again had a 40.0 percent higher odds ratio of success to failure in reducing violence arrests than the violence, no drug arrestees.

For change in violence and drug arrests, the workers' opportunity-provision efforts were associated with a 28.8 percent greater odds ratio of success to failure in reducing levels of both of these types of arrests. The older age groups and the Latin Kings were again associated with higher success-to-failure odds ratios in response to opportunity-provision efforts. The violence and drug arrestees had a 22.2 percent greater odds ratio of success to failure than the violence, no drug arrestees.

For change in drug arrests, the workers' opportunity-provision efforts were associated with a 36.1 percent greater odds ratio of failure to success in reducing drug arrests. However, the violence and drug arrestees had a 38.0 percent better odds ratio of success to failure in reducing drug arrests than the drug, no violence arrestees. The workers' opportunity-provision efforts appeared to be more successful with older youth and the Two Six than with younger youth and the Latin Kings.

We emphasize that "very effective" opportunity-provision services—a combination of job and school services—were more successful in reducing arrests than "very effective" school services alone, particularly in respect to violence arrests. "Very effective" opportunity-provision services also had better results than job services alone in reducing drug arrests.

"Very Effective" Contacts for Brief Counseling Services

Brief counseling of youth about various issues—particularly leaving the gang and reducing violent behavior—was associated with a high odds ratio of success to failure in the reduction of violence arrests, a combination of violence and drug arrests, and drug arrests of the youth.

For change in violence arrests, the workers' counseling efforts were associated with a greater odds ratio of success to failure. The difference was statistically significant ($p = 0.04$). Counseling seemed to be even more effective than job placement and job referral. Higher success-to-failure odds ratios of counseling services in reducing arrests were found for the older compared to the younger age group, and for the Latin Kings. The violence and drug arrestees still had a 24.9 percent higher odds ratio of success to failure in reducing violence arrests than the violence, no drug arrestees.

For change in violence and drug arrests, the workers' counseling efforts (compared to the absence of such efforts) were associated with a 2.1-times-better odds ratio of success to failure in youth reducing their levels of violence and drug arrests. The difference was almost statistically significant ($p = 0.10$). Older youth compared to younger youth, and Two Six compared to Latin Kings, were associated with higher success-to-failure odds ratios. However, with brief counseling, the workers had a 17.9 percent greater odds ratio of success to failure in reducing violence arrests for the violence and drug arrestees than the violence, no drug arrestees.

For change in drug arrests, the workers' brief counseling efforts were associated with a 35 percent greater success-to-failure odds ratio in reducing drug arrests. Nevertheless, the odds ratio of success to failure in reducing drug arrests with "very effective" brief counseling services appeared to be even greater than the odds ratio of success to failure with "very effective" job services, school services, or a combination of the two. The success-to-failure odds ratio for the violence and drug arrestees was 29.0 percent higher than for the drug, no violence arrestees. Older youth had a 47 percent higher odds ratio of success to failure than younger youth in reducing their drug arrests. Also, the Two Six drug, no violence arrestees had a 49.0 percent better odds ratio of success to failure in reducing drug arrests during the program period than the Latin King drug, no violence arrestees. Counseling seemed to be relatively more useful than any other type of service in reducing drug arrests, particularly for the Two Six, who generally were younger than the Latin Kings.

"Very Effective"Contacts for Family Services

Family services included contacting the youth's family, wife, or girlfriend, usually about the youth's gang involvement and related problems. Family contacts on behalf of program youth were most frequently initiated by the youth worker but sometimes by a family member, wife, or girlfriend who requested the worker's assistance. Such contacts included brief counseling or advice and sometimes referring the family member, wife, or girlfriend for services.

For change in violence arrests, family services were associated with a 32.0 percent greater odds ratio of success to failure in youth reducing their violence arrests. The difference was not statistically significant. However, the older age group in particular, but also the Latin Kings, were associated with higher success-to-failure odds ratios of youth reducing their violence arrests. The violence and drug arrestees had a 23.6 percent higher odds ratio of success to failure in reducing violence arrests than the violence, no drug arrestees.

For change in violence and drug arrests, family services were associated with a 72.0 percent greater odds ratio of success to failure in youth reducing their levels of violence and drug arrests. Once again, the older age group and the Latin Kings were associated with higher success-to-failure odds ratios of youth reducing their violence and drug arrests when the workers provided "very effective" family services. The violence and drug arrestees had a 16.7 percent greater odds ratio of success to failure in reducing violence arrests than the violence, no drug arrestees.

For change in drug arrests, the worker's "very effective" family services were associated with a 49 percent greater success-to-failure odds ratio in reducing drug arrests. The success-to-failure odds ratio for the younger age group was 47.0 percent higher than for the older age group, and the Two Six had an odds ratio of success to failure that was 53 percent higher than for the Latin Kings. In the provision of "very effective" family services, the success-to-failure odds ratio for the violence and drug arrestees was 20.0 percent higher than for the drug, no violence arrestees.

"Very Effective"Suppression Contacts

In this set of logistic regression models, we note again that we obtained responses only from project police and probation workers about suppression contacts (e.g., warnings, arrests, probation violations, etc.). The worker-tracking form did not include a question or provide for a response about the youth workers' efforts in direct-suppression or suppression-related contacts, although the debriefing records did (chapter 11). "Very effective" suppression efforts in this model were by the project police and probation workers only.

For change in violence arrests, police and probation workers' suppression contacts were associated with a 67 percent greater success-to-failure odds ratio of youth reducing violence arrests. The oldest age category was associated with a significantly higher success-to-failure odds ratio than the younger age categories, and the Latin Kings were associated with a higher success-to-failure odds ratio than the Two Six. The violence and drug arrestees had a 22.0 percent higher odds ratio of success to failure in reducing violence arrests than the violence, no drug arrestees.

For change in violence and drug arrests, police and probation workers' contacts for suppression were associated with a 7 percent greater odds ratio of failure to success in youth reducing their levels of both violence and drug arrests. Suppression apparently made almost *no* contribution to the success or failure of youth reducing both their violence and drug arrests. The older youth did better than the younger youth, and the Latin Kings did better than the Two Six in the odds ratios of success to failure in reducing violence and drug arrests. The violence and drug arrestees had a 23.0 percent greater odds ratio of success to failure in reducing violence arrests than the violence, no drug arrestees.

For change in drug arrests, suppression contacts were associated with an odds ratio of failure to success in reducing drug arrests that was more than twice as high as it was for nonsuppression contacts. However, the older rather than the younger youth, and the Two Six rather than the Latin Kings, had a higher success-to-failure odds ratio in reducing drug arrests. The violence and drug arrestees had a 57 percent better odds ratio of success to failure in reducing drug arrests than the drug, no violence arrestees.

EFFECTIVENESS OF TARGETING YOUTH

The Little Village Project was more effective in targeting the more violent gang youth than the less-violent and more drug-oriented youth for the reduction of arrests, particularly violence arrests. A range of contacts and services was provided by a team of workers, including outreach youth workers, police, probation officers, and a neighborhood organizer. Each of the workers took a particular but not exclusive approach to providing contacts and services, and worked together in regard to youth in the program.

Each of the worker approaches contributed in distinctive and reciprocal ways to changes in the youth's lifestyle. Suppression contacts, mainly by project police, reduced the youth's interest and attachment to the gang. Job placement, mainly by youth workers and the neighborhood organizer, predicted the youth's spending less time with gang friends and more time with his wife or steady girlfriend. Also, as workers increased contacts and services, program youth reduced their contact with gang friends. The greater the number of contacts and services provided by project team members, the more likely the youth developed realistic income and occupation expectations. Each contact and service, and a combination of these, and other life-course changes predicted a reduction in violence arrests.

Although program youth were exposed to a range of services, most of the youth were provided with individual counseling and somewhat fewer with family contacts and job services. School and suppression services or contacts were provided to the fewest youth, due partially to the fact that youth in the program were on average seventeen or eighteen years old and out of school (with primary interest in jobs), and project police focused on older youth who had records of, or were more likely to be engaged in, serious violence.

Certain types of services predicted the possibility of greater success in the reduction of violence arrests. Job services and individual counseling predicted greater odds ratios of success to failure in reducing violence arrests than did other types of services. School-related services produced the greatest odds ratios of failure to success in reducing violence arrests, particularly for younger youth. Generally, the odds ratios of success to failure in the reduction of violence arrests through the provision of a range of services was higher for the Latin Kings than for the Two Six. However, family contacts and individual-youth counseling produced higher odds ratios of success to failure in the reduction of drug arrests for the younger Two Six than for the older Latin Kings.

In general, age was the most significant predictor of high odds ratios of success to failure in the reduction of violence arrests across the two gangs. Older youth, nineteen years old and over, did better than seventeen- and eighteen-year-olds, who did better than sixteen-and-under youth. However, age was not a significant predictor in the reduction of drug arrests. Youth with arrest histories of violence and drugs did better in reducing their drug arrests than did youth with arrest histories of drugs but no violence. Youth with histories of both violence and drug arrests may have had less specialized or intense commitment to drug-only or violence-only types of criminal behavior, or simply less time to specialize in both types of crime.

NOTES

1. Of the 191 youth with worker-tracking records, the workers did not report the level of effectiveness of services for 7 youth, and these records were eliminated for the analysis.

2. The total preprogram period was four and a half years prior to the youth's entry into the program but varied for each youth depending on the length of his program period. Youth with fewer tracking forms were usually in the program for shorter periods, and their matched preprogram arrest period was shorter.

3. We eliminated five youth from this analysis who were provided only with recreational activities.

4. The odds ratio of failure to success is the reciprocal of the odds ratio of success to failure.

15

Gang and Community Crime Change

In the design of the evaluation of the Little Village Gang Violence Reduction Project, we proposed that a reduction of gang violence at the program-youth level would contribute to a reduction of gang violence at the gang-as-a-unit and community levels as well. Furthermore, we anticipated that a relative reduction of gang violence at the Little Village community level would exceed that of comparable high-gang-crime Latino communities in Chicago. A variety of measures and types of analyses were employed using Chicago Police Department statistics over the five-year preprogram and five-year program periods, that is, the five years of project operations and the five years preceding the start of the project.[1]

We also compared changes in views about the gang-crime problem of residents in high-gang-crime streets and representatives of local organizations in Little Village and Pilsen (the adjoining, almost identical high-gang-crime community) between the first and third years of project operations. The expectation was that, if the project was successful, residents and representatives of organizations in Little Village would perceive a greater relative reduction in the gang problem, especially violence, than residents and representatives of organizations in Pilsen.

GANG-AS-A-UNIT CRIME CHANGES

Key measures of project impact on the gang problem, particularly the serious violence problem, were not only changes in gang homicides, aggravated batteries, or aggravated assaults but also a combination of all three. Our objective was to provide an inclusive measure of change in serious gang violence that might be more reliable than change in only one type of serious gang violence. There were relatively few gang homicides over short periods of time, and the distinction

Table 15.1. Little Village gang as a unit crime statistics

Gang	8/87–7/92	8/92–7/97	% Change	Rank	Target vs. nontarget	8/87–7/92	8/92–7/97	% Change
A) Gang incident data:[a] serious violence incident index [b]								
Latin King	117	155	32.5	2	Latin King and Two Six	165	236	43.0
Two Six	48	81	68.8	3				
Other Latino gangs	51	56	9.8	1	Other Latino and African American gangs	58	79	36.2
African American gangs	7	23	228.6	4				
Total	223	315	41.3	—				
B) Gang offender data:[a] serious violence incident index [b]								
Latin King	208	238	14.4	2	Latin King and Two Six	295	387	31.2
Two Six	87	149	71.3	3				
Other Latino gangs	90	99	10.0	1	Other Latino and African American gangs	111	156	40.5
African American Gangs	21	57	171.4	4				
Total	406	543	33.7	—				
C) Gang offender data: homicide offenders								
Latin King	28	35	25.0	2	Latin King and Two Six	38	57	50.0
Two Six	10	22	120.0	3				
Other Latino gangs	18	20	11.1	1	Other Latino and African American gangs	21	38	81.0
African American Gangs	3	18	500.0	4				
Total	59	95	61.0	—				
D) Gang offender data:[a] drug arrests								
Latin King	65	692	964.6	3	Latin King and Two Six	73	881	1106.9
Two Six	8	189	2262.5	4				
Other Latino gangs	46	123	167.4	1	Other Latino and African American gangs	66	288	336.5
African American gangs	20	165	725.0	2				
Total	139	1169	741.0	—				

Notes
a. Excludes December 1994 data, except for homicides.
b. Includes homicides, aggravated batteries with handguns or other firearms, and aggravated assaults with handguns or other firearms.

between aggravated batteries and aggravated assaults was not carefully made among police districts. We used a measure of drug arrests separately.[2]

TARGET AND NONTARGET GANGS

We compared changes in gang crime for the different gangs in Little Village, which included the target gangs—the Latin Kings and the Two Six—alone and together. The nontarget gangs included the other smaller Latino gangs located mainly on the fringes of the Little Village area—the Two-Two Boys, Deuces, Satan Disciples, and Latin Disciples—and the African American gangs—the Vice Lords and Black Gangster Disciples. Most of the violent gang activity, however, was between the Latin Kings and Two Six.

Serious Gang-Violence Incidents

The two target gangs accounted for 74.0 percent of all serious violent incidents in the Little Village target area in the five-year preprogram period, and 74.9 percent in the five-year program period. There was an increase of 41.3 percent in serious gang-violent incidents by all the Little Village gangs together. Although the Latin Kings were responsible for the majority of all serious violent gang incidents in each period, the increase was greater for the Two Six (68.8 percent) than for the Latin Kings (32.5 percent). Other Latino gangs in Little Village had the smallest increase (9.8 percent) and the African American gangs the greatest increase (228.6, but from the smallest preprogram base; table 15.1, A).

There was considerable difference in the relative proportion of increases in violent gang incidents committed by the target gangs between the preprogram and program periods. We could not, however, determine how similar or different the target gangs were from the nontarget gangs on a range of personal, social, and background criminal characteristics.

Serious Gang-Violence Offenders

There were usually multiple gang-violent offenders present at each gang incident. The overall increase in number of gang offenders (33.7 percent) was slightly less than the overall increase in the number of gang-violent offenses (41.3 percent). The increase in offenders was five times greater for the Two Six (71.3 percent) than for the Latin Kings (14.4 percent). When we calculated the changes in number of offenders between the preprogram and program periods, there was a relatively greater increase in the nontarget gangs (40.5 percent) than in the target gangs (31.2 percent), although not for the other Latino gangs (10.0 percent) (table 15.1, B).

Gang Homicide Offenders

The increase in the number of gang homicide offenders (not the same as the number of gang homicides) was similar to the increase in the number of serious gang-violent offenders. The Latin Kings had more gang homicide offenders than any of the gangs, in both periods, but the increase was greater for the Two Six (120.0 percent) than for the Latin Kings (25.0 percent). The largest increase was in the African American gangs (500.0 percent, but again from a small preprogram base). The lowest increase was in other Latino gangs in the area (11.1 percent) (table 15.1, C).

When we aggregated the number of homicide offenders by target offenders versus nontarget offenders between the preprogram and program periods, the increase was greater in the nontargeted gangs (81.0 percent) than in the target gangs (50.0 percent). Furthermore, the increase in seventeen- to twenty-four-year-old gang-homicide offenders was greater in the Two Six—by 77.1 percent, from 48 to 85—than it was in the Latin Kings—by 15.1 percent, from 126 to 145. Also, while the number of sixteen-and-under Two Six offenders increased by 38.5 percent—from 26 to 36—the number of Latin King offenders decreased by 33.9 percent—from 62 to 41.

In sum, the number of serious violent gang incidents increased relatively more in the target gangs than in the nontarget gangs, but the number of serious gang offenders increased relatively more in the nontarget gangs than in the target gangs. Although the Latin Kings were responsible for more serious gang-violent incidents and had more serious offenders than any other gangs in both the preprogram and program periods, the increases in the program period were consistently greater for the Two Six than for the Latin Kings.

Gang Offender Drug Arrests

We expected there might be a greater increase in drug gang offending than in violence arrests. Indeed, this was the case for all of the gangs. The increase in drug arrests was sharper in the aggregate of the two target gangs (1106.8 percent) than in the aggregate of the nontarget gangs (336.5 percent). Again, while the Latin King gang-offender drug arrests were higher than for any other gang in the preprogram and program periods, the Two Six arrests increased more, percentage wise (2262.5 percent), than they did for the Latin Kings (964.6 percent), although from a smaller base. Again, the increase in gang offender drug arrests (as was the case for serious violent incidents and offenders) was lowest in the other Latino gangs in Little Village (table 15.1, D).

At the gang-as-a-unit level in Little Village, the project appeared to be associated with less of an increase in violence arrests for offenders in the target gangs than in the nontarget gangs but with a greater increase in drug arrests for offenders in the target gangs than in the nontarget gangs. The percent of Two Six serious violent offenders was increasing more than the percent of Latin King offenders.

An adequate comparison of target and nontarget gang behavior was probably limited by the different characteristics of the gangs and, especially, by the fact that the two target gangs accounted for the very large majority of violence and drug behaviors in the area.

COMMUNITY-LEVEL CRIME CHANGES

A comparison of changes in aggregate gang incidents, offenders, or arrests at the community level between the preprogram and program periods may be a more valid indicator of possible project effects than differences between target and nontarget gangs in Little Village. The Little Village target area included six beats in the Tenth District of the Chicago Police Department. These beats were the major serious violent gang-incident locations and hangouts of the two key gangs. Prior to the start of the project, comparable beats in six other districts where Latino gang violence was very high were also identified: six beats in the Eighth District; eight beats in the Ninth District; three beats in the Twelfth District; six beats in the Thirteenth District; ten beats in the Fourteenth District; and fifteen beats (all beats) in the Twenty-fifth District.

The Twelfth and Ninth District were contiguous to Little Village. The three selected beats of Pilsen in the Twelfth District were located to the east and were most comparable to Little Village (based on demographic and socioeconomic factors as well as tradition of gang activity). The eight selected beats in the Ninth District, a community directly south and contiguous to both Little Village and Pilsen, included a growing Latino population and a declining African American, low-income, public-housing population. All of the beats were contiguous within each of the seven districts.

Table 15.2. Gang crime statistics across communities in seven police districts

District	8/87–7/92	8/92–7/97	% Change	Rank
A) Gang incident data:[a] serious violence incident index[b]				
Little Village (10)	237	369	55.7	3
8	58	151	160.3	7
9	197	296	50.3	1
Pilsen (12)	198	304	53.5	2
13	143	306	114.0	5
14	292	573	96.2	4
25[c]	174	439	152.3	6
Subtotal w/o 10	1062	2069	94.8	—
Total	1299	2438	87.7	—
B) Latino gang offender data:[a] serious violence incident index[b]				
Little Village (10)	367	496	35.2	2
8	66	142	115.2	6
9	216	196	9.3	1
Pilsen (12)	330	487	47.6	3
13	210	398	89.5	5
14	383	714	86.4	4
25[c]	204	529	159.3	7
Subtotal w/o 10	1409	2466	75.0	—
Total	1776	2962	66.8	—

District	8/87–7/92	8/92–7/97	% Change	Rank
C) Gang incident data:[a] homicide incidents				
Little Village (10)	39	60	53.9	5
8	4	16	300.0	7
9	33	56	69.7	6
Pilsen (12)	30	39	30.0	1
13	19	25	31.6	2
14	43	61	41.9	4
25[c]	31	41	32.3	3
Subtotal w/o 10	160	238	48.8	—
Total	199	298	49.7	—
D) Gang offender data:[a] drug arrests				
Little Village (10)	106	929	776.4	5
8	65	913	1304.6	7
9	280	2646	845.0	6
Pilsen (12)	116	656	465.5	3
13	168	832	395.2	2
14	819	2339	185.6	1
25[c]	243	1813	646.1	4
Subtotal w/o 10	1691	9199	444.0	—
Total	1797	10128	463.6	—

Notes

a. Excludes December 1994 data, except for homicides.

b. Includes homicides, aggravated batteries with handguns or other firearms, and aggravated assaults with handguns or other firearms.

c. A decision was made to include all beats in the Twenty-fifth District, rather than only the highest, serious gang-violence crime beats, because of a radical change in beat boundaries in the district in 1993. The overall boundaries of the district were not changed.

All the selected beats had particularly high levels of gang violence between 1990 and 1992, and contained mainly lower-income Hispanic populations. Based on 1990 U.S. Census data, each was an area of concentration of first- and second-generation Hispanics, although the proportion of different Hispanic or Latino ethnic groups (i.e., Mexican, Mexican American, and Puerto Rican) varied in each district. However, the ethnic compositions of the populations of Little Village and Pilsen were almost identical, comprising mainly Mexicans and Mexican Americans. It was important also to note that over the course of the program, Pilsen was undergoing gentrification, including a sharp influx by middle-class (mainly white) people from other parts of the city.

Serious Gang-Violence Incidents (District Level)

All selected areas in the seven police districts experienced an increase in the absolute number of serious gang-violent incidents. The increase in Little Village in the five-year program period compared to the five-year preprogram period was 55.7 percent, which was less than the average for the six other districts (94.8 percent), but still slightly higher than in the Ninth District (50.3 percent) and the Twelfth District (Pilsen) (53.5 percent; table 15.2, A).

However, the pattern sharply improved in Little Village when we used the first three-year program period (probably the peak effective period of project operations) versus the first three-year preprogram period in the analysis.[3] During the first three program years, the increase in serious gang-violent incidents was 35.4 percent, the lowest of all districts. The next lowest increases were in the Ninth District (65.9 percent) and the Twelfth District (Pilsen; 72.0 percent).

Serious Gang-Violence Offenders

Where we used the measure of change in numbers of serious violent offenders for Latino offenders only, the Little Village increase was 35.2 percent—the second lowest increase of all the districts (table 15.2, B)—although it ranked third lowest if we used the measure for change in number of serious violent offenders of all racial and ethnic backgrounds. Little Village had the second lowest percent increase of seventeen- to twenty-two-year-old serious violent offenders and the lowest increase of sixteen-and-under serious violent offenders (regardless of race and ethnicity). The percent increase for the sixteen-and-under age group was 8.2 percent, compared to an average of 74.0 percent for the other district areas.

Gang Homicide Incidents

Nevertheless, gang homicides were very high in Little Village in the five-year preprogram period (n = 39), and higher in the five-year program period (n = 60). (We note that there was often more than one offender per homicide incident.) The percentage of gang homicide incidents (53.9 percent) was the third highest of all the district areas in the program period but second highest in the preprogram period. We cannot account for the relatively higher number of gang homicides yet relatively lower number of serious violence incidents in Little Village. We did not control for change in characteristics of population size or age across the periods, or for possible variations in district reporting procedures. Overall, Little Village remained one of the two deadliest gang-violence areas of the city (table 15.2, C).

Gang-Offender Drug Arrests

Gang arrests mainly for drug possession and trafficking increased tremendously in all of the districts. The increase in gang drug arrests was particularly sharp in Little Village—from the second lowest of the seven districts in the preprogram period to the third highest in the program period. Overall, the increase in drug activities was greater than for serious gang violence. The swing from relatively more serious gang-violent activity to more drug activity was especially marked in Little Village compared to any of the other districts. The findings thus far presented suggest that while the project might have had an effect in reducing serious gang violence, it probably had no effect in reducing the gang drug problem at the Little Village community level (table 15.2, D).

SERIOUS GANG-VIOLENCE CHANGE: A RATIO ANALYSIS

We attempted in other, more controlled ways to determine the relative scope and direction of change in serious gang violence in Little Village compared to the other district areas. We employed means and standard deviations of the numbers of reported serious violent incidents for the five-year and three-year program periods compared to their preprogram periods. This was the basis for creating ratio scores and trend graphs to reflect changes in mean scores for each of the districts in relation to the other districts. In other words, we explored not only the level of serious violence changes for each of the different districts from year to year but also the level of change for districts in relation to each other during the preprogram and program periods.

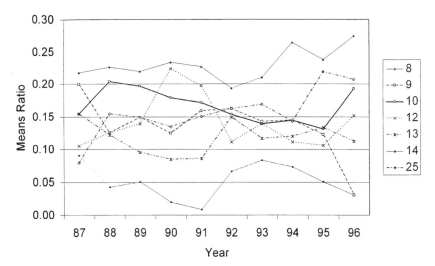

FIGURE 15.1
Ten-year (1987–1996) trend of serious gang-violent crime. Means ratios across seven police districts (8, 9, 10, 12, 13, 14, and 25).

We knew that serious gang-crime incidents increased in each of the districts over the five-year program period. By computing ratio scores, we considered how much they increased in relation to the average, or mean, score for each of the other districts. We did this initially for the five-year program period compared to the five-year preprogram period, and then for the first three-year program period compared to the first three-year preprogram period.[3] Finally, we graphed these changes for both the five- and three-year periods, to look at longer- and shorter-term effects that might be associated with the project staff's initial, more committed period of program activities.

We first examined these ratios on a year-to-year basis over ten years, in all of the districts. Levels of serious gang violence increased in four of the districts and declined in three of the districts—Little Village in the Tenth District, as well as the Ninth and Twelfth Districts. The Little Village relative decline appeared to be consistent from 1988 through 1995. The pattern in the Ninth District seemed to run from a relatively high level to a low level. The Twelfth District pattern was more erratic, starting low, rising in the five-year preprogram period, then declining and rising again in the five-year program period. Overall, there was little to distinguish the year-to-year patterns in the Ninth, Tenth, and Twelfth Districts (figure 15.1). Fluctuations in the Twelfth District were greater than

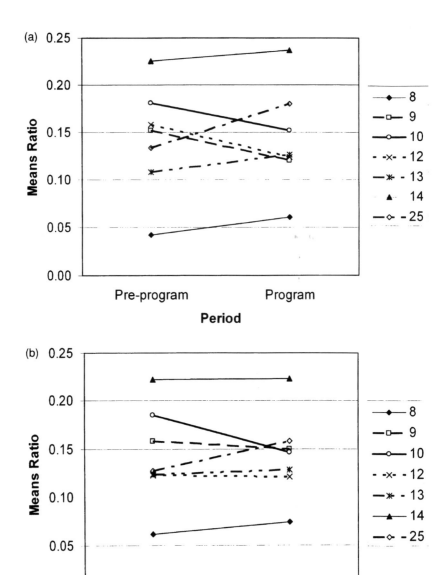

FIGURE 15.2

Comparison of average yearly serious gang-violent crime. Means ratios across seven police districts (8, 9, 10, 12, 13, 14, and 25).

(a) Ten-year comparison: five-year preprogram period (1987–1991) vs. five-year program period (1992–1996).

(b) Six-year comparison: three-year preprogram period (1989–1991) vs. three-year program period (1992–1994).

in the Ninth and Tenth Districts. Sharp changes in population movement and housing patterns in the Ninth and Twelfth Districts might have accounted for some of these fluctuations.

Five-Year Analysis

When we straightened out the up and down fluctuations in each district area, that is, increases and decreases on a year-to-year basis over the ten-year preprogram and program period, the pattern of area decline was very similar in the Ninth, Tenth, and Twelfth Districts. However, the decline in the Tenth District (Little Village) was from the second highest ratio point for serious gang-violent incidents of all seven districts. The Fourteenth District had the highest ratio of serious gang-violent incidents at the beginning of the ten-year period, and it kept rising (figure 15.2a).

Three-Year Analysis

However, the three-year pattern of change (i.e., differences between the first three-year program period and its comparable three-year preprogram period) was most favorable to the Little Village Project. The sharpest ratio decline occurred in the Tenth District, where there was a fairly steep and consistent decline in serious gang-violent-crime ratios over the three-year program period (figure 15.2b).

It was apparent that the decline in serious gang violence in the Tenth District relative to the other districts began in the preprogram period. The patterns of serious gang-violent incidents showed little change in the Ninth and Twelfth Districts during the three-year program and preprogram periods. The actual decline was best sustained during both the program and preprogram periods in the Tenth District.

Although we can make a case for a relative lowering of the serious gang-violent incident rate in Little Village from a very high level over the five-year program period, we can also make a similar case for ratio declines in the Ninth and Twelfth Districts, from lower levels. Little Village did best in the three-year program period versus the three-year preprogram period, and clearly demonstrated the largest ratio decline in mean serious gang violence, compared to all of the other districts. Nevertheless, it was still not clear that the relative decline in aggregate serious gang violence in the Tenth District was necessarily associated with a project effect, even in the first three years of the program period. The trend in aggregate serious gang violence was downward in Little Village at the start of the program and continued downward for the succeeding three-year period. It was clear that the level or slope of decline was best sustained in Little Village compared to the other districts during the first three years of the program period.

HOT-SPOT ANALYSIS

We were also interested in whether the project could have had an effect on the spatial distribution of gang-crime activity in Little Village. We wondered whether serious gang-violent incidents were spreading or becoming more confined during the program period. We mapped the serious gang-violence-index offenses (now including gang armed robberies) by year for the ten-year period for the Little Village and Pilsen areas (Tenth and Twelfth Districts), identifying the areas of densest criminal activity. Concentrations of incidents were determined using Spatial and Temporal Analysis of Crime (STAC) software, developed by the Illinois Criminal Justice Information Authority. Our primary interest was to determine whether the locations and clustering patterns of violence-index offenses changed in Little Village during the five-year program period and if so, whether the changes could be related to the effects of the project. To more clearly determine whether such effects might be program related, we also compared pattern changes that occurred in the comparison community of Pilsen during the program and preprogram periods.

The pattern of clustering, or concentration, of serious violent gang incidents varied somewhat between Pilsen and Little Village. This might have been due in part to the size of each of the communities. The Little Village program area contained six police beats; the Pilsen area had three. Little Village had a larger population, 60,829, compared to Pilsen's 35,433 (U.S. Census 1990, excluding undocumented residents). The two major gangs in Little Village generally had their own distinctive and quite separate turf areas; the three major gangs in Pilsen were situated very close to each other.

There was little change in the gang-turf cluster patterns of serious gang-violent incidents in both Little Village and Pilsen, during both the preprogram and program periods. In general, the clusters in Little Village were smaller, less dense, but spread more widely than those in Pilsen; these patterns changed little between the preprogram and program periods. The size of the gang problem (i.e., number of serious gang-violent incidents) increased in both Little Village and Pilsen. In the physically larger Little Village area, the number of cluster-pattern locations increased slightly, spreading over a wider area. The number of cluster patterns did not increase in Pilsen, but the clusters of serious gang-violent incidents located in the central part of the area grew larger.

The spatial distribution of serious violent gang incidents in Little Village changed only slightly during the program period. The project might have had some impact on dispersing the spatial patterning of serious gang violence in Little Village during the first four program years, relative to the pattern-ing in Pilsen. Serious gang violence remained concentrated on the borders of gang turfs and around school areas, especially the high schools, in both communities.

CHANGES IN RATES OF SERIOUS VIOLENCE

We were also interested in project effects on rates of serious gang violence for seventeen- to twenty-five-year-old males (the target age group) comparing Little Village with Pilsen, using U.S. Census 1990 data. We compared rate changes in serious violent incidents per one hundred thousand males, sev-enteen to twenty-five years old, between the three-year preprogram period (1988–1991) and the three-year program period (1992–1995). We computed the number of serious violent gang-crime incidents (i.e., homicides, aggravated batteries with handguns or firearms, and aggravated assaults with handguns or firearms) for the seventeen- to twenty-five-year-old males per one hundred thousand individuals (the most at-risk group for serious violence) in the to-tal population of each community, assuming no population or age-pattern changes between the preprogram and program periods.

According to the 1990 Census, there were approximately 9,000 males aged seventeen to twenty-five in Little Village, compared to slightly more than 9,800 in Pilsen. Pilsen had a higher density of males in this older, high-risk age category than Little Village. In the preprogram period there were 197 serious gang violent incidents in Little Village—one for every 45.7 males seventeen to twenty-five years old—compared to 152 incidents in Pilsen—one for every 64.9 males seventeen to twenty-five years old. In the three-year preprogram period, the rate of gang violence for this age group was higher in Little Village than in Pilsen.

In the three-year program period, there were 269 incidents of serious gang vi-olence in Little Village—an increase to 1 in 33.4—while the number of incidents in Pilsen increased to 230—an increase to 1 in 42.9. At both time periods, the number of youths at highest risk for serious violence was greater in Little Village than in Pilsen, but the increase in the rate of serious violence incidents in Little Village (12.3) was less than in Pilsen (22.0). In other words, the serious gang-violence rate increased relatively more in Pilsen (33.9 percent) than in Little Village (26.9 percent) during the first three program years, especially considering that the risk population (seventeen- to twenty-five-year-olds) was decreasing in Pilsen, probably because of gentrification, and increasing at a faster rate in Little Village. All of this suggested that the project may have been associated with a greater reduction in the rate of serious gang violent incidents in Little Village compared to Pilsen.

COMMUNITY PERCEPTIONS OF CHANGES IN THE GANG PROBLEM

We were also interested in changes in the perception of the gang problem at the community level, comprising the views of local residents and representatives of agencies and organizations in Little Village and Pilsen during the program period. The Chicago Police Department (CPD) requested that part of the evaluation of the Gang Violence Reduction Project (GVRP) include surveys to determine whether the Little Village community perceived a change in the gang problem that could be associated with the presence of the project. While we could not establish a direct, causal relationship between changes in the behavior of program youth and changes in local residents' and organizations' perceptions of the gang problem, the GVRP was the only intervention project active at the time that was likely to have contributed to any change that may have occurred. The CPD initiated a community-policing strategy in the Tenth District (Little Village) six months after the start of the project, but it did not focus on the gang problem and collaborative service and suppression efforts with youth (Skogan and Hartnett 1997).

Pilsen and Little Village were probably more like each other than any two other communities in Chicago in their concentrations of recently arrived populations of Mexican origin. Many of the same socioeconomic conditions were present, and the same social, economic, cultural, and health institutions served both communities. Table 15.3 compares demographic, socio-economic, and housing characteristics of the two communities, based on U.S. 1990 Census data. Characteristics of ethnicity, gender, income, education, and

Table 15.3. Community characteristics of Little Village and Pilsen—1990 U.S. Census

Census characteristics	Little Village		Pilsen	
	Total	%	Total	%
Population	60,829	—	35,433	—
Households	14,287	—	8,985	—
Males	32,211	52.9	18,934	53.3
Females	28,684	47.1	16,558	46.7
Gender ratio (male vs. females)	113 : 100	—	114 : 100	—
Mexican	52,781	86.8	30,920	87.3
White	3,269	5.4	2,465	6.9
African American	1,479	2.4	317	0.9
Home ownership	5,525	48.4	2,149	23.6
Total housing units	15,579	—	10,258	—
Housing units built 1939 or earlier	8,339	53.5	7,863	76.6
Mean household income	$22,974	—	$22,259	—
Mean family income	$23,445	—	$22,494	—
Per capita income	$6,480	—	$6,345	—
Married couples with own children under 18	7,089	49.6	3,728	41.5
Male unemployment	2,051	11.3	1,397	13.2
Males 17–25 years of age	5,471	24.03	3,495	26.38
Education: less than 9th grade	15,199	53.0	8,899	53.6
Education: 9th to 12th grade	5,367	18.7	2,710	16.3
Education: college	1,929	6.7	1,284	7.7

unemployment were similar. There were more home owners in Little Village and slightly more married couples with children under eighteen.

Data were collected from approximately the same one hundred residents and sixty organization representatives in each of the two communities at each time period. Initial (time I) interviews were conducted in the winter and spring of 1992–1993; follow-up (time II) interviews in the winter and spring of 1994–1995, approximately two years after the initial interviews. The findings were based on changes in responses between time I and time II. Differences between the communities were expressed in Chi-square probabilities, when statistically significant.

RESIDENT RESPONDENT

To develop the initial community resident sample, local households were selected on a cluster-sampling basis from the streets and sections of streets with the highest gang-violence activity, based on CPD incident data. Approximately ten street locations were selected in each community. Project interviewers from the community went to preassigned locations to interview heads of households in the selected streets. Almost all interviews were conducted in Spanish.

Resident respondents in both communities most often mentioned gangs as a problem at time I and time II. Over time, there was a statistically significant decrease in mentioning gangs in both communities, more so in Pilsen—from 92.8 percent to 73.7 percent (p ≤ .001)—than in Little Village—from 80.2 percent to 64.9 percent (p ≤ 0.05). A large proportion of respondents in each of the two communities felt there was "a lot" of gang-motivated violence and gang-motivated property crime. At time I, more than three quarters of all respondents felt there was a lot of gang-motivated violence, and more than two thirds felt there was a lot of gang-motivated property crime. There were some declines in these proportions in both communities at time II, but there were statistically significant declines for changes relating to gang-motivated violence (p ≤ 0.01) and gang-motivated property crime (p ≤ 0.001) only in Little Village.

Respondents were also asked to give reasons for the amount of crime they perceived, both at time I and time II. There was a decrease in both communities in the proportion of respondents who held gangs responsible for crime. The decrease among Little Village respondents was statistically significant, from 58.3 percent at time I to 42.9 percent at time II (p = 0.038). Among Pilsen respondents, the change was smaller, not statistically significant, but still impressive—from 67.0 percent at time I to 53.9 percent at time II. There was a slight increase in Pilsen respondents' mentioning drugs as a reason for crime at time II (34.1 percent) compared to time I (27.8 percent) but a small decrease in Little Village respondents' mentioning drugs at time II (28.6 percent) compared to time I (38.5 percent).

When asked about causes of the gang problem, drugs (using or selling) were mentioned by Little Village respondents almost twice as often at time I (29.1 percent) as at time II (16.7 percent) (p ≤ 0.05). There was less of a decrease in mentioning drugs in Pilsen—from 23.4 percent at time I to 20.0 percent at time II. It was not uncommon in both communities for children to be involved in selling drugs, in part to add to the marginal income of families. While almost three times as many Pilsen respondents (24.0 percent) as Little Village respondents (8.6 percent) generally knew of such families at time

I, the proportion of Little Village respondents who knew such families increased from 8.6 percent to 12.5 percent at time II. Change was imperceptible in Pilsen.

Resident Respondents—Little Village Gang Territories

We also compared differences between resident respondents in the two gang territories within Little Village, approximately sixty in the Latin King territory and forty in the Two Six territory. We wanted to determine if changes in Little Village were similar across the whole community, or whether one gang area was affected more by the project than the other. There were significant differences in the responses of residents in the two Little Village gang areas. The responses of those Little Village residents living in Two Six territory were more similar to those of the residents in Pilsen than to those of the Little Village residents living in Latin King territory.

There were a few notable differences regarding the perception of problems among residents in the two gang territories in Little Village. Gangs were the most serious problem at both time periods for respondents in both gang territories. However, fewer residents in Latin King territory saw gangs as a community problem at time II (55.0 percent) than at time I (81.7 percent). The difference between time periods was statistically significant ($p \leq 0.01$). This was not so in the Two Six territory. More residents there saw gangs as a community problem at time II (82.3 percent) than at time I (77.8 percent). The difference between the Latin King and Two Six resident sample at time II was statistically significant ($p \leq 0.01$).

Residents in both gang territories in Little Village were fairly alike in feeling that there was a lot of gang-motivated violence and gang-motivated property crime in their areas. Differences between time I and time II were much greater for respondents in Latin King territory. The proportion of those who felt there was a lot of gang-motivated violence fell from 80 percent to 50 percent between time I and time II; and for gang-motivated property crime, it fell from 75 percent to 37 percent. These changes were highly statistically significant: gang-motivated violence $p \leq 0.001$ and gang-motivated property crime $p \leq 0.001$. Changes in Two Six territory were very different. There was actually a small increase in the proportion of residents who said there was a lot of gang-motivated violence at time II compared to time I and only a small decline in the perception of a lot of gang-motivated property crime. The differences between the communities at time II were statistically significant for both gang-motivated violence (p ≤ 0.01) and gang-motivated property crime (p ≤ 0.05).

There was also growing concern among residents about the relation between gangs and the drug problem in both gang territories of Little Village. The proportion of respondents in Latin King territory who saw drugs as a cause of the gang problem increased from 16.7 percent at time I to 22.2 percent at time II. The increase in the Two Six territory was much larger, from 16.7 percent at time I to 46.6 percent at time II (p ≤ 0.05). In other words, the increase in residents' concerns about the relation of gangs to drug violence and property-crime problems occurred mainly among residents in the Two Six territory.

ORGANIZATION RESPONDENTS

A different selection process was used to develop a sample of organization respondents. Lists were obtained from various local youth agencies, churches, and major community organizations. Leaders or administrators of local organizations who had knowledge and contact with gang youth and their families were interviewed. These leaders referred us in turn to other organizations. In time, a "snowball" sample emerged. Very few of the organizations targeted in this "snowball" sample refused to participate in the survey.

The types of agencies and organizations whose representatives were interviewed were slightly different in Little Village and Pilsen. Slightly more than 25 percent of the sample in Little Village, and 20 percent of the sample in Pilsen, were representatives of schools or education-related agencies. At time II, significantly more representatives of businesses were interviewed in Pilsen (35.1 percent) than in Little Village (17.0 percent) (p ≤ 0.05). More block-club respondents were interviewed in Little Village than in Pilsen at both time periods. Similar proportions of respondents in both communities were from organizations such as churches, health clinics, youth agencies, community organizations, social service agencies, city organizations, wards, or employment-training centers.

We asked the organization representatives in Little Village and Pilsen the same questions relating to community and gang-crime changes that were asked of the resident respondents. Organizations were likely to be dealing with residents and gang members from the immediate areas where they were located but not necessarily concentrating on a particular gang territory in the community. In general, the perceptions and experiences—and their changes—reported by organization respondents in each community (particularly about the gang problem) were similar but not as strong as those of the residents.

At time I, a greater proportion of organization respondents in Little Village (44.6 percent) rated the community as very dangerous at night, compared to Pilsen respondents (26.3 percent). There was a decline in this proportion in both communities at time II, but it was much greater and of statistical significance only in Little Village—from 44.6 percent to 13.2 percent (p ≤ 0.001). By time II, the proportion of organization respondents in both communities who felt the neighborhood was very dangerous at night was virtually the same (13.2 percent in Little Village and 14.5 percent in Pilsen). At time I, more organization respondents in Little Village (58.9 percent) were likely to think there was a lot of personal crime, compared to respondents in Pilsen (41.4 percent). The proportion of those who thought there was a lot of personal crime declined in both communities, but the change was greater and of statistical significance in Little Village only (p ≤ 0.01).

Almost all organization respondents in Little Village (91.1 percent) felt there was a lot of gang-motivated violence at time I, as did a large proportion of organization respondents in Pilsen (77.2 percent). However, the difference between the two communities at time I was statistically significant (p ≤ 0.05). At time II, there were small declines in this proportion in both communities, but still, three-quarters or more of all organization respondents felt that there was a lot of gang-motivated violence. Similarly, gang property crime was rated quite high in both communities at time I and time II, but declines were greater and statistically significant in Little Village only (p ≤ 0.05). Organizations in both communities continued to view gang property crime as quite serious at both time periods.

Organization respondents were asked to what extent they thought gang members were responsible for *most* of the violence in their communities, not just gang-motivated violence. At time I, a large proportion of organization respondents in both communities—more than 80 percent—saw gangs as being "very much to blame" for violent crime in general, not just for violence related to intergang fights. By time II, declines in this view occurred in both communities, but the decline was greater and of statistical significance only in Little Village— from 85.7 percent at time I to 66.0 percent at time II (p ≤ 0.05). The decline in Pilsen was from 84.5 percent to 74.6 percent. The trend was similar with respect to gang property crime. In Little Village, the decline for gang property crime was statistically significant—from 83.6 percent to 56.6 percent (p $\leq$ 0.01). In Pilsen, gang property crime declined only slightly between the two time periods—from 77.6 percent to 73.2 percent.

Finally, organization respondents said that drug dealing was a major problem in the neighborhoods. They considered it one of the reasons that youth joined gangs, as well as a cause of the overall gang problem. When presented with the statement, "Community children are at risk of becoming involved with drugs," organization respondents were asked to rate the statement as either "mostly true" or "mostly false." At both time I and time II, more than 95.0 percent of respondents in Little Village and Pilsen said that the statement was mostly true.

In general, changes in the perceptions and experiences of the organization respondents were similar to those of the resident respondents in their respective communities but less pronounced and less statistically significant across time periods. Property and personal crimes were perceived as decreasing significantly, more in Little Village than in Pilsen. In both communities, organization respondents saw gangs as the chief reason for crime, and this pattern did not change across time periods.

IMPACT OF THE PROJECT AT GANG AND COMMUNITY LEVELS

In the analyses, we first directed our attention to changes in levels of gang violence affecting the targeted and nontargeted gangs within Little Village. The Latin Kings and the Two Six continued to be responsible for the preponderance of serious gang-violent crimes in the area, but generally they experienced a smaller combined increase in gang homicides, aggravated batteries, and aggravated assaults compared to the other Latino and African American gangs in the area. However, the increase in gang drug crime was particularly large in Little Village. This did not match individual-level findings for program youth, for whom there was a significant decrease in drug arrests.

The Little Village community as a whole experienced a lower rate of increase in serious violent gang incidents and offenders relative to the average of six similar high-gang-crime police districts. In Little Village, the project was associated with the lowest percentage increase of gang-violence incidents in the seven high-gang-crime Latino communities during the first three years of project operations.

A special analysis was conducted to determine whether the ratio of serious violent gang incidents in Little Village increased or decreased relative to the other districts. Based on a five-year preprogram and program-period analysis, we found that the serious violent gang offense ratio decreased in Little Village and two other comparable districts but increased in four other comparable districts. A further analysis of the first three-year program period (when the project was in peak operation) compared to the equivalent preprogram period indicated that serious gang-violent incidents declined more sharply in Little Village than in any of the other six districts over the same period.

In a spatial and temporal analysis of gang crime, the patterning of serious violent gang crime did not vary substantially between the five-year program period and the five-year preprogram period, except that clusters of serious violent gang incidents were somewhat smaller, and more dispersed, in the program period than in the preprogram period in Little Village compared to the key comparison community of Pilsen. Clusters of serious gang-violence incidents were expanding in the high-gang-violence areas in Pilsen. One additional aggregate-level analysis was conducted to determine changes in rates of gang violence during the first three years of the project, using U.S. Census and CPD incident data. The rate of serious violent gang incidents for seventeen- to twenty-five-year-old males increased at a considerably lower rate in Little Village than in Pilsen.

Thus, there was consistent evidence of a deceleration in the serious gang-violence problem at the community level in Little Village compared to other similar communities but also evidence of a substantial acceleration in the gang drug problem. This was in contrast to the reduction of gang drug arrests among program youth during the five-year program period.

Community surveys of residents and organization representatives in Little Village and Pilsen also indicated a significantly greater perceived reduction in gang crime—especially violence—in Little Village than in Pilsen during the first three program years. The perceived reduction was particularly evident in Latin King territory in Little Village. The congruence of research findings at the program-youth, gang-as-a-unit, and community levels consistently provided weight for the argument that the project and its program model accounted for a greater, sometimes significant, amount of reduction of the gang-violence problem in Little Village (although not the overall gang drug problem) than in similar high-gang-violence communities in Chicago between 1987–1991 and 1992–1997.

NOTES

1. These periods do not necessarily match the program-exposure periods of the different youth who were contacted and provided with services.

2. Data on all lethal incidents, arrests, or offenders were generally available. However, these data were missing from Chicago Police Department records for one month, December 1994.

3. Project efforts began to lose momentum during the last two years, when it was uncertain that the Chicago Police Department would sustain the program, and the project staff began to lose heart.

Project Termination

Comprehensive, community-based gang projects that require institutional change are highly vulnerable to failure. Few innovative—if even effective—programs survive, or develop further, unless they serve and sustain important organizational and political interests. The success of the Gang Violence Reduction Project (GVRP) in Little Village, that is, the reduction of gang violence at the individual program-youth level, and probably at the gang and community levels as well, was not sufficient for project survivability and the institutionalization of its interdisciplinary, interorganizational, community-based approach. The program's effectiveness was not sufficient in the context of imbedded, hard suppression police practice and policy, mayoral politics (which emphasized an almost exclusive suppression approach), lack of social-agency capacity for interdisciplinary arrangements around the youth gang problem, and a traditional pattern of local community disorganization in Chicago's gang-problem communities. The death of the Little Village Project could probably have been predicted before the end of the first year of operations, although the program lasted for five years.

Under the terms of the original agreement between the Chicago Police Department (CPD) and the Illinois Criminal Justice Information Authority (ICJIA)—also involving the Cook County Department of Adult Probation (CCDAP) and the University of Chicago (UC) School of Social Service Administration as subcontractors—the Little Village Project (initially more of an idea than a plan for a program) would be funded for one year. The project began during a period of local government and criminal justice–agency leadership transition. New leaders had been elected or appointed to the top positions in Chicago government, the ICJIA, and the CCDAP. I had just completed a research and development project for the creation of a comprehensive community-wide gang program model for the U.S. Department of Justice. I agreed to assist with the development of the Little Village Project. However, the police department's interest and administrative support quickly lagged. I took on initial responsibility for guiding the development of the project and then assumed coordination and direction of project operations for the five-year program period. The original expectation was that the CPD would take administrative charge of the project and would make an early decision whether to continue it by the end of the first year, or soon thereafter. This expectation was not met, even though the program seemed to be working. The CPD was distracted by problems in implementing its community-policing strategy and paid little attention to the project, although it continued to accept funding for it over the entire five years. I had originally agreed to stay on only for a year but remained for five years as the project coordinator before announcing my plan to leave. The CPD then decided that the project approach was not compatible with its mission and should not be integrated into department policy and operations (although three years of federal funding remained).

The process of the project's termination is described using data derived from monthly reports that I submitted to the CPD, biweekly team staff-meeting minutes, and letters and memoranda to and from the CPD and me. Together, the documents trace and explain the steps taken in the project's potential transition and its final termination.

PROJECT TRANSITION

In December 1994, a little more than two years after the project began, no decision about the project's future had been made by the CPD, so I wrote a memo on "thoughts about project transition" to the neighborhood-relations sergeant of the Tenth Police District who had some quasiadministrative responsibility for the project:

> Based on the feasibility and effectiveness of the project, thus far, I would recommend continued if not primary responsibility for administration and coordination [of the project] by the Chicago Police Department, particularly the present neighborhood-relations unit, with the aid of the special tactical unit and close liaison with narcotics and organized-crime units, since a sharp rise in drug possession and drug dealing at the street level is occurring.
>
> In this process [of transition], the University of Chicago would gradually reduce its commitment to administer and supervise the community youth-

work unit. The Chicago Police Department should consider contracting for youth-work services targeted to hard-core gang youth from Neighbors against Gang Violence [the affiliate agency of GVRP], with close oversight from the Tenth Police District. . . .

The University of Chicago would expect to terminate fully its coordination and provision of youth-work services by August 30, 1995. It would begin to transfer coordination and supervision of the youth-worker unit in February 1995 but retain oversight and funding responsibility for the youth-work unit until August 30.

There was no response to the memo. The problem of further developing and transferring the project remained unsolved, pending meetings among representatives of the CPD, the ICJIA, and the UC. The director of the research and development unit (R&D) of the CPD attended a GVRP staff meeting in early February 1996 to further assess the value of the project to the CPD. The then acting director of the ICJIA summarized the project's February 7 meeting with the assistant director of R&D in a memo as follows:

I found our discussion revolved around the following things:

- **Team approach**: Over and over again, everyone stressed the importance of the project being a collaborative effort. It appeared the feeling of the group was that the whole was greater than the sum of its parts. Each project team member believes he or she is better equipped to do his or her job because of the participation of other members of the team.
- **Information**: It was clear to me that those present felt they had access to more information that assisted them in the performance of their jobs than they would if the team was not in place. Information was gathered both in general and [also] relative to specific incidents. I found it particularly noteworthy that police officers Gary and Rob are viewed as "resources" by other police agencies (FBI, ATF, county sheriff).
- **Communication**: Perhaps more important than gathering information is sharing it. Because team members are in constant contact with one another, there are numerous opportunities for passing along information that is directly related to a particular gang member or incident or [that] may fit into an investigation at some future time.

- **Program features:** The program has two primary elements—intervention with the target population (to divert them from the gang or remove them from the streets) and intelligence gathering (to solve crimes or reduce the chance they'll be committed to prison). I, for one, underestimated the significance of intelligence gathering when the program design was first completed. It's also important to be mindful of
  - **Needs and motivation** of gang members who become involved in a gang and why.
  - **Targeting** of resources toward a particular problem or group of offenders. In this case, we were hoping to reduce incidents of violent crime, so the target population included those who were committing violent crimes or causing them to be committed.
  - **The community as a partner:** The success of this type of program will be effected by the extent to which the community is on board and able to do its part. That is, residents need to work with the team, and services need to be in place to be drawn on by the team.
  - **The members of the team:** Needless to say, these should be people who believe in what they will be asked to do and committed to doing the best they can. This is particularly true because they will need to confront and overcome problems between the participating agencies and within their own agencies. A special mention should be made about the outreach youth workers—both their value to the program and their characteristics. The coordinator should be asked to elaborate in particular on the latter, along with their hiring and supervision.
  - **A neutral leader:** One of the reasons the program has been effective is the coordinator. He has been exclusively focused on getting the program to work. All team members know that and respect him for it.
  - **Data collection:** Documentation of impact and ongoing crime analysis has been limited by a lack of data [available to project staff]. I am hopeful some of the department's new efforts in this area—especially ICAM [a new computer program]—will be a help here.
- **New Approach/New Rules:** The police officers present noted it was sometimes hard to take a new approach to their jobs when supervisors were holding them to the "old" performance standards. Sound familiar?

In the monthly report of June 1996 to the CPD's director of R&D, I wrote,

Plans to transfer the project continue. Our Lady of Tepeyac Church and Latino Youth [Agency] also indicate interest in taking responsibility for the project. I will request only a six-month project continuation to facilitate such project transfer. The Chicago Police Department should provide as soon as possible a key managerial officer to assist with this process as well as, ideally, take over responsibility for further development of the Little Village Project, which could include initiation and testing of a similar project in a high-gang–violence, local Chicago African American community.

In the monthly report of August 1996, I noted,

Additional agencies have expressed interest in "running" the project, including BUILD, Cook County Adult Probation, and Juvenile Court Intensive Probation. These organizations are particularly interested in the youth-work component. OJJDP [Office of Juvenile Justice and Delinquency Prevention] copied a letter to me dated August 16, sent by the administrator of OJJDP to the director of research and development, Chicago Police Department, inviting her to submit an application to support the continued implementation of the project:
    Specifically, we would consider your proposal for the enhancement of the existing project in Little Village and potentially the expansion of this project to other neighborhoods through a twenty-four-month project with one hundred thousand dollars, available for the first twelve months. In the second twelve months, we would consider a similar or enhanced level of funding. . . . We are excited about the possibility of partnering with you and the Little Village Project and look forward to your proposal.

In the monthly report of November 1996, I wrote,

A meeting of key CPD headquarters administration personnel, the Tenth District commander and GVRP sergeant, administrative representatives of adult proba-tion, the acting director of the Illinois Criminal Justice Information Authority, and me was held downtown to discuss the future direction of the project. In the course of discussion, considerable concern was expressed by heads of the various police divisions that the CPD was not a social agency and not primarily inter-ested in organizing the Little Village community around the gang problem. The director of research and development raised the issue of cost of the project if it went citywide. The deputy superintendent, however, expressed qualified support for the project idea. He stated that the CPD would in the immediate future focus on the development of a police coordinator role. A full-time sergeant would be assigned to the GVRP from the deputy superintendent's office, to explore the possibility of managing the project. The deputy superintendent and the director of the R&D division also emphasized the importance of determining the feasibility of the project as a citywide model. This should be done as quickly as possible.

From the monthly report of January 1997,

The sergeant assigned out of the deputy superintendent's office met with [selected] project personnel in Little Village and at the University of Chicago but did not appear to be especially interested in project operations. He did not meet with the outreach youth workers or probation officers. He did tour the neighborhood with the project police. He was most interested in available research reports, especially on project outcome. After examining them, he acknowledged the positive effect of the project on older youth but raised questions about the effect on juveniles, only recently the focus of operations and not the primary target of the project. He failed to recognize that program juveniles, although with slightly increased arrests for gang crime, were still doing significantly better than similar unserved comparison gang juveniles.

While he agreed with the finding of superior performance of the Tenth District in regard to lowering the level of gang violence compared to six other districts, he was not sure that including the Eighth District [one of the comparison districts] was a fair one, because the community was in the midst of rapid population change.

The sergeant was interested in the involvement of the public schools in addressing the problem of younger youth about to become gang members. He was also interested in a closer relationship between police and adult probation. The sergeant appeared less interested in preserving or developing a comprehensive approach to the gang problem than in discovering those elements of the project that would be useful for the CPD in coordinating efforts to squash gang crime through justice-system approaches in the city.

In several discussions after the sergeant's visit, the key question among staff, including project police, was whether the sergeant's presence represented an effort to develop and expand the project or to torpedo it.

By the end of December 1996 there was still no evidence that the CPD was committed to sustaining, modifying, or expanding the project. Nevertheless, support for the project was expressed from a variety of sources. Seven agencies and community organizations were interested in assuming responsibility, mainly for the youth-worker component. Preliminary evidence suggested that project outcome at the individual and aggregate-community levels was good, particularly relative to curtailing the growth of the gang-violence problem in other comparable communities of the city.

After four and a half years, I had announced that I would no longer manage the project. I was an academic and a researcher, and not primarily an agency or program director. My original commitment had been to serve as a consultant for one year. My attempts to induce the CPD to take over the project or to partner with some appropriate set of organizations to do so, had not borne fruit to date.

Statistical evidence and the interest of local community leaders appeared not to be sufficient to convince the CPD that the project was not only effective but feasible and should be continued or expanded. The cost of the program was again raised by the R&D director, but the only major additional cost would have been sustaining the youth-worker component, which could have been borne by a youth-work agency through funds from the United Way, various foundations, and other sources. A key stumbling block remained—the CPD was also not prepared to manage an approach to the gang problem that required significant partnership with other agencies or integration of social intervention with its suppression operations. The CPD was also not interested in a program that involved collaboration with outreach youth workers. Community policing was sufficient for its community-organization purposes, particularly if the local community aided suppression activities. The sergeant out of the deputy superintendent's office indicated that the CPD was willing to consider coordination of their gang-suppression activities with adult probation.

CRISIS AND TERMINATION

A staff crisis involving the project youth-work supervisor occurred in early 1997, which was exaggerated and became a flimsy excuse for a decision by the CPD R&D director to raise questions about the department's involvement in the project. Three more years of funding ($1.5 million) for the project remained from the block grant of the U.S. Justice Department's Office of Justice Programs; additional funding by the Office of Juvenile Justice and Delinquency Prevention had also been offered. The CPD superintendent did not respond to this offer.

The CPD R&D liaison lieutenant had stated (with disgust and disappointment, before he departed at the end of the first year of the project) that "the CPD has 'deep pockets.' . . . The CPD does not need grant funds from the federal government to develop or sustain any project it is interested in."

The acting director of ICJIA and I continued to seek the interest and support of public agencies and community leaders to bring about an effective transfer or adaptation of the project. I held meetings with the Pupil Services Section of the Board of Education in January and February 1997 to discuss their provision of one full-time and one half-time crisis caseworker to address the gang problem in elementary and middle schools in Little Village. Specifics of staffing and operations were to be worked out, based on a budget decision of the board.

The acting director of the ICJIA and I held a meeting with the presiding judge of the juvenile court and his administrative probation and court-services staff to discuss how the juvenile court could be more fully involved with project staff around gang youth and community gang situations. Discussions were also initiated with two local organizations—La Villita Community Church and the Latino Youth Agency—to jointly operate the Little Village Project, particularly the youth-worker component, and to enhance social services; both organizations would have to be in close collaboration with police and adult probation.

A citizen's group in the African American section of the Tenth District, concerned with the gang-violence problem in their area, held discussions with the deputy police superintendent and me about extending the project to that area. One of the local aldermen and the congressman from the area expressed support for the project and their desire to see it expanded to the African American area of the Tenth District.

A letter of February 11, 1997, from the director of the CPD's R&D unit to me signaled the beginning of a project crisis. Its basis may have developed two months earlier with a minor project administrative change, when I expanded the supervisory responsibilities of the youth-work supervisor to include collection of time cards from youth-work staff. This had previously been my exclusive responsibility. It emerged that the particular youth-work supervisor at the time, a recent graduate of a criminal justice program at a local university, had begun to allocate more hours of work to certain part-time youth workers than I had originally assigned them to perform. More importantly, the supervisor erased and then added hours to a worker's original time sheets *after* I had approved and signed off on them. The letter from the CPD R&D director also accused the supervisor of intimidating one of the other youth workers. When I found out about these activities, the supervisor was immediately suspended. After I gathered further evidence of the supervisor's irregular actions, I terminated him from the project. Formal investigations followed—by the University of Chicago Accounting Department and the Chicago Police Department—but sufficient evidence was not found for criminal action against the terminated supervisor. All project property in the supervisor's possession was returned, and the costs of his irregular activities (estimated at ten thousand dollars) were adjusted out of the project's grant.

Despite the crisis the project continued its work. A replacement youth-work supervisor was appointed within two weeks. Project youth workers, police, and probation officers continued their normal routines. An additional youth worker was employed; weekly youth-worker meetings and biweekly project team meetings continued.

The key issue of transferring the project and adapting the program model remained. Two local organizations—Latino Youth and La Villita Community Church (both in Little Village, and both familiar with and participants in project operations)—remained interested. Both were viable organizations for taking over parts of the project. A series of meetings were again held with Rev. Mike of La Villita Community Church and the director of Latino Youth, this time involving the sergeant out of the CPD deputy superintendent's office, the director of the Illinois Criminal Justice Information Authority (formerly the acting director), and me. Rev. Mike and the director of Latino Youth were each prepared to take over certain components of the project but not the entire project. Neither organization was interested in collaboration with police and probation. The CPD, in turn, still had not made an official decision as to what to do with the project. In a series of discussions with the sergeant, it became clear that his function had been in fact to explore alternatives to the project, that is, the possible development of a citywide project emphasizing police and probation collaboration and, ideally, closer involvement with the elementary and middle schools around the issue of gang prevention among juveniles but not direct support of an outreach youth-work component.

In early April 1997 the sergeant stated informally to me that the CPD would not extend or transfer the project, and that a letter to me from the police superintendent terminating the project would be forthcoming. It came a month later:

Dear Professor Spergel:

I have recently signed the Illinois Criminal Justice Information Authority Interagency Agreement, which funds the Gang Violence Reduction Project in Little Village through July 17, 1997. At this time, we are contemplating not requesting additional funds for the program beyond this year, although we expect to expand many elements of the model into each of our remaining twenty-four districts in July without the use of grant funds.

I have followed the progress of the Little Village pilot over the past four years via the quarterly reports that you and others have supplied to the department as well as through briefings from my staff. Thanks in large part to your efforts, the program has certainly involved some groundbreaking activity. As you are aware, it has been our intent to learn from the experiences of this pilot and to apply the "best practices" from the program to the work of the other twenty-four district gang tactical teams. To that end, I asked my staff to design a gang tactical strategy that combines and incorporates the strengths of the Little Village Program and CAPS [Community Alternative Policing Strategy, i.e., community-policing] model.

I am reviewing an alternative version of the Little Village program that would capitalize on our current partnerships with other criminal justice agencies as well as the community involvement promoted by CAPS but that does not include the outreach workers that are currently part of the existing agreement. I wanted to share with you our initial thoughts about what this citywide program might look like.

We have benefited a great deal from our involvement in the project. As part of our commitment to expand a gang tactical model citywide, we are currently fine-tuning a pilot in a police area in July. This model incorporates the elements of information sharing, team work, and the targeting and tracking of the most violent gang members. Probation has agreed to continue to provide this population referral to social services as well. We will also be talking with the Illinois Department of Corrections Adult Parole Services and the Office of the Cook County State's Attorney about possible linkages in this effort.

I want to personally thank you for your hard work and dedication in the Little Village Project. I believe that your efforts will lead us to a future model that contains a more focused and effective response to violent gang members in Chicago. I would be happy to hear any thoughts that you might have that would assist us in our expansion efforts.

Sincerely,
Superintendent of Police

On May 9, I responded to the superintendent's letter as follows:

Dear Superintendent:

Thank you for your letter of May 5, 1997. I appreciate your interest in the Little Village Gang Violence Reduction Project, particularly based on our monthly (we did not submit quarterly) reports and extensive research reports.

I agree with you that the project has involved "groundbreaking activity," by addressing the serious problem of gang violence in a fairly comprehensive way in one high-gang-violence Chicago community through the sharing of information, interaction with and coordination of certain key elements of the justice system, youth workers, and local community institutions, especially churches, youth agencies, job providers, and to some extent, schools.

My present concern is that your future development of policy and administration may not be based sufficiently on the complexity of the serious gang problem and the need of police leadership to address it in a comprehensive manner. . . . It is important not only to build partnerships with other criminal justice agencies but also to enhance internal police department coordination and to work closely with the community's educational and employment systems as well as with the social service system. Lack of coordination with these non–criminal justice units is part of the complex gang problem.

The use of outreach workers is difficult but also highly relevant to dealing with the gang problem in an effective way. An appropriate local-agency structure must be found in the community to utilize indigenous and professional human service workers as well as former gang members, under close supervision, to address the problem. This is very difficult and risky

but an essential part of the task of law enforcement and gang-crime reduction. A focused criminal justice approach with only a nominal community
involvement will be inadequate.

There were major design flaws in the Gang Violence Reduction Project.
Perhaps you can rectify them in your future planning. While project staff
functioned well on their own, there was a serious lack of support by various
levels of police administration in integrating the project, or elements of it,
into CAPS or Tenth Police District operations. The project was a relatively
isolated effort in the department for over a four-year period. It could be
that CAPS, as yet, does not deal with hard-core gang youth in a manner that
serves both to control and mainstream them. Unless you contribute to the
development of a more comprehensive focus in your design, I believe the
Chicago Police Department will be stuck with a suppression approach that
will probably not be effective. . . .

I thank you for permitting us to conduct the Gang Violence Reduction
Project pilot program these past years.

Sincerely yours,

Professor Spergel

All staff members were notified in April 1997 of the project's termination, to
be effective July 17, 1997, although project police and probation officers were
not informed by their respective agencies of the termination of their assign-
ments to the project until the end of June 1997. Officer Rob began planning
to transfer to a day shift with the narcotics division downtown; officer Gary
hoped to remain with the Tenth District tactical unit. The Little Village probation unit would remain intact in its current location and expand as part of
a possible cooperative Tenth and Eleventh District police and probation unit
to combat gang crime. Each of the youth workers quickly found employment.
A final effort by Rev. Mike to mount a community-resident and local-agency
protest meeting to sustain the project was not successful.

The CPD idea of a collaborative police and probation arrangement did
not work out. As of the fall of 1999, the coordination of the Cook County
Department of Adult Probation (CCDAP) with the Chicago Police Department
around the gang problem had not developed. In late November 1997, following
the project's termination, the Tenth District commander telephoned me for
an appointment to discuss the increasingly serious gang-violence problem in

Little Village: he wanted to know more about the use of outreach youth workers. The project's former adult probation supervisor wanted to attend the proposed meeting, noting that, since project termination, the probation officers no longer knew what was happening with gangs on the streets of Little Village. The meeting never took place, and as of this writing, a collaborative relationship between the CPD and the CCDAP around the gang problem has still not occurred. In June 2003, almost six years after the project terminated, the rate of homicides in Chicago exceeded that of any other city with a million or more people in the United States. The CPD superintendent's new "plan" to solve the homicide problem remained "red hot." Its focus now was " 'gang strategy teams' in each of the Police Department's patrol areas to meet every week to share information and discuss crime-fighting strategies" (Washburn 2003).

A sharp drop in homicides (including gang homicides) did occur in Chicago in 2004. Violence, including gang violence, was leveling off or declining in many urban areas of the United States, particularly in the largest cities (Egley 2005; Harrell 2005). More recent reports have indicated that youth gang violence is again rising in some of the large urban areas.

AFTERTHOUGHTS

The Chicago Police Department delayed a decision for four and a half years about whether to sustain, modify, or abandon the project. The CPD's singular interest in a suppression approach was too great to overcome, despite the success of the program. Top levels of city government, particularly the mayor's office, citywide social agencies, and other criminal justice agencies as well as the media remained publicly silent, and ostensibly uninvolved, during the course of the discussions about what to do about the project. There was no attempt to utilize the wealth of data about the project's efforts and its effectiveness.

Key and unique elements of the project probably were its team structure and process, that is, the interdependent relationships, approaches, and procedures that developed between the different staff, including police, probation, and outreach youth workers (and to a lesser extent the neighborhood organizer). The team approach, however, did not translate into full involvement and support by administrators of the CPD and the CCDAP. The project's police tactical team and probation officers were largely on their own and did not have sufficient central-office backup and administrative supervision. The CPD and CCDAP did not clearly know or fully understand what their street-level staff on the project were doing. Adequate policy and administrative arrangements for the project were not developed.

Nevertheless, the close interaction between project police and youth workers served not only to provide better targeted and effective police suppression efforts but also helped the project police to become better aware and supportive of the gang youth's needs for employment assistance and social services. The close interaction of team members also required the youth workers to take greater responsibility for supervising and controlling gang-youth behavior, alerting project police about gang incidents and offenders, and at times, assisting them directly and indirectly in their various law-enforcement tasks. Early on, project probation officers developed a close relationship with the project police and often went on patrol with them. In the later years they participated less in joint patrolling, due in part to the increased rigidity of the CCDAP's policies and administrative practices. The CCDAP's inability, or lack of opportunity, to provide probation staff with a design for collaboration with other project team members, and appropriate coordinated arrangements at the policy level with the CPD, were basic problems.

A major limitation of the project was a lack of sufficient resources for purposes of community organizing and inter-justice-agency coordination. I was too involved in day-to-day administration and supervision, worker team coordination, and program evaluation efforts to have more strongly insisted from the beginning that the CPD and the CCDAP meet their administrative and community-leadership responsibilities for supporting the project model. Efforts should have been made, especially by the CPD, not only to integrate community policing with the project but also to involve area and district police commanders as well as CPD youth and narcotics divisions' personnel in collaborating with the project. A community-based and interagency gang-control project cannot be created without considerable commitment and involvement, not only by top community and political leaders, but also by midlevel police department administrative leadership.

A strategic political error may have been the assumption by the director of ICJIA, the head of the CPD's R&D unit, and me that achievement of the program's goals and objectives (and even the availability of federal funding and enthusiastic support) was sufficient to institutionalize a successful, integrated gang program model in Chicago. The reality of project achievement did not make sense in Chicago's political, criminal justice, and social-agency climate between 1992 and 1997, and perhaps still does not today. High-level policy discussions about the nature and accomplishments of the project should have been undertaken earlier with the mayor and political, civic, religious, foundation, and other community leaders. However, this may not have been possible. In the final analysis, Chicago was not ready for a program to substantially reduce the gang problem that also did not meet other interests of the mayor and the city's leaders.

The city's policy of single-minded police suppression against gangs and gang members may have been the mayor's means of maintaining the political support of the "good" local people in Chicago's communities, as well as meeting the interests of businesses, churches, the media, and academic, youth-serving, and other local institutions. While these organized interest groups might disagree with the mayor on other issues, they were passive or united with him on a short-sighted, simplistic, and ineffective policy of arresting and incarcerating gang members—the "bad guys." The key leaders of the city were not aware of or willing to address the systemic and complex nature of the youth gang problem in Chicago in interinstitutional and balanced strategic terms, involving social intervention and job and educational opportunities, as well as suppression targeted to gang youth.

By fighting gangs simplistically, the mayor could politically divert the attention of the city's leaders, residents, citizen groups, and a great variety of organizations from the more basic job opportunities, racial, educational, health, housing, social service, and other problems ailing the city, which contributed to the gang problem and other urban ills. Despite the termination of the Little Village Gang Violence Reduction Project, the comprehensive community-based approach became a key element of program initiatives, supported by the U.S. Department of Justice, local leaders in other cities, and some gang experts around the country, but not without considerable *Sturm und Drang*.

WHAT WE LEARNED, WHICH MAY BE USEFUL TO OTHER CITIES AND LOCALITIES

1. The youth gang problem results not only from the antisocial behavior of gangs and their members but also from the unintegrated, inappropriate, often politicized responses of government leaders, criminal justice and social agencies, community groups, and civic leaders to a complex social problem,

increasingly prevalent across highly mobile societies containing socially disadvantaged and segmented male-youth and young-adult groups.

2. Substantial reductions of gang crime, particularly gang violence (and to some extent drug-related activities), can be achieved—at community, as well as at gang and individual levels—through the implementation of a set of comprehensive and interrelated strategies of community mobilization, social intervention, provision of social opportunities, suppression, and organizational change and development targeted to gang youth in high-gang-crime sectors of a community.

3. In this effort, law enforcement—under the aegis and control of a central unit of government, the mayor's office, or the city council—must be the lead agency, supported and influenced by an interagency and community advisory council, and a street-outreach team of police, probation, youth workers (including former gang influentials from gang-problem areas), neighborhood organizers, and associated school, treatment, and job-placement personnel collaboratively serving, controlling, and targeting problem gang youth.

17

Summary

The key questions this book has tried to answer are how the Little Village Gang Violence Reduction Project developed, what its model of a comprehensive, interdisciplinary community approach was, and to what extent the project was successful in reducing violence of gang youth. The model stressed the integration of several program strategies.

Law enforcement was the primary institutional approach to the youth gang problem. It emphasized use of single-minded suppression, with little interest in collaborating with other approaches. Youth agencies used referral, treatment, or recreational and, occasionally, outreach youth-worker strategies but without collaboration with law enforcement. Educational organizations emphasized gang prevention, cultural sensitivity, and sometimes special education, but mainly zero tolerance. Neighborhood groups—including home owners, business proprietors, and local citizens—quickly called for police to arrest gang youth. While most politicians and lawmakers denounced gang members and recommended extra punishment for them, some gang experts and social reformers believed that former gang members had to be involved in some positive way in addressing the youth gang problem, and that they were essential to successful gang-control and gang-prevention programs.

Each gang policy and program approach was claimed a success. However, none was adequately articulated and tested with empirical research. The Little Village Project was different. It was based on the integration of multiple strategies. It was a test of the capacity and willingness of city political, youth-agency, and community leaders to support a comprehensive, collaborative, and balanced approach to the youth gang problem. Closely associated or interrelated with the project was a prospective, quasiexperimental research evaluation to assess its program process, program-youth outcome, and impact on the community gang problem.

PROJECT FORMATION

In the spring of 1992, just prior to the start of the Little Village Project, a series of changes occurred in city government and selected criminal justice agencies in Chicago, Cook County, and the State of Illinois. A new Chicago mayor was elected, and he appointed a new police superintendent. A former Illinois assistant state's attorney became the director of the Cook County Department of Adult Probation (CCDAP). The then associate director (later the director) of the Illinois Criminal Justice Information Authority (ICJIA) contacted me for a concept paper to create a comprehensive approach to address the worsening gang-violence problem in Chicago.

The idea of the Little Village Gang Violence Reduction Project (GVRP) was quickly accepted with the Chicago Police Department (CPD) as the lead agency, in partnership with the Cook County Department of Adult Probation (CCDAP) and the School of Social Service Administration (SSA) of the University of Chicago. Funding would come from the U.S. Department of Justice's Violence in Urban Areas Program. The goal of the pilot project was to reduce gang homicide, aggravated battery, and assault in six beats of the Tenth Chicago Police District, comprising a mainly Mexican American, low-income working-class community. Violent youth in the two major gangs in the area—the Latin Kings (estimated membership of 12,000) and the Two Six (estimated membership of 8,000)—would be targeted.

The project called for an interagency, community-based team approach to violent gang youth that emphasized a set of interrelated strategies—community mobilization, including formation of a neighborhood advisory group; social intervention through use of outreach youth workers; provision of social opportunities, particularly jobs, training, and access to school programs; a modified suppression strategy by a small group of tactical officers; and organizational change and the development of policies and administrative arrangements to accommodate the new interrelated strategies.

The project was reorganized almost before it began. The commander of the gang-crime unit, a key supporter of the project, resigned, and the patrol division assumed minimal responsibility for the two tactical and two neighborhood-relations officers but not for the project. The Chicago Department of Human Services had initially planned to provide outreach youth workers for the project but did not. With experience as a gang worker and administrator of gang projects, I became responsible for developing the outreach youth-work component. The CCDAP followed through on its staffing commitment, but little collaboration occurred between the CPD and CCDAP. A police administrator was not appointed, and I, by default, became the de facto coordinator of the project. The CPD was minimally interested in the development of the project. It was preoccupied with planning and implementing the Chicago Alternative Policing System (CAPS), its new community-policing program.

ENTERING THE FIELD

The project did not begin in an orderly or carefully planned fashion. It had to make progress in addressing the gang problem in Little Village within a year. I utilized CPD contacts and official crime data as well as outreach youth workers—mainly former leaders of the Latin Kings and Two Six—to determine which gang sections of the two gangs to target.

The youth workers had no trouble contacting members of the various sections of the two gangs. Their members were omnipresent on the streets from early evening until early the following morning. The assistant director and I, together with the youth workers, explained the purpose and structure of the project, emphasizing the objectives of reducing gang violence, getting youth back to school, and referring them for job training and placement. The assistant director and I told the youth workers that police and probation officers would be on the project team, and together they would help protect the gang guys and the local citizens from gang violence.

By the end of the six months, there was preliminary acceptance of the purpose of the project and the role of youth workers, particularly in respect to helping with job opportunities and gaining access again to school and training. Gang youth more freely provided information about gang situations. Communication by youth with other members of the project team, including police, began to occur. Identifying youth for the program was based mainly on the observations of youth workers and gang-violence arrest reports provided by project tactical police. The project police reviewed arrest reports of all Tenth District officers each day, and recommended and confirmed which particular youth should be targeted.

Youth workers responded to project police and probation officers' requests for information about where program youth hung out and the nature of activities of the gang sections, and verified whether a youth was responsible for a particular gang-violent act. Youth workers did not necessarily share information about all forms of crime in which target youth participated. Project police and probation officers were respectful of youth workers and acknowledged the critical importance of their contacts and services. Project police referred target gang youth for help with school problems and job-related placement or training. From the start, relations between the two project tactical officers and the youth workers were remarkably positive. At the invitation of the youth workers, project police met on the street with members of a section of the Two Six, and then with members of a section of the Latin Kings. Project probation officers also quickly developed good relationships with both the tactical officers and youth workers.

The assistant director and I made contacts with local organizations and community groups to support the development of the project. The park department, several Catholic churches, and a protestant community church made gym and meeting-room facilities available to program youth. Contacts were also made with the administrators of the two local Boys and Girls Clubs, the high school, a major Latino community organization, and the three aldermen who represented sections of the Little Village community. A local community activist at one of the local community organization meetings volunteered to help with the creation of a neighborhood advisory group to assist the project in its mission of comprehensively addressing the youth gang problem.

Varied evaluation-research aspects of the project's work developed simultaneously. The CPD liaison lieutenant to the project assisted with access to police data and recommended the development of surveys to measure changes in the community's perception of the gang problem. Interviews of program youth began. Arrangements were made to obtain entire police histories of program and comparison youth. Program records began to be completed by the youth workers, police, probation officers, and later, the neighborhood organizer.

TEAM DEVELOPMENT

A key objective of mine was to develop close team relationships among staff assigned to the project. The project police, probation, and youth workers met together on a regular basis—once every other week and more often as needed. Workers learned to understand and complement the roles of other staff members in achieving the common purpose of gang-violence reduction. Direct and immediate communication and working relationships among team members developed in order to meet ongoing gang problems and crises in the field. Still, each worker acted within the parameters of his respective agency's purposes and regulations.

The physical boundaries used by project staff to carry out their activities varied. The gangs operated mainly in the Little Village area but did engage occasionally in conflict with gangs and commit crimes outside the area. The outreach youth workers mainly confined their work to Little Village but could occasionally, for specific reasons, move out of the area. The police confined their operations to specific beats of the Tenth District. At first, probation officers' caseloads included gang youth from the comparison area. However, probation administrators quickly permitted project probation officers to work primarily with gang youth who resided in Little Village, while still including nongang drug probationers from the comparison community of Pilsen—a neighboring community of identical characteristics.

Collaboration among staff was not easy to manage. Project police officers complained that their collaborative efforts with other workers were not always successful; some of the gang youth referred to youth workers for jobs were still on the streets getting into trouble. They complained that probation did not transfer a particular gang youth quickly enough from general probation to Little Village intensive probation. The youth then committed a gang homicide. The project youth workers and the advisory board's youth-agency-type worker were somewhat competitive. They often worked with the same youth and disagreed about who should provide job services and family contacts. Both project police and probation staff complained that their respective agencies did not sufficiently support their project work, and that agency administrators did not fully understand what their staff members were doing.

SOCIAL INTERVENTION: THE OUTREACH YOUTH WORKER

The project depended heavily on youth-worker outreach contacts and relationships with gang youth. Most of the outreach youth workers from the community had been former leaders or influential members in the particular gangs to which they were assigned. Use of outreach youth workers made for rapid entry into the gang world and easy targeting of hard-core gang youth by the entire project team. Outreach youth workers were present on the streets of Little Village not only during assigned work hours but at other times as well, since most still lived or had friends and family in the community. They had access to information that served law-enforcement and social-intervention purposes. They engaged gang youth individually or in small groups on the street, at home or in family contexts, on athletic fields, in recreation centers, in detention facilities, at school, on the job, and elsewhere about a range of problems. The youth worker was often involved in a variety of tense field situations.

A primary concern of the youth worker was to help the youth stay out of trouble. He was a proactive communicator and mediator between the target youth and his significant others: family, girlfriend or wife, and representatives of social, educational, employment, and criminal justice agencies. The program gang youth was helped to find a job, complete high school, or pursue further education. However, the traditional role of mediating conflicts between opposing gangs was not generally employed by youth workers. It was easier to encourage lulls in fighting and gain agreement from gang leaders or influentials to "get members to stay in their own neighborhoods." Project team members in general were reluctant to formally mediate conflicts, which would mean recognizing the legitimacy of gang leaders and strengthening their influence in enforcing gang norms and contributing to gang cohesion. The stated view of project staff, including the youth workers, was that gangs were illegitimate structures and that gang life was destructive. Gang youth had to be persuaded or constrained to leave the gang as soon as possible.

Youth workers assisted local residents and block clubs in addressing problems that contributed to gang delinquency, such as closing down a bar that catered to underage gang youth and permitted the use and sale of narcotics. They were able to support parents and neighbors at times of gang crises, particularly when shootings occurred and gang members (and nongang youth) were injured or killed. The youth workers collaborated with the project police officers in the exchange of information that was vital to the police suppression role. On the other hand, the youth workers depended on the project police for information about program youth, as well as for assistance in fulfilling their own roles: protecting them from "hard-nosed" and sometimes brutal police officers in the district who at times harassed and tried to arrest youth workers. The project police often vouched for the youth workers' appropriate presence on the street when they were about to be arrested for gang loitering. (Chicago's gang loitering law was later declared unconstitutional.)

There were problems as well as benefits to the project's use of youth workers who were former members of gangs in the area. When a youth worker's performance problem could not be corrected, I separated the worker from the project but also assisted him in finding another position, enabling him to collect unemployment insurance and maintain health insurance, and assuring that he would remain positively connected to the project. The close interaction of workers in the project team also served as a control mechanism to keep the outreach youth workers conforming to project norms and values.

SUPPRESSION AND SOCIAL CONTROLS

Basic goals and objectives of the original CPD proposal for the development of the Little Village Gang Violence Reduction Project were stated in general terms. Given the CPD's history of specialized gang units and focused suppression tactics, change in policy and practice to facilitate collaborative interagency and interdisciplinary teamwork could not readily occur. An administrative group consisting of CPD and CCDAP officials, SSA, and other agency representatives to oversee the project was not created.

A key problem was identifying who in the CPD was responsible for the project. The commander of the gang-crime unit had been expected to be responsible, but he resigned. Then the patrol division, through the local Tenth District commander, was to have some responsibility for administering the project (at 5 percent of time) along with the research and development unit. The deputy superintendent's office was to assure police department interbureau cooperation. In the first three years of project operations, three different commanders in sequence were placed in charge of the Tenth District and the administration of the project. The Tenth District neighborhood-relations sergeant, who was to serve as the commander's liaison to the project, was not clear what his role should be. His major responsibility became developing the new community policing program in the area, which had no relation to the GVRP.

The CCDAP wanted to be the junior partner in the project (with the CPD as the senior partner), but a concept of how the probation officers were to be related to the project was not formulated. The CCDAP administration was in the dark as to what the probation component specifically should do, except to carry out some form of regular probation activity in the area. The original probation supervisor was replaced because he was too rigid in implementing probation procedures in the Little Village unit, which caused the three probation workers to transfer to other units of the department. The new probation supervisor reconstituted the Little Village probation unit but was frustrated because of a lack of clear direction from the CCDAP and their failure to provide adequate support.

Despite, and perhaps because of, the weakness of policy, structure, and support for the roles of project police and probation officers, an unusually high degree of cohesion evolved among members of the project team. Much of this was a response to the performance of the two project police officers, largely detached from certain routines of the Tenth District tactical unit. Still part of the CPD structure as they carried out tactical responsibilities in respect to gangs and assisted other police officers in carrying out their law-enforcement duties, they were also sensitive to the needs of gang youth and able to use the resources of other team members to address the gang problem. The two tactical officers summed up their experiences as follows:

> Nobody really knew what they wanted us to do . . . the first thing . . . we went out and started talking to these guys [gang kids]. We let them know who we are and what we're doing. We put out the word that we are the police. We're the law end of the project . . . but if you have a problem, talk to us. If we can do something, we'll do it. We're not out there just to lock everybody up, because that obviously doesn't work. If you have a problem, like you feel you can't go to your family, the boys on the streets aren't helping you out—maybe we're the connection. We got some guys like street workers who can do something for these guys. Before the project, if a kid came to a policeman and said, "Hey, listen, I got kicked out of school for fighting, and I need to get back. I screwed up," a policeman couldn't do anything.

COMMUNITY MOBILIZATION

The priority objectives at the start of the project were the creation of a street-level team to control gang violence and to provide services to targeted youth. These objectives became a basis for organizing an advisory group to the project, which became a quasi-independent neighborhood organization concerned with the gang problem. The CPD was interested in organizing or using a neighborhood group but not a broad group of key community leaders and agency personnel for a community-wide steering committee to advise and direct the development of the project.

The assistant director and I spent a great deal of time, initially, contacting local agencies, churches, colleges, unions, and business groups to develop access to education, training, and jobs for program youth. Special interest and concern about the youth gang problem were expressed by several Catholic churches and a local protestant community church; several Boys and Girls Clubs, the local high school, a job agency, and one of the three aldermen in the wards representing the community were also interested.

A local community activist, with a background as a local alternative-education worker and community organizer, offered to bring agencies, local organizations, and residents together to form an association to support the project. By early spring of 1993, the community activist and the pastor of a local protestant community church had developed a small advisory group. Several community meetings were held, and local citizens expressed concerns about the gang problem. The Catholic churches, two Boys and Girls Clubs, a job agency recruiting workers for factories in the suburbs, one of the local aldermen, and several residents became board members of Neighbors against Gang Violence (NAGV). Application for a state charter as a nonprofit organization was made and awarded. Funding applications also went to local and national foundations and a state agency.

NAGV stated that its goal was "to reduce gang violence in the Little Village Community." Its objectives included establishing four chapters in high-gang-violence areas, recruiting two hundred members, initiating activities to bring the community together, and placing twenty hard-core gang members on jobs or in training. Funding was received from a state agency and a local community foundation. However, there was little effort in organizing residents, businesses, and local agencies by the two NAGV organizers. Several community-wide meetings were held, but attendance was sparse. A good deal of time was spent participating in and organizing recreational activities for GVRP program youth. However, a large and successful community memorial service and mass meeting was held to honor youth victims of gang violence. The interest of NAGV focused more and more on placing youth in jobs and conducting group meetings for parents, some of whose children were not GVRP targeted program youth.

A series of crises occurred in mid-1995 that had long-term effects on the development of NAGV. A gang graffiti paint-out was conducted with one of the project gangs but without contact or involvement of GVRP staff. A youth was shot and killed, and the mother of the victim sued NAGV. Tensions increased between the NAGV board, the community organizer, and project youth-worker staff. Project police officers were also upset that the NAGV organizer charged them with false arrest of a neighborhood youth. Conflict developed between the organizer and the NAGV board. She was accused of "double dipping," obtaining funds from the GVRP and a state grant for the same effort. Community cross-agency meetings were infrequently held. The NAGV organizer became increasingly interested in direct service to youth and less in assisting the project with mobilizing and coordinating community and agency interests in addressing the gang problem. NAGV and GVRP efforts, separately and together, were insufficient to develop an effective neighborhood advisory group for the project and mobilize agency and community interest in the youth gang problem.

THE PROJECT EVALUATION

The research evaluation of the Little Village Gang Violence Reduction Project attempted to assess the complex dimensions of gang-program development, outcome, and community impact. Multiple sources and levels of data and different units of analysis were used in the evaluation. Of primary interest was the effect of the program on reducing violence for target gang youth. Program youth interviews and self-report data, as well as official arrest histories of program and comparison youth were collected. Gang and community-level gang incident and arrest data were also gathered. Field observations of gang situations and individual youth and family behaviors were obtained. Worker-service or program-tracking records were employed to describe key program activities and worker contacts provided to program youth by the team.

The analysis was concerned with types and dosages of project contacts and services to different gang youth. Measures of change had to be constructed to determine, for example, whether changes occurred in the youth's identification with the gang, his rank in the gang, time spent with gang and nongang friends, gang involvement of parents and siblings, or time spent on the job or with a wife or girlfriend—and whether such changes contributed to a reduction or increase in violent and other criminal behavior. A typology of gang youth was created based on arrest histories to determine what kinds of worker contacts and services were most effective with what types of gang youth.

The effectiveness of the Little Village comprehensive gang program had to be assessed not only in terms of significant changes at individual-youth, gang, and community levels but also in terms of changed policy and developing local community-agency structures and interorganizational relationships that contributed to effective program strategy. Not only did the project have to be successful in accounting for specific crime changes, but if successful, it also had to lead to institutional change and the development and sustaining of a comprehensive, city- and local neighborhood–wide program to reduce the youth gang problem.

CHANGES IN SOCIAL CONTEXT OF PROGRAM YOUTH

There were 195 youth from the two gangs—Latin Kings and Two Six—in the program sample, of whom 127 were interviewed three times in annual periods during the course of the five-year program to ascertain their perceptions of change in community institutions, agency programs, gang membership status, gang structure, peer relationships, family life, employment, educational experience, personal and household income, and future job and income aspirations and expectations. Program youth indicated many changes. They came to view the Little Village community as a better place to live. They were less concerned about family victimization from gang crime. Individual and household income increased slightly more for the Two Six than the Latin Kings. Illegal income was a smaller proportion of individual and household income than legal income but was a larger proportion of total income for Latin Kings and their households. Relationships with mothers, fathers, and siblings continued to be generally positive. The quality of relationships between gang youth and their wives or steady girlfriends was only moderately positive at the time I interview and deteriorated by the time III interview. There was some increase in household health and mental-health crises.

Aging out of the gangs seemed to be correlated with perceived changes in community and personal factors. Toward the end of the program period, many youth in the program declared they were no longer active members of the gang. The drop was particularly marked for the Latin Kings. Educational levels and employment increased for members of both gangs. Latin Kings school dropouts decreased from 52.3 percent to 35.4 percent, and Two Six dropouts decreased from 43.6 percent to 25.8 percent. Latin Kings employment increased from 35.7 percent to 48.2 percent; Two Six employment jumped from 30.9 percent to 63.3 percent. While occupational aspirations fell and occupational expectations rose, income aspirations and expectations remained relatively high for members of both gangs.

354
CHAPTER 17

SELF-REPORTED OFFENSE CHANGES IN RELATION TO LIFE-COURSE CHANGES

Program youth were asked whether and how many times they had committed any of sixteen offenses typical of gang members in Little Village. Focus was on serious offenses, especially violence. The analysis was not statistically controlled for preprogram criminal record or length of time in the program, as it was in later multivariate analyses using arrest data. We found extensive, if not extraordinary, reductions in self-reported offenses and self-reported arrests by almost all program youth between the time I and time III interviews. Most of the reductions were highly statistically significant. There were reductions in serious violence offenses from a mean of 15.5 to 3.6 per youth, and a reduction in drug-selling offenses from a mean of 4.1 to 2.8 per week per youth (but this reduction was not statistically significant). There were also declines in offenses when the units of analysis were the gang (Latin Kings or Two Six), cohort (I, II, or III, that is, entry points of youth into the program), and age group (nineteen and older, seventeen and eighteen, sixteen and younger). The oldest group, nineteen and older, already had the lowest mean level of self-reported offenses at the time I interviews. The seventeen- and eighteen-year-olds self-reported the highest level but also the greatest reduction of offenses at the time III interviews.

We wondered whether there was a correlation between the reduction in self-reported offenses and arrests and changes in life-course and life-space factors. One surprising correlation was the youth's relationships with wives or steady girlfriends and their self-reported offenses. Surprisingly, a poorer or more conflicting relationship with a wife or steady girlfriend between the time I and time III interviews was correlated significantly with a reduction in self-reported total offenses, violence offenses, and property offenses at the time III interview. Unlike the youth's relationships with mothers, fathers, and siblings, problematic or conflict relationships with wives or steady girlfriends tended to result in reduced levels of offending over time. This could be explained by pressures from wives or steady girlfriends for the program youth to reduce their levels of involvement with the gang. Also, an increase in the amount of time spent with wives and steady girlfriends at the time I or time III interviews was significantly correlated with a reduction in self-reported total offenses, violence offense, and serious violence offenses at the time III interviews.

Certain life-course and life-space factors seemed to be good predictors of reductions of different types of self-reported offenses. The variables in the best multiple regression model that predicted reduced total offenses included the youth's contact with a probation officer, more rather than less time spent with a wife or steady girlfriend, and being nineteen years or older. The variables in the best model predicting reduced violence offenses were the youth's satisfaction with the community, his avoidance of gang situations, and more rather than less involvement in treatment for personal problems. The variables in the best model predicting reduced drug-selling activity were more rather than fewer relatives in jail, having a wife or steady girlfriend, and spending more rather than less time on a job.

PROJECT-WORKER CONTACTS, SERVICES, AND STRATEGIES

We used worker-tracking data of 191 program youth to look at the nature of worker services and dosage (that is, duration, frequency, and intensity)—brief counseling or advice, family contacts, school and job-related services, and suppression efforts. An average of 2.4 project workers were in contact with 191 program youth an average of sixteen times per month over a program period of 29.2 months. An average of 1.7 youth workers contacted 179 program youth an average of thirteen times per month; an average of 1.6 project police officers contacted fifty-eight youth an average of 7.7 times per month; and an average of 1.8 project probation officers contacted twenty youth an average of 7.4 times per month. The neighborhood organizer contacted twenty-five program youth an average of 5.6 times per month.

Different types of services or controls were provided to varying numbers of program youth: 84 percent of youth were provided with counseling; 52.8 percent with family-related services; 50 percent with job-related services; and 38.0 percent with school contacts or referrals. Of the sample of fifty-eight youth contacted by project police, 64.9 percent were provided with suppression services. Surprisingly, the police provided school-related contacts for 31.6 percent of youth. An estimated 14.8 percent of all services provided by youth workers were also suppression-related services.

In addition to worker-tracking records (completed by all workers), more detailed process records were completed by eleven youth workers, in response to a specific set of questions asked by a project researcher, for a subsample of sixty-five program youth. Of the total contacts provided by these youth workers, 41.5 percent were to individual youth. Substantial numbers were also made with family members of youth (13.5 percent) but fewer with groups of gang youth (12.1 percent). More than three times as many contracts were made with individuals as with groups of gang members. Of the total field contacts, some were made with project probation officers (8.0 percent), project police officers (6.2 percent), other project youth workers (6.0 percent), neighborhood organizer (3.9 percent), and local community leaders, agency personnel, and residents (6.3 percent).

The youth workers developed different patterns of services and activities depending on the different gangs they served. The Two Six youth workers were relatively more oriented to direct-service contacts with individuals, gang sections, and family (61.3 percent of total contacts), compared to the Latin King workers (49.6 percent of total contacts). The Latin King workers were relatively more oriented to project police, probation officers, and community leaders (38.2 percent of total contacts), compared to the Two Six workers (27.2 percent of total contacts). These differences could be partially accounted for by the following: (1) Two Six workers were a little younger than Latin King workers; (2) Two Six youth were younger than Latin King youth; and (3) the Latin King youth had more extensive criminal records, especially for violence.

ARREST CHANGES: PROGRAM AND COMPARISON YOUTH

Our most rigorous analysis of the effectiveness of the Little Village Gang Violence Reduction Project was based on use of Chicago Police Department arrest-history data. Arrest data were of special importance from a police-policy perspective. Changes in arrest patterns, not self-reported offenses, were the coin of law-enforcement operations and police-policy decision making. For our purposes, both arrest and self-reported offense data, plus detailed program information, were critically important for evaluating program success. We were given access to police and court records for research purposes and examined changes in arrests for all 195 program youth; a matched "quasiprogram" group of ninety youth gang co-arrestees who were on the periphery of the program and provided with some limited (mainly recreational) services; and a matched "true" comparison group of 208 youth who were provided with *no* services or contacts by project workers.

There were no significant differences among the three samples in race or ethnicity, gender, and age. The race or ethnicity of program, quasiprogram, and comparison youth was predominantly Latino, mainly Mexican American. We examined only males in our arrest-change analyses, although there were a small number of females in each of the samples (program sample—four; quasiprogram sample—three; comparison sample—four). The mean age of youth in each of the samples in the preprogram period was almost identical (program sample—17.98 years; quasiprogram sample—17.86; comparison sample—17.95). There was no significant statistical difference between the ages of the Latin Kings and the Two Six in the samples as a whole.

In the preprogram period, total mean arrests were as follows: program sample—4.57; comparison sample—4.01; and quasiprogram sample—7.75. While there was no statistically significant difference between program and comparison samples, there was between the quasiprogram sample and each of the other samples—program and comparison. When we examined preprogram serious violence mean arrests, we found a similar pattern: program sample—0.79; comparison sample—0.82; and (significantly different) quasiprogram sample—1.35. Again, the pattern was the same comparing preprogram mean total violence and property arrests for the samples. The pattern of arrests was more similar for the three samples in respect to preprogram mean arrests for drug crimes and such crimes as mob action, disorderly conduct, and obstruction of a police officer. We appeared to have well-matched samples, particularly for the program and true comparison youth.

Using general linear model statistical analysis of variance, we found that program youth reduced their levels of total violence arrests, serious violence arrests, and drug arrests significantly more than did comparison youth and quasiprogram youth during the program period compared to the preprogram period. The reduction of serious violence arrests was more than 60 percent greater for program than for comparison seventeen- and eighteen-year-olds—the highest-rate offenders in that age group—controlling for other variables in the equation. The project had an across-the-board effect in reducing the levels of arrests for serious violence for all age groups in the program sample in relation to the comparison and quasiprogram samples. The project was particularly successful in reducing drug arrests for program youth compared to comparison and quasiprogram youth, who showed increased drug arrests. Program youth showed nonsignificant greater reductions in arrests for other types of arrests such as mob action, disorderly conduct, and obstruction of a police officer but no difference in the reduction of total arrests (mainly property crimes). The most significant reduction in all types of arrests was by the nineteen-and-older youth across the three samples and, especially, in the program sample.

ARREST CHANGES FOR DIFFERENT TYPES OF GANG YOUTH

Youth gang members were differentially engaged in certain types, or combinations of types, of offenses—violence, drug selling, property, and other types of crime. We were interested mainly in violent gang offenders. Project staff members were continually making distinctions between shooters and potential shooters, and those who were less interested in violence and more interested in drug or other criminal activities. Staff were expected to target shooters and potential shooters with special services, opportunities, and controls. It was important, therefore, to determine whether the program engaged different kinds of gang youth and whether the program was more effective with one type, or subgroup, of gang youth (particularly those youth more engaged in or predisposed to violence) than with other subgroups of gang youth.

A total of 418 youth in our three samples had arrest histories during either or both the five-year preprogram period and five-year program period. We classified each youth into one of four major arrestee and offender categories, or types, based on total arrest charges in the ten-year period: violence, no drug; drug, no violence; violence and drug; and "other," that is, youth with no record of violence or drug arrests but of other arrests—property, disorderly conduct, mob action, status offenses, and so forth. While youth in all of the samples were arrested more often for "other" offenses, our primary interest was in youth arrested for violence or drug crimes—the crimes that presumably most distinguished gang-youth offenders from other, nongang youth offenders.

To understand whether the program had an effect on arrest changes for different kinds of youth, we again conducted a general linear model analysis focusing on arrest changes but now including the subsample typology. We found that the program-youth violence, no drug, and violence and drug arrestee subsamples did significantly better in the reduction of serious violence arrests and total violence arrests than the equivalent comparison and quasicomparison subsamples. Also, program youth in the drug, no violence, and the violence and drug subsamples reduced their levels of drug arrests compared to the equivalent comparison and quasiprogram subsamples, but these differences were not statistically significant. The typology was useful in demonstrating that the project targeted and was most effective in reducing violence arrests for those youth in the gangs who had a high commitment to, or potential for, violence.

SERVICES AND OUTCOME

Based on analysis of program tracking records, we found the great majority (88.9 percent) of youth in the program were appropriately targeted for worker contacts and services. The findings indicated that the youth who may have had only the briefest contacts with youth workers (11.1 percent) were less violent and delinquent than youth who had multiple contacts.

The findings showed that when contacts included job-related services, opportunity provision (job and school services), family counseling, and individual-youth-counseling services, the odds ratios of success to failure for program youth in reducing arrests (particularly violence arrests) were higher than if the contacts did not provide these particular services. The odds ratios of success to failure in contacts that involved school services alone were low. We also found that "very effective" job-related services and "very effective" individual-youth counseling (particularly by outreach youth workers) predicted higher odds ratios of success to failure in reducing arrests for violence than did other types of "very effective" services.

Generally, the odds ratios of success to failure in the reduction of violence arrests through the provision of a range of services were higher for the Latin Kings than for the Two Six. However, family contacts and individual-youth counseling produced higher odds ratios of success to failure in the reduction of drug arrests for the younger Two Six than the older Latin Kings. Age was the most significant predictor of high odds ratios of success to failure in the reduction of violence arrests. Youth nineteen years old and over did better than seventeen- and eighteen-year-olds, who did better than the sixteen-and-under youth. However, age was not a significant predictor in the reduction of drug arrests. Also, certain arrestee types—youth with arrest histories of violence and drugs—did better in the reduction of drug arrests in response to services and controls by workers than did youth with arrests for drugs, but no violence. Similarly, youth with arrest histories of violence and drugs did better in the reduction of violence arrests than did youth with arrests for violence, but no drugs. Youth with histories of both violence and drug arrests may have been less committed to either violence or drug crimes than the "quasispecialist" violence or drug offenders.

GANG-AS-A-UNIT AND COMMUNITY CRIME CHANGES

In the design of the evaluation of the Little Village Gang Violence Reduction Project, we proposed that a reduction of gang violence for program youth would contribute to a reduction of gang violence at the gang-as-a unit and community levels. Furthermore, we anticipated that a reduction of gang violence at the Little Village community level would exceed that of comparable, high-gang-crime Latino communities in Chicago. A variety of analyses were employed, using Chicago Police Department aggregate crime statistics, to test these propositions.

In Little Village, the Latin Kings and Two Six together continued to be responsible for the preponderance of serious gang-violent crimes in the area, but they experienced a smaller combined increase in gang homicides, aggravated batteries, and aggravated assaults than did the other constellations of gangs together (Latino and African American) in the area. The Little Village community as a whole experienced a lower rate of increase in serious violent gang incidents between the preprogram and the program years, relative to the average of six similar, high-gang-crime police districts with predominant Latino populations. Little Village was associated with the lowest percentage increase in serious gang-violent incidents compared to any of the other six comparison high-gang-crime Latino communities during the first three years of the project. Using both U.S. Census and CPD data, we found the rate of increase of serious violent gang incidents for seventeen- to twenty-five-year-old males was less (26.9 percent) in Little Village compared to Pilsen, its almost identical comparison community (33.9 percent), during the first three program years compared to the equivalent preprogram years.

In a spatial and temporal analysis of serious gang-violent incidents, the patterning of such gang crime did not vary substantially in the five-year program period compared to the five-year preprogram period, except that clusters of serious gang-violent incidents were somewhat smaller and more spread out geographically in Little Village than in Pilsen. Importantly, the results of community surveys of residents and representatives of organizations indicated a significantly greater reduction in gang crime, especially violence, in Little Village than in Pilsen between the first and the third years of the project. The reduction perceived by residents was particularly sharp in the Latin King territory within Little Village.

PROJECT TERMINATION

The success of the Gang Violence Reduction Project in reducing gang violence in Little Village at the individual program-youth level, and probably at the gang and community levels, was not sufficient to ensure the project's continuation and the adaptation of the comprehensive community-based model in Chicago. The expectation that the CPD would make an early decision whether to continue the project by the end of the first year of program operations did not materialize. The CPD, distracted by problems of implementing its community-policing strategy and its decades-long tradition of lumping the gang problem into one simple ball of gangs, drugs, and violence—gang members were only to be suppressed—paid little attention to and was uncertain what to do about the project, although it continued to accept funding for it for the five program years. I had agreed to stay on for a year but stayed for four and a half years and then announced my plan to leave the project in six months. Subsequently, the CPD determined not to continue sponsorship of the project, although three years of federal funding remained. A variety of local youth agencies and community organizations offered to continue operation of the youth-work component of the project, although none wanted to collaborate closely with the CPD in a comprehensive effort.

A key conceptual and political stumbling block was that the CPD was not prepared to manage an interdisciplinary approach to the gang problem that required significant partnership with other agencies and collaboration of social intervention with its suppression strategies. The CPD leadership was not interested in cooperating with outreach youth workers, and its expressed interest in coordinating gang-suppression efforts with adult probation was not realized. The youth gang problem was complex, basically interrelated with socioeconomic and racial or ethnic problems inherent in the structure and politics of government and interorganizational relationships in Chicago. In the 1990s, Chicago was not ready for effective policies and programs leading to a reduction of the youth gang problem, which required significant collaboration and integration of strategies.

More recently, Chicago and other cities and jurisdictions, with the concern and aid of funds from state and federal legislatures, have begun to support comprehensive gang-program projects. Government, criminal justice, public-health, social-agency, business, education, civil-rights, and other community leaders have slowly become aware that separate strategies of suppression, prevention, social intervention, and even local citizen involvement are insufficient to successfully address the youth gang problem. Comprehensive, integrated strategies may, in addition, be critical in building the broad coalitions and community support, as well as the organizational change and development necessary to tackle the mix of basic problems of community disorganization, poverty, segregation, racism, rapid population movement, and organized crime that generates the youth gang problem.

References

Alinsky, Saul. 1946. *Reveille for radicals.* Chicago: University of Chicago Press.

Asbury, Herbert. 1971. *Gangs of New York: An informal history of the underworld.* New York: Putnam. (Originally published 1927, New York: Alfred A. Knopf.)

Austin, David M. 1957. Goals for gang workers. *Social Work* 2 (4) (October): 43–50.

Berleman, William C. 1969. The value and validity of delinquency prevention experiments. *Crime and Delinquency* 15 (4) (October): 471–78.

Berleman, William C., Janis R. Seaberg, and Thomas W. Steinberg. 1972. The delinquency prevention experiment of the Seattle Atlantic Street Center. *The Social Service Review* 46 (3) (September): 323–46.

Bernstein, Saul. 1964. *Youth on the streets: Work with alienated youth groups.* New York: Association Press.

Bibb, Marilyn. 1967. Gang-related services of mobilization for youth. In *Juvenile gangs in context: Theory, research and action,* ed. Malcolm W. Klein, 175–82. Englewood Cliffs, N.J.: Prentice-Hall.

Bickman, Leonard. 2000. Summing up program theory. In *Program theory in evaluation: Challenges and opportunities,* ed. P. J. Rogers, T. A. Hacsi, A. Petrosino, and T. A. Huebner, 103–12. San Francisco: Jossey-Bass.

Block, Carolyn R., A. Christakos, Ayad Jacob, and R. Przybylski. 1996. Street gangs and street crime: Patterns and trends in Chicago. In *Research Bulletin.* Chicago: Illinois Criminal Justice Information Authority.

Brace, Charles L. 1973. *The dangerous classes of New York and twenty years' work among them.* New York: Wynkoop and Hallenbeck.

Braga, Anthony A., David M. Kennedy, and George E. Tita. 2005. New approaches to the strategic prevention of gang and gang-involved crime. In *The modern gang reader,* ed. J. Miller, C. L. Maxson, M. W. Klein, 368–79. 3rd ed. Los Angeles, Calif.: Roxbury.

Browne, Philip W. 2004. Finding solutions. *Los Angeles Daily News*, October 3.

Bursik, Robert J., Jr., and Harold G. Grasmick. 1993. *Neighborhoods and crime*. New York: Lexington Books.

Caplan, Nathan S., Dennis J. Deshaies, Gerald D. Suttles, and Hans W. Mattick. 1967. The nature, variety, and patterning of street club work in an urban setting. In *Juvenile gangs in context: Theory, research and action*, ed. M. W. Klein, 194–202. Englewood Cliffs, N.J.: Prentice-Hall.

Carney, Frank J., Hans W. Mattick, and John Calloway. 1965. Street club work practice. Chicago: Chicago Youth Development Project.

Chicago Tribune. 2004. Working their way down the list. Editorial, December 2, sec. 1.

Cloward, Richard A., and Lloyd E. Ohlin. 1960. *Delinquency and opportunity: A theory of delinquent gangs*. Glencoe, Ill.: Free Press.

Coleman, James S. 1974. *Youth, transition to adulthood: Report of the panel on youth of the president's science advisory committee*. Chicago: University of Chicago Press.

Cooper, Charles N. 1967. The Chicago YMCA detached workers: Current status of an action program. In *Juvenile gangs in context: Theory, research and action*, ed. M. W. Klein, 183–93. Englewood Cliffs, N.J.: Prentice-Hall.

Covey, Herbert, C. 2003. *Street gangs throughout the world*. Springfield, Ill.: Charles C. Thomas.

Crisis Intervention Network. 1981 (May 11). Operational procedures for crisis teams/probation unit. Philadelphia.

Curry, G. David. 1995 (July). Responding to gang-related crime and delinquency: A review of the literature. Prepared for Abt Associates and the National Institute of Justice. Department of Criminology and Criminal Justice, University of Missouri, St. Louis.

Darden, Oliver A., Irene F. Peinsley, and Peter Digre. 1985 (April 8). Crisis Intervention Network annual review. First draft. Unpublished.

Decker, Scott H. 2003. Policing gangs and youth violence: Where do we stand, where do we go from here? In *Policing gangs and youth violence*, ed. S. H. Decker, 287–93. Belmont, Calif.: Thompson Wadsworth.

———. 2004. *Understanding gangs and gang processes*. Indianapolis: National Mayors Gang Task Force.

Decker, Scott H., and G. David Curry. 2003. Suppression without prevention, prevention without suppression: Gang intervention in St. Louis. In *Policing gangs and youth violence*, ed. S. H. Decker, 191–213. Belmont, Calif.: Thompson Wadsworth.

Doty, Earl F., and Hans W. Mattick. 1965 (August 1). The Chicago Boys Club's S.T.R.E.E.T.S. Project. Chicago: Chicago Boys Club.

Eccles, Jacquelynne, and Jennifer Appleton Gootman, eds. 2002. *Community programs to promote youth development*. National Research Council and Institute of Medicine. Washington, D.C.: National Academy Press.

Egley, Arlen, Jr. 2005 (June). Highlights of the 2002–2003 National Youth Gang Surveys. In *OJJDP fact sheet*. No. 1. U.S. Department of Justice, Office of Justice Programs, Office of Juvenile Justice and Delinquency Prevention.

Egley, Arlen, Jr., J. C. Howell, and A. Major. 2004. Recent patterns of gang problems in the United States: Results from the 1996–2002 National Youth Gang Survey. In *American youth gangs at the millennium*, ed. F.-A. Esbensen, S. G. Tibbetts, and L. Gaines, 90–108. Long Grove, Ill.: Waveland Press.

Fattah, David. 1987. The House of Umoja as a case study for social change. *Annals of the American Academy of Political and Social Science* 494 (November): 37–41.

Grennan, Sean, Marjorie Britz, Jeffrey Rush, and Thomas Barker. 2000. *Gangs: An International Approach*. Upper Saddle River, N.J.: Prentice Hall.

Hagedorn, John. 1988. *People and Folks: Gangs, crime and the underclass in a rust belt city*. Chicago: Lake View Press.

Harrell, Erika. 2005 (June). Violence by gang members. In *Crime data brief*. NCJ208875. U.S. Department of Justice, Office of Justice Programs, Bureau of Justice Statistics.

Hobsbawm, Eric J. 1963. *Primitive rebels: Studies in archaic forms of social movement in the 19th and 20th centuries*. 2nd ed. New York: Praeger. (Originally published 1959, under the title *Social bandits and primitive rebels*. New York: W. W. Norton.)

Howell, James C. 2000 (August). *Youth gang programs and strategies: Summary*. National Youth Gang Center. Institute for Intergovernmental Research. Washington, D.C.: U.S. Department of Justice, Office of Juvenile Justice Programs, Office of Juvenile Justice and Delinquency Prevention.

Howell, James C., and Scott H. Decker. 1999 (January). The youth gangs, drugs, and violence connection. In *Juvenile justice bulletin*. Washington, D.C.: U.S. Department of Justice, Office of Justice Programs, Office of Juvenile Justice and Delinquency Prevention.

Hyman, Irwin A. 1984. Testimony before the Subcommittee on Elementary, Secondary, and Vocational Education of the Committee on Education and Labor, p. 82. U.S. House of Representatives, January 24.

Kass, John. 1995. Latinos slam gang politics. *Chicago Tribune*, 27 February, Chicagoland section, final edition, p. 1.

Kirkpatrick, David D. 2005. Congress rethinks battle of mandatory sentences. *New York Times*, May 11, national edition, sec. A, p. 16.

Klein, Malcolm W. 1965. Juvenile gangs, police and detached workers: Controversies about intervention. *Social Service Review* 39 (2) (June): 183–90.

———. 1968 (July). *The Ladino Hills project.* Los Angeles: Youth Studies Center, University of Southern California.

———. 1969 (July). Gang cohesiveness, delinquency and a street-work program. *Journal of Research in Crime and Delinquency.* Pp. 135–166.

———. 1971. *Street gangs and street workers.* Englewood Cliffs, N.J.: Prentice-Hall.

———. 1995. *The American street gang.* New York: Oxford University Press.

———. 2004. *Gang cop.* Walnut Creek, Calif.: AltaMira Press.

Kobrin, Solomon. 1982. *Sociological aspects of the development of a street corner group: An exploratory study.* Institute of Juvenile Research, Department of Public Welfare, State of Illinois.

Kontos, Louis, David Brotherton, and Luis Barrios, eds. 2003. *Gangs and society: Alternative perspectives.* New York: Columbia University Press.

Los Angeles County Probation Department. 1982. The purpose and objectives of group guidance. Los Angeles.

Los Angeles Daily News. 2004. Our opinions: Gangbusting agency. December 21.

Marburger, John H., III. 2005. Wanted: Better benchmarks. Editorial. *Science* 308 (May): 1,087.

Mattick, Hans W., and Nathan S. Caplan. 1962 (April 1). Street Work, Community Organization, and Research. The Chicago Youth Development Project. Chicago: Chicago Boys' Clubs.

Merton, Robert K. 1957. *Social theory and social structure.* Glencoe, Ill.: Free Press.

Meyers, Jim. 2000. Retired gangsters gang up on youth. *Youth Today* 9 (10) (November): 40–43.

Mihalic, Sharon, Katherine Irwin, Delbert Elliott, Abigail Fagan, and Diane Hansen. 2001 (July). Blueprints for violence prevention. *OJJDP Juvenile Justice Bulletin.* U.S. Department of Justice. Office of Justice Programs. Office of Juvenile Justice and Delinquency Prevention.

Miller, Walter B. 1957. The impact of a community work group program on delinquent crime gangs. *Social Service Review* 21 (4): 390–406.

———. 1962. The impact of a "total-community" delinquency control project. *Social Problems* 10 (2): 168–91.

———. 1982. Personal communication.

Mobilization for Youth. 1961 (December 9). A proposal for the prevention and control of delinquency by expanding opportunities. New York.

Moore, Joan W. 1990. Gangs, drugs, and violence. In *Drugs and violence: Causes, correlates, and consequences,* ed. M. De La Rosa, E. Y. Lambert, and B. Gropper, 160–76. Research Monograph No. 103, Rockville, Md.: U.S. Department of Health and Human Services, National Institutes of Health, National Institute on Drug Abuse.

————. 1991. *Going down to the barrio.* Philadelphia: Temple University Press.

Morley, Elaine, Shelli B. Rossman, Mary Kopczynski, Janeen Buck, and Caterina Gouvis. 2000 (November). *Comprehensive responses to youth at risk: Interim findings from the safe futures initiative.* Washington, D.C.: U.S. Department of Justice, Office of Juvenile Justice and Delinquency Prevention.

National Institute of Justice (U.S. Department of Justice). 2004 (December). Solicitation for proposals: Evaluations of Office of Juvenile Justice and Delinquency Prevention FY 2003 and discretionary fund projects. Appendix: Evaluability assessments with prefaces. Chicago Project for Violence Prevention/Cease Fire, 3–24. SL000694

New York City Youth Board. 1960. *Reaching the fighting gang.* New York.

New York Times. 1994. Ft. Worth pays gangs to fight crime. May 13, Midwest edition, sec. A, p. 13.

Norman, Alex J. 1963. Working with juvenile gangs and their members. Paper presented at the Institute on Special Service for Groups' Service and its Activities. Pasadena, California. Special Service for Groups: Los Angeles, California.

Piehl, Anne Morrison, David M. Kennedy, and Anthony A. Braga. 2000. Problem solving and youth violence: An evaluation of the Boston Gun Project. *American Law and Economic Review* 2 (1): 58–106.

Proyecto Intercambio, Latino Youth, Inc. 1990 (December). Report on the Pilsen/Little Village youth needs assessment project. Chicago.

Reed, Winifred L., and Scott H. Decker. 2002 (July). *Responding to gangs: Evaluation and Research.* Washington, D.C.: U.S. Department of Justice, Office of Justice Programs, National Institute of Justice.

Roth, Norman R. 1961 (July). *Reaching the hard-to-reach.* Syracuse, N.Y.: Huntington Family Centers.

Sampson, Robert J., and John H. Laub, eds. 2005. Developmental criminology and its discontents: Trajectories of crime from childhood to old age. *The Annals of the American Academy of Political and Social Science* 602 (November): 12–45.

Schlossman, Steven, and Michael Sedlak. 1983. The Chicago Area Project revisited: A board note prepared for the National Institute of Education. Santa Monica, Calif.: Rand.

Schubert, Jane G., and Louis O. Richardson. 1976 (23 November). *Youth gangs: A current perspective.* Revised ed. Washington, D.C.: U.S. Department of Justice, Law Enforcement Assistance Administration, Office of Juvenile Justice and Delinquency Prevention.

Shaw, Clifford R., and Henry D. McKay. 1942. *Juvenile delinquency and urban areas.* Chicago: University of Chicago Press.

Shireman, Charles H. 1958. *The Hyde Park youth project (May 1955–May 1958)*. Chicago: Welfare Council of Metropolitan Chicago.

Short, James F. Jr. 1985. The level of explanation problem in criminology. In *Theoretical methods in criminology*, ed. R. F. Meier, 51–72. Beverly Hills, Calif.: Sage.

Short, James F., Jr., and Fred L. Strodtbeck. 1965. *Group process and gang delinquency*. Chicago: University of Chicago Press.

Sivilli, June S., Robert K. Yin, and M. Elaine Nugent. 1995 (March). *Evaluation of gang intervention: Final report*. Cosmos Corporation. Washington, D.C.: U.S. Department of Justice, National Institute of Justice, Office of Justice Programs.

Skogan, Wesley G., and Susan M. Hartnett. 1997. *Community policing, Chicago style*. New York: Oxford University Press.

Skolnick, Jerome H. 1992. Gangs in the post-industrial ghetto. *The American Prospect* 8 (Winter): 109–20.

Snodgrass, Jon. 1976. Clifford R. Shaw and Henry D. McKay: Chicago criminologists (draft paper). *British Journal of Criminology* 16 (January): 1–19.

Spergel, Irving A. 1964. *Slumtown, Racketville, Haulburg: An exploratory study of delinquent subcultures*. Chicago: University of Chicago Press.

———. 1966. *Street gang work: Theory and practices*. Reading, Mass.: Addison-Wesley.

———. 1969. *Community problem solving: The delinquency example*. Chicago: University of Chicago Press.

———. 1972. Community action research as a political process. In *Community organization: Studies in constraint*, ed. Irving A. Spergel, 231–62. Beverly Hills, Calif.: Sage.

———. 1995. *The youth gang problem: A community approach*. New York: Oxford University Press.

Spergel, Irving A., et al. 2000 (September). Evaluation of the gang violence reduction project in Little Village. Chicago: School of Social Service Administration, University of Chicago.

Spergel, Irving A., and Ron Chance, eds. 1992. *Technical assistance manuals*. School of Social Service Administration, University of Chicago, in cooperation with the Office of Juvenile Justice and Delinquency Prevention, U.S. Department of Justice.

Spergel, Irving A., Susan F. Grossman, and Kwai Ming Wa. 1999. Reducing youth gang violence in urban areas: One community's effort. *On Good Authority* 2 (5) (March): 1–4. Chicago: Illinois Criminal Justice Information Authority.

Spergel, Irving A., and Kwai Ming Wa. 2000a. Combating gang violence in Chicago's Little Village neighborhood. *On Good Authority* 4 (2) (August): 1–4. Chicago: Illinois Criminal Justice Information Authority.

———. 2000b. Outcomes of the Little Village Gang Violence Reduction Project. *On Good Authority* 3 (3) (August): 1–4. Chicago: Illinois Criminal Justice Information Authority.

Spergel, Irving A., Kwai Ming Wa, and Rolando Sosa. 2002 (October). *Evaluation of the Mesa Gang Intervention Program (MGIP)*. Chicago: School of Social Service Administration, University of Chicago.

———. 2003 (October). *Evaluation of the Riverside Comprehensive Gang Program*. Chicago: School of Social Service Administration, University of Chicago.

———. 2006. The Comprehensive, Community-Wide Gang program model: Success and failure. In *Studying youth gangs*, ed. J. F. Short Jr. and L. A. Hughes, 203–224. Walnut Creek, Calif.: AltaMira Press.

Swans, Bennie J. 1981 (May 11). Crisis intervention procedures for crisis teams. Philadelphia: Crisis Intervention Network.

———. 1985. Crisis Intervention Network, Inc. Revisions Corrections. Philadelphia: Crisis Intervention Network, 3 pp. (mimeo).

Thornberry, Terence P., Marvin D. Krohn, Alan J. Lizotte, Carolyn A. Smith, and Kimberly Tobin. 2003. *Gangs and delinquency in developmental perspective*. New York: Cambridge University Press.

Tita, George, K. Jack Riley, and Peter Greenwood. 2003. From Boston to Boyle Heights. In *Policing gangs and youth violence*, ed. S. H. Decker, 102–30. Belmont, Calif.: Thomson Wadsworth.

Valdez, Avelardo, and Stephen J. Sifaneck. 2005. Getting high and getting by. In *The modern gang reader*, ed. J. Miller, C. L. Maxson, M. W. Klein, 322–27. 3rd ed. Los Angeles, Calif.: Roxbury.

Venkatesh, Sudhir Alladi. 2000. *American project: The rise and fall of a modern ghetto*. Cambridge, Mass.: Harvard University Press.

Washburn, Gary. 2003. Hillard plans united front on murder. *Chicago Tribune*, June 6, sec. 2, p. 7.

Webb, Vincent J., and Charles M. Katz. 2005. A study of police gang units in six cities. In *The modern gang reader*, ed. J. Miller, C. L. Maxson, M. W. Klein, 380–92. 3rd ed. Los Angeles: Roxbury.

Welfare Council of Metropolitan Chicago. 1960. *Breaking through barriers*. Chicago.

Index

ACE (Alliance for Community Excellence), 59, 138, 141. *See also* United Neighborhood Organization (UNO)

African American community, 331

Alinsky, Saul, 6, 12

analysis of variance explaining CPD arrest changes, 250–51; for drugs, 260–62, *261*; for other offenses, 262–64, *263*; for property, 257–59, *259*; for serious violence, 254–57, *255*; for special police gang-activity, 264–66, *265*; in total arrests, 251–54, *253*; in total violence 257, *258. See also* arrestee typology

Arata, Louis, xviii

arrestee typology

—based on youth arrests for violence and drugs, 270

—construction of, 271–73, *273*

—frequencies of arrests by subsample in, 273–76, *274*

—similarity of patterns of arrests using self-reported offenses, 276–79, *278*

—subsample arrest changes for: drug arrests, 282; other arrests, 282; serious violence arrests, 281; total arrests, 280–81; total violence arrests, 281–82

—value for program development, 269–70, 283

Asbury, Herbert, 4

Austin, David M., 9

Avila, Javier, xvii

Barrios, Elisa, xviii

Barrios, Luis, 23

Bartollas, 25

Block, Carolyn R., xvii

Block et al., 270

Boys and Girls Clubs, 57, 151, 351

Boys Club, 5, 10

Brace, Charles L., 5

Braga, Anthony A., 18, 19, 24

BRIDGES program of Los Angeles, 20

Brotherton, David, 21

BUILD, 331

Bursik, Robert J., Jr., 24

Suburban Job Link, Inc., 41, 138, 142, 143, 149, 150

Swans, Bennie J., 14

team development, 344; boundary issues in, 72–74; building structure for, 66–67; collaboration in, 74–77; coordination in, 65–66; information exchange in, 67–70; institutional relationships in, 77–78; youth worker sharing information in, 70–92

Ten Point Coalition, 18

tenth district neighborhood relations unit, 147

Tita, George K., 23, 24

Torres, Angelo, xvii

TWO. See Woodlawn Organization, The

Two Six, 67, 70, 71–73, 86–87, 97, 101, 103–4, 140–42, 146–51, 172, 228, 246, 296–99, 301–2, 306–8, 321–22, 324, 344–46, 353–54, 357, 359–60

U.C. (University of Chicago). See School of Social Service Administration, University of Chicago

United in Peace, 144

United Neighborhood Organization (UNO), 59, 141, 143

urban disorder, 11, 15

urban riots. See urban disorder

U.S. Department of Education, 144

U.S. Department of Justice, Office of Justice Programs, xviii, 327, 341; Bureau of Prisons, 78; comprehensive gang program approaches, 21–24; delinquency prevention (OJJDP), 21–22, 27, 331, 333; office of community oriented policing services

(COPS), 21, 22, 23; violence in urban areas program, 30, 344

U.S. Office of Economic Opportunity, 12

Valdez, Avelardo, 270

Venkatesh, Sudhir Alladi, 20, 25

Victory Outreach, 152

Wa, Kwai Ming, xviii, 22

Washburn, Gary, 339

Webb, Vincent J., 17, 18

Welfare Council of Metropolitan Chicago, 7, 153

Woodlawn Organization, The, (TWO), 12; the Youth Manpower Project of, 15, 20

Woods Charitable Trust, 141–42, 143, 147

worker debriefing record contacts, 227–39, 222; in criminal justice system, 237–39, 238; gang-related, 232–33, 234; job, 233, 235; school, 237, 236; target gang differences in, 239–42, 239; types of contacts/services provided in, 229–32. See also worker tracking record contacts for services

worker tracking record contacts for service results: arrestee types in, 296–302, 297; effectiveness of, 302–4; effects of targeting of, 287–89; related to life space/life course changes, 289–93, 292; specificity of, 293–96, 295; youth targeted in, 285–86, 286

worker tracking record contacts for services, 217–22; athletics, 226–27; family contacts, 224; individual youth counseling, 223; job referrals, 225;

About the Author

Irving A. Spergel has been trying to understand and address the youth gang violence problem for over fifty years. He has been troubled, if not appalled, that social scientists and gang workers do not communicate with and learn from each other. This may explain, in part, why little progress has been made in addressing the problem. Social scientists spend time theorizing, describing, and analyzing gang phenomena and pay almost no attention to what to do about the problem. Gang workers, police, agency directors, and policymakers are convinced that what they do or recommend is effective with no hard data to back up their convictions.

Spergel is the George Herbert Jones Professor Emeritus in the School of Social Service Administration, University of Chicago. He has a master's degree in social work from the University of Illinois, Urbana, and a PhD in social work from Columbia University. He has been a street gang worker, supervisor, and gang program director in New York City and Chicago, and he has conducted street gang and community-based research and program evaluations in cities across the country. He was a United Nations consultant on youth work to the Hong Kong government and a consultant on the development of social work and youth work training programs in Hong Kong and Russia. His major teaching experience at the University of Chicago has been in group work, community organization, and community development, as well as youth gangs and gang work. His most recent effort has been the development of a Comprehensive Gang Program Model, applying and testing it in six cities, sponsored by the Illinois Criminal Justice Information Authority (1992–1997) and the Office of Juvenile Justice and Delinquency Prevention, U.S. Department of Justice (1995–2003). Spergel is widely published in professional social service and social science journals, and in state and national agency reports. He has also published five books, including *The Youth Gang Problem. A Community Approach* (1995).

Made in the USA
Lexington, KY
22 June 2017